TROUBLE

Nigeria Since the Civil War

Edited by
Levi A. Nwachuku
G. N. Uzoigwe

To John, a genuine friend, whose intellectual progressivism and compassionate humanism have always inspired me.

Levi

University Press of America,® Inc.
Dallas · Lanham · Boulder · New York · Oxford

Copyright © 2004 by
University Press of America,® Inc.
4501 Forbes Boulevard
Suite 200
Lanham, Maryland 20706
UPA Acquisitions Department (301) 459-3366

PO Box 317
Oxford
OX2 9RU, UK

Library of Congress Control Number: 2003114129
ISBN 0-7618-2712-9 (paperback : alk. ppr.)

Dedication

To our Parents Rev. Moses Akalazu Nwachuku
and Evangeline Mberunma Nwachuku; Nze
Thompson Okebata Uzoigwe and Esther Ereh Uzoigwe.

CONTENTS

PART I: HISTORICAL OVERVIEW

CHAPTERS

                         G. N. Uzoigwe

Okechukwu Okeke

Gloria Ifeoma Chuku

G. N. Uzoigwe

FOREWORD

Nigeria's post-colonial development has always received an inordinate amount of attention from political and social analysts because of its demographic attributes (e.g., it is Africa's most populous state and most educated society) and the numerous developmental crises its peoples have endured, now for two full generations as an independent nation state. *Troubled Journey: Nigeria Since the Civil War 1970-1999*, edited by Levi Nwachuku and Godfrey N. Uzoigwe, is the latest of a number of case-study probes into Nigeria's unique experience as a modern African state. It pulls together a talented group of Nigerian historians who have been close students of Nigeria's "troubled journey" since independence day on October 1, 1960 and more precisely since the conclusion of its devastating Civil War – 1967-1970.

The design of the volume is particularly apt. The authors focus on the variety of political regimes - and interim regimes - that have attempted the multi-faceted task of governmentally harnessing the massive and intricately complex geo-political unit that Nigeria is. And within the regime-focused case-study chapters, each author has wisely favored the volume's readers with a skilled and rigorous attention more to historical process and dynamics than to formalistic schema of presentation and analysis. The inevitably intricate layers of what might be called societal and cultural complexity that make up that geopolitical unit called Nigeria, cannot be assumed to be at the finger tips of readers of this volume. Therefore, case-study chapters that historically tutor, so to speak, are clearly what is required.

The contributing authors have also exhibited a keen capacity to distill a prominent or regime-shaping motif or theme within their chapter presentations, and this serves the readers of the volume well indeed. For, within the lifecycle of the nine Army Regimes - plus several interim improvised regimes and one transition democratic regime - there have been rather complicated maneuvers and political gyrations among leading figures and their networks (not to mention similar maneuvers and political gyrations among citizen sectors of society) which must be rendered graspable by readers. Finding an appropriate distillation motif or theme to lend an immediate meaning or understanding to political maneuvers and gyrations is, therefore, of utmost serviceability to readers.

In this regard Professor Uzoigwe of Mississippi State University sketches in chapter one an informed and concise overview of Nigerian history from precolonial times to 1960, providing thus the necessary background why Nigeria's journey to stability and unity has been troubled. Professor Nwachuku of Lincoln University takes up the story from 1960 and surveys Nigerian history to 1999. He searched for and located a keen distillation motif for helping readers to grasp the significance of the mania of wealth-acquisition-through-politics in post-Civil War Nigerian development. Nwachuku refers to this as a "new morality." From the late '70s onward, Nigeria's oil fields produced two million and more barrels of rich oil (low in impure ingredients) per day, which means a lot of revenue was available to a succession of nine army-fueled regimes, save for periods of declining oil prices and periods of run-away state debts to foreign bodies.

In looking back over a generation of post-Civil War governance in Nigeria as the chapters in this volume do and uncover more developmental failures than successes is clearly a let-down. One feature of the analytical success of each chapter in this volume is that each author grasped what was systemically unique about developmental failures associated with the particular Nigerian regime studied. And conversely, where there were a few instances of development successes, again authors grasped what was systemically serviceable to such successes. Dr. O. N. Njoku performed this analytical task very well in Chapter 3, I thought, identifying General Yakubu Gowon's special capacity to translate his regime's policies in a manner that helped many citizens view the interplay between citizens and regime's policies as part of a "covenant." Which is to say, that the Gowon regime exhibited an outreach-to-Nigerian-citizens aura that seemed to many thoroughly genuine — that is not nakedly self-interested for those running the regime. This capacity of the Gowon regime helped much in fashioning the rehabilitation of secessionist Igbo and other Eastern Nigerians as *bona fide* members of post-Civil War Nigeria. Of course, there were inevitably some imperfections associated with the Gowon regime's Igbo-rehabilitation process, for many Igbos suffered from the Gowon regime's property restoration practices.

Professor Gloria I. Chuku also brought an apt understanding to the too brief Murtala regime - July 1975-February 1976 - with her conceptualization of it as a "purification-questing regime," I thought. A regime, that is, which might be called ascetic-driven, at least in the first instance anyway. Ascetic-driven regimes are sparked by a passion, a mystique, an overweening fear/anxiety, etc. The early Bolshevik regime under Lenin comes to mind, perhaps; and even more appropriate today, the Kemalist regime in World War I Turkey. There were several others.

Above all, one should be aware that a "purification-questing regime" in developing countries like Murtala's Nigerian government (July '75-February '76) must be willing to run risks with its very existence. But risks that are systemically serious - developmentally enhancing, that is - not frivolous or elite-self-serving risks. And this, as Chuku informs us, the Murtala regime - almost among Nigeria's nine Army-ruled post-Civil War governments was willing to do. As Chuku observed: "One of the most pressing problems that were facing Mohammed's administration was the reorganization of the armed forces. The program of reorganization and demobilization of the army was aimed at reducing its strength from some 250,000 to some 100,000 soldiers. . . .About a total of 216 officers were affected by the purge exercise at the end of November 1975. Lower down in the ranks of the army, many officers were dismissed or retired, but it was said to have been done with speed and care, for those dismissed were either extremely lax in their duties in the past or were involved in large scale financial corruption or were even said to be absent from their units without reason for long periods. A total of about 115 corrupt and inefficient police officers were also retired or dismissed." (p. 64 Chuku Chapter)

What particularly interested me while reading the shrewd portrayal of the Murtala regime was this: Why hasn't crisis-riddled and generally modern failure-riddled Nigeria produced more Murtala-type ascetic-driven or passion-driven attempts to govern? And thus by extension, why indeed haven't crisis-riddled and modern failure riddled post-colonial African regimes generally spawned more instances of ascetic-driven or passion-driven attempts at governance to date? This topic is waiting - anxiously - for its appropriate author, I believe.

In our volume at hand, the Nwachuku chapter (on the Obasanjo interim regime), the Uzoigwe chapter (on Shagari transition democracy), the Nwachuku chapter (on Buhari dictatorial era), the Dibua chapter (on cynical-populist or pseudo-populists Babangida regime '85-'93), and the Okeke chapter (on hyper-dictatorial Abacha era and aftermath) - all of these chapters inform readers of the vast variety of the sway of what Professor Nwachuku dubbed the "new morality" (the use of government to fuel the wealth-questing mania) in the life-cycle of the regimes that have dominated post-Civil War Nigeria. The corruption-mediated route via governance to wealth in post-Civil War Nigeria took on full-fledged kleptocratic dimensions in each of the regimes mentioned above. This route to wealth and class-efficacy, in short has deep roots in the modern sector of Nigerian society as well as between the modern and traditional sectors. As such, perhaps as in Saudi Arabia, Nigeria's "new morality" can be vanquished not through normal politics (democracy-mediated politics), but only through an extra-ordinary politics, which is what the ascetic-driven Murtala regime and politics were.

It should be noted that all of the regime-focused chapters in *Troubled Journey* point out a major failure caused by the pervasive presence of the "new morality" in all of the post-Civil War Nigerian regimes. That failure was the ability to cultivate genuine political trust patterns of convoluted alienation, which took hold throughout Nigerian life. Not only did all the nine Army-ruled regimes since the Civil War experience wide political alienation to one important degree or another among Nigeria's citizens, but the interim Shagari elected government analyzed by Professor Uzoigwe in Chapter 6 experienced popular alienation as well. Under such circumstances amounting to a kind of kleptocratic-caste barrier between popular society and ruling elites, in any developing country, popular society has virtually only one expressive political outlet to employ, namely, some kind of upheaval-political response, some kind of political eruption if you will. And though such upheaval-political response could be directed explicitly toward the illegitimate ruling elites and the regime they control, such popular political eruptions are also what might be called "internalized communalist upheavals" – riots within popular society, riots betwixt-and-between segments of popular society. Since the Civil War, Nigerian political life has been saturated with such riots within popular society. Uzoigwe, in Chapter 6, reports some 22 riots between 1979 and the 1990s (p.158)!

The keen analyst of the Shagari era that he is, Professor Uzoigwe recognizes that the politics of what I call "internalized mass eruptions" seldom if ever fundamentally alters dysfunctional regimes like those Nigeria has experienced since the end of the Civil War. As suggested in

Professor Chuku's chapter, erupting popular forces require assistance and direction from within some sector of the ruling elites, and the elite-sector most likely to supply such outreach-to-erupting-popular-forces has attributes like the Murtala regime of '75-'79 Chuku analyzed, that is, shaped by ascetic-values, influenced by passions based upon ideas and an ethos that constitute a higher-order-of-existence than that based upon materialistic obsessions, on wealth acquisition through naked political and governmental maneuvers and manipulations. Like Chuku in her chapter on Murtala, Uzoigwe concludes his analysis of the Shagari transition-democracy regime (1979-1983) suggesting that what was missing under Shagari was a Murtala-like leadership understanding. As Uzoigwe put it: The important point to note is that Shagari ...seemed ...to be oblivious of the fact that the most effective antidote to military intervention in politics is good governance. And it will be difficult to conclude, given the evidence at our disposal, that under Shagari Nigeria enjoyed good governance. It would appear that he was unable to implement "The Essentials of Good Government and the Obligation of Leadership" [Precepts], taught by Usman dan Fodio [the 19th century Hausa-Fulani Caliphate leader] which Shagari himself summarizes in a 1967 book that he authored with a Mrs. Jean Boyd. An important and relevant section of this teaching is the injunction of rulers to undertake regular "assessments" of their officials to find out if any of them has acquired "unexplained wealth." Any such wealth, it was stressed, must be confiscated. The ruler is further enjoined to listen to his people's complaints and to avoid even the appearance of favoritism (p. 158).

Ascetic-driven or passion-driven leaders and their regimes mean usually authoritarian governance of some sort. The costs of authoritarian governance to citizens and society are, we know quite well, extremely burdensome and cruel. But can they also carry in their wake a new order in African situations probed in this volume - like the Nigerian situation? Is there a benign variant of the passion-driven governance that Murtala had in mind for Nigeria? Is it possible to mediate and tame a Murtala-type regime in Nigeria and elsewhere in Africa? Of course, these queries would be moot if the current American-dominated global capitalist world system awake to its moral obligations to weak and poor and fledgling regions -Africa, prime among them, fashion serious Marshall Plan options for them, convince over-fed citizens to undergo the sacrifices required to put such options into place for a generation or more in the world's poor corners. We can dream, can't we .....

MARTIN KILSON

Frank G. Thomson
Research Professor
Harvard University
November 2001

PREFACE

This book began as the result of discussions on problems facing Nigeria among university colleagues as the country was on the verge of inaugurating General Obasanjo's second coming. Our discussions centered on the tortuous, troubled, and turbulent experiences that have characterized Nigerian history since independence. Twenty-nine years of military dictatorship and nine years of what could be described as visionless and failed democratic experiment took a near fatal toll on Nigeria's life. Neither the respective military regimes nor the civilian ones succeeded in putting neither a viable "public system" in place, nor a "systematic leverage" that could assure development and growth in Nigeria.

We observed that the problems that have adversely affected Nigeria's social, economic, and political development are rooted in its past. To understand these problems, one has to examine the regimes of those who ruled Nigeria since the civil war. We chose the period after the civil war because that event is a benchmark which marked a departure from the intent of those who designed Nigeria. Britain, Nigeria's colonial ruler that led the country into independence may have believed that it had successfully created a unified nation from ethnic groups which, over the centuries, had developed their respective identities and operated as independent sovereignties. The civil war belied that belief and exposed the reality of the fragile state of the Nigerian nation-state. During Nigeria's first Republic, politicians, in moments of crises, talked loosely about the possibility of secession. Such talks were at the time regarded as hot air induced by emotions that would not endure. However, with the civil war, resulting from the declaration of independence by the Eastern Region, the possibility of the disintegration of Nigeria became a reality.

Nigeria has, since the war, been haunted by tremors of disintegration and general Yakubu Gowon, who prosecuted the civil war had as his motto: "To keep Nigeria one is a task that must be done." It is not certain that those who have led Nigeria after the reintegration of the seceded region appreciate the extent to which the political unification of Nigeria needs serious attention. Alongside the problem of unity are other problems which have defied efforts at solution. These problems include systemic corruption in all its ramifications, absence of systemic leverage for nation-building, overwhelming military influence in the nation's politics, persistent economic depression, absence of national focus and the state's inability to provide security of life for its citizens.

This book focuses on the administrations of those individuals who have led Nigerians in a journey which, at best, has been troubled. The various contributors have comprehensively examined how each regime performed. The views expressed are entirely theirs and they do not blame anyone for any errors of fact, omission, or interpretation. They do, however, hope that their contributions would induce redemptive discussions among Nigerians so that solutions to the problems now confronting Nigeria can be found and its journey ahead would become a safe and progressive one.

Given several recent books on Nigeria and its political culture one may wonder why this book is needed at this time. We believe that *Troubled Journey: Nigeria Since the Civil War* is the first systematic and comprehensive study of Nigerian history from the end of the Civil War in January 1970 to May 1999 when the present Olusegun Obasanjo administration came to power. It is a major contribution to the on-going debate about what the trouble with Nigeria has been and still is. We note that historians of Nigeria, unlike their counterparts in the social sciences in particular, have not seriously entered the debate. This is the first major attempt to do so.

Although available evidence indicate rather ominously that the state of Nigeria has not been good-and is still not good-for reasons generally agreed upon, and that the country's journey toward unity, stability, prosperity and nationhood has been painfully troubled, we nevertheless believe that it would be unhistorically and, certainly, risky to write off Nigeria as a failed project as some are wont to do. Nigeria is so well-endowed and so important a country to be so glibly written off. Moreover, because the Nigerian state, like any other state, is a living organism the possibility and, indeed, the probability exists that Nigerians today are better prepared to deal with the complexities of this century than they were in dealing with the nightmares of the 20th century. We believe that practically most things that could possibly go wrong for Nigeria have already gone wrong. The country has consistently bent but never broke. We believe also that Nigeria's problems, although for Africa, at any rate, have tended to be of maximum severity, are still more general than unique. *Troubled Journey*, then, is a refreshing departure from the existing literature on Nigeria which is replete with forecasts of uncertainty and even of doom.

The problems that have characterized Nigeria's social, economic and political history, we repeat, are squarely rooted in its past. To understand and perhaps appreciate those problems the historical approach is, in our view, the best methodology. Thus, the first chapter of this book is a succinct overview of Nigerian history from the earliest times to 1960, the year of Nigerian independence from British colonial rule; and the second chapter takes off from that date and provides an informed survey of the country's history since independence. The remaining chapters discuss the various rulers of Nigeria, regime by regime, since 1970, analyzing their strengths and weaknesses. The final chapter provides a prospectus for the future. By also taking a stand against military dictatorship, visionless and corrupt political leadership, and the moral decay that has afflicted Nigeria especially since independence, the book, obliquely, is a reconciliation of the externalist and internalist interpretations of modern African history. We chose to close the book in 1999 because the return to civil rule under the leadership of Obasanjo is still a work in progress.

Troubled Journey is expected to be of great interest to students and scholars of Nigerian history, African history, political science, economics, sociology, literature, religion, African studies, international studies and world history. It should also be of use to politicians and the general reader who care about the future of Nigeria in particular and of Africa generally because Nigeria is, indeed, a microcosm of or, in the words of Ali Mazrui, "a metaphor for Africa." For us Nigeria, essentially, is a peg on which the book hangs ideas on democracy and development in erstwhile decolonized plural societies.

Levi A. Nwachuku   G. N. Uzoigwe
Lincoln University   Mississippi State
Pennsylvania   University

                        November 2002

ACKNOWLEDGMENTS

Numerous individuals have contributed to the completion of this project. The staff of the Langston Hughes Memorial Library, Lincoln University, Pennsylvania were of much help to us. In this regard, special thanks go to Professor Emery Wimbish, Head Librarian; Professor Edward Gibson, Special Collections Librarian; Ms. Doris Hughes, a staff member of the Special Collections; and Ms. Brenda Snider of Lincoln University's Instructional Media Center. Ms. Stella Odilli helped in collecting materials on chapters five and seven. To all of you, we say "thank you."

We acknowledge with much appreciation the financial support from Mississippi State University, Starkville, which enabled one of us to conduct research in Nigeria for chapters six and eleven. We must not fail to record the assistance we received from the librarian and staff of the Mitchell Memorial Library, Mississippi State University. Peggy Boner, Secretary, Department of History, Mississippi State University and her staff, Dr. Lonna Reinecke and Patsy Humphrey were of immense help to us. To all of them we extend grateful thanks.

We also thank Mrs. Martha Parisan, Secretary of the History Department, Lincoln University, and Ms. LaShaunda Allen, a student at Mississippi State University, who were the pillars of the project. They typed the manuscripts and Patsy Humphrey, Peggy Bonner, and Jennifer Parker (all of the Department of History, Mississippi State University) put them in the form that the publishers would accept. We acknowledge also with gratitude the dedication shown by the copy-editor, Janet Watson, in finally getting the manuscript ready for publication; and Lorraine Watson who provided substantial help with the indexing and many hours of proofreading.

In Nigeria the librarian and research staff of the Nigerian Institute of International Affairs went beyond the call of duty to facilitate this project. We thank them most sincerely. Barrister Ejide Ukelonu, Research Fellow at the Institute, did an excellent job in identifying important materials for writing chapters six and eleven. We thank her most sincerely.

We also owe intellectual debt to the numerous scholars whose works were useful sources for our project. We acknowledge, too, the contributions of those informants who freely shared their experiences and ideas with us. At Tulane University, New Orleans, the contents of this book formed the subject of an undergraduate seminar in the Spring of 1999 conducted by one of us. The exchange of ideas in this seminar was most helpful to us in this project.

Finally, we reserve what is left in our reservoir of thanks for our wives-Ugochi Nwachuku and Patricia M. Uzoigwe. They showed understanding, tolerance, and support even as we relocated our time and attention away from family needs to the writing of this book. To both of you, we are grateful.

L.A.N.   G.N.U

MILESTONES IN NIGERIAN HISTORY, 1960-1999

1960
October 1.   Nigeria becomes independent

1963
October 1.   Nigeria becomes a republic

1966
January 15.   First Military Coup d'Etat
July 29.   Second Military Coup d'Etat

1967
May 27.   Creation of twelve states. Four Regions abolished.
May 31.   Eastern Nigeria secedes. Republic of Biafra declared.
July 6.   Nigerian Civil War begins.

1970
January 12.   Civil war ends.
October 1.   9-point program for return to civil rule in 1976
                 announced by Gowon.

1972
February.   First Indigenization decree promulgated.
                 Nigeria adopts Naira as national currency.

1973
November.
Announcement of Provisional population census results: 79.76 million population figure later annulled.

1974
October 1.
Return to civilian rule indefinitely postponed by Gowon

1975
July 29.
Third military coup, Mohammed Regime begins
October 18.
Constitution Drafting Committee is inaugurated (CDC).

1976
February 3.
Creation of nineteen states.
February 13.
Fourth military coup (abortive). Mohammed assassinated. Olusegun Obasanjo becomes military Head of State.

September 14.
CDC submits report.
December.
Local government reforms announced

1977
January.
Second Indigenization decree promulgated
October 6.
Constitutional Assembly inaugurated (CA).

1978
March.
Promulgation of Land use decree.
September 21.
1979 Constitution promulgated. Ban on politics lifted.

1979
October 1.
Shagari inaugurated as civilian president. Second Republic begins.

1980
December.
Fundamentalist Muslims riot in the north: the Maitatsine Riots.

1983
December 31.
Fifth military coup. Buhari assumes power.

1985

August 27.   Sixth military coup. Babangida assumes power.

December 20.   Seventh coup (Vatsa coup) but the coup fails.

1986

January.   Announcement of return to civil rule by October 1.

February.   Babangida sneaks Nigeria into the Organization of Islamic Conferences (OIC).

1987

September.   Creation of two more states (Akwa Ibom and Katsina).

1988

May 11.   Inauguration of Constitution Assembly (CA).

1989

May.   Promulgation of a new constitution.

1990

April 22.   Eighth military coup led by Major G. Orkar fails.

1991

August 27.   Creation of 11 more states

December 12.   Federal capital moves from Lagos to Abuja.

1992

March 19.   Census returns announced: 88.5 million population reported

October.   AFRC annuls presidential primaries, dissolves NRC and SDP executive committees and appoints caretaker committees.

November.   Presidential election postponed to June 12, 1993.

December 5.   National Assembly is inaugurated.

1993

January 2.   Transitional Council headed by Ernest Shonekan appointed.
NDSC replaces AFRC.

June 23.   Presidential election annulled. NEC and transition program suspended.

August 27.	Babangida 'steps aside'. ING named, with Ernest Shonekan as Head of State.
November 10.	Lagos High Court declares ING illegal.
November 17.	Ninth military coup, Abacha assumes power and dissolves all democratic and transition programs.

1994

June.	M.K.O. Abiola proclaims himself as Nigeria's president.

1995

July.	Another Constitutional Conference begins.
July 27.	Constitutional Conference submits report.
November 10.	Ken Saro- Wiwa is executed.
November 11.	Nigeria is expelled from the Commonwealth.

1996

October 1.	Creation of six more states and 138 Local Government Areas (LGA).

1998

June 7.	Sani Abacha dies suddenly.
June 8.	Abdulsalaam Abubakar becomes Nigeria's ninth military ruler.

1999

May 29.	Olusegun Obasanjo becomes President. Third Republic Begins.

PART ONE

HISTORICAL OVERVIEW

Map of Nigeria showing major Nigerian Peoples

Chapter 1

Nigeria to 1960: An Overview

G.N. Uzoigwe

INTRODUCTION

Nigeria is a complex but compact country. It has a long history. Over two hundred and fifty clearly identifiable and vibrant groups of people live there. This is why Nigeria is usually described as an ethnic mosaic. Before the imposition of British colonial rule early in the twentieth century, each of these groups was a nation in its own right. In the context of modern Nigeria, however, they are now described as ethnic or sub-national groups. This is a testimony to the triumph of historical forces. For the history of modern Nigeria is essentially the series of processes—admittedly agonizing, slow, and sometimes incoherent-- through which the country has been evolving absent-mindedly into nationhood. We would like to suggest here that the conventional thinking that regards Nigeria as a mere historical expression is flawed because it is not based on a serious study of history. Neither is Nigeria a mere geographical expression. There is, in fact, a natural unity to Nigerian history and geography. The authors of this book feel that Nigeria is essentially a unity, and that this essential unity should continue. As General Olusegun Obasanjo said:

> Yes, we have no common indigenous language; yes, we have no common religion; yes, we have slight differences in culture; but we do have common history, common practices, common interests, common destiny and common threat and danger facing us. ... If Switzerland can remain one country, why not Nigeria? If India can continue to survive as a country, why not Nigeria? ("We Must Keep Hope Alive" in *Tell Magazine*, no 23, June 7, 1993, p.14)

It is not helpful, therefore, to be concerned with the unique and particular in Nigerian history. In this chapter the concern is more with the general than with the particular. This is what makes history significant and interesting.

GEOGRAPHY AND ENVIRONMENT

Bounded on the North by the republics of Niger and Chad, on the East by the Cameroon Republic, on the South by the Atlantic Ocean, and on the West by the Benin Republic (the former Dahomey), Nigeria is located in the eastern corner of the Gulf of Guinea--an arm of the Atlantic Ocean--in West Africa. Lying between 4 and 14 degrees North Latitude and 3 and 14 degrees East Longitude, Nigeria covers an area of about 924,000 square kilometers. This ranks it as the second largest country in Africa; the largest is the Sudan Republic. Even so, Nigeria's geographic expanse is such that it is about the same size as Pakistan and Bangladesh combined, and larger than the total area of France and Italy. The country's major landmarks are the great River Niger (from which it derived its name) and its major tributary the River Benue. The two rivers join together around Lokoja in the present Kogi State where they neatly dissect the country and thence flow majestically together through the Niger Delta into the Atlantic Ocean. The other important rivers include the Kaduna River, Sokoto-Rima River, Osun River, Cross River, Imo River, and Anambra River. It is interesting to note that these names are the official names of the states through which these rivers run. Nigeria lies entirely within the tropics. The Nigerian environment is characterized by two broad vegetational climatic and economic zones: the Forest Zone and the Grassland (Savannah) Zone. The average annual temperature in the Forest Zone (the South) is 80 degrees Fahrenheit (27 degrees Celsius); that of the

Grassland Zone (the North) is 100 degrees Fahrenheit (38 degrees Celsius). There are two predominant seasons. The rainy season lasts from April to October, and the dry season lasts from November to March. The wettest areas of the South, along the Coast, receive an average annual rainfall of about 38 centimeters (about 150 inches) while the driest part of the North averages annually 64 centimeters (about 25 inches) of rainfall.

The Forest Zone is usually divided into the thick tropical forest of the Southern Coast and the tall-grass "derived Savanna" belt of Southern Nigeria. The Grassland Zone is also conventionally divided into the natural savanna of the Middle Belt and the almost desert conditions of the Far North. Although human activity has become less dependent than ever before on the local climatic conditions, the pattern of economic activities of the various zones has not changed significantly. The South-West, for example, which is drier than the rest of the South and "has a double maximum rainfall regime with a short dry season in August," can support two crops each year, in contrast to the one crop raised in other, wetter, regions of Southern Nigeria. The Middle Belt, whose climate is transitional between the South and the Far North is consequently a zone of mixed economic culture. There, the food crops of the South are cultivated side by side with those of the Far North. The main agricultural products of this drier region include millet, wheat, guinea corn, groundnuts (peanuts), and cotton. The agricultural products of the more humid South include timber, palm oil and kernel, rubber, cocoa, kola nuts, cassava, yams, rice, fruits, beans, and a variety of vegetables. The Middle Belt is noted particularly for the cultivation of yams, tomatoes, potatoes, soybeans, carrots, and onions. The Mambila Plateau and the Obudu mountain ranges, whose climate is semi-temperate, produce tea, coffee, and wheat. Livestock are also raised in the various zones. The most important economic resources of the country include petroleum, which is produced in the Forest Zone. The export of crude oil accounts for about 90 percent of Nigeria's foreign earnings. Nigeria is the world's sixth greatest producer of crude oil. The production of Liquefied National Gas (LNG), a resource that abounds in the South, is on the way. It is hoped that the facilities will be ready shortly. It is estimated that when fully in production, LNG will replace petroleum as the country's leading foreign exchange earner. Other natural resources mined in the Southern Zone are coal, iron, marble, asbestos, salt, clay and limestone. In the Grassland Zone, uranium, gold, tin, tantalite, and columbite are found.

Conventional wisdom puts Nigeria's population between 120 and 150 million people. However, the last official census, not ratified, put the figures at slightly over 88 million to the consternation of international and Nigerian experts on population. Equally peculiar, is the revelation in the census that Nigerian men outnumbered women. Whatever is the case, Nigeria is the ninth or tenth most populous country in the world. It is by far Africa's most populous county. It is, in fact, variously estimated that one in four or one in five Africans is Nigerian.

The subject of this book, then, is a country that is one of the most generously endowed in the world, physically, economically, and—especially—in terms of human resources. It is an African power with the potential to exercise a greater influence in the world. If Nigeria lives up to its great potential, it will become Africa's great giant and will assume the natural leadership of the Black World. It is only when this promise is achieved that the Blacks all over the world will receive the respect they seek but which has not been given to them. The many people who are descendants of those scattered throughout the world in the African Diaspora may well be looking to the nation of Nigeria as a champion of their causes.

ANCESTRY OF NIGERIANS

How did the saga of Nigeria begin? It is clear that the history of Nigeria did not begin with the Royal Niger Company or with European imperialism generally. The coming of Europeans is only one phase in the evolution of contemporary Nigeria.

Although some strides have been made in Nigerian Archaeology, it is fair to state that relative to much of the rest of Africa, West Africa (including Nigeria) is archeologically very much understudied. The evidence that has been uncovered, however, suggests that man has inhabited the Nigerian area since the Early Stone Age. Stone implements that are 40,000 years old have been discovered. There exists, also, numerous rock-paintings, human skeletons and other evidence of prehistoric settlements that attest to the antiquity of the ancestry of Nigerians.

Nigeria's best known early culture, the Nok civilization, flourished for seven centuries, beginning in 500 B.C.E. and lasting until 200 C.E. in the Middle Belt of central Nigeria. This makes the civilization of Nok contemporaneous with the civilization of Ancient Greece. The artifacts of Nok civilization, which have been discovered so far, include clay figures that rank among the oldest sculptures in Africa. In this civilization, there was a tradition of working in metals evidenced by the presence of smelting furnaces, iron slag, and iron and tin manufactures. The Atili and the oil palm tree were used for food, fuel and medicine.

Another ancient Nigerian civilization is that of Igbo-Ukwu, which flourished in the present Anambra State of Nigeria. Knowledge of this civilization has been detailed by Thurstan Shaw in two monumental volumes entitled *Igbo-Ukwu: An Account of Archaeological Discoveries in Eastern Nigeria* (London: Faber and Faber, 1970). Although the Igbo-Ukwu artifacts have been dated to the 9th century A.D., there is no doubt that the culture that produced such a highly skilled level of professional and artistic workmanship took centuries to evolve. There is evidence that by the first century of the Christian era, the Igbo-Ukwu culture had spread to other parts of Igboland and even beyond. For one thing, the Nri Igbo culture has been identified as an offshoot of Igbo-Ukwu culture. And the influence of the Nri in the evolution of modern ways of Igbo life is well recognized. Worth noting, also, is the Nri claim to have founded the Igala monarchy at Idah. They also claim a history of performing ritual functions in the coronation of the Benin Obas [kings]. These claims, as far as I am aware, have not yet been fully authenticated, but they do suggest, at least, evidence of early interaction. According to Shaw, Igbo-Ukwu culture was characterized by the existence of a priest-king who presided over a highly ritualized religion. The Igbo-Ukwu civilization had a diversified economy, which depended on agriculture, hunting and a complex network of internal and external trade involving non-Igbo peoples. Like the Nok people, the Igbo-Ukwu had iron-working skills. They also worked in bronze and copper, and had beautifully decorated pottery.

We asserted earlier that Nigeria has a basic geographical and historical unity. Geographically, a look at the river system reveals an essential unity that made possible relationships between groups. The vegetational zones also dovetail beautifully into one another; and because the borders are open and fluid, migrations of peoples have never been obstructed. Historically, then, Nigerians have never lived in isolation of one another. It is true that Nigeria did not really emerge as a political entity until the amalgamation of 1914, but in reality, if Nigeria was a historical accident, then, surely, it was an accident anxiously waiting to happen.

The myths of origin of Nigerian peoples show an interesting correlation. If we note, with respect, the traditions of such Nigerian peoples as the Ibibio, the Edo and the Ife, we can discover much. Some of these groups claim that their populations have always lived in their present locations and did not migrate from anywhere. However, the majority of Nigerian peoples claim to have migrated from somewhere. We know, for example, that the Fulani, over a long period, migrated into Nigeria from the regions of Fouta Djallon and Fouta Toro, that is, from Sierra Leone, Guinea and Senegal. The grassland was not always as arid as it is today. Before the Sahara became a desert area, the land was fairly fertile, and it supported a relatively large population. Following the desiccation of the Sahara after about 8000 B.C., the displaced peoples began to migrate into the drying bed of what was left of Lake Chad. The indigenous populations of Borno State, the majority of whom are Kanuri, resulted from these population movements. The Hausa, Yoruba, Efik and some Igbo claim, too, to have migrated into Nigeria from Egypt and various regions of the present Middle East. Although these claims appear romantic, it is a fact that both the dessication of the Sahara and the final collapse of Ancient Egypt in 341 B.C.E. resulted in large scale population movements southwards. This suggests that these traditions should be looked at again more closely, more dispassionately, and in the wider context of African history. Within Nigeria itself, nevertheless, population movements continued over the centuries. From these movements the numerous Nigerian peoples and cultures developed. In terms of culture values, occupational specializations and political structures, the groups adapted themselves according to the conditions of the geographical zones they occupied.

The major groups of the Forest Zone include the Yoruba, Edo, Ijo, Ibibio, and Igbo. The Yoruba-speaking peoples occupy the south western part of Nigeria and are dominant in Lagos, Ogun, Oyo, Ondo, and Kwara states. Originally a grassland people, the Yoruba were pushed toward the south where they were forced to adapt to forest conditions. Ethnically and linguistically homogenous, they were never ruled by a common government until they became the subjects of an European power. And yet they all share common traditions and claim a common ancestry which they trace to Oduduwa, the fabled founder of the Ife dynasty at Ile-Ife (*literally,* "the house of spreading"). Ife thus became the "father-kingdom" of the other Yoruba kingdoms and Ile-Ife became the national capital, so to speak, of all Yoruba. The most important Yoruba kingdoms included Oyo, Egba, Ijebu and Owu. Each was independent and was ruled by a king, called the *Oba.* Each king had a specific title. For example, the Oba of Ife is called the *Oni* and is regarded as the spiritual head of all Yoruba. A unique feature of the Yoruba, among Africans, is that although a predominately agricultural people, they are the most urbanized people on the continent. The largest towns include Ibadan, Eko, Ogbomosho, Oshogbo, Ilorin, Abeokuta, Ilesha and Ede.

To the east of the Yoruba are the Edo-speaking peoples. The Edo are historically famous because of the Kingdom of Bini (which later became an empire) and their bronze work, acclaimed to be among the best in the world. The Edo and Yoruba have cultural and political similarities. For example, the artists who sculpted the internationally renowned bronze heads of Edo are thought to have drawn their inspiration from Ile-Ife. The Bini monarchy, whose king is also called Oba, is said to be of Yoruba origin. Unlike the Yoruba, however, the Edo were united under a common government. It is also claimed that Eko (Lagos), a Yoruba town, was founded by the Edo people. The Yoruba and Edo languages are classified as belonging to the Kwa sub-group of the Bantu family of languages.

The Ijo constitute the majority group in the Eastern Delta in the present Balyesa State. Although they are one of Nigeria's oldest and largest ethnic groups, they have not received enough attention in the existing texts on general Nigerian history. The Ijo maintain that they have existed in their present habitat for thousands of years. Rejecting the notion that they were derived from the Igbo or the Yoruba, they claim that their language does not bear close resemblance to either the Kwa or the Benue-Congo sub-groups of languages and to have existed as a separate group. However, the Nigerian magazine *Legacy* classified it as one of two parts of the Ijoid sub-group, the other being Defaka. What is clear is that they beautifully adapted themselves to the harsh and peculiar conditions of their environment. They developed small-scale kingship institutions, probably between 1200 and 1400 A.D., and founded city-states. It is not clear why, in spite of the antiquity of the people, they took so long to evolve a monarchial tradition. External stimulation may have accounted for the rise of such an institution.

The Ibibio constitute the largest group in the basin of the Cross River. They do not have a common tradition of origin, probably, it is claimed, "because of the absence of a unitary political authority over them in the past." Because of this some scholars have asserted that the Ibibio were "a people of hoar antiquity" who had forgotten from where they came. What seems probable is that the Ibibio migrated into their present location from two major corridors, the Igbo and the Nigeria/Cameroon. In contrast to the Efik with whom they share close linguistic affinities, the Ibibio did not establish any large-scale political institutions.

With this love of limited government, the Ibibio share some similarities with the Igbo who, together with the Hausa and the Yoruba, constitute the majority sub-national groups within the Nigerian nation-state. Unlike the Ibibio, however, the Igbo did establish some kingdom-states, especially among the Onitsha people, the Oguta people, and the

Western Igbo. The Igbo are concentrated in Imo, Abia, Anambra, Enugu, Rivers (the southeastern Igbo) and Delta (the western Igbo). It is claimed that the Igbo-speaking peoples began emerging as a distinct group about six thousand years ago. The scanty archaeological evidence available to us suggests that the Igbo have been in their present locations for thousands of years, possibly since as early as 3000 B.C.E. Although there are folkloric claims by the Igbo of affinity both to early Egyptians and early Hebrews, based as they are on what has been described as "the rich profusion of superficial similarities", there is no conclusive evidence that the Igbo migrated into their primary core areas of Nri-Awka and Amaigbo-Orlu axis from anywhere. There is, however, enough evidence detailing their dispersal from the core to the frontiers. The Igbo are essentially farmers and village dwellers. Today, the largest Igbo towns include Onitsha, Enugu, Owerri, Aba, Umuahia, Abakaliki, Afikpo, Orlu, Okigwe, Asaba, and Agbor. Many people of Igbo descent live also in the town of Port-Harcourt.

The Grassland Zone is divided into the Middle Belt and the Far North. The Middle Belt has the largest concentration--180 in number--of Nigeria's ethnic groups. The two most prominent ones are the Nupe of the Middle Niger River Valley in the west and the Tiv of the Benue Valley in the east. The Belt crosses Nigeria from west to east and from south to north. Today, it includes the following areas: Kwara State, Kogi State, Niger State, Plateau State, Adamawa State, Taraba State and Southern Zaria (a part of Kaduna State).

The Nupe-speaking peoples occupy what may be described as "Nigeria's heartland". "Kin Nupe" (the Land of Nupe) is an extensive area encompassing parts of Niger State and the former Kwara State. Abuja, the new capital of Nigeria, is located on its eastern border. The Nupe are the majority group in the emirates of Bida, Agae, Pategi-Lafiagi and Lapia. They have been in occupation of the Middle Niger for thousands of years. In Zugurma in Kontagora, Shona and share districts of Ilorin as well as at Egan of Koton Karge, they constitute compact minorities. The tradition of origin of the Nupe is not clear. They did not establish a centralized political system until about the fifteenth century when they were stimulated to do so through contact with the Igala kingdom whose political overlordship they had earlier acknowledged. The political system thus established was an arrangement that resembled the Yoruba system in some respects. Their settlement pattern is also similar to that of the Yoruba. Like the Yoruba, the Nupe belong to the linguistic group of Kwa. Of great significance in the history of the Nupe is the ability of its leaders to forge a nation out of a group that is heterogenous but contiguous. Important also is Nupe's location on the Niger between the Benue and Kaduna rivers.

It has been suggested that "the ultimate homeland of the Tiv" may be placed "in the Obudu hills area". It was from this area that they expanded to their present location in the Benue Valley. Their expansion brought them into contact with Jukun who were to exercise profound spiritual influence over them. They provided a typical example of what anthropologists call "stateless societies". The largest political unit was the family compound. That was why British officials saw them as "a people divided against itself." Warlike, virile and truculently independent, contact with the Jukun and the Idoma could not stimulate the Tiv to form large political units. Today, their major town is Makurdi, the capital of Benue State. The Tiv language also belongs to the Kwa linguistic group.

The major groups of the open Savannah of the Far North are the Hausa, the Fulani and the Kanuri. This belt also straddles Nigeria from west to east and stretches from northern Zaria in the south to the borders of Nigeria with the republics of Niger and Chad in the North. Today it encompasses the following states: Kebbi, Sokoto, Katsina, Kaduna, Kano, Jigawa, and Borno.

The Hausa-speaking peoples are found throughout the Grassland Zone of West Africa. In Nigeria, however, they are dominant in Kebbi, Sokoto, Katsina, Kano and Jigawa states. Their Hausa language which is most generally spoken throughout West Africa is also the lingua franca of the grasslands peoples of Nigeria. The curious thing about the Hausa is that although they are ethnically varied, they are culturally and linguistically homogenous. Their language bears no relationship to those of the groups we have discussed so far. They claim to have migrated into Nigeria directly from Baghdad. Muslims since the fourteenth century, their claim of origin is not unrelated to this fact. The Hausa founded a number of city-states which were independent of one another until the Fulani conquerors from the North subjugated them early in the nineteenth century. The Hausa are famous farmers, stock rearers, artisans and traders. The Fulani are an interesting group. They have no territory or state that they can call their own. And yet since the beginning of the nineteenth century they have been dominant in Nigerian politics. Like the Hausa, they are found all over West Africa. Fulani settlements extend eastwards to the upper Nile. In Nigeria, having conquered the Hausa among whom they had settled, they imposed their political and religious systems on them; but the Hausa absorbed them culturally and linguistically. Today, the Fulani are divided into two: the Cattle Fulani and the Settled or Town Fulani. They are devout Muslims.

Like the Hausa-Fulani, the Kanuri are also Muslims. They are a group who have been influenced culturally by the Arabs of North Africa, largely through Islamization. The Kanuri converted to Islam as early as the eleventh century but its spread was limited. Although the Fulani failed in their efforts to conquer the Kanuri during the nineteenth-century Jihad, the aftermath of that movement was the spread of Islam in Borno State where the Kanuri are the dominant group. Although many of them own large herds of cattle, which the Shuwa-Arabs and the cattle Fulani rear for them, most of them are farmers and traders.

We have so far attempted an examination of the ancestry of Nigerians using the major ethnic groups as case studies. We can see that Nigeria's basic unity is historically validated. Geographical factors facilitated rather than hindered the interaction of Nigerian groups. Except for the Hausa language the other Nigerian languages belong to the same family. However, the Hausa language has been a unifying factor in the grassland zone. We can see that although no power before the British was able to impose its authority over Nigeria as a whole, processes of political integration were going on, in varying degrees, before the colonial period. If the British had not come, the process would have continued. The outcome, however, can only be speculated.

STATE FORMATION

A common feature in Nigerian history has been attempts by various societies to organize themselves into systems of governance they considered appropriate for their needs. Broadly, these systems may be grouped into three: the non-centralized societies, the centralized societies, and the empires. All of them shared certain basic characteristics.

The non-centralized societies were basically small-scale societies. They varied from those like the Tiv who lived in villages of a few hundred people to those like the Ibibio and some Igbo groups who lived in larger villages of a few thousand people. Their basic political and social until was the village; and lineage governed political and social relations. A group of those villages constituted a town, or what is called today in Nigeria an autonomous community. Although there was usually a senior village in this arrangement, the equality of the villages was emphasized. Traditionally suspicious of kingship and other forms of authority, the Igbo and the Tiv especially, practiced what may be described as a diffused democracy, which to a visitor sometimes has the appearance of anarchy. But it was nothing of the sort; everything was well ordered. The Igbo and Tiv, too, place a lot of stress on leadership qualities, competence, integrity and individual achievement. Consultations and debates preceded any decision and consensus was the goal. There is no suggestion that everybody was equal to everybody else in these societies, but deliberate efforts were made to minimize social stratification.

The best examples of Nigerian societies that were non-centralized included the Igbo (with the exceptions already noted), Ibibio, Ijo, Tiv, Idoma, Angass, Yako, Mbembe, Ekoi, and the pre-jihad Fulani. It can be seen that this political system operated throughout Nigeria's geographic zones. It should also be pointed out that all these groups eventually evolved their peculiar brands of kingship of varying power and scale. Even the Tiv whose primordial political structure was so fragmented that "the compound" was the only group for which "someone was responsible", have evolved the concept of the Tor Tiv (the ruler of all Tiv).

The centralized societies were those that evolved large-scale or fairly large-scale political structures. The states of the Grassland Zone tended generally to be larger than those of the Forest Zone. These states were ruled by kings variably known as Emirs, Obas, Ezes, Igwes, and so forth. Unlike the European monarchs who were representatives of God on earth, they were divine kings who were, more or less, gods on earth. The knowledge of iron technology and the possession of cavalry (in the grassland zone) enabled them to subdue and control their neighbors. Other factors that stimulated centralized state formation included Islam, long distance trade, the trans-Sahara trade, and the Atlantic slave trade. Trade with the Europeans and cultural diffusion may also have contributed to this development. Because the nature of Nigerian kingships resembled that of Egypt, it is believed by many that the idea might have been diffused from here. There is as yet no concrete evidence to support this theory.

A system of centralized states is also widely spread throughout the country. In the Far North they included the Hausa states of Kanem-Borno, Kano, Katsina, Zaira, Zamfara, Gobir, and Sokoto. In the Middle Belt, the most prominent were the Jukun, Igala and Nupe. In the West they included Ife, old Oyo, Ijesha, Eko, Owo, Ondo, Ekiti (all Yoruba states), Benin (Edo), Aboh (Igbo), and Itsekiri. And in the East they included Membe, Okrika, Kalabari, Bonny, Opobo, Ijo (the Niger Delta States); the city states of Old Calabar; Igbo-Ukwu, Nri, Onitsha, and Oguta (Igbo states). Theses centralized states or kingdoms had common characteristics: centralized authority, hereditary rulership, high stratification, extensive bureaucracies and court systems; elaborate titles and honors, a citizen militia and, in some cases, standing armies. In the Northern kingdoms, Islam was a cohesive force.

Ancestors of today's Nigerians also founded empires. These empires included various kingdoms under a ruler who had incorporated them, in usually a sort of federal or confederal arrangement. They were, therefore, larger than the kingdoms and less centralized. The most important of these empires included Kanem-Borno, Oyo, Benin, and the Sokoto Caliphate. But the warlike Caliphate was more or less in retreat until British colonialism provided for it a conducive atmosphere that made possible the peaceful diffusion of Islam.

The histories of these state-systems discussed above show clearly that Nigerians had always had a lot in common in spite of their obvious differences; that they always interacted broadly and diffusely with one another; that this interaction was not always characterized by hostility; that they had influenced one another over the centuries; and that until the coming of the Europeans no power was able to bring them under one political umbrella.

EXTERNAL INFLUENCE

Euro-centric scholarship in Nigerian history has tended to lay more emphasis on external influences than on the internal developments that we have been discussing. Of course, external factors have played a significant role in the evolution of Nigerian society and culture. That Arabs, through the process of Islamization, played an important role in shaping Nigerian history and culture is not in dispute. Also conceded is the impact of Christian Europe from the fifteenth century. Both the Trans-Saharan Slave Trade and the Atlantic Slave Trade must constitute the negative results of their impact. But the introduction of Islam and Christianity, on the whole, must also be conceded as beneficial. In the first instance, they brought Nigerians into contact with the wider world and introduced them to Islamic learning and Western education through which they widened their horizons. Secondly, the two religions not only stimulated the process of political centralization but also made it possible for Nigerians to know one another better than it was possible hitherto.

British conquest of Nigeria by the close of the nineteenth century was the culmination of a long process of impact which, starting with the slave trade and its suppression, led to the occupation of Lagos in 1851. In 1861 Lagos was formally declared a British colony. The expansion of the

Lagos colony initiated the conquest of Nigeria. British colonialism of the twentieth century with its policy of divide and rule vitiated much of the good intentions of colonial officials as well as of successive British governments. So also did the latent racist attitudes embedded in the philosophy of colonialism. Eurocentric scholars are wont to recount *ad nauseam* the great achievements associated with British administration of Nigeria. Some of these are admitted. But a close look at the post-colonial history of Nigeria would suggest, surely, that the British, on the whole, did a shoddy job of their stewardship. As the following chapters show, the post-1960 history of Nigeria is mainly a narrative of the unsuccessful efforts so far by Nigerians to resolve the difficulties created by the British. It may not be an exaggeration to note that British colonialism whether it be in Canada, India, Middle East, Egypt, Sudan, Uganda, Kenya, Zambia, Zimbabwe, South Africa and so on had created similar difficulties and had left a lot for others to resolve and clear while British critics speak thoughtlessly of the inability of Africans to rule themselves. Even some Africans, especially Nigerians, confronted with a myriad of problems facing them since independence have unfortunately come to accept this myth. Some have even suggested that the British should be recalled to re-colonize Nigeria!

Please do not misunderstand me. I am not suggesting - not even remotely- that the Nigerian leadership have been doing a fair job since independence. Nor am I seeking to absolve them totally from Nigeria's post-independence traumas. Far from it. I am saying that faced with the problems created for them by British colonialism- perhaps the most efficiently ruthless of its kind since the fall of the Roman Empire - which they were ill-prepared to handle, they compounded these problems by succumbing to pressures arising from primordial sentiments, sub-national self-interests and personal ambitions.

Let me illustrate with a few examples. First, the North-South dichotomy did not exist in the pre-British period. The imaginary line - for that is exactly what it is - dividing the North and South was a British creation. While British colonial officials were subjugating Nigeria from the South, George Goldie's Royal Niger Company (RNC) was doing the same from the North. Both groups competed with each other as if they were serving different powers. Finally, a truce, more or less, was called. The sphere of influence of the Royal Niger Company was to become the Protectorate of Northen Nigeria or the Sudan Province of the Selbourne Committee Report of 1898; the sphere of influence of the British officials in Lagos became the Protectorate of Southern Nigeria. Thus was begun the lopsided nature of the Nigerian federation that post-colonial attempts at state creation have not yet resolved.

Secondly, the so-called amalgamation of the two protectorates in 1914 was not undertaken for the purpose of unifying the country really, but essentially as a fiscal measure. The Protectorate of Northern Nigeria was unable to raise enough revenue to be viable; therefore, the surplus revenue from the Southern Protectorate was used to develop the North. That process has continued ever since. The political repercussion of this arrangement, which has developed into an article of faith in Nigerian politics, is still very much evident.

Thirdly, Nigeria's pre-Independence constitutions-- the Selborne Report (1898); the Clifford Constitution (1922); the Richard's Constitution (1946); the MacPherson Constitution (1951) and the Lyttleton Constitution (1954)--were never intended to mold a united Nigerian nation. On the contrary, these constitutions have been described as "products of the mental reservations by the British about treating Nigerians as one entity". The result was the entrenchment of regionalism and sectionalism in Nigerian political life. The 1951 Constitution, which created the Nigerian federation--but still allowed the North to be larger than the East and West put together--made Nigeria an unstable federation. To compound the problem, the British also decided (without sufficient evidence) that the population of the North was more than that of the South. That decision has also remained an article of faith in Nigerian politics. Every "census" from the colonial period to the present has religiously preserved the population ratio. This ratio has been used for the such important matters as allocation of political representation, the creation of states, the creation of local governments, recruitment into the armed forces and so on. Thus we see that its earliest planners knowingly built conflict and instability into the Nigerian body of politics.

Fourthly, the present educational imbalance between the South and the North also resulted from British colonial policy. In deference to the wishes of the Northern emirs, for whom successive British administrators had the greatest respect, Christian missions were not allowed to operate in the North for a long time. And since these missions were the crucial apparatus for Westernization and Western education, within a short time, the North began to lag behind, as far as Western education was concerned. And because literacy in English was a requirement for recruitment into the British colonial service as well as for admission into the post-secondary institutions, most people of the North rapidly became disadvantaged in these respects. It should also be noted that these emirs were careful to ensure that their children and relations received Western education and, therefore, availed themselves of the opportunities it conferred. It should be also noted that since the 1950's a deliberate quota policy in both employment and admission into post-secondary institutions has operated in favor of the North, a policy that the beneficiaries had came to regard as a right and not a favor. Post-colonial Nigerian governments, led practically by Northerners, have pursued this policy so relentlessly that many Southerners have come to regard it as discriminatory and unfair. They do not see why they should be made to pay indefinitely for the past decisions of Northern emirs who wanted to ensure that their subjects should not be educated enough to enable them to challenge their unprogressive and autocratic rule. The bitterness engendered by this system is one of the difficulties that have made Nigeria's journey troubled.

Finally, recruitment into the colonial army and police was also lopsided in favor of the North. This has continued after independence. It was true that during the colonial period and before the Nigerian Civil War, the bulk of the officer corps was Southern simply because of their superior educational qualifications. By the 1970's that advantage enjoyed by the South had been swiftly eroded. Now the Yoruba and the Igbo have become disadvantaged in that respect also. The result is that all the successful military coups in Nigeria have been led by Northerners. In short, the North has a stranglehold on any Nigerian government. This is a legacy of British colonial policy.

Reflecting on the issues discussed above, members of the Political Bureau set up by the Federal Government of Nigeria in 1986 with a mandate to fashion an appropriate political system for the country, noted that

> The major political legacies of the colonial period can be summarized as follows: weak constitutional and institutional bases for development-oriented policies; unbalanced federation; regionalism which engendered mutual jealousy and fear erected barriers against free movement of people and goods; governance in which the masses were perceived as an exploitable group and leadership unaccountable to the people; regionally based political constituencies; and educational system that alienated the educated from his cultural milieu.

The criticisms, therefore, of British colonial administration in Nigeria made in this chapter are neither flippant nor the figment of the author's imagination. The Nigerian Civil War (1967-1970) may be seen as, in large part, as a bloody but unsuccessful attempt to solve these problems. The administrations of Yakubu Gowon (1967-1975), Murtala Mohammed (1975-1976), Olusegun Obasanjo (1976-1976); Shehu Shagari (1979-1983); Muhammed Buhari (1983-1985), Ibrahim Babangida (1985-1993); Sani Abacha (1993 - 1998); and Abdul Salaam Abubakar (1998 - 1999) have all equally failed to solve Nigerian's problems and not for want of trying. At a national conference held at Abuja in 1993 attended by a select group of Nigerian intellectual, academic, political and military elite (at which I had the honor to be an active participant), the theme was "to be or not to be" and it was unanimously resolved that Nigeria should be. That such an idea was even contemplated after thirty-three years of existence as an independent nation was mind-boggling, to say the least. But that the voices of disintegration, if any, were silent was a testimony to the fact that the Nigerian federation, its problems notwithstanding, will continue in the interest of all Nigerians, Africans, the African Diaspora, and the global community generally.

CONCLUSION

Needless to say, any overview of the history of a country as large and complex as Nigeria, to be meaningful, must inevitably be skeletal and selective. It has been demonstrated that although Nigeria has enormous geographic expanse, its compactness and easy internal and external accessibility from one point to the other facilitates relations between groups. The country is well endowed in its economic potential. It has a large and vibrant population. It has, therefore, most of the ingredients that make for greatness. The ancestry of Nigerians as well as the major movements in its pre-colonial history reveal that Nigeria is not the mere historical expression that conventional wisdom believes it to be. It was pointed out, nevertheless, that external influences - Arabic and European-did play a major role in the evolution of contemporary Nigeria. European influence, principally British, played a crucial role in the modernization of the country. This has left in its wake both positive and negative results. The tasks ahead for Nigerians are to fine-tune, so to speak, and adapt the positive legacies of colonialism to suit contemporary needs and to eliminate the negative aspects that are threatening to destroy the nation state. To explain Nigeria's troubles in the context of the failure of the post-colonial leadership alone has become the conventional wisdom of the internalist interpreters of Nigerian history. This approach is seriously flawed. Equally flawed is the externalist interpretation that fails to credit the work of the colonizers with any beneficial results, accidental or otherwise. A balanced study of the Nigerian past must assign appropriate weight to the two interpretations.

SUGGESTIONS FOR FURTHER READING

Adiele Afigbo, *Ropes of Sand: Studies in Igbo History and Culture* (Ibadan: University Press, 1981).

Obaro Ikirne (ed.), *Groundwork of Nigerian History* (Ibadan: Heineman, 1980).

John N. Oriji, *Traditions of Igbo Origin: A Study of Pre-colonial Population Movements in Africa* (New York: Peter Lang, 1990).

Richard Olaniyan (ed.) *Nigerian History and Culture* (Ibadan: Longman, 1985).

Lambert U. Ejiofor, *Igbo Kingdoms: Power and Control* (Onitsha: African Publishers, 1982).

Arthor Nzeribe, *A Manifesto for the Third Republic* (London: Kilimanjao Publishing Company, 1988)Robert S. Smith, *Kingdoms of the Yoruba* (London: Methuen, 1969).

Sam Epelle, *The Promise of Nigeria* (London: Pan Books, 1960).

Chinua Achebe, *The Trouble with Nigeria* (Enugu: Fourth Dimension, 1983).

Okwudiba Nnoli, *Ethnic Politics in Nigeria* (Enugu: Fourth Dimension, 1978).

Obaro Ikirne, *In Search of Nigerians: Changing Patterns of Inter-group Relations in an Evolving Nation-State* (Ibadan: Impact Publishers, 1985).

I.A. Akinjogbin and S.O. Osoba (eds.) *Topics on Nigerian Economic and Social History* (Ille-Ife: University of Ife Press, 1980).

Okon Edet Uya (ed.) *Contemporary Nigeria: Essays in Society. Politics and Economy* (Buenos Aires, Edipublisa, 1992).

J.F. Ade Ajayi and Bashir Ikara (eds) *Evolution of Political Culture in Nigeria* (Ibadan: University Press Ltd., 1985)

Michael Crowder (ed.) *History of West Africa Vol. I* (London: Longman, 1971).

Michael Crowder, *The Story of Nigeria* (London: Faber and Faber, 1996).

James S. Coleman, *Nigeria: Background to Nationalism* (Berkeley: University of California Press, 1958).

Nwanna Nzewunwa, *A Source Book for Nigerian Archeology* (Lagos: National Commission fc Museums and Monuments, 1983).

James O. Ojiako, *Nigeria: Yesterday, Today, and ...* (Onitsha: Africana Educational Books, 1981).

Mahdi Adamu, *The Hausa Factor in West African History* (Zaria: Ahmadu Bello University Pre 1978).

Alan C. Bums, *History of Nigeria* (London, 1956).

C.R,Niven, *A Short History of Nigeria* (London: Longman, 1952).
Athur Northern Cook, *British Enterprise in Nigeria* (London: Frank
    Cass, 1964).
The Conch: Nigeria 1975, Vol. V., Nos. & , 1975.

Dr. Nnamdi Azikiwe
Governor General 1960-1963
President 1963-1966

Chapter 2

A Survey of Nigerian History
Since Independence

Levi A. Nwachuku

INTRODUCTION

Britain began to make serious efforts towards Nigeria's independence after the end of the Second World War. These efforts were due to a combination of the impact of the war and the activities of the Nigerian nationalists. Much has been written on the salutary effects of this war on the aspirations of the colonized for their political freedom. The war, which can be seen as a European civil war, had the effect of challenging major European practices of the time. These included colonialism, state-sponsored racism, and fascism. The war ended, destroying Fascism and state-sponsored racism, and paved the way for the eventual end of colonialism. In 1941, Britain and the United States affirmed that the Second World War was a struggle for the vindication of democracy. This affirmation was expressed in the Atlantic Charter of August 1941. The Charter affirmed the right of all peoples to choose their own form of government. Although Winston Churchill exempted Great Britain's colonial subjects from this right, these subjects could not escape the dismantling effects of the charter on colonialism. It is this dismantling effect that, in part, induced in Britain "the loss of will to govern her colonies."[1]

In Nigeria, Britain's "loss of will" to continue governing her dependencies was exacerbated by the activities of the nationalists. These activities, however, led to several constitutional conferences after World War II. From 1947 to 1958, five Constitutional Conferences were held in London. The last London Conference, in 1958, was attended by 114 Nigerians. Nnamdi Azikiwe and Obafemi Awolono were among these delegates. The colonial disengagement conferences eventually ushered in independence for Nigeria. On October 1, 1960, after dominating them for the better portion of half a century, Great Britain transferred political power to the Nigerians.

The British left Nigeria with a sense of an accomplished mission, with a feeling that she had created a Nigerian state out of many separate nations. To the British, Nigeria was a success story of her colonial adventurism. Excited by Nigeria's peaceful transition to independence, Margery Perham, a student of British colonialism, commented that "the leadership, at least, of independent Negro Africa is there for Nigeria to take."[2]

At least, superficially, Nigeria at independence showed much promise of success. An appreciable percentage of the population had acquired political sophistication. The Nigerianized bureaucracy was moderately technocratic. The civil servants were efficient. To a large extent, they were driven by patriotism. Endowed with natural resources, Nigeria's economy had the potential for fostering self-sufficiency. Before their departure, the British had developed Nigeria's cash crops, in particular cocoa, cotton, oil palm, rubber and tea were grown. In the northern region , soya beans, peanuts and cotton were grown. Indeed, from the end of World War II through the end of Nigeria's first Republic, Nigeria's economy was largely sustained by the agricultural sector. As a matter of record, the seeming success of Nigeria's first years of statehood entitled the country to be considered as one of the happier creations of Britain's imperial adventure. However, as the Nigerian story unfolded, it became obvious that the new nation seriously needed national coherence.

Nigeria's independence did not immediately terminate her political association with Great Britain. For three years, 1960-1963, Nigeria still maintained political allegiance to the British crown. After 1963, however, Nigeria ceased to recognize the British crown as her titular head and became an independent republic. The move toward a republican status reflected Nigeria's conviction that true independence meant complete dissociation from whatever would seem to be British intervention in her political affairs. This political persuasion was apparent in the radical reaction that Nigerians exhibited against the retention of Peter Stallard, a Briton, as the private secretary of Sir Abubakar Tafawa Balewa ,the Prime Minister of Nigeria. If Nigeria was free from British colonial domination, would it be wise to retain a Briton as the private secretary of an independent Nigeria's Prime Minister? The contradiction ushered in a "Stallard must go" movement, and Peter Stallard was relieved of his appointment. In the same spirit of nationalism, the Anglo-Nigerian Defense Pact was annulled in 1962. The pact, which had its roots in the resumed constitutional conference in 1958 stipulated that Nigeria would provide Britain with facilities to run tropicalization trials of aircraft both above land and sea, and that Nigeria would also grant Britain rights for over-flying and air staging facilities.[3] Many Nigerians also questioned the wisdom of retaining Major-General Christopher Welby-Everard, a British officer, as the General Officer commanding the Nigerian Army.

Nigeria sought further affirmation of her independence by proclaiming a non-aligned posture in foreign policy issues. But this was the era of the cold war. The colonial experience made it difficult for it to translate its proclamation of neutrality into foreign policy practice. In essence, Nigeria could not be neutral in issues that involved Britain, in particular issues of diplomacy and economy. Nigeria depended heavily on trade with England and British citizens owned many companies in Nigeria. Nigeria found itself taking positions that were pro-British and pro-Western. It was politically pragmatic for Nigeria to lean toward Britain and its allies. A pro-Western posture did not contradict Nigeria's claim to sovereignty. These postures were simply acts of political pragmatism.

THE TEST OF THE NIGERIAN STATE

At the inauguration of Nigeria's independence, the prospect for democracy in the new nation seemed promising. In spite of the fact that the various political parties were ethnically and regionally based, the political parties that contested with each other in the Federal elections for the independence parliament were somehow able to create a government that appealed to the majority of Nigerians. But the hopes which attended Nigeria's independence did not sustain their grip on the country. As

Nigeria grew older in independence, its political and economic fortunes began to decline. In the first five years of independence, Nigeria experienced several crises, largely political in nature, which challenged the basis of its claim to a politically united nation. By the seventh month of its seventh year of independence, Nigeria was engulfed in a gruesome civil war. The civil war lasted until January 1970. Nigeria's history since the end of the war has largely been the story of a nation desperately in search of a national symbol of allegiance, a consensus leadership and a national ideology. One is prompted to conclude that the British defined as a country a geographical area, which has far too little political cohesion. Whatever national cohesiveness which Britain may have imposed, eluded the Nigerians when the colonial power left. Among the crises which shook the foundations of Nigerian unity were the census crisis of 1962-1963, the creation of the Mid-West region, the appointment of a vice-chancellor for the University of Lagos, the military coup d'etat, 1966, and the declaration of secession by the people of Eastern Nigeria on May 31, 1967.

CENSUS CRISIS, 1962-1963

The census exercise of 1962 was the first post-independence national enumeration. The three major regions of Nigeria at the time - the North, the West, and the East - recognized the importance of the census. Regional representation in the federal parliament was proportional to the population. The North's political domination depended on its large population. The other regions felt that an accurate 1962 census would reject northern claims to a large population, and diminish the basis of its political power in the central government. The census, it was hoped, would also guide the federal government in the distribution of regional economic and welfare programs. Walter Schwarz put it correctly when he said, "from the outset, the ...[census] was submerged in politics, with politicians and tribal leaders out to win."[4]

Unfortunately the census results were disputed. There were allegations that the Eastern and northern regions had inflated their figures. J. J. Warren, the Federal census officer, wrote the census off "as false and inflated,"[5] and the federal government did not publish the results. Had the results been accepted, the North would have lost its numerical dominance, since it had 22.5 million people as against 23 million in the southern regions, including Lagos.[6] Because of its political strength in the federal parliament, it is reasonable to suggest that the North was instrumental in the invalidation of the 1962 census. The political mood of the south was one of disenchantment, bordering on an inclination toward political separation from the North, a precursor of the later Biafran conflict. Kalu Ezera, a member of parliament from the south, described the mood: "Opinion in the south was rapidly and widely inclining to the dangerous view that secession of the south from the North would be the only answer to a continued Northern domination."[7] In 1963, a recount was undertaken. It gave the Northerners numerical superiority over the other regions. The Eastern Region rejected the results. The census had become a flash point for inter-regional conflict. The coalition between the northern led political party--Northern Peoples Congress (NPC) and the Eastern led political party--National Council of Nigerian Citizens (NCNC), weakened and finally dissolved in 1964. Perhaps of even greater significance, however, is the revelation of the deepening of schism, which developed between the Igbo of the East and the Hausa-Fulani of the North. During a Federal House of Representatives debate on the 1963 census, a member from the East commented that:

> Since the publication of the preliminary figures [census 1963] which theNCNC rejected, Nigerian unity seems to be in mortal peril. Northern Minister of Land, on behalf of his government, promised to dispossess the Ibos of their property as well as the earlier threat to remove them from the civil service of that region.[8]

Replying to the comment, a Northern member of parliament said, "it is no concern of this parliament what they do in the North, let them [Igbos] go home."[9] These statements were made by members of parliament whose parties were in coalition in governing the newly independent nation. There was a crisis of disunity and disagreement within the governing parties. It was an ominous sign of an impending fracture in the nation. Unfortunately, the parliament failed to collectively condemn statements that had the potential to ignite the fire of inter-ethnic discord. At independence, Nigeria emerged as a federation of three regions-- Northern, Western, and Eastern.

CREATION OF MID-WEST REGION

Each of the three major regions, North, West and East, had a numerically dominant ethnic group. The Hausa-Fulani were dominant in the North. The Yoruba and the Igbo were dominant in the West and the East respectively. However, each region also contained other ethnic groups, though numerically minor, that could qualify for separate regions. In the East, ethnic groups from the riverine areas wanted their own state, to be called Calabar-Oil-Rivers (COR). In the North, the non-Hausa-Fulani people, the Idoma and the Tiv, in particular, under the leadership of J. S. Tarkar wanted a Middle Belt State. The federal government was controlled by a coalition of the NCNC, which had strong Igbo support, and the NPC, which was Hausa-Fulani based. Neither party supported the aspirations of the minorities in the East and in the North for separate states.

Obafemi Awolowo, the popular Yoruba leader of the Action Group political party, had argued in favor of creating states along ethnic configurations. Awolowo and his party were in opposition to the NPC and NCNC in the federal parliament. They supported the creation of states for the minorities in the East and North respectively. However, the dominant ethnic group in each of these regions did not support creating states out of them. But the Federal parliament controlled by parties whose support comes from the East and the North respectively, voted in favor of creating a Mid-West State, although they opposed doing the same in their own respective regions. The Action Group opposed the creation of a Mid-West State. Their opposition was based on two factors: First, the Western Region was not willing to diminish its size. Creating the Mid-West Region would involve reducing the size of the Western Region by one third in terms of area. The second factor of objection was based on the refusal of the federal parliament to carve out states from the North and the East. The irrationality of the policy seemed obvious at least to the government of the Western Region and Yoruba politician Chief Samuel Akintola, the then premier of the Western region, argued that to create only the Mid-West Region while neglecting the aspirations of the minorities in the other regions was unfair.[10]

The Yoruba would also argue that the Mid-West Region was created on the dictates of ethnic politics. Consequently, they would see the dismantling of their region as a punitive measure meted out by the Hausa-Fulani and the Igbo, whose political parties dominated the federal parliament. The creation of the Mid-West State, revealed Nigeria's potential for inter-ethnic crises. Perhaps to avoid endangering Nigerian unity, the Yoruba, in the end, acquiesced.

LAGOS UNIVERSITY VICE-CHANCELLORSHIP CRISIS, 1965

The broadening of the gulf of ethnic disharmony was manifested further in the crisis which arose from the appointment of the Vice-Chancellor of Lagos University in 1965. Professor Eni Njoku, an Igbo, was appointed Vice Chancellor of the University of Lagos in 1962 by the Prime Minister for an initial three-year period, after which he could be re-appointed. At the expiration of Dr. Njoku's first term of office, the Provisional Council of the University refused to re-appoint him. The council argued that it was desirable to have a change in the university's leadership in order to facilitate the smooth running of the affairs of the institution. Consequently, the council recommended that Dr. S. O. Biobaku, a Yoruba by ethnicity, should be appointed. Many students, primarily Igbo, protested against the non-reappointment of Dr. Njoku. The council regarded the protest as a manifestation of fear by the Igbo that other ethnic groups were out to supplant them everywhere. One could argue that replacing an Igbo Vice-Chancellor with a Yoruba Vice Chancellor was induced by ethnic consideration. This argument may have merit. The University, located in a region that is geographically Yoruba, would be seen as a Yoruba University and should be led by a Yoruba. But the University as a federal institution, should not be run on a purely ethnic basis.

However, it would be politically naive to argue that the replacement of Eni Njoku as vice-chancellor of Lagos University was devoid of ethnic consideration. Eni Njoku was not found to be intellectually deficient, nor academically incapable, nor administratively a failure. He was, indeed, an internationally known and respected biochemist whose initial appointment was due to his excellent academic record. The view of G. F. Layu in this episode is instructive. "Anyone who knows Nigeria is painfully aware of the menace of tribalism which threatens the country's unity. What has happened in the University of Lagos . . . is one more example of the effects of this menace."[11] The crisis worsened the Igbo-Yoruba relationship, which was already marred by mutual suspicion.

PRELUDE TO THE FIRST MILITARY COUP

In December 1964, the Independence Parliament, which had been inaugurated on December 12, 1959, was dissolved. That parliament had been led by a pragmatic but fragile coalition of the Northern Peoples Congress (NPC) with 126 seats and the National Council of Nigerian Citizens (NCNC) with 66 seats. In opposition was the Yoruba dominated Action Group (AG). This parliamentary arrangement made it seem as if the Igbo and the Hausa-Fulani ruled Nigeria leaving the Yoruba and other smaller minorities out. The independence parliament revealed how tenuous Nigerian unity was.

In 1964, the first post-independence federal elections would polarize Nigeria into two hostile political camps. In that year, the NPC and the NCNC coalition collapsed. The Igbo-based NCNC and its affiliates coalesced with the Action Group and its allies to form the United Progressive Grand Alliance (UPGA). In response, the Hausa-Fulani based Northern Peoples Congress and its allies joined with Samuel Akintola's Nigerian National Democratic Party (NNDP) to form the Nigerian National Alliance party (NNA). The NNA enjoyed strong support in the Northern region, and the UPGA was southern-based and supported. Both political parties looked to the federal election to test their national strength and popularity.

The political atmosphere in the country was tense. The UPGA alleged that there were plans by the NNA to harass their members and candidates during the campaigns and elections. In the West, the NCNC headquarters in Ibadan was attacked. Action Group cars were burned and the houses of prominent UPGA members were damaged.[12] Against this background, the UPGA decided to boycott the elections.[13] In spite of this decision, the elections were held on December 30, 1960 as scheduled. The NNA won more seats since none of its candidates participated in the boycott. As the results of the elections showed, the decision of the UPGA to boycott the elections seemed, in retrospect, unwise. Of the 312 federal seats, the NNA won 200. Suspecting that the UPGA would contest the results on the grounds of their boycott of the election and the alleged electoral irregularities, the political leaders agreed to form a broadly based government in which the major political parties participated. In this coalition, political influence tended to favor the North. After all, the NNA, Northern-based, secured 200 seats of the 312 seats. It was widely believed that the broad-based compromise saved the Nigerian federation at least temporarily, from descent into disintegration.

WESTERN REGION ELECTION OF NOVEMBER, 1965

The virus of political instability that had affected the federal government spread to the Western Region and created an impasse in that region's 1965 election for a new assembly. The incidence of chaos reached a climax when the election degenerated into a campaign to plead the cause of the Yoruba. The manifesto of Samuel Akintola's Nigerian National Democratic Party testifies to the feeling of alienation that had gripped the Yorubas:

> Since 1944, the people of Western Region have been feeling as if they did not belong to the federation of Nigeria. They have not been in a position to share the amenities and fruits of labour emanating from the Federal Government and which other parts of the country share and openly flaunt before their eyes.[14]

For Nigeria, the year 1965 embodied fundamental contradictions. In this fifth year of independence, Nigeria stood tall among African nations. It was very active in the still-ongoing struggle to liberate African nations from the shackle of European imperialism, racism, and political powerlessness. Nigeria was a nation driven by a sense of destiny, amply qualified to lead the African continent. But the internal dynamics of the country revealed a nation tormented by forces of disintegration. Ethnicity remained a growing and dangerous threat to national unity. Following the census crisis, the appointment of Lagos University Vice Chancellor and the 1964 federal elections, secessionist talks escalated beyond the realm of just simple hot air. The Western Region election, which took place on October 11, 1965, would test Nigeria's capacity for overcoming political crises. The Nigerian National Alliance Party, a combination of the Northern Peoples' Congress, and the Nigerian National Democratic Party, contested the election along with the United Progressive Grand Alliance, a combination of the Action Group Party and National Council of Nigerian Citizens. The election revealed that intra-ethnic acrimony as well as rivalry among the Yoruba was intense. The root of this unhealthy situation among the Yoruba would be traced to the Awolowo-Akintola political conflict at the Eighth Annual Congress of the Action Group Party in 1962.

During the 1965 election, each party accused the other of all sorts of electoral malpractice. Feelings gave way to violent action, and the counter-accusations produced undesired casualties. There were more than

70 deaths, including two customary court judges. Several courthouses were burnt. The printing workshop of the Nigerian *Tribune*, the AG supported newspaper published in Ibadan, the capital of the Western Region, was also totally destroyed by fire. From October 11, the day of election, to October 23, curfew was declared in the Western Region. The region had become a raging river of humanity. Riots and vandalism were commonplace. The lives of the citizens were in peril and the leaders could not contain the violence. In the western region, newspapers produced by UPGA supporters, such as the *West African Pilot* (of Lagos), and the *Outlook* (of Enugu), were banned. If anyone was caught reading them, the individual would be fined $150.00 or given a sentence of six months in jail. If anyone in the West was discovered listening to the Eastern Nigeria Broadcasting Service, the person would be fined $37.50 or jailed for two months. In retaliation, newspapers that were controlled by the NNA were banned in the Eastern region, the home of NCNC and the UPGA. Those papers were *The Times*, *The Express*, and *The Post* of Lagos.

At the end of the election, Akintola's NNDP claimed victory. The opposing party, the United Progressive Grant Alliance (UPGA) led by Alhaji Adegbenro, contested the results of the election. Chief Samuel Akintola's NNDP leaders arrested Alhaji Adegbenro and a good number of UPGA leaders and charged them with "unlawfully forming an interim executive council for the government of Western Nigeria."[15] They were released without bail. Disturbed by the political crisis, leading Yoruba Obas met to resolve the crisis. They did not succeed in that effort.

In spite of electoral malpractice, and in spite of the admission of E. E. Esua, the Federal Electoral Officer, that there were anomalies in the electoral process, the official electoral results favored Akintola's NNDP. The refusal of the UPGA to accept that verdict plunged the Western region into a state of "suspended revolution,"[16] since political authority could no longer be located. The stalemate in the Western Region would signal the final collapse of the fledgling stability of the federal government. It is, nonetheless, ironic that as the NNA and the UPGA were warring in the Western Region, the same parties were prepared to coalesce at the Federal level. UPGA ministers were ready to serve in the national coalition government following the embattled 1964 federal elections.

Alhaji Abubakar Tafawa Balewa
Prime Minister 1960-1966

THE COUP D'ETAT OF JANUARY 15, 1966
AND THE SUBSEQUENT BREAK UP OF
THE NIGERIAN FEDERATION

As the political conflict in the Western region continued to persist, Nigerians began to be disillusioned with their politicians, whose self-centered activities were becoming irrelevant to the problems confronting the nation. Politicians were self-indulgent, the ministers in particular. Worst still, the nation was immersed in an orgy of corruption. Immediate post-independence high expectations were rapidly yielding to collective disappointments. Popular suspicion of the government reached an unprecedented height. It was at this juncture that the military intervened. On January 15, 1966, a military coup ended the first Nigerian Republic, and the country faced a future of uncertainties. The coup claimed the lives of Sir Abubakar, Tafawa Balewa, Ahmadu Bello, Samuel Akintola and Festus Okotiebo. The influence of these political leaders had determined the shape of events in Nigeria's history since its independence. Many Nigerians felt that the army, unpolluted by the corruption of politics, would be better able to lead the country into progress and stability.

Different sections and sectors of the country gave their approval to the military takeover. Intellectuals who had been resentful of the nepotism shown in appointments were pleased at the demise of a system that had fostered nepotism. Workers who had been experiencing hardship in making a living but seeing their political leaders wallowing in financial extravaganza hoped that a military regime would bring them relief. The United Labor Congress, in supporting the coup, argued that the action of the army "will aid the struggle of all true patriots against economic and social injustice, political fraud, tribalism, nepotism and the excesses of a few power-drunken politicians."[17] Even the Northern Peoples' Congress (NPC) that had enjoyed hegemonic control of Nigeria's politics showed, at least, initially, appreciation for the military intervention. On January 18, 1966, five days after the coup, the NPN issued a release signed by Alhaji Hasina Adaji, Minister of State. The release said:

> The party regards the transfer of authority as the only solution to the many recent problems facing this country. The party gives its unqualified support to the military regime and to the Major General in particular... we call on all the peoples of Nigeria irrespective of tribal origin or political persuasion to rally round the new military government so as to make easy its great and noble task.[18]

On the whole, there seemed to be a national feeling of joy, and a collective sigh of relief. On January 17, 1966, Lagos University students carried placards reading "Tyranny is ended. New era of peace and justice."[19] But the coup did not end tyranny or usher in peace and justice. It, instead, would preside over the birth of a new Nigeria with an uncertain future.

For a little over five months, the military coup enjoyed national approval. However, two misunderstandings expedited the evaporation of that jubilation. The first misunderstanding grew from the pattern of killings during the coup. A national political leader from western Nigeria was assassinated, as was one such from the Mid-west region. Two leaders from the Northern Region were also assassinated. However, no national political leader from the East was killed. No Igbo political leader was a casualty of the coup. The regions that lost their leaders began to see the coup as an Igbo plot. John de St. Jorre wrote: "But for the federal government and many others, it was the tribal pattern of killings as much as the ethnic origins of the killers that provides the most damning evidence to support the Igbo conspiracy theory."[20]

From the above comment, it would be correct to argue that the northerners as well as many westerners, because they lost some of their political stalwarts, sincerely believed that the coup was an Igbo design; that the Igbo were attempting to use military means to reverse what they perceived as the political hegemony of the North. However, Walter Schwarz seemed to have captured the true essence of the coup when he said: "Others see it-perhaps more accurately-as a sincere attempt at a national and radical revolution, planned without thoughts of tribal advantage, but which later came to be contaminated and perverted by tribalist consideration."[21]

The second misunderstanding emerged from Decree 34. Aguiyi Ironsi, the most senior officer in the army became Nigeria's leader as a result of the coup, and to maintain national unity was a major goal. He, therefore, issued Decree No. 34, which abolished the federal system in favor of a unitary one. However, the northern section of the country was not enthusiastic about the decree and openly opposed it. The negative reaction to the decree indicated that the military government had misread the mood of a section of the nation that it opted to govern.

The January 15 coup, as it happened, was a prelude to Nigeria's disintegration. Barely seven months thereafter, a second coup took place on July 29, 1966. General Johnson T.U. Aguiyi Ironsi, who became the Head of the Nigerian Military Government after the overthrow of the First Republic, was brutally assassinated along with Adekunle Fajuyi, his host

Major General Aguiyi Ironsi
Head of State
January 1966-July 1966

in Ibadan. The manner in which these men were killed reveals the dark side of human nature. The killing was described thus:

> Finally, major Danjuma (second in command of the Fourth Battalion) took some of his men upstairs, confronted and questioned the Supreme Commander (Major-General Aguiyi Ironsi), saluted him and ordered his arrest. The general was led downstairs to join the others. The three captives (the Western governor, Fajuyi, who with great gallantry, refused to leave his guest and commander, and Ironsi's A.D.C. were now stripped and their hands tied behind their backs with wire. They were flogged, tortured and then put into separate police vans. The captives were ordered out and led along a footpath off the right side of the road. These Northern officers and men beat and tortured the captives so badly that their bodies were swollen and bleeding profusely...the supreme commander and the governor who were almost dead by now, were separately finished off by a few rounds of machine-gun fire.[22]

Lieutenant-Colonel Yakubu Gowon, a northerner, became the Commander-in-Chief of the Nigerian Military Army and the Head of the Military Government. The July coup d'etat generally seen as a "return match," was a reaction of the Northerners, who as a result of the first coup, had lost their political power at the federal level. The coup was accompanied by a massacre of Nigerians of Eastern origin. Estimates of the massacre ranged between 10,000 and 50,000 dead.[23] Most of the victims were Igbo. The new military government claimed that it could not control the massacre and, therefore, should not be blamed. The massacre in the north resulted in the mass exodus of Easterners, largely Igbo, to their homeland. At this point, Nigerian unity suffered its greatest setback, and the Head of the Military Government reflected this situation in his broadcast on August 1, 1966:

> I have now come to the most difficult part, or the most important part, of this statement--I am doing it conscious of the great disappointment and heartbreak it will cause all true and sincere lovers of Nigeria and of Nigerian unity....As a result of the recent events and the other previous similar ones, I have come to strongly believe that we cannot honestly and sincerely continue in this wise, as the basis of trust and confidence in our unitary system of government has not been

> able to stand the test of time...suffice it to say that, putting all
> considerations to the test--political, economic, as well as
> social--the base for unity is not there or is so badly rocked not
> only once but several times.[24]

The statement was ominous for the cause of Nigerian unity.

Understandably, the pogrom that took place before and after the second coup d'etat strained the relationship between the North and the East. The inability of the military government to stop the killings made the easterners fear that their general security could not be guaranteed by the new Military Government. Because of this, on May 30, 1967, Colonel Chukwuemeka Ojukwu, the Military Governor of Eastern Nigeria, made the proclamation of secession, saying, "aware that you (Easterners) can no longer be protected in your lives and in your property by a government based outside Eastern Nigeria...I do declare that all political ties between us and the Federal Republic of Nigeria are hereby totally dissolved"[25]

Thus, six years after independence, the solidarity of Nigerian unity was tested and found wanting. A military coup d'etat in January 1966, followed by a civil upheaval later in the year, created a situation which led to the disintegration of the country. To nullify the secession of the Republic of Biafra, the rest of Nigeria declared war on July 6, 1967. For thirty months (July 6, 1967 to January 12, 1970) the two states, Biafra and Nigeria, were at war with each other. To the Nigerians, this struggle was a war for unity to preserve the federation. But to the Biafrans, it was a war for survival. On January 12, 1970, the war ended with a proclamation by General Gowon that there was "no victor and no vanquished." Biafra was reincorporated into Nigeria. But the old Nigeria would have to be rebuilt in order to accommodate a section that sought to break away.

Ardent supporters of the Biafran cause were bewildered by Biafra's defeat. On examination of the birth and death of Biafra, one discovers that the Biafran experiment was doomed to a short life. Major-General Alexander Madiebo, in a brilliant expository, *The Nigerian Revolution and the Biafran War*, discussed factors which he believed made Biafra fail. Among the factors were: (1) Inadequate weapons; (2) Failure to take initiative following the counter-coup of July 1966; (3) Foreign support for Nigeria; (4) Crisis of confidence within the Biafran army; (5) President Ojukwu saw himself as the sole effective policy-maker in a time of national struggle.[26]

Judging from the above factors, it would appear that Biafra was a premature experiment, at the time. The initiators of the experiment underestimated the need for careful thought, careful analysis and careful planning. However, given the urgency of the crisis, the above lapses were expected. It is this underestimation that the Nigerians and other foes of Biafra exploited. When the northerners engaged in systematic destruction of innocent Igbo lives, both in the army and the civilian sector, it behooved the Igbo to have challenged the cruel aggression of the northerners by revenging in the field of aggression. The failure to have done this gave the northerners a psychological advantage that aided their effort against the Igbo. During World War II, it was the failure of England and France to challenge Hitler's march into the Rhineland that strengthened his courage in the pursuit of his *Lebensraum* for the Germans. When the former decided to call a halt to Hitler's conquest of other nations, Hitler had been well entrenched in his occupations of the territories. A world war became inevitable. Again the second World War showed that a careful plan yields desired results. Hitler did not begin his conquest overnight. He planned and invested resources and mobilized his nation around his plans. Ojukwu's leadership was deficient in the requirements needed to execute the Biafran struggle. In a struggle for survival, it is risky for one to rely on other people's assistance for success. The Biafran leadership placed too much hope on the contributions of foreign support. There was over confidence in the perceived sympathy of some foreign powers. The Biafran leadership did not seem to distinguish between the humanitarian attitude of some of the sympathetic foreign nations and their political inclinations. These nations were unwilling to allow the Biafrans to starve to death. They were equally unwilling to support an independent Biafran State. Therefore, for the Biafran leadership to have assumed that the people of the United States, for example, who contributed much to the alleviation of hunger in Biafra would also give the Biafrans political and military support was an exercise in futility.

An independent Biafra would belie England's claim of colonial success in Nigeria as it pertains to national political unity. Also, European business interests in Nigeria favored a united Nigeria. The West may have felt that an independent Biafra would cut it off from the supply of oil, more so as the Biafrans and the Nigerians were each seeking Soviet Russia's support. Biafra, then, became a casualty of global geopolitical considerations.

In the final analysis, the division into more states was lethal for the Biafran cause. When Yakubu Gowon created states in the Eastern Region, he dismantled the region's geographic solidarity. The Efik and the Ibibio became more interested in the affairs of the South-Eastern

State, which had been created for them. The people of the Rivers were consolidating themselves in their newly created identity. The Igbo were consigned to what Gowon called East Central State. Since the leadership of the Biafran war was largely in the hands of the Igbo, the Biafran war was seen as an Igbo affair. Understandably, the peoples of the South Eastern states as well as the Rivers States became lukewarm in sacrificing their lives for a cause which had become increasingly identified with Igbo hegemony. The Nigerian forces exploited this vulnerability. They encircled the Biafran enclave by controlling the neighboring states, one by one. It is probable that if the South Eastern State and the Rivers State had meaningfully cooperated with the Igbo of the East Central State, the Nigerians could not have easily defeated the Biafrans.

AFTER-MATH OF THE CIVIL WAR: A FEDERAL OMNIPOTENCE

The Nigerian Civil War produced after-effects, which in many respects, transformed Nigeria's geopolitics, and gave birth to a new social ethics and redefined Nigeria's economic base. Prior to the Nigerian Civil War, the regions had enjoyed an impressive measure of autonomy. The national government, in some aspects, exercised only peripheral authority. However, during the period preceding the Nigerian Civil War, General Aguiyi Ironsi, Nigeria's first Military Head of State, promulgated Decree No. 34 on May 24, 1966. This abolished political regionalism and transferred all powers to the central government. General Aguiyi's argument was that regionalism fostered ethnicity that was detrimental to Nigeria's unity. However, the decree's intent was not appreciated by all sections of Nigeria. The people of the Northern Region resented the measure. They felt that centralization would subject them to southern domination. This centralization would continue, however. Subsequent governments, after General Ironsi, centralized the Nigerian State and extended its reach by dominating the powers of the states. During every military regime, the central government appointed the chief executives of every state who in turn appointed their respective cabinets that would also be approved by the Federal Military Government. Federal agencies superintended most of the activities of the states. This Federal presence dominated the political as well as the economic landscape of the states. It took much effort by the citizens of the various states to convince the Federal Government to even allow states to build their own universities.

The loss of state autonomy was not a product of popular will. The framers of the independence constitution did not intend the center to have pervasive powers. The military, which dominated Nigerian politics for more than a quarter of a century, regarded political centralization as essential to their purpose. It is a convenient governing mechanism. Alongside centralization, the Federal Military Government circumscribed the press, stamped out political debate and overtly freed itself from political checks. The State Secret Service became a familiar agency of the national government.

Centralization of political authority raises a sensitive issue in post civil war Nigerian politics. Who dominates the center? Nigeria is an ethnically heterogeneous society. Much concern is generated about the nature of the composition of the central authority. The power that dominates the center also rules the other sections of the country. The post-civil war period has witnessed the weight of political authority in the center shifting in favor of the Hausa-Fulani ethnic group. From 1960 to 1998, eleven individuals served as Nigeria's Executive Heads of State. Of these, eight (Abubakar Tafawa Balewa, Yakubu Gowon, Murtala Mohammed, Shehu Shagari. M. Buhari, Ibrahim Babangida, Sani Abacha Abdulsaluam) were from the Northern Region; two (Obasanjo, Shonekan) from the Yoruba ethnic group in the Western Region and one (Aguiyi Ironsi) an Igbo from the Eastern Region. He ruled for only six months before he was assassinated by northern soldiers. Thus we see that political power in Nigeria during the period has been strongly dominated by the Northern oligarchy.

SOCIAL ETHICS

After the Civil War, Nigeria developed new social ethics in which wealth determined social elevation and defined justice. The pursuit of wealth became the object of this new morality and its accumulation became an important agendum of most Nigerians. This has produced an ignoble culture of corruption in almost all facets of Nigerian life. Almost every agency of the state carried the virus of corruption. Ministries rarely execute their projects, yet financial allocations are made for such projects. The postal delivery system is a failure. Mail from overseas countries were usually opened by postal workers looking for foreign currencies. Reports abounded of overseas residents who complained that letters to their relations in Nigeria did not get to them. Bribery in transactions became the rule rather than the exception. It became a common practice to inflate the cost of contracts. Government finances are regarded as public property for looting by those employed by the state. In a statistical analysis of corrupt nations in the world, Nigeria ranks at number one. As in any corrupt society, not everyone has equal access to wealth. Those denied access to wealth, use whatever means is feasible to obtain riches. Armed robbery, prostitution, ritual killings and "419" (obtaining business by fraud) are all actions that have been taken in this pursuit.

THE IGBO EXPERIENCE

There is no doubt that the civil war's effect on Nigeria exposed all Nigerians to new experiences. However, the effects on the Igbo need special discussion. Before the war, the Igbo participated in Nigeria's politics and bureaucracy. They were respected citizens. Confident, energetic, enterprising and evincing an appreciation of self-worth, they saw themselves as a people destined to play a positive role in the promise of Nigeria. It is, perhaps, that ebullient self-confidence, that faith in their indomitable spirit that encouraged the Igbo to challenge the central government when the latter attacked them on July 6, 1967. Employing well-orchestrated propaganda, the Igbo leadership successfully mobilized the minds of their people to fight an enemy they believed would easily be defeated. However, the outcome of the war belied the reality of that belief. After having sacrificed their youth, having failed to achieve their goal of independence, the Igbo suffered social and psychological injuries. Enemy soldiers violated and abducted Igbo women. This experience caused them torment and physical scars. It was a moral injury done on the Igbo society. The Igbo experienced disorientation and decenteredness. Since the end of the Nigerian Civil War, the Igbo have become the symbol of political and social marginalization.

The civil war did not argue well for the relationship between the Igbo and their neighbors. During the war, many Igbo who owned property in Port-Harcout abandoned it and sought safety in their villages. As the Igbos left, the other people of Port Harcourt claimed the abandoned properties and refused to return them to their owners when the war ended. This situation soured the relationship between the people of the Rivers State and the Igbo. A feeling of mutual suspicion dogged their relationship and made political partnership between the two groups almost impossible to achieve. In 1979, when Nigeria returned to a democratically elected government, inaugurating the Second Republic, the two Igbo neighboring states, Rivers and Cross River, voted for a northern-based political party, which the Igbo did not support. Opinion polls in those neighboring states revealed that they voted not out of support for the northern-based party, but out of spite and dislike for the Igbo.

For the Igbo, the post civil war experience produced a strange contrast of selfish individualism and communal cooperation for community development. Most people were more concerned with personal survival than worrying about the survival of a neighbor. This was a sharp change from the lifestyle enjoyed before the civil war. It was commonplace in Igbo communities for a community as a whole to pay for the education of any of its sons in universities overseas. Before the war, communities collected money to support any of their industrially enterprising sons in an economic adventure. An Igbo community believed that the progress of any of its members reflected the progress of the entire community. Conversely, the misfortune or the lack of progress of any member of the community was essentially the failure of the community as a whole. However, the Igbo inclination to collective and communal assistance seemed to have faded away with the civil war. During the civil war, many Igbo suffered from disillusionment, embitterment, disorientation and physical need. This experience taught the Igbo the individualistic nature of the struggle for survival. Some parents, searching to provide for their children during the war, lost their lives, leaving the children to fend for themselves. Survival defined the emotional chemistry of the Igbo. During the war, it was a matter of both the survival of the state of Biafra and also the survival of the individual. The survival of Biafra essentially meant the sacrifice of the individual Igbo, and by extension, a negation of the survival of the individual. In the end, the primacy of individual survival outweighed the need for Biafran survival. The pursuit of collective or communal security gave way to the pursuit of individual survival. Because of the Biafran War, the individual Igbo developed a greater consciousness for self-survival and became less interested in being his brother's keeper. The war, however, did not altogether destroy the cohesive social fabric of the Igbo. Instead, it reinforced their sense of unity. The Igbo learned from the war that they live in a social and political environment hostile to their survival. They appreciated the fact that Nigeria could not offer them help or opportunities for economic survival. They took their economic destiny in their own hands. Barely two years after the civil war, one could hardly notice that the Igbo areas had experienced a devastating civil war. The

Igbo had rebuilt their region and embarked upon economic adventures that argued well for their prosperity. Imo State, in the heartland of the Igbo people, is the only state that built its own airport, although the Nigerian federal government built airports for the other states. Today, many Igbo communities raise funds to provide themselves with electricity and water. They have become the architect of their region's social engineering. Before the war, people of Igbo extraction would erect palatial buildings in other regions of Nigeria where they are not indigenous. The lessons of the Civil War taught them to seek security of property in their own states.

NIGERIA, 1970-1980: THE BOOM DECADE, AN OVERVIEW

The history of Nigeria from 1970 to 1980 is a story of a nation enjoying an economic boom. Commercial output of crude oil in Nigeria, which began in December 1957, blossomed into the major source of the country's wealth by the 1970s. Nigeria's problem was "not money, but how to spend it," the Nigerian war leader, Gowon, boasted. Nigeria was producing more than 2 million barrels of crude oil petroleum daily. The country was, however, guided by the regulations of the Organization of Petroleum Exporting Countries (OPEC), of which it became a member in 1971. During this decade, Nigeria loaned the World Bank $324 million (In 1971, one Nigerian Naira was equal to $135.00. The exchange rate is 2003 is the exact reverse: one U.S. dollar now purchases N135 in the autonomous market) to be repaid in ten installments at eight percent interest.[27] Also Nigeria introduced Universal Primary Education (UPE), and built five more federally supported universities each at Jos, Calabar, Sokoto, Maiduguri and Kano. In order to produce enough teachers, many teacher-training institutions were built. The building of a new capital at Abuja was begun. Indian engineers were commissioned to revitalize the railroad systems. On the recommendation of Jerome Udoji's Salary Commission, Nigerian workers received a 133 percent pay hike.[28] The workers received one-year arrears of salary. Nigeria hosted the World Black and African Festival of Arts and Culture in which more than 35,000 performers participated. The Nigerian government invested 33 million dollars in the event, including building a national arts theater modeled after Bulgaria's Palace of Sports and Culture. The theater cost six hundred thousand dollars.[29] Unmindful of the unhealthy effect of the expenditure on its foreign exchange reserve, Nigeria worsened the situation by relying heavily on imported food and manufactured products for its economic comfort.

Believing that the good health of the economy would continue, the government introduced optimistic national development plans. The first of the plans (for 1962 through 1968) laid a good foundation for Nigeria's industrial growth. The Second National Development Plan (for 1970 through 1974) and the Third National Development Plan (for 1980 through 1985) called for N3.27 billion and N10.7 billion investments respectively by the government.[30] The decade of the 1970's witnessed an unprecedented migration of Nigerians from the rural environment to towns and cities. Many who had sustained their lives by farming abandoned that calling and moved to cities in search of the new wealth. This caused the gradual abandonment of agriculture and consequently a national dependence on imported food. The agricultural sector lost its place as the premier source of Nigeria's foreign exchange earning. As urbanization further developed, it brought with it greater incidents of such social problems as prostitution, ghettos, traffic problems, poverty, robbery, and other urban-associated dilemmas. The government may not have anticipated these problems and was ill prepared to find solutions for them.

However, there were indications that Nigeria was riding on the crest of prosperity. This prosperity induced a get-rich-quick attitude in the society. As would be expected, this outlook produced greed and corruption. Thus, the decade of the 1970s witnessed not only an economic boom but also a boom in corruption. Unfortunately, the economic boom evaporated as the decade lapsed into history, but the corruption boom would grow to new heights in the coming decades. It was equally unfortunate that as the petro-naira (petroleum-based currency) was visible in the 1970s giving economic comfort to the Nigerians, Nigerians were denied the experience of democratic government. For nine of the ten years of this decade, Nigerians chafed under the anvil of military dictatorship. The military relinquished power in October 1979 only to return in December 1983.

NIGERIA, 1980-1990S: THE TROUBLED
YEARS, AN OVERVIEW

With the birth of the Second Republic, Nigerians felt relieved that democracy had returned. There was a general feeling that the decade of the eighties would be an improvement on the one that preceded it. The economy did not, at the time, indicate signs of collapse. The political landscape did not show cracks and potholes. It was not recognized then that the outward manifestation of political and economic stability masked an inner turbulence, which was propelling Nigeria toward national decline. The second democratic experiment survived for only 51 months, however. In December 1983, the Republic ended when the Nigerian military overthrew it.

The failure of the experiment has been attributed to unbridled corruption, unchecked extravagance defined by gross economic mismanagement, electoral fraud and poor political leadership. Whether these factors were the legitimate cause of the demise of Nigeria's second experiment in democratic government is difficult to confirm. A more detailed analysis of the Second Republic is found in chapter six. What is certain, however, is that the democratic government was not given the opportunity to solve the problems that confronted it. Indeed, during the Second Republic, Nigerians did not experience any devastating economic crisis. Essential commodities could be afforded by average Nigerians. The National Party of Nigeria (NPN), the ruling political party, attracted support across the country, from many ethnic groups. Although there were allegations of rigging and other unfair practices during elections, still, Nigerians accepted the results in order to prevent the Nigerian Army from seizing power. When the military, under General Muhammadu Buhari, took power in December 1983 it was argued that the problems surrounding the elections invited the army to take over the government.

By 1981, Nigeria had begun to experience a downward slide in its economy. Very suddenly, essential commodities became scarce by April 1984. Inflation rose to an unprecedented level. Workers were laid off. The laying off exercise even extended to the universities. Nigerian's currency, the naira, began to depreciate. Development projects were halted. The government began to ration essential commodities. Some state governments responded to the depressed economy by cutting down on capital projects. In Imo State, Governor Ike Nwachukwu, who was in office from 1984 to 1986, introduced what came to be known as the "Imo Formula." By this formula, workers in Imo State public service were to be paid according to their respective productive capacity. In simple terms, if a public servant's productive capacity amounted to only eighty percent of his salary, he would lose twenty percent of his salary for that month. This formula raised some troublesome issues. How would the productive capacity of a worker be measured? It would appear that the Imo Formula was concerned with improving the productive capacity of any employee rather than a reaction to a depressed economy. Eventually, the Imo formula translated into delayed payment of salaries to the state civil servants. Civil servants in many states would go for months without receiving their salaries. Eventually, non-payment of salaries to state civil servants became a national occurence. Only workers in the Federal Public Service were certain that they would be paid their salaries at the end of the month. The non-payment of salaries to workers produced a predictably negative effect on the work ethic of public servants. Workers seemed to regard public service more as a mere past time rather than a committed responsibility for the service of the nation. They went to work if and when they chose. Those of them who controlled budgets and allocations, found any means feasible to embezzle funds. The economic situation produced two classes of Nigerians: the few very wealthy who exploited the system to their advantage and the abject poor who had no access to the possibilities of exploitation. For average Nigerians, their political destiny was uncertain, the economic situation precarious and daily existence at best, extremely troublesome. As the political and economic condition deteriorated, Nigerians felt that the military had lost legitimacy. It was no longer a viable instrument that could restore political and economic stability. On the contrary, the military failed to give the Nigerians the very stability and security of life, which it had claimed as its excuse for overthrowing democratically elected governments.

As the 1980s ended, the chemistry of the Nigerian body politic continued to expose the imbalance in the distribution of the country's assets. A true federal character in the distribution of assets continued to elude the Nigerians. The military rulers allowed ethnic considerations to determine national policy directions. Major political appointments in federal establishments continued to favor Nigerians of northern origin. The Yoruba ethnic group continued to enjoy the domination of the federal bureaucracy. This was largely because the federal capital was located in their geographic zone. Ethnic groups, considered as minorities, did not relent in their preference for alliance with the North, indeed, with the Hausa-Fulani political oligarchy. They sometimes received crumbs of political favor in return. The Igbo ethnic group continued to experience political as well as economic neglect. Sometimes, this neglect was tantamount to an effort at economic strangulation. In the late 1980s, there was a repeat of the policies of the 1970s, which dealt a lethal blow to the economic sustenance of Igbo businessmen. In the 1970s, the federal government banned the importation of second-hand clothes as well as stockfish. These commodities had been vital to Igbo importation businesses.

Since the late 1970s, the Igbo dominated the interstate transportation system--"the luxury bus" phenomenon. This is a public transportation system privately organized. But in the late 1980s, the federal government introduced a state run public transportation system with cheaper fare. This was perceived as the federal government's design to close viable avenues of Igbo economic progress. Thus, for the Igbo ethnic group, the decade of the 1980s was not one of political and economic contentment, but one of a continuous quest for the relevance of the federation of Nigeria to their existence.

As the decade of the nineties dawned, Nigeria's political uncertainties and economic situation continued to get worse. Inflation had become uncontrollable. Workers' wages fell far below expenditure. College graduates could not find employment. Institutions of higher learning remained closed for more periods than they were open. Industrial output fell below capacity. Many Nigerians began to leave for overseas nations in search of greener pastures.

Nigeria witnessed the highest rate of brain drain in its history. Many university lecturers began to leave Nigeria for universities in the United States of America. Nigerian workers smuggled themselves into Italy and other European countries seeking employment picking tomatoes, harvesting other crops, and performing other menial tasks in the worst of conditions on subsistence wages. On June 12, 1993, hope was rekindled when the Nigerians elected a civilian government to be headed by Alhaji Moshood Abiola. It was a short-lived reality. The military government under General Ibrahim Babangida nullified the election and appointed Ernest Shonekan to hold the instrument of power, if only temporary. It was, indeed, a very temporary appointment. On November 17, 1993, General Sani Abacha seized power restoring the military to power. Generals Babangida and Abacha will be remembered in history as the two leaders who nullified the national will of the Nigerian peoples by overturning their mandate. After the nullification, there was an intensified call for the abdication of the military from Nigerian politics. General Sani Abacha had drawn a program to restore democracy to Nigeria. By his program, an elected government would be installed in October 1998. The popular suspicion was, however, that Abacha would succeed himself as a civilian president. General Abacha died suddenly on on June 8, 1998. He was succeeded by General Abdulsalam Abubakar. Thus, at the close of the 20th century, the statement of Anthony Kirk-Greene and Douglas Rimmer, in their book, *Nigeria Since 1970*, becomes instructive. They said: "We cannot pretend to see clearly the future of Nigeria; not even the immediate future."[31] However, in chapter eleven we attempt the difficult task of assessing the problems and prospects of the Nigerian nation-state in the 21st century.

ENDNOTES

1. Kalu Ezera, *Constitutional Developments in Nigeria*, 2nd Edition, London: Cambridge University Press, 1964, 133.
2. Margery Perham, *Colonial Reckoning*, N.Y.: Alfred Knopf, 1962, 88.
3. House of Representatives Debates (Nigeria), 1960, 56-58
4. Walter Schwarz, *Nigeria*, N.Y.: Frederick A. Praeger, 1968, 158.
5. Ibid., 159
6. Loc cit.
7. Ezera, *Constitutional Developments*, 281-2.
8. House of Representatives Debates (Nigeria) , April 1, 1964: 1418
9. Loc cit.
10. *West Africa*, April 21, 1962, 423.
11. G. F. Layu, *Letter to the Editor*, *West Africa*, July 24, 1965, 826.
12. *West African Pilot*, May 24, 1964.
13. Schwarz, *Nigeria*, 164-169.
14. Cited in Ibid., 179.
15. West Africa, October 23, 1965, 1194.
16. *West Africa*, November 13, 1965, 1183.
17. *West Africa*, January 22, 1966, 83.
18. Loc cit.
19. Loc cit.
20. John de St. Jorre, *The Nigerian Civil War.* London: Holder and Stoughton, 1972, 45.
21. Schwarz, *Nigeria*, 194.
22. *Before and After*, Volume 7: Enugu: Eastern Region Government, January 18, 1964, 46-47.
23. C. Odumegwu Ojukyu, *Biafra*, N.Y.: Harper and Row, 1969, 17.
24. Edited by Anthony H. M. Kirk-Greene, *Crisis and Conflict in Nigeria: A Documentary Source Book 1966-1970*, London: Oxford University Press, 1971, Vol. I., 197.
25. Cited in Ibid., 451-452.
26. Enugu, Fourth Dimension, 1980, 377-384.
27. *Africa Report*, January-February, 1975, 27.
28. *West Africa*, January 6, 1975, 25.
29. Africa Report, July-Aug., 1975, 25-26.
30. Anthony H. M. Kirk-Greene and Douglas Rimmer, *Nigeria Since 1970: A Political and Economic Outline*, N.Y.: Africana Publishing Company, 1981, 142.
31. Ibid.,156.

PART TWO

FROM GOWON TO

ABUBAKAR

General Yakubu Gowon
Head of State
July 1966-1975

Chapter Three

Era of Misguided Good Feeling: Yakubu Gowon and the Birth of a New Nigeria, 1970-1975

O. N. Njoku

BACKGROUND

The surrender of the secessionist Biafran military command to the Nigerian federal forces on January 15, 1970 began the second phase of General Yakubu Gowon's rule as military Head of State of Nigeria. At the news of the Biafran surrender, Nigerians poured into streets and village squares in jubilation. There was a general feeling that Nigeria was on the threshold of a golden era.[1] An atmosphere of high expectations and euphoric feeling pervaded the nation. The cessation of hostilities offered an opportunity for a "fresh start."[2]

This chapter examines the rule of General Yakubu Gowon after the close of the Nigerian Civil War, the event that was the basis for the mood of optimism and euphoria prevalent in Nigeria at the time. It will be argued that at the end of the war, Gowon had an excellent opportunity to initiate a purposive and radical program that could launch the country into a period of positive economic and social transformation. The signposts to the future appeared inviting, and Gowon's early gestures encouraged optimism. But having won the war, Gowon proved neither able to heal the country's wounds satisfactorily nor to consolidate the peace. It seems also that Nigerian's themselves fell victim to the "conspiracy of optimism" and failed to recognize some fallacies in the theory of a fresh start. The ultimate criterion for judging a government is the quality of life of the majority of the governed. The program that a government sets for itself to accomplish is also a convenient and objective yardstick for accessing its degree of success. The discussion that follows of the Gowon regime is based on these two premises.

SILVER LINING

A convergence of events during the early part of the "new era" looked very promising. After thirty months of a bitter civil war, all Nigerians had good cause to heave a sigh of thanks and relief. Many had survived the conflict by acts of providence. Although the Igbo lost the war, they won the admiration of Nigerians, indeed of the international community as well, by their heroic courage and ingenuity.[3]

But prolonged fighting and mutually recriminatory propaganda had narrowed sympathies and stiffened prejudices on both sides of the divide. Fear of another anti-Igbo pogrom was widespread and real not only among the Igbo themselves but among also foreign leaders. Thus appeals for magnanimity in victory came to Gowon from different world leaders including Pope Paul II.[4] The apprehensions, however, turned out to be largely unfounded. On January15, 1970, Major General Philip Effiong of the Biafran Armed Forces handed over to Gowon at Dodan Barracks, Lagos, a document of surrender "in a very cordial, casual and friendly atmosphere."[5] This was achieved without overt external mediation and has been likened to the surrender of General Robert Lee of the Confederacy army to General Ulysses S. Grant of the Union army during the American civil war.

In his response to Effiong, Gowon stressed the need for reconciliation, saying that in the war there was "no victor, no vanquished."[6] In his broadcast to the nation later on that day, Gowon again sounded reassuring and magnanimous:

We guarantee the personal safety of everyone who submits to the federal authority. We guarantee the security of life and property of all citizens in every part of Nigeria, and equality in political rights. We also guarantee the right of every Nigerian to reside and work wherever he chooses in the federation as equal citizens of one united country.[7]

To the Igbo in particular and ex-Biafrans in general, apprehensive of the fate that awaited their return to the Nigerian fold, the broadcast was most reassuring. Already in 1968, the federal government had established the National Rehabilitation Commission (NRC) with the primary purpose of bringing relief to the victims of the war. At the cessation of hostilities, the Commission proceeded to execute its mandate with some vigor. It suffices for now to note that the establishment of the Commission helped to raise the expectations of the war victims. Another boost to the national optimism was the launching of the Second National Development Plan (NDP), 1970-74. The plan presented a socialist ideal, stressing that

A just and egalitarian society puts a premium on reducing inequalities in interpersonal incomes and promoting balanced development among various communities . . . . It organizes its economic institutions in such a way that there is no oppression based on class, social status, ethnic group or state.[8]

Gowon thus promised to build Nigeria into a great and dynamic economy with bright and equal opportunities for all.

Then on the 10th national independence anniversary, he unveiled a nine-point program which, he announced, was aimed at healing the wounds of the civil conflict and steering Nigeria back to the path of peace and social harmony based on shared values. The nine-point program emphasized: (1) reorganization of the armed forces; (2) implementation of the Second NDP and repair of damage and neglect of war; (3) eradication of corruption in the national life; (4) settlement of the issue of creation of more states; (5) preparation and adoption of a new constitution; (6) introduction of a new revenue allocation formula; (7) conduction of a national population census; (8) organization of genuinely national political parties; and (9) organization of elections and installation of properly elected governments in the states and in the center.[9] Gowon had, as it were, made a covenant with the people. The challenge was to keep it. His reassuring and optimistic pronouncements helped greatly to generate an atmosphere of good feeling among Nigerians. Surging crude oil prices which hit the roof in 1973 providentially ensured a stable financial base for actualizing the national dreams.

Gowon's political stature and popularity soared nationally and internationally. He had rescued the nation from the brink of disintegration, and his simplicity and seeming candor endeared him to many Nigerians. He had demonstrated magnimanity in victory, and ex-Biafran leaders were only obliged to demonstrate their loyalty to the authorities. British journalist John de St. Jorre remarked that "while the black man has little to teach us about making war, he has a real contribution to offer in the art of making peace."[10]

In some quarters Gowon was described as "Nigeria's Abraham Lincoln."[11] Streets and public institutions were named after him and some musicians made recordings singing his praise. The name "GOWON" was interpreted as an acronym for the slogan "Go On With One Nigeria." No Head of State before him had enjoyed so much poplar and unalloyed support and admiration. But time and events gradually showed that national optimism was misplaced and the euphoria misguided.

RECONSTRUCTION AND REHABILITATION

The civil war had wrought enormous destruction of lives and property in Eastern Nigeria. Igboland in particular, the central theater of the war, had suffered greatly. All over Igboland, roads and communication infrastructures were in ruin. Hundreds of residential and commercial buildings , markets, schools, churches and hospitals had been partially or completely destroyed. Men, women and children emerging from the war looked like living skeletons. They were pathetically malnourished. Most of the people had seen their means of livelihood blighted by the war, their villages and farms put to the torch. Eastern Nigerian business owners and public servants had had to flee their places of work in other parts of Nigeria to their home villages during the civil disturbances of 1966-67.

Physical reconstruction of war damages and rehabilitation of the victims of the war was the first real test that faced the Gowon regime. The NRC was charged with this task. The Commission had three goals: to reasonably compensate those people whose property had been destroyed or damaged as a result of the civil war, to resettle and assist all those who had had to flee their normal places of residence or business, and to reconstruct all roads, bridges and public buildings damaged or destroyed during the war. The Commission had also the responsibility of coordinating the relief efforts of other organizations, including state governments.

It is not certain exactly how much money was allocated to the Commission by government and what practical results were achieved. According to Oyetunji Aboyade and Allison Ayida, the NRC was distributing three thousand tons of relief materials such as food, clothing and drugs and spending N2.4 million on relief operations in 1970.[12] The Commission is said to have made available to the East Central State Rehabilitation Commission eleven million naira to aid relief in the state. Under its food for work program, the state commission distributed food items, equipment and construction materials to various communities and organized groups. These included Indian hoes, axes, native hoes, shovels, pick axes, cement and corrugated iron sheets. One of the most significant accomplishments of the NRC was the reconstruction of the Onitsha main market. At that time, this market was said to be the largest market in sub-Saharan Africa. Other facilities that received attention were the Eastern Nigeria Railway and the airports at Enugu, Port Harcourt, and Calabar. Many roads and bridges were also rehabilitated.

Official sources praised government efforts in reconstructing war damages. Ukpabi Askia, the Administrator of East Central State, described in 1971 the progress made in the reconstruction and rehabilitation process as a "modern miracle."[13] This was the official viewpoint; other sources disagree.[14] Axel Harnet-Seivers has observed that the federal funds made available for the program were very small compared to the estimates on war damages made by federal government experts.[15] Compared to the estimates, which ran into several hundred million Nigerian pounds, the funds were insufficient. In September 1971, a government owned newspaper, *Renaissance,* reminded Nigerians that "thousands of our people are still living on the fringe of starvation."

Allegations of official corruption and nepotism dogged the Commission at all levels. Relief materials reached only a small number of the people who needed them most. Often the quantities were grossly inadequate, rarely arriving in time. Sometimes the materials were hijacked for the use of high-ranking officials and army officers or sold to businessmen and women who resold them at exorbitant prices. A foreign observer was baffled to witness on March 19, 1970 an auction sale of relief materials valued at over 0.5 million sterling at Apapa, Lagos.[16]

Four days later, Maurice Foley, British Parliamentary Under-Secretary of State, expressed concern about a report of a British visitor to the Eastern states. The reporter, said to be "usually pro-Federal Government of Nigeria," stated, among other things:

> It is really a terrible situation down there... A few
> miles from Uli [in Igboland], there are thousands of people
> literally starving and the Federal Government refuses to allow
> relief planes to land there. Instead, they had to unload at
> Lagos where a lot of the relief supplies are stolen...and a lot
> more [are] rotting on the wharfs in the Lagos docks...Most of
> the food that gets   through [to the East] is for the Nigerian
> Army....[17]

The Federal Government had refused offers of relief aid from countries such as Israel and Norway, which it suspected of having aided the Biafran cause. The victims of the war were hurt the most as a result of the federal government's action. The pangs of hunger and disease and the agony of defeat continued to haunt them. The promise of reasonable compensation to all those people whose property had been destroyed during the civil war was observed in the breach, not in the fulfillment. The victims, many of whom were people of property who had settled in other parts of Nigeria, were left on their own to devise how best to rebuild their shattered means of livelihood.

As for roads and communications, these were deliberately neglected to the point that many roads were called death traps. Z. A. Bonat has remarked that "for many years, after the war, roads and telegraphs in the war affected areas...remained in a very poor state."[18] This situation contributed to hamper the distribution of relief materials. For some years after the war, many schools in the ECS continued to conduct their classes under trees, in church buildings and in thatched, mud houses. When a well-known television personality satirized government as always 'ear-marking' projects but hardly ever 'eye-marking' them, he was promptly relieved of his position.

In the final analysis, the burden of reconstruction and rehabilitation fell on the local communities themselves, as shown by Gloria Chuku and E. O. Egboh. Some communities received assistance in food, clothing, medical and technical services from semi-governmental and non-governmental humanitarian organizations.[19] From 1970-72, UNICEF spent 2.4 million sterling in reconstructing damaged school building while the USAID spent 200,000 in the repair and equipping of 858 school buildings.[20]

USAID also provided helicopters to the ECS for air-lifting relief food to communities inaccessible by road. The Cooperative for American Relief Everywhere (CARE) was also involved in the reconstruction of schools, bridges, and culverts and in the rehabilitation of damaged or abandoned rural water supply equipment, as at Aji in Nsukka Division.[21] The commercially essential Niger bridge, which links the Western and the Eastern states, was rebuilt by the West German government at the cost of £6 million (British pounds). In relation to the resources available to them, the foreign bodies perhaps made a greater positive impact on the rural communities than did the Commissions.

Although most civil servants employed by the government of the former Eastern Region (divided in 1967 into East Central, Southeastern, and Rivers states) were reabsorbed by their respective new state governments, Federal civil servants who had fled their posts as a result of the civil war had great difficulty regaining their jobs. A decree in August 1970 provided for the dismissal of civil servants found to have supported succession by more than fulfilling their normal official duties. The looseness of the wording of the decree gave room for petty personal vendettas. It is known that the decree was applied selectively. In those departments where manpower was in short supply–for example, communications– a fair number of returning civil servants were reabsorbed. In other departments, especially the 'lucrative' ones such as the Department of Ports Authority and the Department of Customs, only very few applicants were rehired. By February 1971, only eleven percent of applications, totaling less than one thousand, had been favorably considered.[22]

The Dismissed Officers Petition of 1980 was sent to President Shehu Shagari by thousands of members of the police force, prison services, and the army who had been dismissed from their jobs, and so had lost their pension entitlements. The few Eastern soldiers and policemen who were reabsorbed were subjected to such daily taunts, indignity, and humiliation even by their juniors that a number of them chose to retire prematurely from service.

It was, however, the messy issue of "abandoned property" which most nakedly demonstrated that government's "no victory,...no vanquished" declaration was mere sloganeering. During the disturbances of 1966 and 1967, scores of thousands of Igbo men, women and children were massacred in different parts of the country, particularly the north. Those who escaped fled their places of work to the relative safety of their Igbo homeland. In their flight, they abandoned various types of property: domestic effects, residential and business buildings, plantations, and undeveloped plots of land.

It would be recalled that during his January 15, 1970 broadcast to the nation, Gowon had affirmed "the right of every Nigerian to reside and work wherever he chooses in the Federation." He also assured the nation of "the security of life and property of all Nigerians in every part of Nigeria." Coming directly from the Head of State, these assurances had given those people who had to abandon their property in different parts of the country optimism about their chances of recovering them.

In a few states, such as Lagos and North Central States, arrears of rent collected by government agents on residential and commercial building and other properties were given to their returnee owners along with the property. For such lucky ones, the rent received and the property recovered made rehabilitation less traumatic than for others. In some other states, Rivers and Cross River in particular, the abandoned property issue developed into a major problem. The governments of these state, with the acquiescence of the Nigerian federal government, summarily acquired most of this property.

Acting unilaterally, the state governments fixed the prices they paid for the sequestrated property. The owners of the property were not allowed any bargaining power. A sizeable number of the returnees, most of them Igbo, received no compensation at all. This was usually at the flimsiest excuse, such as incomplete documentation. In the Rivers State alone, the Igbo lost property estimated in the 1970s at £56 million including 5,600 buildings, undeveloped land, plants and machinery.[23]

It is worth noting that some of the sequestrated properties were later sold by the Rivers State government to other Nigerian citizens described as indigenous inhabitants ("indigenes") of the state. A bona fide Nigerian could be a non-indigene within the Nigerian federation. Gowon turned his back at this anathema, which made caricature of his solemn pledge, namely, the freedom of every Nigerian to reside, work and own property in any part of the county. Not a few of the victims of the "abandoned property" policy died without recovering their estates. They died of frustration and broken hearts, the ultimate price of raised hopes and dashed expectations. In the view of Sam Mbakwe, the confiscation of Igbo property, especially in Rivers State, was nothing short of "reparation [sic] for the loss of war."[24]

Some banking and currency regulations of the Nigerian government compounded the rehabilitation problems of the war victims. In January, 1968, the Biafran currency was invalidated. Then followed the Banking Obligation (Eastern States) Decree of 1970. By this decree, any account in any bank in the former Eastern Nigeria which was operated after the declaration of the Republic of Biafra stood invalidated. Thousands of people of the former Eastern Nigeria lost all of their life's savings.

The federal government further ordered all those people who were in possession of Biafran currency to submit this at designated banks. The time allotted for this exercise was so short and the centers for surrendering the currency so few that only a small proportion of potential depositors could exchange their Biafran "confederate dollars" for Nigerian naira. Of the estimated £B135 million in the possession of residents of the eastern states at the end of the war, only £B16.5 million was submitted at the end of the exercise in April 1970.

Then in May, the federal government decided on a flat rate payment of £N20 to each depositor. It made available only £N4 million for disbursement to depositors, thus limiting the number of recipients to not more than a paltry two hundred thousand, in a region of high population. As Harneit-Sievers put it, the currency exchange was "a most obvious symbol of post-war discrimination against the Igbo by the federal government."[25] The actual beneficiaries from the exercise were the federal officers who were in charge of it. They were said to have devised various ways to manipulate the exercise in order to enrich themselves.

It is clear that all these measures could not have been intended to rehabilitate the victims of the war and reintegrate them into the Nigerian society. On the contrary, they were punitive and designed to "reconstruct" ex-Biafrans out of, rather than into, the mainstream of the Nigerian economy. Many informed observers[26] hold the view that these punitive measures were the brainchild of Obafemi Awolowo, Federal Minister of Finance at the time. It is widely believed that Awolowo's primary objective was to install and entrench his own ethnic group in an unassailable dominant position in the political economy and administration of Nigeria. Before the civil war, the Igbo and the Yoruba groups had been rivals for the economic and administrative control of the country. The outcome of the war put the Igbo at a severe disadvantage; the Yoruba were in a more favorable position. Awolowo tried to consolidate this *post bellum status quo*. The timing of the Indigenization Decree of 1972 was largely aimed at ensuring that the Igbo, emerging from the war acutely short of cash, did not buy a substantial number of shares of the enterprises affected by the Decree.

Another covertly anti-Igbo measure introduced by the federal government was a ban on the importation of used clothing items, textile fabrics and stockfish. The ban affected the Igbo adversely in three ways. First, these lines of business had been dominated by the Igbo before the war. Aba in Igbo country had been the center of the business. The ban stifled the efforts of Igbo importers to reopen credit and commercial lines with their foreign partners after the war. Second, as we have seen, during the immediate post-war era, the Igbo were an impoverished group. Most of them had lost all their belongings and personal effects to the war. Men, women and children emerging from the war were scantily clothed or not at all. New clothing items were out of the reach of most families; used clothes were more affordable. Third, as a result of wartime privations, Igbo men, women and children emerged from the war malnourished and emaciated to the bone. Kwashiorkor was endemic; the people, especially children and pregnant mothers, were in dire need of protein. Cattle and fish, the chief local sources of protein, had been dislocated by the war. These became relatively too expensive for most Igbo families to afford. A relatively short while later, the severe drought of 1972-74 and the rinderpest epidemic that hit the Sahel–Savanna parts of northern Nigeria decimated the livestock. This further raised the price of meat.

Unable to afford the traditional sources of protein, many families resorted to eating boiled animal hides, products of home butchering that in good times had been saved to sell to the shoemakers. Fish might have been a cheaper source of protein. It is worth noting that the ban on the import of the aforesaid items hit the most vulnerable groups in post-war Nigeria. It should also be noted that no ban was placed on the importation of non-essential, luxury items such as "Uncle Ben's rice," corn flakes, cigarettes, and frozen chicken.

ECONOMIC MISMANAGEMENT

The immediate post-war economic prospects of Nigeria appeared very promising. The 1970-74 Plan described Nigeria as fortunate in having the resource potential in men, material and money "to lay a solid foundation for a socioeconomic revolution in black Africa."[27] The chief economic aspirations of the Plan were three-fold: self-reliance, defeat of neo-colonial forces in Africa" and achievement of the highest possible growth rate per capita income. Fortunately for Nigeria, there was a continuous flow of revenue from the oil wells to the federal coffers. In 1970, for instance, revenue from oil stood at N166.4 million, accounting for 26.3 percent of total government revenue; in 1975, the figure had shot up to N4,271.5 million, accounting for 77.5 percent of the national income.[28]

But the radical engineering required to bring about the envisaged "socioeconomic revolution" was conspicuously lacking. Managerial incompetence, sheer bankruptcy of vision and major errors of policy were among the forces which conspired against plan implementation and attainment of national goals. Agriculture, the bedrock of the Nigerian economy, was criminally neglected by officialdom; so were the farmers who composed the majority of Nigerians. The contribution of agriculture to the GDP fell from 48.23 percent in 1970 to 23.95 percent in 1975 while the value of agricultural exports fell from 32.38 percent to 5.23 percent during the same period.[29] Before the civil war, Nigeria used to produce all but five percent of her food needs. By 1974, she was producing less than sixty percent.

The impact of this development was sobering. Rural neglect accelerated the movement of rural youth to urban areas with adverse socioeconomic consequences. Food imports, mostly for the urban elite, became a huge drain on the national revenue. The period marked the small beginnings of the craze for imported pre-cooked instant rice, tinned milk, frozen meat, apples, and similar products. The mania developed over the years, and by the time of Shehu Shagari's regime, it was a malady of staggering proportions. The idea of self-reliance and balanced economic growth had been thrown out of the window, and undue reliance on petroleum brought about 'monocultural vulnerability.'[30]

Industrial manufacturing was a central theme of the 1970-74 plan document. The plan aimed at increasing the contribution of the sector to the GDP and also promoting indigenous participation via progressive indigenisation in both ownership and management of economic enterprises. During 1971-73, the government established a number of economic and technical institutions to achieve its economic goals. These Institutions included the Nigerian National Oil Corporation (renamed Nigerian National Petroleum Corporation), the Industrial Training Fund, the Nigerian Bank for Commerce and Industries, the Nigerian Agricultural Bank and the Nigerian Enterprises Promotion Board. However, time and events later proved that it takes more than institutional framework and money to achieve national economic objectives. The industrial philosophy of the government was outmoded and flawed, anchored on a policy of industrialization via import substitution. Import substitution is nothing more than the consolidation, refinement and expansion of the inherited exploitative colonial system. This system of manufacturing relies on imported critical components of technology. It is, therefore, a recipe for perpetuating technological dependence because it denies the local economy opportunity for innovation and research.[31] The import substitution strategy involves the final or "mature" stages of manufacturing; it may give an illusion of economic growth but this is usually without development.

As Yusufu Bala Usman observed, Gowon's economic program was doomed to failure because it sought to preserve the status quo.[32] It is true that during the Plan period the contribution of industry to the GDP grew at a phenomenal pace. However, this was fueled by surging petroleum prices. This did not lead to greater self-reliance but rather to greater strategic external reliance.[33] Change was lacking where it mattered most: the undergirding structure of the economy. If an auto-centric, self reliant and balanced economy was to be attained, a prerequisite step was to dismantle the existing neo-colonial structure. Yet the Biafran experience shows quite clearly that a mine of indigenous know-how, which could be exploited to radically transform the economy, abounded in the economy.[34] But this was not to be.

Perhaps nothing shows more clearly the fallacy and cosmetic nature of government's industrialization strategy than the Nigerian Enterprises Promotion Decree of 1972, implemented in 1974.[35] The Decree, an expression of economic nationalism, was aimed at enabling Nigerians to assume control of the commanding heights of their national economy. It divided all foreign enterprises in Nigeria into two schedules. Schedule One, comprising twenty-two small-scale enterprises, was to be reserved exclusively for Nigerians while Schedule Two, comprising thirty-three large-scale ventures, was to have at least forty percent Nigerian equity participation. Shares totaling 54,051,000 were eventually transferred to Nigerians.

Despite the nationalistic posturing of the decree, it effected little real change in the country. As Bade Onomide observed: "Unfortunately, indigenization has preserved imperialist domination of capital, technology and management in the large enterprises of the sensitive sectors of the economy like oil, manufacturing, [and] construction . . . ."[36] The Decree enabled only a few rich and well connected Nigerians to buy a large proportion of the shares in foreign firms and to become armchair managers of the firms.

Neo-colonial habits and structures remained deeply entrenched. By having local bourgeoisie as window-dressers, the multi-national corporations were actually accorded greater protection than before. It was like modernizing the "indirect rule" system, states P. Heinecke.[37] The decree also tended to widen and deepen existing cleavages between social and economic groups, as will become evident shortly.

The dominance of the industrial sector by foreign interests is best exemplified in the petroleum industry. The creation of NNOC in 1971 was intended to increase the participatory capacity of the federal government in all aspects of the industry. But Nigeria failed to develop the capacity to explore, refine or market oil in the world market, independently of the multi-national oil corporations.

The grip of multinationals such as Shell, British Petroleum, and Ashland on the petroleum industry was acknowledged even by government in the 1970-74 plan document. The Irikefe[Judicial Tribunal on Crude Oil Sales was embarrassed when it found out how ignorant the NNOC and its successor, NNPC, were of crucial happenings in the oil sector. The tribunal revealed that yearly, Nigeria was being swindled of billions of naira by the multinationals. The dubious oil production sharing arrangement between NNOC and the Ashland Oil Company in 1973 is one scandalous example.[38] Only a tiny fraction of Nigerian's crude oil was refined locally. As Akasun Abba and others have stated, "No country can genuinely develop which exports its major natural resources."[39]

The failure of government to manage the petroleum industry in particular and the nation's economy in general was conspicuously brought home to ordinary Nigerians by the constant fuel shortages that plagued the country. Endless and frustrating gasoline and kerosene queues became a familiar sight in one of the world's major oil producing countries. Cooking and industrial gas were in acute short supply, although a staggering daily average of 60.7 million cubic meters of gas, the equivalent of four hundred thousand barrels of crude oil per day, was being flared with reckless inconsideration.[40]

Just as petrol stations were jammed with queues of vehicles, so were the ports congested with shipping. During 1973-75 in particular, Lagos ports were so hopelessly congested that ships had to wait for months on the high sea before docking. After several months of endless and frustrating waiting on the high sea, some ships discharged their cargo in the ports of the neighboring states of Togo and Ghana. Often much of a ship's cargo got spoiled and became unusable as a result of the long waiting period. Whatever happened, Nigeria incurred huge demurrage every day a ship waited in the ports. This amounted to hundreds of millions of naira.[41] Port congestion itself reflected the inefficiency of the national transport system. The Second National Development Plan amply recognized the central place of a cheap and efficient system of transportation in resource mobilization. To this end, the plan allocated to the transport sector 23.7 percent of the total budgeted public capital investment.[42] Some roads and bridges were rehabilitated or constructed during the plan period; some rehabilitation work was also done on the railways. Nevertheless, the huge amount of expenditure the sector gulped was not matched by greater efficiency or rationality, nor yet by the promotion of national economic integration and self-sufficiency.

The disarticulation of the transport system showed most strikingly with respect to rural-urban and rural-rural linkages. The urban bias of government development programs is well known. Although over seventy percent of Nigerians were rural dwellers, planned rural investment during the 1970-74 period was only 18.2 percent. In comparison, 81.8 percent went to the urban areas.[43]

Disparity in economic and social infrastructure between town and country found expression also in income disparity between the two. While urban dwellers enjoyed the gains from oil, the rural dwellers remained "submerged in a degrading culture of poverty and decimating diseases."[44] Indeed, the oil boom widened the gap in social and economic welfare between town and country.[45]

Staggering disparities existed even between the urban centers. An industrial survey in 1973 by the Federal Office of Statistics showed that sixty percent of the total manufacturing capital stock in the country and much of the total manufacturing employment were based in one state alone, Lagos.[46] Less than ten percent of the Nigerian population resided in this state at the time. Inequality in resource distribution reflected power disparities between rural and urban centers and among the urban centers themselves. Power and wealth go hand in hand; wealth can either buy power or power conscripts wealth.

CORRUPTION, EXTRAVAGANCE AND INEQUALITY

In his October 1, 1970 broadcast to the nation, Gowon lashed out at public officers who had illegally enriched themselves through abuse of office. He vowed to wage an unrelenting war on corruption and wasteful and ostentatious display of wealth. The position of Gowon in this matter is not surprising because the First Republic was terminated by the army in 1966 because of the alleged corruption and embarrassing extravagance of the politicians.[47]

Ironically, Gowon's regime soon got enmeshed in a maze of corruption, extravagance and ostentatious display of wealth that made the sins of the First Republic politicians seem saintly. "After the defeat of secession," writes Bala Usman" the Gowon regime sank further and further into a morass of corruption, waste, incompetence and repression."[48] The cankerworm was permissive both among the military and the civilian public servants, in particular the state governors and ministers. As corruption became increasingly overt among public officers, public outcry grew louder and more persistent.

Two particular incidents hit the national headlines. In an affidavit sworn to at a Lagos High Court on July 13, 1974, Joseph S. Tarka, Federal Minister of Communication, was openly accused of corruption and abuse of office by Godwin Daboh, a Lagos-based businessman. Tarka stuck to his ministerial post, ignoring the accusation. Gowon himself apparently ignored the whole business. Thankfully, sustained press criticisms forced Tarka to resign his post to the relief of the Head of State.[49]

Barely one month after Tarka's resignation, another scandal hit the Gowon regime. On May 29, 1974 and again on August 13, 1974, Aper Aku, a Tiv man, who later became Governor of Benue State, wrote to Joseph Dechi Gomwalk, Governor of Benue-Plateau State, accusing him of nepotism and "financial wrong doings.[50] Although the letters were widely circulated, the Federal Government ignored them. Then on August 31, 1974, Aku swore to an affidavit in the Jos High Court, again accusing Gomwalk of financial wrong doing in contract awards and expenditure of public funds.

But Gowon summarily cleared Gomwalk of any wrong-doing, describing the allegation as a malicious fabrication. However, a probe panel set up by Gowon's successor, Murtala Ramat Mohammed, headed by Justice Alfa Belgore contradicted Gowon:

> We have come to the conclusion that the records of Mr. Joseph Dechi Gomwalk as military governor ...[involved] great corruption and ignoble arrangements to waste government money and therefore gain from such waste for himself, his cronies and his family.[51]

Aper Aku was vindicated at last. It is not certain that Gowon himself was corrupt. However, in using the weight of his high office to shield his corrupt officials, he laid himself open to suspicion of the same crime.

In the army, allegations and rumors of dishonesty and abuse of office were rife. The Pay and Records section allegedly kept alive lists of "ghost" soldiers whose salaries and emoluments went into the pockets of the officers in charge. The Supply and Transport section was so often said to be engrossed in diversion of supplies, fictitious bookkeeping, and warehousing that it was nicknamed "Supply and Thief."[52] All these wrong-doings were committed with impunity and created the impression of official backing. It is significant that after seizing power from Gowon, Murtala Mohammed promptly dismissed a number of allegedly corrupt high-ranking army officers, including state governors, describing them as a disgrace to their profession.

It was in the award of contracts that corruption appeared most prevalent and systematized. In this, both army and civilians were serious offenders. A rapid increase in oil wealth led to massive public construction works such as roads and bridges, public buildings and army barracks as well as supply of equipment. Government was enticed to play a more and more central role in the development process. The actual values of contracts were routinely highly inflated, the excess going into the pockets of awarding government officials. A survey of comparative unit cost of building and civil engineering projects between Nigeria and other African countries in 1979 showed that building costs were highest in Nigeria by fifty to one hundred percent.[53] Almost overnight, especially from 1973, the number of private millionaires—even billionaires--increased. Their newly found wealth was deeply rooted in the pillage of the state. When university students demonstrated against the corruption of his regime, Gowon reacted in a high-handed manner.

Sudden easy money bred the propensity for extravagance and ostentatious display of wealth both at the official and private levels. Dazzled and stupefied by ever-flowing wealth from the oil wells, the government embarked upon a variety of ego-boosting projects. The All-African Games, the ECOWAS games, the Scout Jamboree, the Black and African Festivals of Arts and Culture (FESTAC), an international trade fair, and an anti-apartheid conference were some of the grandiose fanfares to which Nigeria committed herself. The preparation of these extravaganzas involved, among other things, the construction of the National Stadium, the National Theater, a trade fair center and the FESTAC village all in Lagos. These and other selected projects gulped billions of petro-naira. On January 1, 1978, the *Sunday Standard* carried an editorial which complained that Nigeria "spent a whopping 90 million naira to build a trade fair center for suckers from other countries to make business at our own expense." On May 3, another newspaper, the *New Nigeria*, lamented that "within a year billions of naira was wasted on FESTAC, Trade Fair . . . ."

It was a sign of the times that Gowon was quoted as saying that Nigeria's problem was not money but how to use it. He was probably echoing Clement Isong, Governor of the Central Bank of Nigeria. Isong had lamented that Nigeria was piling up foreign currencies but had "nowhere to invest them properly."[54] Yet rural neglect and urban squalor remained endemic even in Lagos. Defense and security consumed a staggering amount of money yearly while education and health were accorded much less attention. The budgeted expenditure on these heads were as follows:

	1970	1971	1972	1973	1974	1975
Defense & Security	N190.8M	N401.6M	N607.1M	N588.1M	N822.8M	N1803.2M
Education & Health	N 20.2M	N 30.7M	N 55.3M	N 61.6M	N240.2M	N 930.8M

Source: Central Bank of Nigeria, 1976

The government's priorities seemed inverted. Gowon had promised to reorganize the army, which was overgrown. It had increased in size from about 8,000 in 1966 to about 250,000 in 1970 as a result of the exigencies of the war. Instead of downsizing the army with the return of peace, he proceeded to construct modern barracks to replace existing ones.

Ostentatious display of wealth along with distorted priorities was not confined to the government. The *nouveaux riches* also lived a life of conspicuous extravagance. They were easily identifiable by their flowing agbada robes or expensive western style suits, imposing estates, and posh cars. Some owned private jet planes. Summer holidays by entire families in some of the most expensive resorts in Europe and America became a regular part of their lifestyle. Though this group constituted no more than one percent of the population of the country, they controlled well over thirty-five percent of its wealth.

The opulence and extravagance of this minority contrasted sharply with the degrading penury of the majority. As J. I. Elaigwu, Gowon's admiring biographer, states, his officials were given to a "display of conspicuous consumption amidst abject poverty of the masses."[55] Standing in contrast with the expensive and stately mansions of these newly rich were the shanties and slums of the abject poor. In Lagos, this was reflected in the cases of Victoria Island and Ikoyi vis-à-vis Ajegunle and Maroko. That hundreds of Lagos dwellers slept under bridges was no secret.

The mismanagement, corruption, and squandermania which accompanied the oil wealth led to galloping inflation. They also led to a widening of the income gap between the upper and the lower ends of the income scale, which widened the social and economic distance between classes, even between similar white-collar classes such as businessmen and civil servants.

Any attempt to assuage the pangs of inflation compounded the situation. Udoji salary awards, backdated nine months, suddenly released into circulation N370 million. Hyper-inflation became unavoidable and quickly blighted the gains of the awards. Labor unrest followed. Strike followed strike in quick succession despite the ban on strikes. Shortly before the curtain fell on his regime, Gowon described Nigeria's socioeconomic malaise, aptly enough, as "want in the midst of plenty."[56] This was, in effect, an admission of failure on the part of his government.

University lecturers were among the working groups who lived among "want in the midst of plenty." When they went on strike, demanding fairer conditions of service and salary, Gowon bullied them into submission by threatening to use force to eject them from their official residences and to have their leaders arrested. Gowon thus set the example which subsequent military heads of state have, unfortunately, continued to use in their fight against university lecturers and quality higher education in Nigeria.

"Want in the midst of plenty" bred frustration and social maladjustment as rising expectations hit the rocks. Frustration frequently led to alcoholism and drug addiction. Girls turned to prostitution. The unwanted babies of their clients were abandoned in street corners, hospitals, garbage dumps and toilets. Among the young men, armed banditry became rife, and was not deterred by the summary executions known as "firing". In some cities such as Lagos and Benin, whole sections became dangerous as "area boys" took over and dared law enforcement officers to venture into their domain. A virtual "state within a state" was emerging. The social fabric was under siege, indeed.

FOREIGN POLICY

The post-civil war environment in Nigeria provided Gowon with a fine opportunity to pursue an active foreign policy. Gowon's foreign policy was greatly influenced by the fact of national affluence and security considerations arising from the civil war. As Bolaji Akinyemi states, there was "a greater degree of national cohesion" than had been the case since the country's independence.[57] Perhaps more important was the sudden wealth the country was enjoying.

During and after that war, national security assumed a central place in Nigeria's foreign policy calculations. The country is surrounded by neighbors that have always had strong ties with France, their former colonial ruler. France itself seemed somewhat sympathetic to Biafra and its attitude was deemed by Nigeria to influence that of the Francophone countries. Some of these countries, such as the Ivory Coast and Gabon, had accorded diplomatic recognition to Biafra. Some former British colonies---notably Tanzania and Zambia--did, too.

To establish cordial relations with her immediate neighbors in particular and other West African states in general, therefore, was the chief priority of Gowon's administration. Such a cordial relation was seen as "a real insurance for guaranteeing security and stability at home."[58] Good neighborliness would also foster cooperation in the development and utilization of shared natural resources and create investment opportunities for Nigerian capital. It was against this background that Nigeria spearheaded the formation of such bodies as the Niger Basin Commission, the Chad Basin Commission and the Economic Community of West African States (ECOWAS).

Nigeria was also intent on playing a central role in the affairs of Africa in particular and the Commonwealth and the Black Diaspora in general. To eliminate all forms of colonialism and racism in Africa was also a central objective of Gowon's foreign policy. This, he assumed, was only logical, as Nigeria is the most populous black nation in the world. Nigeria thus adopted Afro-centrism as the basis of its foreign policy. The Organization of African Unity (OAU) provided a convenient platform for Nigeria to make its influence felt in the continent.

Technical and economic assistance was extended to many African states and other countries—Caribbean countries, for example-- outside Africa peopled by persons of African ancestry. Nigeria committed millions of naira to fund and sustain ECOWAS. The Nigerian government shouldered the disproportionate cost of running the Organization of African Unity (OAU), made substantial outlay for the African Development Bank and sold crude oil at concessionary prices to needy African states when the Yom Kippur War of 1973 caused crude oil prices to skyrocket. Lagos also gave out a huge sum of money to expand the Commonwealth Fund for Technical Cooperation and volunteered to pay the salaries of civil servants in Grenada when that country was in financial stress.

Free of financial dependence on any country, Lagos could pursue a large measure of independent foreign policy. While maintaining strong links with the West, Gowon's administration moved Nigeria to a non-aligned position. Lagos extended diplomatic recognition to the People's Republic of China, and developed close cooperation with the Soviet Union through the Ajaokuta iron and steel project. Nigeria spearheaded opposition against the white minority regime in Rhodesia (now Zimbabwe), the apartheid regime in South Africa and supported liberation movements in Angola, Mozambique and other colonized countries in Africa.

ECOWAS was by far the greatest achievement of Gowon's administration in foreign affairs. The body has been described as a manifestation of the desire for cooperation and as a product of determined "search for collective self-reliance in the global context."[59] No doubt, although the achievements of ECOWAS have fallen far short of its dreams, it has continued to serve as the pivotal instrument for cooperation among West African states. Succeeding governments, for good or ill, have continued Gowon's policy of keeping Africa the centerpiece of Nigeria's foreign policy.

But Gowon's foreign policy cost Nigeria staggering amounts of foreign exchange. Yet little tangible dividends accrued to the country from the foreign ventures. Indeed, his foreign policy lacked a cardinal principle in any nation's foreign policy, namely, "self." As Okordian Ozemonye argues, "self remains the hub of any nation's foreign policy."[60] In other words, self-interest ought to be the chief determinant of a nation's foreign relations. This is why it is often said that in international affairs, a country has permanent interests but not permanent foes or permanent friends.

It is not easy to justify most of Gowon's foreign policy actions by the criterion of national self-interest. For instance, Gowon paid the salaries of civil servants in Grenada, a country of little or no strategic, political, or economic interest to Nigeria. His foreign policy was conspicuous for its "adoration-value" rather than "use-value" or "respect-value." Most of Gowon's foreign policy actions were embarked upon to boost the image of Nigeria as "the big brother" and "the giant of Africa," not to advance the country's interests.[61] It was to satisfy his "adoration psyche" that Gowon embarked upon such extravaganzas as the All Africa Games, ECOWAS Games, FESTAC, International Scout Jamboree. As shown earlier, these were merely escapades that gulped huge amounts of foreign exchange from the country. Yusufu B. Usman has argued that Gowon's foreign policy brought no economic benefits to Nigeria. Nor did it lead to the liberation of the country from neocolonialism.[62]

One would think that such actions would be reciprocated. But the shabby manner in which Nigerians were expelled from Equatorial Guinea and Ghana [63] seems to show the contempt with which those African states hold Nigeria.   Yet Nigeria got hardly anything in return, not even gratitude, a situation which made Akinyemi pose this question: " . . . why, in spite of the goodwill shown by Nigeria towards her neighbors, have we not always got from them the desired level of understanding?"[64]

By posturing as the "big brother," "the giant of Africa," Nigeria probably instilled fear of domination into other African nations and stirred up hidden hatred.   In any case, it was not too long before Nigeria's ambitious foreign commitments became too burdensome for the economy and "the giant" began to show that it has feet of clay.

As domestic problems began to overwhelm his administration towards its end, Gowon tried to find solace in "personal summitry"[65] and globe trotting. Between January 1975 and his overthrow six months later, he made three overseas trips. In one of the trips—the Commonwealth Summit in Jamaica—he spent two long weeks, as if he were a Head of State with no pressing problems at home.

BROKEN COVENANT

As a soldier–head of state, Gowon was expected to be a man of prompt and decisive action, and his words were expected to be his bond. But he was well known for vacillation and inaction even over crucial national issues, and for reneging on his promises instead of meeting them.

The 1973 population census is a case in point. It was generally acknowledged throughout the country that the exercise was fundamentally flawed and that whatever final figures that were to be published would not receive public endorsement.   Gowon vacillated on the matter while acrimony built up between ethnic and geographical groups. The matter lingered until Mohammed succeeded him and promptly canceled the census results, to the relief of most Nigerians. Gowon also dithered over the choice of a new federal capital, even though overcrowding and ecological concerns were making it increasingly difficult for Lagos to continue to cope as capital of the country. Here, again, a final decision on the matter awaited the regime of Mohammed.

Three broken covenants in particular seemed to have brought the curtain down on the Gowon regime. These were the issue of creation of more states, change of state governors and return to civilian rule. In his October 1, 1970 broadcast to the nation, Gowon had promised to review, by 1974, the issue of creation of new states, realizing that there was widespread demand for it. The promised date came and passed but Gowon failed to honor his promise, to the exasperation of most Nigerians. As Elaigwu puts it, Gowon "resorted to a technique he had used before:" he "tucked the state issue under the carpet."[66]

As we mentioned earlier, Gowon's state governors openly abused their office and corruptly enriched themselves at the expense of the governed. By 1973, the demand for change of the governors was widespread. Even Gowon's top military officers openly told him that his continued retention of the governors in office had put the credibility of his regime on the line. On the fourteenth independence anniversary of the country, Gowon, for the third time, promised to reassign his governors. The date for this reassignation, March 31, 1975, came and passed, but again he procrastinated. By his inaction, Gowon created the impression that he was "the poodle" of the governors. A columnist in *Daily Times* of 2 August, 1975 wondered if Nigeria was short of capable hands. All of the governors had been in office since 1967.

It was the question of return to civilian rule that drove the final nail on the coffin of the Gowon regime. In 1970, Gowon had promised to return Nigeria to civilian rule in 1976. "We shall hasten and try to complete the program earlier, if possible,"[67] he added. But in his October 1, 1974 broadcast to the nation, Gowon announced that "the target date of 1976 is . . . unrealistic for returning Nigeria to civil rule."[68] He then went on to accuse aspiring politicians of unrestrained sectional politicking and intemperate utterances and writing. He charged that the people had learned no lessons from the country's past experiences.

By this announcement, Gowon parted ways with the vast majority of Nigerians who had become tired of military rule. Few people gave credence to his reasons for postponing his handover to an unnamed date. Most Nigerians believed that he was feigning an excuse to prolong his stay in office. Some prominent opposition ministers, such as Aminu Kano and Anthony Enahoro, openly dissented from his decision. Gowon also estranged his top military officers, including some of his closest aides, such as Joseph Nanvel Garba, then Commander of the Brigade of Guards.

By then the clouds were darkening fast on the regime. His national rating had plummeted to its lowest ebb. On 28 July, 1975, nine years to the day Aguiyi Ironsi was toppled from power in a bloody military *coup d'etat*, the curtain fell on Gowon, too. Jubilations greeted his exit in most parts of the country. Even before his fall, the newspapers which had sung his praise in the immediate post-war years had already started to chant with glee his requiem. The press described his regime in the most uncomplimentary language. The *Nigerian Tribune* of August 1, 1975 described it as "nine years of misrule and failure." The *London Guardian*, asserting that the regime was one of drift and inertia, welcomed its overthrow and expressed surprise "that it did not come sooner." How times had changed!!

CONCLUSION

At the end of the Nigerian Civil War in 1970, Gowon rode the crest of national popularity and acclaim. His simplicity and seeming candor endeared him to most Nigerians. His relative magnanimity to many ex-Biafran high-ranking officers had won him national and international admiration. At the outset, his regime held out enticing prospects of a new era of collective and individual prosperity, harmonious social integration and equity.

To his credit, Gowon introduced a number of positive innovations: the National Youth Service Corps program, new economic policies, the change from left to right hand drive in automotive transportation, and the decimalization of the currency. He was one of the chief architects of the Economic Community of West African States, and, aptly enough, was elected its first president.

But all these achievements appear modest against the background of the unique opportunity he had to bring about radical transformations of the Nigerian society and political economy. With respect to his nine-point program, only the new revenue allocation formula was fashioned out and implemented. Even here, controversy has continued to dog the formula. A population census which gulped millions of naira ended as a nullity.

Corruption, extravagance and distorted social and economic priorities characterized the administration, the very malaise Gowon vowed to uproot from the Nigerian society and government. He had pledged to rid the Nigerian economy of its neocolonial strangle-hold, but the indigenization decree entrenched and refined this condition by giving the multinational corporations a sort of indigenous "protective coloration."

Gowon won the war to keep Nigeria one, but proved unable to take charge of the country. He was naive and myopic if he assumed that the harrowing experience of the war was of itself sufficient to create a new Nigeria and new Nigerians. The notion of a fresh start lured the Nigerian leadership into a mood of optimism and elation that proved to be misguided. As a perceptive observer advised, "The federal victory has not remade Nigeria, it has only provided an opportunity to do so."[69] Such remaking could only have come through a well articulated and consistently pursued program of radical social, economic, and political engineering. This in turn would be anchored on a sound intellectual formulation of a liberal policy that would transcend the narrow particularisms of sectional groups.

Gowon was not fitted for this sort of endeavor; nor did he demonstrate steadfastness of resolve to carry his own program through. He, therefore, could not bring the vast majority of the people on board the new ship of state. The physician needed to heal himself first.

ENDNOTES

1. John Oyinbo, *Nigeria: Crisis and Beyond*, London: Charles Knight & Co., Ltd., 1971.
2. T. N. Tamuno and S. C. Ukpabi, Eds., *Nigeria Since Independence*, Vol. VI. Ibadan: Heinemann, 1989, 81.
3. Elizabeth Isichei, *History of Nigeria*, New York: Longman, 1983, 472-474; Stremlau, *The International Politics of the Nigerian Civil War, 1967-1970*. Princeton: Princeton University Press, 1977.
4. Nwankwo, Arthur A., *Nigeria: the Challenge of Biafra*, Enugu: Fourth Dimension, 1980.
5. Elaigwu, J. Isawa, *Gowon: The Biography of a Soldier-Statesman*, Ibadan: West Books, 1986
6. Paul Obi-Ani, "The Post-War Social and Economic Reconstruction of Igboland, 1970-1983," M.A. Thesis, University of Nigeria, Nsukka, 1997.
7. Yakubu Gowon, *Unity, Stability and Progress: The Challenge of the 2nd Decade of Nigeria's Independence*. Jos: Government printer, n.d.
8. Federal Republic of Nigeria (FRN). *National Guideline for the Projection of Nigeria's Philosophy and Action*. Lagos: Minister of Information, 1971, 141.
9. Gowon, *Unity*, 168.
10. *The Nigerian Civil* War. London, Hodder and Stoughton, 1972, 407.
11. Elaigwu, *Gowon,*.137.
12. A. Aboyade and O. Ayida, "The War Economy in Perspective," *Nigerian Journal of Econoimc and Social Studies*, Vol. 13, 1971, 13-32.
13. Ukpabi Asika, 1971-72 Budget Speech, Enugu, Government Printer, 1971, 4.
14. Obi-Ani, "Post War. . .Reconstruction," *op.cit.*
15. "No Victor, No Vanquished?: Reconstruction and Reintegration After the Nigerian Civil War," Berlin, Unpublished, n.d., .6.
16. Gloria I. Chuku, "The Changing Role of Women in Igbo Economy, 1929-1985," Unpublished Ph.D. Thesis, University of Nigeria, Nsukka, 1995, 313.
17. Cited *Ibid.*, 313.
18. See "Agriculture" in M. O. Kayode and Y. B. Usman, (ed.), *Nigeria Since Independence: The First 25 Years*, Vol. 2, *The Economy*. Ibadan: Heinemann, 1989, 142.
19. Edmond Egboh, Community *Development Efforts in Igboland*. Onitsha: Etukokwu Publishers, 1987; Chuku, "Changing Role of Women."
20. O. Oyediran, (ed.), *Nigerian Government and Politics Under Military Rule*, 1966-79. London: McMillan, 1979.
21. East Central State Rehabilitation Commission (ECSRC), 1971, 14.
22. *Ibid.*
23. *Nigeria, Federal Military Government's View on the Reports of the Panel on Abandoned Properties in the Former Eastern States.* Lagos: Government Printer, 1975.

24. Sam Mbakwe, quoted in *National Concord*, February 22, 1988.

25. Harneit-Sievers, "No Victor, No Vanquished," 5.

26. Chinua Achebe, *The Trouble with Nigeria*. Enugu: Fourth Dimension Press, 1983.

27. FRN. *Building the New Nigeria: National Development Plan, 1970-1974*, Lagos Government Printer, 1970, .32.

28. P. O. Sada, "The Changing Pattern of Income Distribution and Standard of Living in Nigeria," Kayode and Usman, *Nigeria Since Independence*, 236.

29. Akasun Abba, et al, *The Nigerian Crisis: Causes and Solutions*, Zaria: Gaskiya Corporation, 1985, Chapter I.

30. Bade Onomide, "The Performance of the Economy," in Kayode and Usman, *Nigeria Since Independence*, Chapter 11.

31 C. C. Onyemelukwe, *Economic Development: An Inside View*. London: Longman, 1974.

32 Yusufu B. Usman, *The Manipulation of Religion in Nigeria*. (Kaduna: Vanguard Publishers, 1987, 27.

33. Samuel Kodjo, "Self Reliance as a Consequence of a Meaningful Understanding of Development," *The Nigerian Journal of Development Studies*, Vol. 3, Nos. 1 & 2, April/October, 1983.

34. O. N. Njoku, "Traditional Economy and Nigeria's Industrial Future: Reflections form the Field and History," *Humanities* (Abraka), 1, 1 (1990). See also R. N. Ogbudinkpa, *The Economics of the Nigerian Civil War and its Prospects for National Development*. Enugu: Fourth Dimension, 1985.

35. FRN. *Nigerian Enterprises Promotion Decree*, 1972, Degree No. 4. Lagos: Government Printer, 1972.

36. Onomide, "Performance of the Economy," 281.

37. *Freedom in the Grave: Nigeria and the Political Economy of Africa*. Okpala: Asekome Publishers, 1986, 65.

38. FRN. *Report of Oil Sales Tribunal*, 1980, 25.

39. Abba, et al, *The Nigerian Crisis*, 84.

40. Abba, *loc. cit.*

41. Isichei, *History of Nigeria*, 475.

42. Abba, *Nigerian Crisis*, 101.

43. Onomide, *Nigerian Since Independence*, 297.

44. *Ibid*, 292.

45. Sayre P. Schotz, "The Nigerian Economy Sicne the Great Oil Increase of 1973-74," *Africa Today*, 29 (1982); O. N. Njoku, 'Broken Covenant: A Historical Reflection on the Nigerian Economy Since Independence, *Indian Journal of African Studies*, VI, 1 (1983); C. A. Nweke, "Inequality and Instability in Nigeria: The Political Economy of Neo-Colonial Development," *Journal of Development Studies*, 1, 1 (1981).

46. FRN. *Industrial Survey*, 1973.

47. Adewale Ademoyega, *Why We Struck: The Story of the First Nigerian Coup*. Ibadan: Evans, 1981.

48. Usman, *Manipulation of Religion*, 43.

49. Elaigwu, *Gowon*, 187-88.

50. *Ibid,*.88-89.
51. Benue-Plateau State: *Report of the Panel Investigation of Benue-Plateau Houses' Contract Procedure and Matters Related to Misconduct of Public Officers* . . . , Jos: Government Printer, 1975.
52. Elaigwu, *Gowon*, 194.
53. FRN. *Report of the Ministerial Committee on the Causes of the Excessive High Cost of Contract in Nigeria*, Lagos: Government Printer, 1981, 37.
54. F. C. Okoli, "Nigeria in Africa: the Dilemma of Misplaced Priorities," in G. A. Nweke, (ed.), *Proceedings of the Policy, 13th Annual Conference of the Nigerian Society of International of International Affairs*. Ibadan University, 11-13 November, 1985, 239.
55. Elaigwu, *Gowon*, 185.
56. Isichei, *History of Nigeria*, 474.
57. O. Aluko, "The Civil War and Nigerian Foreign Policy," *Political Quarterly*, April, 1974.
58. Bolaji Akinyemi, "Twenty-five Years of Nigeria's Foreign Policy," in A. G. Nweke, ed., *Proceedings of the Nigerian Society of International Affairs*, 35.
59. *Idem*; Aluko, "The Civil War," *loc. cit.*; Adebayo Adedeji, "Collective Self-reliance in Developing Africa: Scope, Prospects and Problems," in A. B. Akinyemi et al (eds.), *Readings and Developments on Ecowas*. Lagos: Nigerian Institute of International Affairs, 1984.
60. "Between Foreign Policy and Hypocrisy," *The Observer*, December 25, 1996, 9.
61. Okoli, "Nigeria in Africa," *loc. cit.*
62. See his *For the Liberation of Nigeria*. London: New Beacon, 1979.
63. A. Osuntokun, *Equatoria Guinea-Nigeria Relations: The Diplomacy of Labour*. London: Oxford University Press, 1978.
64. Akinyemi, *Readings and Developments on ECOWAS*, 35.
65. Promise Abali, "Nigerian Foreign Policy inHistorical Perspective, 1960-79: An Analysis." B. A. Project, Nsukka, 1998.
66. *Gowon*, 185.
67. Gowon, *Unity*, 168.
68. Elaigwu, *Gowon*, 199.
69. Tamuno and Upabi, *Nigeria Since Independence*, 8.

General Murtala Ramat Mohammed
Head of State
July 1975-February 1976

Chapter 4

Quest for National Purification:
Murtala Mohammed's New Vision,
1975-1976

Gloria I. Chuku

INTRODUCTION

On July 29, 1975, the Nigerian Armed Forces, in a bloodless coup, deposed General Yakubu Gowon while he was attending the Organization of African Unity (OAU) Summit in Kampala, Uganda. Brigadier Murtala Ramat Mohammed (1938-1976), then the Inspector of Signals in the Nigerian Army and Federal Commissioner for Communications, became the new Head of State and Commander-in-Chief of the Armed Forces.[1] In his first broadcast to the nation on July 30, 1975, Murtala Mohammed accused Gowon's government of insensitivity and inaccessibility. He said that Gowon had let the country drift and that his government had, since the end of the civil war, been characterized by lack of consultation, indecision, indiscipline and neglect.[2] He immediately cancelled the contentious 1973 census results, and retired some public officers in a clean-up campaign popularly known as his "purge exercises" or the "removal exercises."

In the October 1, 1975 broadcast marking the fifteenth anniversary of Nigeria's Independence, Murtala Mohammed announced that the country would be returned to civil rule by October 1, 1979.[3] He outlined the transition program, which consisted of a 5-stage agenda with a detailed timetable of what had to be done at each stage. Elements of the program included appointment of a Constitution Drafting Committee in October 1975 to work on a preliminary draft. New states would be created by April 1976. A Constituent Assembly would be formed in October 1977. This Assembly would ratify the draft constitution by October 1978. By October 1978, elections to legislative and executive offices at the local government, state and federal levels would be held.[4] The 1966 ban on political parties and local government reforms would be lifted in time for this election.

This chapter examines how well the Murtala Mohammed administration was able to address the important issues he raised earlier. The regime's civil and service purge, the creation of more states and relocation of the federal capital as well as the transition to civil rule program are discussed. The revolutionary structure of Mohammed's government, his leadership style and foreign policy are also examined. How did Mohammed tackle some of the contentious issues such as the abandoned property problem, and the 1973 census figures, which were capable of threatening the unity of the country if not properly and promptly addressed? How did he tackle the economic problems of the time? What was the position of women in his regime? How did he regard the religious bodies in the country? Above all, what could we say was his legacy to Nigeria? Is it correct to say that he left no legacy because of the briefness of his regime? Or can we say that his regime's legacy to Nigeria was the quest for national purification? If the response to the last question is on the affirmative side, how did he pursue national purification in the country? In an attempt to address the above questions, this chapter starts with his public service purge because of its topicality to the regime's quest for national purification.

CIVIL AND PUBLIC SERVICE PURGE

A comprehensive purge of those in public employment began a few weeks after Murtala Mohammed came to power. The exercise started with the governors, the police and the federal and state civil services. It soon extended to the various public corporations, boards and companies, the universities and finally, the army. Popularly referred to as "Operation Deadwoods," the scale of this comprehensive retrenchment and retirement of public employees was unprecedented in the whole of Africa.[5] It resulted in the firing of some ten to eleven thousand government employees, representing more than fifty percent of all federal government employees. It was more drastic in its early than in its later phase.

On September 16, 1975, the government of Murtala Mohammed appointed a three-man panel to examine the assets of former military governors, the former administrator of the East Central State and some former federal commissioners with the aim of finding out whether they misused their offices in order to acquire personal wealth. This panel was to make recommendations regarding these assets. On February 3, 1976, ten days before he was killed, Mohammed (who had promoted himself to the rank of General in January, 1976) announced his government's decisions on the report of the panel. Of the eleven former military governors and the administrator of East Central State, only two, Brigadier Mobolaji Johnson (of Lagos) and Brigadier Oluwole Rotimi (Western region) were not found to have "grossly abused their office." Assets worth over ten million naira, which had been misappropriated by ten of the governors were forfeited to the State.[6] All officers of the rank of General and the equivalent in other services including Police Commissioners and Inspector General of Police were retired. All retired military officers were said to have received their full benefits and all honor. General Gowon, for example, was paid his full pension and a substantial monthly sum through the Nigerian High Commission in London when he was at the University of Warwick in England as an undergraduate student in political science.[7]

One of the most pressing problems that were facing Mohammed's administration was the re-organization of the army. The program of re-organization and demobilization of the army was aimed at reducing its strength from around 250,000 to about 100,000 soldiers. It was stated that to keep the army at the larger size, to arm and equip the existing divisions with sophisticated weapons would absorb 60 percent of the country's national income.[8] Indeed, the Chief of General Staff of the Supreme Headquarters, was reported to have said that the Nigerian Army was "completely immobile without the right equipment and without shelter; it was almost the only army in the world where serving soldiers died of old age."[9] The re-organization of the army seemed inevitable. But the deteriorating economic situation in the later part of 1975 made the exercise increasingly unrealistic because the government was no longer in a position to finance such a costly and extensive exercise as the resettlement of demobilized military personnel. However, about a total of

216 officers were affected by the purge exercise at the end of November 1975. Lower down in the ranks of the army, many officers were dismissed or retired, but it was said to have been done with speed and care for those dismissed were either extremely lax in their duties in the past or were involved in large scale financial corruption or were even said to be absent from their units without reason for long periods.[10] A total of about 115 corrupt and inefficient police officers were retired or dismissed.[11] Paradoxically, in the face of this colossal purge, about 14 military officers were promoted to the rank of General, including General Mohammed.[12] This promotion caused discontentment and dissatisfaction among the rank and file, and also received wide criticisms from the public because it was inconsistent with the aims and ideals of the July coup.[13]

Although military personnel were affected by the purge, civil servants constituted the overwhelming number of public officials who were dismissed. This was because, according to Henry Bienen and Martin Fitton, who studied the soldiers, politicians and civil servants in Nigeria,[14] a large number of civil servants were intimately linked in factional alliances with military officers under Gowon's regime. Their increasing visibility and the perception among elites and non-elites in Nigeria that the civil service was a political actor made them more vulnerable to the house-cleaning of the new regime. Most of the high level civil servants who had been closely linked with the Gowon regime were not tolerated by the Mohammed regime.[15] From August 13, 1975, civil servants were no longer permitted to attend and participate in meetings of the Executive Council unless specifically invited to do so. Thus, a significant number of the civilian commissioners who were members of the Council were academic people and technical experts rather than politicians or civil servants.

It was widely acknowledged that by the time General Mohammed was assassinated in February 1976, several thousands of federal employees had either been retired or dismissed.[16] In addition, seven vice-chancellors of federal universities were replaced, including one dismissed because of "conduct unbecoming of an academic."[17] But, between September and October 1975 alone, Murtala Mohammed's government had dismissed and retired over 10,000 civil servants, members of the armed forces, teachers and university staff, top officials and staff of parastatals on grounds of "inefficiency, declining productivity, old age, misconduct, ill-health, doubtful integrity and divided loyalty." Deadwood and unproductive workers were retired with benefits. It was a countrywide purge, which started at the federal level and later moved to the states.

Paradoxically, this exercise gave rise to the greatest criticisms as well as the greatest praises of Mohammed's administration. Critics have accused the regime of carrying out a countrywide purge based on blanket and unproven allegations. According to C.O. Taiwo,[18] this well-meaning measure was marred by being hurriedly executed, unevenly applied and in a number of cases manifestly unjust. He went further to say that the effect on the teaching service was a reduction of the teaching force where the remaining serving teachers suffered a sense of insecurity and a lowering of morale. It was observed that the morale of the workers in general was so affected that a year later, General Obasanjo (who succeeded General Mohammed as the Head of State) was still complaining of low morale in the federal civil service. This low morale may have led to the persistence of old and discredited patterns of behavior.

Mohammed was also criticized for destroying the security of tenure of office in the civil service. In some cases, the purge degenerated into witch-hunting. It was said that many people who did not commit any offence lost their jobs. Indeed, in some exceptional cases, elements of personal vendettas and animosities occurred and in others, there was an element of arbitrariness. People were applying excessive caution in their work to the point of paralysis; civil servants became increasingly reluctant to offer advice or to assume responsibility. One could say that the civil service purge of 1975 still remains a sore point in the record of Mohammed's administration because of these criticisms. As Eghosa Osaghae[19] aptly observes, it was uncertain how the purge was to check corruption as a vast majority of those retrenched were people from the lower rungs such as messengers, cleaners, drivers and clerks whose share in the corruption practices of the past was nowhere near that of their bosses who had recommended them for retrenchment. To L. Adamolekun,[20] the colossal and premature retirements, dismissals and imprisonment of men of the armed forces damaged military confidence and disrupted the continuity in the administration of the military. It was, in fact, reported that already in September 1975, the authorities had acknowledged that the exercise had caused "concern, panic and uncertainty in the ranks of serving officers."[21] J.I. Elaigwu[22] has opined that General Mohammed's death was partly motivated by the declared intention of the government to demobilize the army.

Whatever the criticisms and the purported effects of the military demobilization and reorganization exercise on the force, the government and the country at large, the Mohammed administration took some positive steps towards improving the military. From 1975 onwards, the administration of the military witnessed a revitalized program of reorganization. For example, command responsibility was vested in the respective service chiefs, thus enhancing quick decisions. Under this regime, too, a program for demobilization of both ex-servicemen and regular soldiers was given priority. Barracks provisions received urgent attention. Award of medals to deserving troops was reinstated as a morale-booster.[23]

Although it is true that we cannot rule out totally the incidence of innocent people becoming victims of the overhaul, the exercise, no doubt, was a major step towards the national purification which Mohammed envisioned. It was a well-meaning measure intended to make workers productive and efficient. It was one of the measures taken by the regime to arrest the moral decadence prevailing within the society. And although the exercise was by no means uniformly applied in every state, department or corporation (because the opportunities for corruption varied widely while suitable replacements were not always at hand), many were removed who were corrupt, inefficient and very old to be remain in office. In most cases, the retrenchment or compulsory retirement was based on the information from personal files, audit reports, police files and reports from numerous committees set up by government to investigate particular scandals. This was perhaps why some Nigerians praised the campaign especially at the initial stage.

However, when government recognized the inadequacy of some of the methods used in the purge, it became increasingly concerned not only about the many cases of wrongful dismissal but also about the unsettling effects of the operation on the administration and on the country as a whole. Government consequently took some measures to make some amendments. It made repeated appeals to serving officers to reassure them of a normal course of justice in the future. It also made it clear that allegations should be laid out in specific terms and an affected person should have the opportunity of a hearing. A Monsignor Pedro Martin's panel was constituted immediately to look into cases of injustice and victimization.

In the New Nigerian newspaper, the Head of State, Murtala Mohammed was quoted of saying that "the aim has been to strengthen the services and there is no intention whatsoever of allowing the exercise to degenerate into witch-hunting."[24] Similarly, the Chief of Staff assured the administrators that "it is not our intention to over-scrutinize every decision and single out every small infringement or departure from regulations." He announced that the exercise was therefore concluded at the end of

November "because it had an unsettling effect on the services; everybody can now settle down to a calmer life."[25]

In spite of these criticisms, the Mohammed purges seemed to have been accepted as reasonably well-directed. According to M.J. Dent,[26] "his purges were different from the past and met with an all-Nigerian acceptance. The regime conducted a purge which was wholesome in volume but much less than revolutionary in severity." Dent felt that a real element of objectivity now entered the process of contract awards. He saw that the personal performance of public officials improved enormously. For instance, people arrived to work on time, worked harder and spent less time on private business. However, total success would have required a change in the ethics of the Nigerian society. To achieve this desired change is very difficult because it required a drastic change in the fundamental attitudes of Nigerians. This was because the Nigerian people have been involved in a long period of "unbridled capitalism (frantic pursuit of wealth) in business for conspicuous consumption." Therefore, one can conclude that the purge exercise had only partial success.

The purge, might have helped to instill confidence in the ability of Nigerians through its reform of the country's civil service, the armed forces and quasi-government agencies. Although the exercise took only four months, there was continuing strictness in the application of standards as disciplinary action was taken against those who fell below these standards. Chinua Achebe's observations would help to illustrate the positive effect of the purge on Nigerians. In his *Trouble with Nigeria*, Achebe describes the situation. "On the morning after Murtala Mohammed seized power in July 1975, public servants in Lagos were found `on seat,' traffic that had defeated every solution and defied every regime vanished overnight from the streets. Why? The new ruler's reputation for ruthlessness was sufficient to transform in the course of only one night the style and habit of Nigeria's unruly capital."[27] But, this dramatic change in the behavior of Nigerians failed to endure. Even before Mohammed was assassinated a few months later, Nigerians were returning cautiously to their old ways.

In his New Year broadcast in January 1976, the Head of State stressed once more that the massive pruning in the country's civil service was intended to weed out the corrupt, the inefficient, the unemployable and the redundant, and that the exercise was now completed. While urging officials and workers to be in the vanguard of the crusade for creating a disciplined and well-ordered society, which upheld the dignity of labor, hardworking and judicious management of public funds, he acknowledged that the exercise had enhanced efficiency and produced a new and positive sense of responsibility. According to a *Daily Times* report, the new sense of responsibility and dedication to duty had been amply demonstrated by the several committees the Federal Military Government set up to look into some important issues in the development of the nation. The report goes on: "The way and manner these various committees accepted the call to national duty, the utter ruthlessness with which they grappled with the problems, the comprehensiveness of their reports and the frankness of their recommendations proved conclusively that Nigeria is endowed with men and women of caliber with absolute degree of I.Q. (Intelligent Quotient)."[28] The report gave credit to the purge for the diligence, frankness and commitment of the committee members.

TRANSITION TO CIVIL RULE

In October 1975, Murtala Mohammed announced a Constitution Drafting Committee (CDC) headed by Chief Rotimi Williams. This was in line with his announcement of the 5-stage program of military disengagement from Nigerian politics. He had previously made the basis of his administration very clear thus: "we are committed to a federal system of government."[29] He therefore charged the Committee to consider a constitutional framework that would respect and promote the "federal character principle." This was formalized and institutionalized in the 1979 Presidential Constitution. It is not our concern here to debate the strengths and weaknesses of the federal character principle, and whether it is appropriate for the unity and survival of Nigeria as a nation-state because some other works have treated the matter extensively.[30] The CDC was made up of 50 members (predominantly academics and lawyers) with a minimum of 2 representatives from each state, apparently putting the federal character principle into practice. Incidentally, there was no female member.[31]

It was decided after a decade of unsettling and largely ineffective changes to undertake a systematic but conservative local government reform in the country. The Federal Military Government took the initiative in September 1975, and directed each state government to set up a commission to appraise the problems involved in the reorganization of the local government system and to submit proposals that would increase the responsibilities of local authorities and encourage participation in governance at the grassroots level. They were asked to indicate what type of staff and finance that would be needed to carry out the proposed decentralization. In a conference held at Kaduna in December 1975, it was generally agreed to have a uniform system of local government throughout Nigeria as proposed by the Federal Government.[32] Thus, by 1976, discussions were held throughout the country on the reorganization of local authorities. This was regarded as an essential step for the indirect election to the Constituent Assembly. The change of pace was quite remarkable. Later, when General Obasanjo took over as Head of State, there was no slacking of tempo.

In line with his goal to sweep-clean, give direction and provide the constitutional foundations of good government, Murtala Mohammed also embarked on addressing unresolved and contentious issues inherited from the immediate past regime. He promptly cancelled the controversial 1973 census results and continued working with the 1963 figures. This was in spite of the fact that the 1973 census results were favorable to the North where Mohammed came from. Dent observed that, "only Mohammed had sufficient status as a northerner to persuade northern notables that this cancellation was a necessity."[33]

Other issues such as the creation of additional states, the removal of the Federal Capital from Lagos to a more appropriate site and the abandoned properties problems were also treated. These were volatile issues. If not promptly and carefully addressed, they were capable of delaying or even undermining the transfer of power to civilians slated for October 1, 1979.

RELOCATION OF THE FEDERAL CAPITAL

Although plans to relocate the federal capital were started under Gowon's regime, it was under Mohammed that action was speeded up to make it realizable. As soon as the Head of State announced his 5-step political agenda, a committee was appointed to advise the government on a more appropriate or suitable site for the nation's capital. The Committee went to work immediately. Some of its members visited Islamabad (in Pakistan) and Brazilia (in Brazil) for the purpose of gathering information for the task before them. The Committee, after a thorough examination of proposals before it, advised government to designate a virgin site near Abuja as the country's new capital. This was because the site satisfied the criteria of centrality, good and tolerable climate, land availability and use, adequate water supply, low population density, physical planning convenience, security and multi-access possibility. The area was not within the control of any of the three major ethnic groups in the country (Hausa-Fulani, Yoruba or Igbo).

In the February 3, 1976 broadcast, the Head of State announced the acceptance of the Supreme Military Council (SMC) of the recommendation by the panel on the relocation of the Federal capital from Lagos to a Federal Territory of about 8,000 square kilometers in the central part of the country. Thus, Abuja, the nation's new capital, was born. Lagos was accorded "special area" status, as were Kaduna and Port Harcourt. The principle of federal character with regard to the decentralization of power was again at work here.

CREATION OF MORE STATES

With the belief that the creation of more states was to bring government nearer to the people while at the same time ensure even development within a federal structure of government which Nigeria had adopted, the Head of State, Murtala Mohammed appointed a 5-man panel headed by Mr. Justice Ayo Irikefe on August 7, 1975. The panel was charged to hear evidence all over Nigeria and to make recommendations to the Supreme Military Council on the need to increase the number of states in the Nigerian federation. The Federal Military Government also charged the panel to make ethnicity the least important of the criteria it would use in recommending for the creation of new states.

The panel went to work immediately and on December 23, 1975, it submitted its report. No time was also lost in acting on its recommendation. After studying the report, the Head of State on February 3, 1976 announced that the SMC had decided to create seven new states, bringing the total number of states in the Nigerian federation to nineteen.[34]

History has shown that the proliferation of states in the Nigerian federation has not eradicated the problem of the minorities and even of ethnicity. However, Mohammed's creation of a 19-state structure was widely applauded. This was so especially when he stated that the states were no longer to be described by reference to geographical points such as North and South, East and West in order to erase memories of past political ties and emotional attachments. Instead, states were now named on the basis of historical significance such as old kingdoms, or geographical landmarks such as rivers.[35]

On February 12, 1976, a six-man commission headed by a Supreme Court Judge, Mr. Justice Muhammadu Nasir, was set up to look into boundary problems arising from the creation of states.[36] The creation of additional states and the relocation of the federal capital were handled with an admirable mixture of the three elements of popular consultation, expert opinion and decisive military action.

ABANDONED PROPERTY ISSUE

It was under Mohammed's regime, five years after the end of the civil war, that the issue of abandoned property in the three states that comprised the former Eastern Region was purposefully tackled. A five-man panel headed by Colonel S. Daramola was set up for this task on September 8, 1975. Based on the panel's recommendation, the Head of State in his February 3, 1976 broadcast announced the federal government's decision on the abandoned property issue. The federal government allocated N14 million to enable the Rivers and South-Eastern State governments to pay a flat rate of N500 per annum for every building property as rent arrears to make up for the previous five-year period from 1970 to 1975.

The federal and state governments were to purchase some of the buildings concerned. Some were to be sold to the indigenes of the state that were required to pay a fair price to respective former owners. Non-indigenes who were interested were also given the opportunity to buy part of the building property. Those who lost their buildings as a result of the war were not left out. They received "appropriate" compensation from the state governments concerned. All those interested in buying the buildings were advised to go to the commercial banks and the Nigerian Building Society for financial assistance. Mohammed also announced the setting up of a Special Tribunal to determine all disputes arising from the disposal of abandoned property in the states affected.[37] He also set up a panel to advise government on the future of the Northern States Interim Common Services (NSICS) and the Eastern States Interim Assets and Liabilities Agencies (ESIALA). Following the panel's recommendation, NSICS and ESIALA were disbanded.

LEADERSHIP STYLE AND POLITICAL STRUCTURE

General Murtala Mohammed's leadership style was greatly influenced by his background. A devout Muslim from an aristocratic family of Kurama quarters, Kano, Mohammed was "tough, inflexible, strong-minded and aggressively intolerant."[38] He was fearless and steadfast. He was "constant and unchangeable in his resolves; and the military regime under his leadership had been characterized by his personal qualities of toughness, imperturbability and swiftness of decision and implementation."[39] Murtala Mohammed was said to have given Nigerians a new sense of nationalism, revolutionary and progressive approach to government. His actions were said to be almost without exception motivated by his total commitment to the aspiration of the people. It was partly because of this visible token of identification with ordinary people that won him great support and acceptance of his seemingly harsh corrective rule. Ironically, it also cost him dearly, his life. Unlike his predecessors, Mohammed like President Jimmy Carter of the United States, shunned formalities and ostentation, and was generous even to those he had overthrown.

Perhaps a few quotations from people's impression about his government and leadership style will make the picture clearer. To M. J. Dent, "The formidable powers vested in Mohammed were rendered tolerable by his populist style of power without pomposity. He dispensed with the vast escorts and security precautions that had cluttered the style of both the Gowon and the Ironsi governments. He was easily accessible in the Dodan barracks and drove almost unescorted in his Mercedes".[40] He shunned the elaborate security paraphernalia associated with previous governments in the country, especially in the Gowon era. Dent continues, saying that in the enforcement of his reforms, emphasis was laid where it was most needed. The regime emphasized and symbolized honest and energetic administration, structural reform and the building of national unity. Mohammed took the most radical reforming action and was to be identified with the progressive cause. Unlike his predecessor who had to rule by cautious consensus, Mohammed's social background allowed him to take firm decisions and avoid compromise. The Mohammed government kept the rules of good government. It did not make change for change's sake but concentrated on those changes that were necessary and could be made to stick. It sought to unite and not to divide the nation. Dent concludes: "for the first time, Nigeria under Mohammed has had a decisive government commanding real popular support. His administration was considered to have done more in six months than previous governments in ten years. And this degree of support for the government of Mohammed was demonstrated by the wave of popular anger that greeted the abortive coup of February 13, 1976 in which Mohammed lost his life."[41]

According to K. Panter-Brick, "nationalism or patriotism, reached a quite high pitch under the brief leadership of General Murtala Mohammed, expressing itself most strongly in the conduct of foreign policy but also in widespread demand for national ideology which would point the way for all to follow. In contrast to its predecessor, Murtala's administration had more clearly defined objectives and the government seemed determined to execute them promptly. There was an almost unprecedented degree of administrative activity in the first months of Mohammed's rule as various commissions were created to investigate and report on issues outstanding from the previous regime."[42] For E. Oyedele,[43] the Murtala Mohammed's administration emphasized probity. Although it was like a flash in the pan, the regime endeared itself to the hearts of Nigerians by its sweeping reforms and temporary restoration of sanity into the public service. Mohammed's administration has been said to be a corrective government. Dent has described it as a mid-way between the two extremes of military caretakership and military revolution. This, he said, has been the broad aim of the vast majority of the Nigerian military rulers, which found its most practical application during the six-month period of military rule under Murtala Mohammed. "For the first time" he says, "Nigeria experienced genuine corrective government where issue after issue was taken up, enquired into systematically and dealt with effectively by decree or administrative action."[44]

Some others have described Murtala Mohammed as a mobilizational leader.[45] According to Elaigwu, the mobilizational personality of Mohammed assisted in a prompt and efficient execution of his programs and policies. As a mobilizational leader with the rhetoric of a radical reformer, Mohammed had little patience for bureaucratic process. He demonstrated this as soon as he came to power by shocking the system out of the lethargy of pervasive corruption that had typified the last days of the Gowon regime. He had little patience for the politics of reconciliation. Elaigwu argues that Mohammed's greatest mistake was his excessive use of the mobilizational style in an essentially reconciliatory situation. This mistake, Elaigwu opines, partly caused Mohammed's assassination. He acknowledges, however, that his six months in office had given the country a sense of direction and augmented the new federal structure created by Gowon. "A nationalist at heart," he says "Murtala

Mohammed had transformed himself from a secessionist to a Nigerian patriot."[46]

In comparing the leadership styles of Gowon and Murtala Mohammed, Elaigwu[47] concludes that Nigerians are too impatient for a leader of Gowon's temperament, and yet too `egalitarian' and `democratic' in values for Murtala's mobilizatonal style. But Lindsay Barrett[48] believes that the dynamic political stance of the regime was being operated with a sense of style and charisma of Mohammed, which "effectively blanked out the milder and blander style of the Gowon era."

We could say that Murtala Mohammed was an impetuous but pragmatic leader with enormous drive and energy. He was a bold and fearless officer, attributes which affected his leadership style. Many Nigerians felt that he was the type of leader they needed at the time. He quickly and effectively addressed such intractable issues as the 1973 census, the creation of new states and a new federal capital, the plan to return to civil rule and the divisive effects of pan-regional bodies like the Interim Common Services Agency (ICSA) and the Eastern States Interim Assets and Liabilities Agency (ESIALA). He was a pragmatist who assembled a battery of highly educated, intelligent and innovative Nigerians as advisors on the making and implementation of major policies. He took decisions on urgent matters for which he later sought the SMC's approval. Although his critics accused him of personal ambition and running a closed government after he elevated himself to the position of General in January 1976, Mohammed's history of low profile, transparency and accessibility in government has not been rivaled in post-colonial Nigeria.

Murtala Mohammed created three organs of government at the federal level: the Supreme Military Council (SMC), the National Council of States (NCS); and the Federal Executive Council (FEC). There were also executive councils at the state level. The SMC was the highest body in the hierarchy providing the general policy guidelines within which the affairs of the nation were conducted. It was made up of 22 members (all military men and the commissioner of police, now called the Inspector General of Police). There was no female member. The NCS provided the forum for state representation in the discussion of matters affecting their interests. In a federation as Nigeria, the state governors should have direct and unhindered access to the highest levels of national decision-making. Thus, even though the governors were no longer members of the SMC under the new dispensation, they were reporting to the office of the Chief of Staff, Supreme Headquarters. The Federal Executive Council conducted and directed the daily affairs of the nation. The FEC provided for a substantial civilian participation in government, serving as an effective link between the populace and the military members of the Council. It was made up of 25 federal commissioners (13 armed forces members and 12 civilians), yet no woman was a member. Mohammed's administration was said to be the first to attract intellectuals to government. It was the first time the highest number of people from the academic circle was appointed into important political offices.

The above government structure made up of the SMC, NCS and the FEC was a welcome departure from the previous system, which concentrated too much power in the hands of one man. However, the system centralized authority in state-federal relations. In this case, orders came down from the center, giving general guidelines and deadlines for particular projects to be carried out such as the retirement of public officers in 1975 and the local government reforms in 1976. The Federal Government took a number of other steps to centralize authority. For example, it took over the *New Nigerian* (a newspaper then owned jointly by the six northern states), and acquired the majority of shares (60 percent of the equity) in the *Daily Times* (the largest newspaper concern in the country). In November 1975, the Federal Military Government announced that it had taken over all the country's radio and television networks. These measures no doubt added to the leverage of the federal center; and the nature of military rule made these actions fall outside the parameters of litigation by states.[49]

Just as a typical military regime, Mohammed's administration relied on decrees. But his decrees were often based on the reports of various panels, commissions and committees he had set up (thereby paying heed to public opinion). Some of his important decrees included Criminal Justice (Miscellaneous Provisions) Decree 1975, No. 30; Decree No 31 – Public Complaints Commission Decree 1975; Decree No. 32 – Constitution (BASIC Provisions) Decree 1975; Decree No. 35 – Petroleum Production and Distribution (ANTI-Sabotage) Decree 1975; and Decree No. 38 – Corrupt Practices Decree 1975.[50]

SOCIO-ECONOMIC PROGRAMS

Murtala Mohammed's government touched all facets of Nigerian society – the economy, agriculture, communication and gender issues. Because of space constraints, this chapter does not go into a detailed discussion of how Mohammed's policies and programs affected the sectors mentioned above, but only highlights salient issues.

The Economy

On August 15, 1975, an eleven-man Anti-Inflation Task Force was set up by the Federal Military Government. Its goals were to examine the current inflationary tendencies in the economy and identify their causes and review the fiscal, monetary and other anti-inflationary measures being pursued; and to recommend, bearing in mind the economic and social objectives of the country. The Task Force was also asked to recommend short and long-term policies, and measures that could effectively contain inflationary pressures in the national economy.[51]

Mohammed's administration tried to strengthen and diversify Nigeria's economic linkages both with the West and elsewhere; and to expand the economic role of the state alongside and in alliance with multinational capital. The regime also tried to stimulate private Nigerian capital through state intervention; and provide the central government the ability and capability to determine and implement public policy in the national interest. The 1975-76 Budget introduced wide tariff changes designed to reduce the cost of production as well as to encourage new local production. Indigenization[52] decree that emphasized nationalization of major industries was strengthened. The Federal Military Government under Mohammed's regime started clearing and decongesting the wharves of an armada of shiploads of cement and other imported goods that clogged the country's main ports where the nation was paying astronomical sums of money as demurrage penalties to overseas shipping companies. Murtala Mohammed stopped the petrol shortage in the country and imported food and other essential materials from wherever he could get them cheapest. It was reported that the sum of N44 million was released for the purchase of essential commodities that were scarce in Nigeria; and that he also subsidized beef prices to make life bearable for the Nigerian populace.[53]

Agriculture

On December 22, 1975, the Federal Government established 14 institutes[54] to undertake research into various fields of the country's agriculture. These were aimed at improving agricultural production of food and to make the country self-sufficient. To what extent these institutes succeeded in achieving the motives for their establishment is a matter of future research outside of the scope of this chapter. The Federal government also embarked on the reform of the marketing boards. A land use decree was promulgated.

Communication

Apart from taking over some newspapers, the radio and television networks as observed earlier, Mohammed modified and consolidated a massive telecommunications expansion scheme in the few months of his leadership. Under Mohammed, government control of the press was tightened.

Religion

Mohammed's policies did not leave untouched the religions of the people because he believed that the various religious bodies in the country had a great task to perform towards the unity and integration of the nation. The government in 1975 therefore constituted a Nigerian Pilgrims Board for the effective conduct of holy pilgrimages. The Board was inaugurated in Kaduna on September 11, 1975. Through the Board, government started providing an effective control of the conduct of pilgrims in order to minimize their perennial suffering. The exercise ceased to be an individual affair. Nigerians pilgrims had to plan and travel as a group with some form of government assistance.

Mohammed urged Moslems and Christians to use religious values to work together for the future of their country. He urged them also to improve on their religious life in order to bring discipline to the nation and shun large-scale bribery, corruption and inefficiency. In a goodwill message to the National Episcopal Conference of Nigeria held at Onitsha from September 9-14, 1975, the Head of State asked the attending Catholic bishops to identify what role the church should play in the move to remold the nation. By implication, this task was also given to the various religions in the country, for to accomplish the arduous task of nation-building confronting the administration, these religious bodies needed to work together as partners in progress and shun all forms of religious intolerance capable of threatening the unity of Nigeria as a nation-state.

Trade Unionism

Trade unionism in Nigeria during this time was fractionalized. The Federal government, therefore, took even-handed corrective action to deal with the warring factions of the left and the right. Over more than 250 labor unions in Nigeria were reorganized into 8 organizations under the umbrella national union, the Nigerian Trade Union Congress (later called the Nigerian Labor Congress). The reorganization made it possible for government to monitor the unions more closely and often manipulate them when necessary. A commission of enquiry was set up to investigate trade union finances, and a strict prohibition was placed on receipt of any money from outside the country.

Education

By Decree Nos. 20, 22 & 23 of 1975, the federal government took over control of the universities of Benin, Ife, and Ahmadu Bello, which were formerly state universities. It created 6 new ones, bringing the total number of federal universities to 12 (including the earliest three: the University of Ibadan, the University of Nigeria, Nsukka, and the University of Lagos). On September 25, 1975, the administration appointed 4 vice-chancellors for the new university institutions to be sited: Professor Gilbert Onuaguluchi (Unijos); Professor A. Ayandele (University of Calabar); Dr Shehu Galadanci (University of Sokoto); and Professor Essien Udom (University of Maiduguri). Also appointed were 3 principals – Malam Mahmud Tukur (University College, Kano); Professor Tekena Tamuno (University College, Ilorin); and Professor D.E.U. Ekong (University College, Port Harcourt).[55]

Primary education, previously a state matter, was brought under federal control. The move to implement Universal Primary Education was intensified under the Murtala Mohammed regime. Although it was not operational in his lifetime, the scheme took off still in the same 1976 under General Obasanjo after Mohammed was murdered.

Bribery and Corruption

In his task of fighting bribery, corruption and inefficiency, Murtala Mohammed established the Corrupt Practices Investigation Bureau and Special Tribunal to handle corruption. He also established a

Public Complaints Commission (or the Ombudsman) on October 3, 1975 headed by a Chief Commissioner, Alhaji Yusuf Maitama Sule. However, the government's cleansing programs wore a human face. Thus, shortly after Mohammed took over, he announced a reduction in criminal sentences for certain offences, especially hemp-smoking, which gave him the image of a champion of the underdog.

Women and Gender Issues

Generally, we could say that the Murtala Mohammed administration neglected women in his appointments. That was why there was no female member in the three organs of government at the Federal level and also in the 50-man Constitution Drafting Committee. Neither was there any woman among the 30 Federal Permanent Secretaries sworn in on November 21, 1975. But when on 28 October, 1975, a delegation of the National Council of Women's Societies visited the Head of State and complained of this neglect, he assured them of his government's commitment to equal rights for men and women.[56] He informed them that government was embarking on a gigantic educational program in which women would have abundant opportunities to develop their potentials. He also assured them that his government endorsed fully the aims, aspirations and activities of the Women's Societies, and that government expected women to contribute their quota in all spheres of national life because he believed that they were the hands that rock the cradle they should also play a role in ruling the nation. But, how can this role be realized if women were marginalized and worse still excluded entirely from participating in decision-making processes, especially at the national level due to their non-appointment to positions of authority? The Head of State promised that women would be given full opportunities and equal consideration with men at all levels of the national endeavors. This promise he tried to keep by appointing in the same year, a few women to the office of state commissioners. In the 1976 local government elections under military supervision, women in Northern Nigeria finally acquired the right to vote, though not without some resistance. A few women ran for positions in public office, but less than 10% of the elected were women.[57]

FOREIGN POLICY

The Murtala Mohammed era is probably best remembered for the dynamism and Afrocentric character of the foreign policy pursued by his regime. He projected Nigeria on the foreign front to match the leadership desired of its size, wealth and power. He threw his weight behind the eradication of colonialism, racism and apartheid in southern Africa. In Nigeria, he abruptly postponed indefinitely a visit to Nigeria by Queen Elizabeth II of Britain and her husband, the Duke of Edinburgh, originally scheduled under the Gowon administration to take place from 14 - 23 October 1975. A team of seven British Broadcasting Corporation (BBC) correspondents was summarily refused entry into Nigeria at the Ikeja International Airport in August 1975. It was also during his tenure in July 1975 that the 1972 Indigenization Decree was actually implemented.

According to O. Aluko,[58] General Mohammed and his lieutenants had little regard for diplomatic niceties. He announced in November 1975 that Nigeria would do everything possible to stop African countries from being used as tools by imperialists and racists. For him all African countries belong to one single family within which any means could be used to bring an erring member back to the fold. It was this belief that made Murtala Mohammed champion the cause of African liberation from colonialists, imperialist oppression and exploitation. This was demonstrated openly in the Angolan crisis.

The swift and unequivocal recognition and support the Mohammed government accorded the Popular Movement for the Liberation of Angola (MPLA) in Angola and the brush-off it gave Henry Kissinger, the US Secretary of State, in the face of U.S support for the South African-backed UNITA and FNLA, brought Nigerian support to the forefront of African and World affairs more than ever before. On January 11, 1976, he attended the Addis Ababa extra-ordinary summit conference of OAU on liberation struggles in Africa. He condemned apartheid South Africa's involvement in Angola and the unedifying role which the U.S. was playing in African liberation struggles. He therefore urged African heads of state and governments to invite the MPLA President, Dr. Augustinho Neto "to take his place of honor among us in this assembly."[59]

Murtala Mohammed's role in liberation struggles in Africa probably informed Y.B. Usman to observe that "the patriotic and decisive stand on Angola in the face of the powerful western campaign, and his eloquent _expression has made Murtala Mohammed one of the greatest heroes and martyrs of the African revolution and the emancipation of the black man all over the world." [60] For T. Otegbeye,[61] Mohammed's greatest contribution was Nigeria's stand in Angola where he called the bluff of the American President and the CIA and persuaded African leaders to recognize the MPLA government headed by Neto. Lindsay Barrett who has written extensively on the Nigerian military has this to say about the foreign policy of Murtala Mohammed:

> In foreign policy, Murtala's government had stunned the world with its bold and unexpected support for the left-wing liberation movements of Southern Africa. The Angolan victory tested this policy and Nigeria's self-confidence as the leader of African intercontinental politics was suddenly enhanced. The perception of military leadership as a force for direct political achievement was extended from the domestic to the international plane.[62]

The role of Mohammed in the Angolan liberation movement had led some to describe his foreign policy as socialist in orientation. Dent,[63] for example, says that in foreign affairs, Mohammed's government was at its most, socialist. His full support to the Angolan civil war and the stringing rebuke with which he replied to a rather patronizing letter circulated by the United States to African Heads of State in this issue earned Mohammed increased support as a spiritual defender of Africa against South African and American interventions. The anti-American crusade, including military and material support to the MPLA and diplomatic shuttles, was estimated to have cost Nigeria over US$20 million.[64] Mohammed was therefore seen as a major threat to America's foreign policy in Africa. This was critical in view of the prevailing Cold War politics between America and her allies on the one side and the Soviet Union and their own allies on the other side. The MPLA victory was a major defeat for the foreign policy of the United States, especially since Angola was tied in with its strategic Southern Africa interests. Many Nigerians believed that the assassination of Mohammed in the Dimka's abortive coup had a US link as the latter was determined to eliminate the threat by Nigeria.

EXIT OF A HERO AND SOLDIER-STATESMAN

Good things, they say, do not last long. Lieutenant Colonel Buka Suka Dimka and his men assassinated General Murtala Mohammed on February 13, 1976 on his way to his office. It was a black day for Nigeria. Nigerians had lost within a twinkling of an eye, their "God-sent" leader who has come to purify the country. There were widespread spontaneous demonstrations by workers, students and traders in major Nigerian cities, especially Lagos. Offices, markets and shops were deserted. Thousands of people wept openly on the streets in the cities. It was reported, "Never in the history of Nigeria has the death or assassination of a Nigerian leader received as much ringing condemnation as that of the late Nigeria's Head of State, General Murtala Ramat Mohammed."[65]

Excerpts from Nigerians' glowing tributes to Mohammed will buttress the above point. S.G. Ikoku,[66] an economist/politician has this to say: "what we owe General Mohammed is to work even more painstakingly for the realization of the dynamic, disciplined and self-directed nation he toiled so hard to build." The Association of University Teachers in its tribute urged the SMC to "uphold the dignity of the Blackman to defend his race and nationhood for which General Mohammed stood throughout his life."[67] In the same line, the Progressive Front of Nigeria Labor Movement and Democratic Union Resistance Committee urged the SMC to "rigorously guard against foreign intervention and interference in the radical policies the nation has been pursuing (under Mohammed)."[68] To the then Chief Justice of the Federation, Mr. Justice R.A. Alexander, Murtala Mohammed was a "dynamic and dedicated national leader, who has left his footprints on the sands of time. The judiciary was aware of the progressive plans for reforms and reorganization he was actively considering for the judiciary. No one can doubt his dedication to the cause of the nation, his words and actions show that he was first, a Nigerian patriot."[69]

The Nigerian nation mourned Mohammed, but its consolation is that it is not life itself that matters but what one puts into it. Mohammed is said to have put all his life into the service of Nigeria. According to a *Daily Times* report, "the nation's consolation was that Mohammed had ably begun the struggle for the establishment of an egalitarian society, devoid of embezzlement of public funds, of corruption, tribalism and nepotism."[70] Fred Ohwahwa and E.P. Uzoanya[71] have observed that after Mohammed was assassinated, his six-month rule has continued to evoke feelings of nostalgia among articulate Nigerians. In retrospect, his regime seems to have signaled the end of the golden years of military dictatorship in Nigeria. According to them, within six months, Mohammed single-mindedly tackled corruption, embarked on a mass purge of the civil service and put the country's foreign policy at its loftiest height yet. He remains the yardstick for measuring Nigerian leaders. Here lies the perpetuation of his status as a national hero. To Professor Adele Jinadu, Director General, Administrative Staff College of Nigeria (ASCON), Badagry, in the 1995 Murtala Mohammed memorial lecture, "our fascination with General Murtala Mohammed is a central element of his political significance which, simply put, is that most of us see in him intimations of what we ought to be but are not; we see in him the model political leader."

Perhaps, one of the greatest tributes came from Murtala Mohammed's successor, General Olusegun Obasanjo who has this to say: "I believe and feel strongly committed to all we have been doing. I pay him no better tribute than to continue in the spirit with which he handled this country – that of complete dedication."[72]As promised, Obasanjo continued with the policies of General Mohammed such as Nigeria's central position in African affairs (as seen in the support of the Patriotic Front in Rhodesia [Zimbabwe] in 1978-79; hosting of the World Festival of Black and African Arts and Culture [FESTAC] opened by General Obasanjo on 15 January 1977 which was attended by thousands of people from over 50 different countries of Africa, the Caribbean, the Americas and Australia); local government reforms; universal primary education; and above all the program for return to civil rule on October 1, 1979.

CONCLUSION

Murtala Mohammed's regime, though brief, was full of achievements. It was therefore not surprising that his regime enjoyed wide popularity throughout the country. His transition to civil rule program endeared him to the political class in the country. His cancellation of the 1973 census results helped to ensure his popularity in the South. The rigorous, no-nonsense approach of his regime further boosted his image. The creation of more states in early February 1976 won him the admiration of most creation of state agitators. Many people[73] believe that Mohammed was a star destined to leave the stage when the ovation was loudest, a meteor burning itself up with the fire of its enthusiasm. For this group of people, the regime was too young to have lost its glamour. The opposition struck at a time when Mohammed's personal popularity and the credibility of his government had reached a peak of acceptability in the nation. As some have noted, however, his death came too soon for one to be able to assess clearly the nature of the legacy that he might have left as an individual.[74] S.C. Ukpabi[75] has observed that Murtala Mohammed had sought to revitalize the body politic and eliminate those problems, which militated against Nigeria's economic and social development, but notes that the degree of success he would have had in finding permanent solutions to Nigeria's political and social problems is now a matter for conjecture.

It is true that Mohammed left the stage too soon. Historical evidence has shown that he did not leave without making a great impact on Nigeria and its people. It is also true that he made mistakes like any other human being, but many of his countrymen would say that they were of the heart and not of the head. Some of his policies and programs attracted powerful enemies (local and foreign) and tremendous jealousy. But on balance, he was a unique person who gave this country a remarkable sense of direction, a feeling of purpose and meaning. His administration gave the dying country life and hope when there was despair. A *Sunday Times* assessment noted that Murtala Mohammed's government "rekindled the hope that Nigeria could yet be a great nation and a source of pride to all black people all over the world. It set before everybody the vision of a great Nigeria. General Mohammed did what most people thought was totally impossible. He took up the leadership of the country at a time the ship of state was drifting aimlessly on a sea of confusion. The odds he faced were absolutely staggering and would have daunted a less determined soul."[76] But he stood firm. No doubt, General Murtala Mohammed and his administration would be remembered for the great achievements made. Although he would also be remembered for the devastating effects his purge have continued to have on the Nigerian civil service system, and the university administration, most importantly, however, he would be remembered for his quest to purify Nigeria as a nation.

And yet "one may also wonder" as Professor G. N. Uzoigwe wondered in his comments on this chapter, "how Mohammed would have handled the consequences of his actions had he lived long enough. It is one thing," he continued, "to disorganize institutions overnight, ride roughshod over certain administrative and other practices, issue directives to be carried out 'with immediate effect' and so forth at the point of a gun; it is another to ensure that such changes are sustained under democratic governance which Nigeria must evolve, sooner than later, if it would continue to receive the support and respect of the international community." Mohammed's "apparent disregard for his personal safety," he suggested, "during a quest for national purification which inevitably hurt many individuals, big and small, admittedly well-meant, smacked either of incredulous carelessness or a lack of proper understanding of the country he was trying to purify or of someone openly courting martyrdom." It will be left to future historians to deal with these issues when the archives and Mohammed's personal papers are made accessible. Clearly, the successor regime of General Olusegun Obasanjo, as we shall see, demonstrated the difficulties that lay ahead.

ENDNOTES

1. Murtala Mohammed was chosen to replace Yakubu Gowon because of his enormous popularity in the army. According to Ian Campbell, "Army Reorganization and Military Withdrawal" in K. Panter-Brick ed. *Soldiers and Oil: The Political Transformation of Nigeria*, (London: Frank Cass & Co. Ltd.), 1978, 58-100, Murtala Mohammed was chosen to lead the government because although often impetuous, he seemed particularly to the young officers, to possess the requisite qualities of drive and determination for a Head of State.

2. R. Uwechue (ed.) *Africa Today* (London: Africa Books Limited), 1992, 1462; and *Nigeria Year Book* (Lagos: A *Daily Times* Publication), 1976.

3. It should be recalled that Nigerians (especially politicians and some military officers) got frustrated and disappointed with General Gowon's administration when on the October 10, 1974 broadcast, he announced formally an indefinite postponement of the plan to return the country to civilian rule in 1976. This indefinite postponement of the transition to civil rule prompted the military to carry out a change of leadership in the bloodless palace coup of July 29, 1975.

4. J.O. Ojiako, *13 Years of Military Rule*, 1966-1979 (Lagos: *Daily Times* of Nigeria Ltd Publication, not dated), 102.

5. Shehu Othman, "Nigeria: Power for Profit – Class, Corporation, and Factionalism in the Military" in D.B. Cruise O'Brien, John Dunn & Richard Rathbone (eds.) *Contemporary West African States* (New York: Cambridge University Press), 1991, 126.

6. Uwechue, *Africa Today*, 1462; and M.J. Dent, "Corrective Government: Military Rule in Perspective" in Panter-Brick, *Soldiers and Oil*, 114-116. On July 31, during the swearing-in ceremony of new governors, Brigadier Murtala Mohammed reminded them that the former governors were removed because of allegations of graft and misuse of public funds and widespread dissatisfaction with their personal conduct. There had been complaints of ostentatious living, flagrant abuse of office and deprivation of people's rights and property. Other allegations were perversion of time-honored government procedures, nepotism and favoritism, as well as the desecration of traditional rulers. All these gave the impression that the states were run as private estates (See Ojiako, *13 Years of Military Rule*, 79.).

7. Dent, "Corrective Government," 119; J.I. Elaigwu, *Gowon: The Biography of a Soldier-Statesman* (Ibadan: West Books Publisher Limited), 1986, reprinted in 1987; and Ojiako, *13 Years of Military Rule*,

79. The payments ceased when the Obasanjo Government became "convinced" of prima facie evidence linking Gowon to the February 1976 abortive coup during which Mohammed was murdered.

8. Campbell, "Army Reorganization and Military Withdrawal," 84.

9. *Daily Times*, 13 January 1976; New Nigeria, 13 January 1976; and *Sunday Times*, 18 January 1976.

10. Dent, "Corrective Government," 119.

11. Dent, "Corrective Government," 119; and Ojiako, *13 Years of Military Rule*, 91. According to the latter source, the retired officers included 1 Inspector General of Police, 1 Deputy Inspector General, 3 Commissioners, 3 Deputy Commissioners, 10 Assistant Commissioners, 13 Chief Superintendents, 18 Superintendents, 20 Deputy Superintendents, and 46 Assistant Superintendents including 2 women – "the terror of danfo and molue" drivers, Mrs. M. Oyebade, popularly known as mama Toyin, and Mrs. Clara Ogbomudia, the wife of the former Mid-West State Governor.

12. Campbell, "Army Reorganization and Military Withdrawal," 85-86; and Ojiako, *13 Years of Military Rule*, 130.

13. For example, the *New Nigerian*, 13 January 1976 reported that the students' union at the University of Ibadan, which had enthusiastically endorsed the new government and its energetic measures to curb corruption, now expressed "utter disgust and disappointment at the promotions which were completely out of tune with the low profile hitherto adopted by the regime."

14. Henry Bienen and Martin Fitton, "Soldiers, Politicians and Civil Servants" in Panter-Brick, *Soldiers and Oil*, 152-153.

15. Dent, "Corrective Government," 119; and Ojiako, *13 Years of Military Rule*, 91. Among the senior federal civil servants retired or dismissed were 5 Permanent Secretaries and the Chairman of the Federal Public Service Commission, Alhaji Sule Katagum. He was replaced by one Professor Ogan from Rivers state. Dan Ibekwe was appointed as the Attorney General of the Federation.

16. Bienen and Fitton, "Soldiers, Politicians and Civil Servants," 53. This source was corroborated by H.N. Nwosu, "The Role of Public Administration in Political Development" in E.C. Amucheazi (ed.) *Readings in Social Sciences: Issues in National Development* (Enugu: Fourth Dimension Publishing Co. Ltd.), 1985, 29-40; and S.C. Ukpabi, *Strands in Nigerian Military History* (Zaria: Gaskiya Corporation Ltd), 1986, 126. According to the latter, there was reorganization of the bureaucracy, which resulted in the compulsory retirement of about 11,000 public servants within a period of 8 weeks alone in 1975.

17. The dismissed Vice-Chancellor was not unconnected with business interests. See Dent, "Corrective Government," 120.

18. C.O. Taiwo, *The Nigerian Education System: Past, Present and Future* (Lagos: Nelson Pitman Limited), 1986, 168.

19. Eghosa E. Osaghae, *Crippled Giant: Nigeria since Independence* (Bloomington & Indianapolis: Indiana University Press), 1998, 83.

20. L. Adamolekun (ed.) *Nigerian Public Administration 1960-1980: Perspectives and Prospects* (Ibadan: Heinemann Educational Books Nigerian Ltd), 1985, 20.

21. *New Nigerian*, November 22, 1975.

22. Elaigwu, *Gowon: The Biography*, 193.

23. Ademolekun, *Nigerian Public Administration*, 20.

24. *New Nigerian,* 20 October 1975.

25. *Daily Times*, 22 November 1975.

26. Dent, "Corrective Government," 118.

27. Chinua Achebe, *The Trouble with Nigeria* (Enugu: Fourth Dimension Publishers), 1983, 1.

28. *Daily Times*, 1 January 1976, "No Laxity, Please," Mohammed, 1.

29. Olusegun Obasanjo, *Not My Will* (Ibadan: University Press Limited), 1990, 57.

30. For such debates on the Federal Character Principle, see I.U. Ukwu (ed.) *Federal Character and National Integration in Nigeria* (Kuru: NIPSS), 1987; and P.P. Ekeh & E.E. Osaghae (eds.) *Federal Character and Federalism in Nigeria* (Ibadan: Heinemann), 1989.

31. K. Panter-Brick, "The Constitution Drafting Committee" in Panter-Brick, *Soldiers and Oil*, 292; and Ojiako, *13 Years of Military Rule*, 103-104.

32. A.Y. Aliyu, "As Seen in Kaduna," in Panter-Brick, *Soldiers and Oil*, 270.

33. Dent, "Corrective Government," 126.

34. Ojiako, *13 Years of Military Rule*, 132, recorded the states as: Anambra (Enugu), Bauchi (Bauchi), Bendel (Benin), Benue (Makurdi), Borno (Maiduguri), Cross River (Calabar), Gongola (Yola), Imo (Owerri), Kaduna (Kaduna), Kano (Kano), Kwara (Ilorin), Lagos (Ikeja), Niger (Minna), Ogun (Abeokuta), Ondo (Akure), Oyo (Ibadan), Plateau (Jos), Rivers (Port Harcourt), and Sokoto (Sokoto).

35. See Note 32.

36. The Commission was charged to:

"Examine the boundary adjustment problems identified by the Irikefe Panel on the creation of state;

Specify which areas of Andoni and Nkoro in Opobo Division of the Cross River State should be in the Rivers State and which areas of Ndoni should form part of the Rivers and Imo States;

Investigate and define the boundaries of any other areas, district or division which might be brought to the notice of the Panel;

Define inter-state boundaries, especially in case of inter-governmental official disputes; and

Make recommendations on the fore-going terms and any other matters incidental to boundary adjustment in the new states structure (culled from Ojiako, *13 Years of Military Rule*, 132).

37. *Nigeria Year Book*, 1976 (Lagos: Daily Times Publication), 1976, 53; and Ojiako, *13 Years of Military Rule*, 96 & 131.

38. O. Aluko, *Essays on Nigerian Foreign Policy* (London. Boston.Sydney: George Allen and Unwin), 1981, 242.

39. O. Awolowo, "Tribute to Mohammed, the great Nigerian," *Daily Times*, February 17, 1976.

40. Dent, "Corrective Government," 116 & 117; and Eliagwu, *Gowon: The Biography*, 255 & 275. According to the latter, the price of the low profile exhibited by Mohammed proved to be very expensive. He never moved to the official Dodan Barracks residence of General Gowon. He remained in his house in Ikoyi and drove to work at Dodan Barracks. It was not unusual for the General to drive in the streets without adequate security. Once, the *Daily Times* carried a picture of the General, driving in a Volvo car in the usual heavily jammed Lagos traffic.

41. Dent, "Corrective Government", 117.

42. Panter-Brick, "Introduction," 6.

43. E. Oyedele, "The Military, Politics and the National Question," in Abdallahi Mahadi, *et al* (eds.) *Nigeria: The State of the Nation and the Way Forward* (Kaduna: AREWA House), 1994, 520.

44. Dent, "Corrective Government," 104 & 114.

45. J.I. Elaigwu, "Federalism and National Leadership in Nigeria," *Publius: The Journal of Federalism*, 21(1991): 126 & 137.

46. Elaigwu, "Federalism and National Leadership," 138. In his earlier work, Ealigwu, *Gowon: The Biography*, 67, has observed that Murtala Mohammed was the leader of northern army officers who championed the cause of northern secession in 1966 and the bombing of Lagos.

47. Elaigwu, Gowon: *The Biography*, 302, states that a leader of reconciliation relies for his effectiveness on qualities of tactical accommodation and capacity to discover areas of compromise between otherwise antagonistic viewpoints. He remains in control as long as he is

successful in politics of compromise and synthesis. To Elaigwu, Nigerian examples were Tafawa Balewa and Yakubu Gowon.

48. Lindsay Barrett, "The Return of the Military: 3, The Long Handover," *West Africa*, 23 July 1984, 1488.

49. Elaigwu, "Federalism and National Leadership," 138.

50. *Nigerian Year Book*, 1976, 29; and Ojiako, *13 Years of Military Rule*, 103.

51. *Nigeria Year Book*, 1976, 34.

52. Indigenization was one of the main objectives of the second and third national development plans (others included self-reliance and industrialization). The aim was to place control of the economy in the hands of Nigerians, and ensure that they were the main beneficiaries of the country's resources. Unfortunately as Osaghae, *Crippled Giant*, 100-101, rightly observes, indigenization did not mean nationalization which implies transfer of `ownership' of the economy from foreigners to nationals but was part of an overall program of elite accumulation within the parameters of the given social order, and involved the transformation of the distributive rather than productive sectors of the economy to a different or "higher" level of dependency. It allowed the Nigerian capitalist class to work out more acceptable terms of `compradorization' with its foreign benefactors.

53. *Sunday Times*, 15 February 1976, front page.

54. These were the Cocoa Research Institute of Nigeria; Forestry Research Institute of Nigeria; Kainji Lake Research Institute; Lake Chad Research Institute and Leather Research Institute of Nigeria. Others were National Animal Production Research Institute; National Cereals Research Institute; National Horticultural Research Institute; and National Veterinary Research Institute. The rest were the Nigerian and Marine Research; the Institute of Oceanography; Nigerian Institute for Trypanosomiasis Research; and the Rubber Institute of Nigeria. (See from Ojiako, *13 Years of Military Rule*, 129).

55. Ojiako, *13 Years of Military Rule*, 101.

56. *Nigerian Year Book*, 1976, 40.

57. C. Vereecke, "Better Life for Women in Nigeria: Problems, Prospects and Politics of a new National Women's Program," *African Study Monographs*, 14, 2(1993), 240; and Gloria Chuku, "Breaking Ethnic Barriers and Urban Interethnic Conflicts: The Gender Imperative," in *The Transformation of Nigeria*, ed. Adebayo Oyebade (Trenton, NJ: Africa World Press), 2002, 372-73.

58. Aluko, *Essays on Nigerian Foreign Policy*, 240.

59. *Nigeria Year Book*, 1976, 42; and Ojiako, *13 Years of Military Rule*, 130.

60. Y.B.Usman, *For the Liberation of Nigeria: Essays and Lecture 1969-1978* (London: New Beacon Books Ltd), 1979, 70.

61. Tunji Otegbeye, "General Murtala Ramat Mohammed – Hero of the African Revolution," *Daily Times*, 19 February 1976, 7.

62. Barrett, "The Return of the Military," 1488.

63. Dent, "Corrective Government," 128.

64. Osaghae, *Crippled Giant*, 107.

65. *Daily Times*, 16 February 1976, "The unkindest Cut of all," Daily Times opinion, front page.

66. S.G. Ikoku, Daily Times, 17 February 1976.

67. *Daily Times*, 17 February 1976.

68. *Daily Times*, 17 February 1976.

69. R. A. Alexander, "The nation's Consolation," *Daily Times*, 18 February 1976, 3.

70. *Daily Times*, 18 February 1976, 2. See also *Daily Times*, 19 February 1976, "He did greatest good in shortest time."

71. F.Ohwahwa & E.P. Uzoanya, "20 Years After Murtala Mohammed: A Hero?' *The Guardian on Sunday Magazine*, February 11, 1996, 61.

72. Uwechue, *Africa Today*, 1464.

73. An example of such writers is Okechukwu Okeke, *Hausa-Fulani Hegemony: The Dominance of the Muslim North in Contemporary Nigerian Politics* (Enugu: ACENA Publishers), 1992.

74. Barrett, "The Return of the Military," 1488.

75. Ukpabi, *Strands in Nigerian Military History*, 125-126.

76. *Sunday Times*, 15 February 1976, front page.

General Olusegun Obasanjo
Head of State
February 1976-September 1979

Chapter 5

Vision Betrayed?: Olusegun Obasanjo, 1976-1979

Levi A. Nwachuku

INTRODUCTION

On February 13, 1976 General Murtala Mohammed was assassinated in a military counter-coup led by Lt. Colonel B. S Dimka. General Obasanjo, who was Mohammed's second in command, was sworn in as Nigeria's fourth military Head of State, on February 14, 1976. A few weeks short of his thirty-ninth birthday, Obasanjo became the first Nigerian of Yoruba provenance to govern the country. He would also be the first military Head of State to voluntarily transfer power to a democratically elected government. A native of Abeokuta in Ogun State, Obasanjo's education was rooted in military training as he joined the army soon after his graduation from Abeokuta Baptist High School.

Obasanjo has impressive military credentials. Commissioned in 1959,he was sent to several overseas training courses in England as well as in India. In the United Kingdom, he attended the Royal Military College of Science and Engineering at Shrivenham, Berkshire. To his credit, General Obasanjo was described as the "best commonwealth student ever," to pass out of the Royal Military College.[1]

General Obasanjo was an active participant in the Nigeria/Biafra War in support of the Nigerian military effort to defeat Biafra. At the outbreak of the conflict, General Yakubu Gowon appointed him the Commander-in-Chief of the Second Area Command, in Ibadan. As the war progressed, Obasanjo took over the command of the Third Marine Commando Division of the Nigerian Army. This Division is credited with presiding over the end of the Nigeria/Biafra War.[2] General Obasanjo exploited the challenges of the war to demonstrate the strength of his character and his commitment to achievement and success.

Obasanjo's star in the military would rise. Under General Gowon's regime, Obasanjo was appointed Commissioner of Works and Housing, an appointment that owed much to his engineering background. He relinquished this post to become Chief of Staff, Supreme Military Headquarters. In more ways than one, General Obasanjo's military career was free of tragedies or setbacks, free of those cathartic moments that crystallize purpose and define motivation.

Nigeria's political culture since independence had favored Northern leadership of the country's political arena. Obasanjo may have felt uneasy when given the mantle of leadership of Nigeria. In his inaugural speech, Obasanjo said, "I have been called upon against my personal wish and desire to serve as the new Head of State. . ."[3] Placed in historical perspective, the new Head of State did not possess psychological motivation for the job that "chance" thrust on him. Unlike his predecessors, who felt that their leadership of the Nigerian government was a divine right, Obasanjo would see himself as laboring in the shadow of Northern political hegemony, merely at the edge of the spotlight and, indeed, on the periphery of meaningful power. General Murtala Mohammed had laid a foundation for a revolutionary government as reflected in the measures he introduced. Obasanjo stated in his statement that his predecessor's policies would continue. He said, "we are all now obliged to continue with these policies laid down by the Supreme Military Council under the dynamic leadership of General Mohammed."[4] General Obasanjo, perhaps conscious that he lacked the ethnic credential expected of Nigerian leaders, would govern with caution, and would no doubt, take some distance from his predecessor's style and policies.

Obasanjo inherited the same problems which marred the ousted Yakubu Gowon's regime and which the assassinated Murtala Mohammed was attempting to solve. Before the outbreak of the Nigeria/Biafra War, Gowon created twelve states. States creation would become an almost perennial demand by different sections of Nigeria. General Obasanjo's government would inherit the task of stabilizing the seven new states, which he and his predecessor had created in February 1966. These states were Imo, Ondo, Benue, Ogun, Gongola, Niger and Bauchi.

Corruption was a debilitating left over from Mohammed's government. It was becoming entrenched in Nigerian social, economic and political culture. In 1966, Gowon's regime had pledged to rid Nigeria of bribery, corruption and nepotism. Nigerians expected the military government to live up to this pledge. But Gowon's government could not clean up the country. Ayo Fasanmi, National General Secretary of National Anti-Corruption of Nigeria, in an article captioned, "Corruption Rides On!"[5] deplored the unrealistic and superficial efforts the Gowon regime exerted against corruption. It was a general feeling that the cleansing of the nation was beyond Gowon's reach. This was reflected in an article which appeared in the London Observer, February 23, 1972 entitled, "Can Gowon Halt Corruption in Time?." The Mohammed regime would inherit this problem which would be passed on to the Obasanjo government.

Nigerians had hoped that the military assignment would be temporary. It was, evidently, this understanding that made Gowon's regime promise a return to civilian rule in 1976. However, Gowon did not redeem this promise. Because of Mohammed's untimely death, Obasanjo would be saddled with the responsibility of returning Nigeria to a democratic state. To his credit, he did so. How he achieved this is discussed later.

THE ECONOMY

A fragile economy was among General Obasanjo's inheritances from the short-lived regime of General Murtala Mohammed. The buoyant economy, which defined General Gowon's nine-year leadership, had begun to slide into the sunset at the time of Obasanjo's government. Industrial establishments were not developed enough to sustain the needs of Nigerian consumers. In 1977, industrial activities were only contributing eleven percent to the gross domestic product. Manufacturing concentrated largely on food, tobacco, beverages, roofing sheets, suitcases, electronics, and automobile assembling plants established by Peugot, Volkswagon and Mercedes-Benz companies respectively. Industrialization was handicapped by the lack of infrastructural support. Electricity supply was inadequate and erratic; communication was antiquated. Roads were not developed. Industrial raw materials were imported. The Indigenization policy in the industrial and manufacturing sectors scared away foreign investors. In 1976, the Federal Military Government took over 120 companies owned by non-Nigerians in Lagos States, Kano, Borno, Oyo, Plateau, Rivers, Bendel and Cross River. The foreign owners had violated the indigenization decree by refusing to sell shares to Nigerians.[6]

The Indigenization Decree was inaugurated in 1972. Many observers thought that it was politically ill conceived and economically unsalutory. All Nigerians should have been given the opportunity to participate in the rewards of the indigenization process. The decree was passed barely one year after the end of the Nigeria-Biafra War. Biafrans, the Igbo in particular, had been marginalized--they were on the periphery of the Nigerian State. Devoid of resources, outside the mainstream of the power structure, the Igbo were not in a position to buy shares in the companies foreigners were selling. Not all Nigerians, therefore, heralded the advent of the indigenization decree. In the economic context, indigenization did not promote growth in Nigerian economy. Nigerians who took over the foreign companies did not possess the technical know-how for running the companies. A majority of them could not provide a stable financial support for the companies. The companies that were hit hardest were those that were controlled solely by Nigerians. Indeed, some of these companies could not survive. General Obasanjo was not discouraged by the gloomy state of the industrial sector. Believing that strengthening the industrial base is an economic insurance policy for the country, he earmarked N15 billion for industrial development.[7] Since the end of the Nigeria-Biafran War, particularly in the period between 1972 and 1974, the petroleum sector sustained Nigeria's economy. It accounted for the better portion of 95 percent of the country's export earnings. However, at the time General Obasanjo became the head of the Federal Military Government, revenue from oil exports had begun to diminish. A global oil glut had set in. There was an increase in the production of oil from new sources in the countries that were outside the Organization of Petroleum Exporting Countries (OPEC). Oil production from the United Kingdom and Norwegian sectors rose to 396 million barrels in 1977 from 192 million barrels that were drilled in 1976.[8] General Obasanjo would have to deal with the problem of creating a balance between the imperative of economic development and the handicap produced by scarce financial resources.

The economic crisis engendered by drop in oil revenue was exacerbated by Nigeria's inability to feed its people. The years of oil boom had diverted attention away from agriculture. Ironically, the agricultural sector had been Nigeria's major export earner from its independence in 1960 to the end of the First Republic in 1966. During this period, the agricultural sector fed the Nigerian populace. However, when agriculture was neglected, Nigeria had to depend on imported food for survival. In 1976 when Obasanjo became the Head of the Nigerian Government, N441 million was spent in importing food. In 1977, food import rose to N770 million and inflation registered forty percent.[9] To Obasanjo, the economic crisis was seen in the context of a "battle of food." He tackled the food shortage with determined intensity. His administration mobilized Nigerians to support "Operation Feed the Nation" and "Grow More Food." A national council consisting of military personnel and federal commissioners for trade, information, cooperatives and supply, education and finance was appointed to take charge of the campaign, which involved encouraging schools, colleges, universities and individuals to grow all types of food crops.[10] Essentially, this was a mass mobilization for food production. Private investors were equally asked to invest in food production projects. Foreign investment in agriculture rose by 40 percent. Investors received a ten percent investment allowance. In the 1978/79 budget speech, General Obasanjo's government allocated N372 million and pledged its assistance to farmers to provide them with improved seeds, seedlings and fertilizer. The efforts expended in rehabilitating the agricultural sector did not yield the expected dividend in food production. Food importation continued and reached astronomical dimensions beyond Obasanjo's tenure. Although this regime did not fulfill the aspiration of the Nigerians in food production it, nonetheless, called attention to the crisis of food shortage by the redemptive measures it inaugurated.

Land-Use Decree.

In the spirit of reform, General Obasanjo's regime saw a need to reform the land use system in the country. To this effect, a panel was set up in 1977 to study various land use systems in Nigeria. Following the panel's report, the Federal Military Government issued a land-use decree in 1978. By this decree, the governor of each state would control and manage all land in urban areas of the state while all other land outside the urban areas would be under the control and management of the Local Government Area (LGA) in which it was situated. Theoretically, by the decree, all land in Nigeria would be held in trust by the Government on behalf of the people. It would eliminate monopolization of land ownership by a group. This would make it possible for the government to develop the land for the benefit of all. The decree placed a limit on the amount of land an individual could possess. It also placed a limit on the number of years an individual could own a piece of land. The limitations and restrictions only pertained to undeveloped land. An individual would not be allowed to hold indefinitely more than half an hectare in any one state at any one time.

It is difficult to assess the effectiveness of the Federal Government's implementation of the land policy. The policy, by definition, took land away from the traditional owners and entrusted it in the hands of bureaucrats who would act for the governor of a state or chairman of a local government area. However, in reality, traditional landowners claiming the sanctity of ancestral right, argued that they, and not the government, had the natural right of ownership of land in their territory. It was only natural to maintain that ancestors bequeathed the land to them. Nonetheless, the new land policy accelerated land development in various parts of the country. Individuals with financial ability, were able to buy land and develop it for either residential purposes or commercial purposes. The land policy, however, did not produce the prodigious dividend in agriculture as expected. Agricultural land fell victim to speculators. Indeed, import of goods including food items increased by forty-two percent as General Obasanjo's regime was winding down.[11] The government could not effectively execute the new land policy. The natives still continued to control land sale particularly in the rural areas. The buyer only paid a nominal fee to the government to obtain a certificate of occupancy. Whatever may be said of the land policy, its greatest achievement is that the policy communalized land ownership and nationalized it under government control.

SOCIO-CULTURAL FORCES

Corruption

General Obasanjo, in his inaugural speech, indicated that he would continue with his predecessor's programs. One of the programs was the effort to sanitize Nigeria's social fabric. Nigeria suffered from perennial social malaise rooted in widespread corruption. An editorial by one of the national papers commenting on the corruption that engulfed Nigeria said, "of all the ills that have so long befallen this country, lack of fair play, unequal opportunities, bare-faced cheating in high places remain the most malignant. "[12]

A high official commented, "I would not go to the extent of saying that everybody is corrupt in Nigeria, but most of our leaders—military and civil—are readily corrupt."[13] The proclivity toward corruption was not limited to those in authority, but extended to many other Nigerians, especially to those who regard the practice as a means of sharing the nation's wealth. In this context, a Nigerian lawyer described this social evil as "democratic corruption," seeing it as "a way of redistributing wealth" in the country. Beyond this, the get-rich-quick syndrome gripped the psyche of many Nigerians, and Brigadier Emmanuel Abisoye, the Adjutant General of the Nigerian army, reflected this thinking when he said, "the present [Nigerian] society encourages the belief that each man is entitled to acquire as much as he can through whatever means."[14]

General Obasanjo, like his predecessor, took measures to rescue the country from this social disability. A permanent Corrupt Practices Investigation Bureau and Special Tribunal was established to handle all cases of corruption in all sectors of the nation's economy. Unfortunately, the effort to rid the country of corruption was more symbolic than realistic. The failure to eliminate corruption was, in large measure, due to the fault that those in a position to implement the anti-corruption measures were themselves the symbols of corruption. General Obasanjo would serve out his term in office without succeeding in his attempt to cleanse the nation's social pathology.

"Education President"

Historians will cast an enduring light on General Obasanjo as the "Education President." His regime inaugurated the federal government's National Policy on Education, which regards education not only as a constructive social force that can be used to foster redress of imbalances among a people, and also as the greatest investment that a nation can make for the development of its socio-political as well as economic and human resources. In promulgating the national education policy, the government emphasized life-long education, universal basic education, and opportunity for the individual to pursue any field of study that would help meet the developmental needs of the nation. To support life-long education, adult education centers were established in many cities in the states. Adult-education systems were not only planned to give an opportunity for learning to those who were less fortunate in having educational opportunity earlier, but were equally intended to provide opportunities for in-service training. This was demonstrated in the number of many Nigerians who were sent to different overseas countries to augment their expertise in their respective areas of interest.

The educational policymakers noted the intellectual as well as motivational diversity among the nation's children. Some are intellectually precocious, and feel not sufficiently challenged by the normal school system. For such children, the policy advocated establishing special schools for the gifted. There are children who are physically and mentally handicapped. For these groups, special education programs were to be created, tailored to the needs of the individual. The educational policy was also concerned with how education could address specific needs of the nation. To this end, schools were encouraged to participate in agriculture and special schools of agriculture were built and the number of universities and polytechnics were increased to accommodate the population of students. Some of the students enrolled in science programs.

In September 1976, the Universal Primary Education (UPE) scheme was introduced. Any Nigerian child, on reaching the age of six was expected to be enrolled in primary school. General Obasanjo described the UPE scheme as "making the dawn of a new era in the history of education in Africa." The scheme "would make education a right and not a privilege for all Nigerians," declared General Obasanjo.[15] Women would also benefit from the scheme. General Obasanjo captured the essence of the universal primary education when he said, "gone are the days when the rightful place for a woman is in the kitchen because it is now universally accepted that when one educates a woman, one educates a nation."[16] Indeed, the scheme was not only a right for education but also a mandate for education. It opened the door of opportunity for women in particular, toward social, economic and political empowerment. About 2.5 million children spent their first day at school on the first day of the Universal Primary Education. This number swelled the primary school population that day to eight million pupils. By 1980, when Nigeria's Third Development Plan would expire, all children at the age of six would be required to be enrolled in primary school.

Unfortunately, not all parents were enthusiastic in exploiting the opportunity to send their children to school. Many state governments in the North had to persuade parents to allow their children of school age to attend school.

With the introduction of the UPE scheme, there was a huge increase in the numbers of school children in primary schools. This created a need for classrooms, trained teachers, and teaching materials. It was estimated that during the first phase of the program 160,000 extra teachers would be needed. This addition would enlarge the teaching population to 300,000 for the first-phase period. Due to shortage of teachers, Nigeria recruited teachers for primary school from Sierra Leone.[17] A healthy economy was needed to sustain the UPE scheme. By 1977, the government had spent over N16 million to implement the scheme. The Federal Military Government, as well as the state governments, began to build colleges of education as well as teacher training schools. From another angle, the UPE scheme had a multiplier effect. The government was confronted with how to accommodate the needs of the primary school leavers. Jobs were not enough to accommodate the primary school leavers and not much alternative safety net for them. There was, therefore, a need to build adequate post primary schools, which would provide opportunities for primary school leavers to pursue either vocational education that would make it easier to get jobs as soon as they graduated or continued further with post secondary institutions. As a result, high schools proliferated in the country. Many technical institutions were also built. Every state built a polytechnic, either federally financed or state financed.

Many of the students who graduated from either the polytechnic institutions or the teacher training colleges preferred to gain admission into universities. To this end, the Obasanjo regime increased the number of universities from the four that existed during the First Republic to eleven the first generation universities were located in Ibadan, Ife, Nsukka and Zaria. The new universities were located in Maiduguri, Kano, Sokoto, Ilorin, Calabar, Port Harcourt and Lagos. At the same time, groundwork was laid for the future establishment of universities of technology at Owerri, Yola, Bauchi, Abeokuta and Minna. Although higher institutions were established, many qualified students still could not find places in them.

For students whose areas of specialization were not offered in Nigeria and for some of the students who, because of inadequate places in the existing universities, could not gain admission, the government made plans for educating them in some overseas countries. A majority of them were given either federal or state scholarships. For instance, in the 1977-1978 school year, a thousand Nigerians were sent to France to study medicine, architecture and engineering.[18] The Federal Military government created many opportunities for students to be educated. A Student Loan Board was created in 1977, and N3,144,000 was earmarked for loan assistance to needy students. At first installment, 798 students received the award.[19] General Obasanjo further expanded educational opportunities for students, especially for those attending technical schools and teacher training colleges, by providing tuition-free education for them.   To harmonize and standardize admission processes with institutions of higher learning, a central admissions board was established. The board, created February 13, 1978, was known as the Joint Admission and Matriculation Board (JAMB). It set examinations for those seeking admission into colleges.[20] The JAMB placed students into various colleges. Furthermore, the Federal Government took over schools, teacher training institutions, technical colleges and universities from private owners as well as state controlled ones.[21] The Federal Government also built two secondary schools in each state. One would be for girls and one for boys.[22] During Obasanjo's last year in office, his regime abolished tuition fees for secondary school students in 1979.[23] In his continuing interest in educational development, General Obasanjo's government established the Nigeria Institute of Social and Economic Research (NISER).   NISER was intended to provide consultancy services to Federal and State governments in the areas of economic and social development, as well as to conduct research in those areas.[24]   The government also set up a National Teachers' Institute (NTI) to monitor and improve educational and teaching standards. The Institute would organize programs for training and certification of teachers.[25] In the same philosophy rooted in improving education, Obasanjo's administration established a National Board for Technical Education (NBTE). The Board, *inter alia*, would advise the government in all aspects of technical education including making recommendations as to the remuneration and condition of service of the teaching staff and products of technical institutions.[26] Along the same line, a National Science and Technology Development Agency was established. This agency would promote, coordinate and finance scientific research.[27] To improve the technical manpower in Nigeria, the Obasanjo regime entered into several bilateral agreements with various overseas nations. Prominent among these were the United States, France, West Germany, Hungary, Italy, Britain, Poland, Canada, Yugoslavia, Rumania, and India. About 500 Nigerians were sent to these countries.   They were to undergo crash programs on technical education in community colleges and universities. Most of the courses they took were veterinary science, forestry, industrial engineering, architecture, surveying, agriculture, plumbing, electronics and tractor engineering.[28] Much financial investment was made in training Nigerians overseas as well as in importing foreign instructors to fill the need in the teaching sectors of the Education Industry. This investment drained

Nigeria's much needed foreign reserve. Nevertheless, it was sound policy to develop the nation's educational section. As result of the Universal Primary Education Scheme, school populations exploded. This explosion necessitated building secondary and vocational schools to receive the end product of the UPE Scheme. Most of the secondary and vocational school graduates would continue their educational quest in universities. If well funded and correctly planned, these various institutions would be able to redeem the educational and developmental needs of the nation. Indeed, five years after Obasanjo left office, training of Nigerians had virtually ended except in cases where there were overseas benefactors. Although there were crisis of stability in terms of funding of the different educational programs, the efforts, nonetheless, spoke well of General Obasanjo's interest in education as a vehicle for national development. He could rightly be called "the Education President."

FOREIGN POLICY

General Obasanjo's foreign policy posture did not deviate in content and context from that of his predecessor. His style was, however, assertive and continuously demanding. Colonel Joseph Garba, the Federal Commissioner for External Affairs, outlined Nigeria's foreign policy objectives: Nigeria intends to aid less fortunate countries through recognized agencies; she supports the economic objective of the United Nations Organization; she will emphasize the paramountcy of Nigeria's national interest. She would be guided by commitment to a fight against racialism and colonialism. To implement her desire to aid less fortunate countries, in February 1976, Nigeria entered into a contract with the African Development Bank to create a "Nigeria Trust Fund." Nigeria made 80 million dollars available for loans to needy African countries. In the same spirit, Nigeria gave scholarships to students from Southern African countries that were struggling against the strangulation of European colonialism. Students from South Africa and Rhodesia were given places in Nigerian schools, colleges and universities.[29]

The Federal government demonstrated an uncompromising distaste for the racialism and colonialism that were prevalent in Southern Africa. On October 12, 1977, after talks with President Jimmy Carter of the United States, General Obasanjo called upon the United States and the Western countries to end their investments in apartheid South Africa. He argued that armed liberation struggles by the oppressed in Southern Africa was not only justifiable, but was bound to succeed.[30] Nigeria's anti-racialist and anti-colonial stance was not only vocal and symbolic; but was demonstrated by financial support. On July 5, 1976, the Nigerian government presented 250 million dollars to the Mozambique government for the liberation struggle in Zimbabwe.[31] Furthermore, the government gave substantial cash to Angola, Mozambique and Namibia for their struggles against colonial oppression and racism. Nigeria even =established a public trust fund with $7.2 million for Southern Africa Relief.[32] Although Nigeria made immense contributions to the Liberation struggles in Africa, she maintained that she regards her role in Africa as only mediatory. She argued that no African country has the right to claim leadership of the continent[33] In the same breath, Obasanjo's government rejected any effort by any power to impose its will on Africa. It is against this background that Joseph Garba, the Commissioner for External Affairs, opposed the creation of a Pan-African Military Force because it was an idea initiated by the French. Commissioner Garba said:

> We do not need security solutions manufactured in Paris or Moscow or Washington or London . . . We remain firmly opposed to any new scramble for Africa. . . we reject any attempt to recolonize Africa in the guise of a permanent African Security Force.[34]

Suspicious of the feasibility and the practicability of creating a politically United States of Africa, Nigeria historically felt more comfortable with regional economic cooperation. The Obasanjo administration, guided by the above philosophy, invested effort, support and funds in establishing the Economic Community of West African States (ECOWAS). ECOWAS, to Nigeria was regarded as "an area of concentrated development" and as a "link of unity."[35] Like its predecessors, the Federal Military Government, argued for a nonaligned posture. This was demonstrated when Nigeria supported the MPLA, which most Angolan nationals also supported. The West, and the United States in particular, supported the UNITA, which opposed the MPLA.

During Obasanjo's first year as the Head of State, Nigeria's relations with the United States as well as Britain suffered some setbacks. Ironically, the United States and Britain had been regarded as Nigeria's traditional friends, considering the fact that, at the time, United States businessmen had at least one billion dollars invested in Nigeria, which was also the United States' second major supplier of crude oil. Nigeria was dismayed by the possibilities of the American Central Intelligence Agency infiltration in the country. And when General Murtala

Mohammed was assassinated, some Nigeria students carried placards implying a link between the incident and the Central Intelligence Agency. [36] Anti-American demonstrators were regular among Nigerian university students, who burned American flags and urged that the American Gulf Oil firm be nationalized.

Lt. Colonel B. S. Dimka's alleged implication of General Yakubu Gowon in the coup d'etat that resulted in the assassination of Murtala Mohammed adversely affected Anglo-Nigerian relations. At the time, General Gowon was in Britain as a graduate student. The Obasanjo administration demanded his extradition to face charges in Nigeria. The British government denied the extradition request and thus set off a diplomatic friction between the two countries. Sir Martin LeQuesne, the British High Commissioner to Nigeria, left for London on March 4, 1976. To Nigeria, Britain was keeping a "wanted man" and this was an "unfriendly act." However, the diplomatic rift was soon over. The relation between Nigeria and Britain is deeply rooted in history and could not easily be destroyed.

POLITICAL DEVELOPMENT

The Constitution

General Obsanjo's regime witnessed several political events. The most important was the military disengagement from politics. Before his assassination, General Murtala Mohammed had set up a mechanism for the return of the country to a civilian regime. Obasanjo was saddled with the responsibility of implementing the program of military disengagement. On October 7, 1976, the government formed a draft constitution committee. Drafting a new constitution was one of the items on the program for transition to a democratic civilian government. The Constitution was anchored on principles such as freedom, equality, and justice in the hope of promoting good government and welfare to all persons in the country. Haunted by forces of disintegration, the Constitution sought to provide mechanisms that would assure the unity of the country. The Constitution emphasized the essence of "federal character" as a sustaining instrument of national integration. It was hoped that the essentials of "Federal Character" would guarantee a state of "balanced domination" which would eliminate inequality in the exploitation of Nigerian wealth as well as its potential among the diverse ethnic groups of the country.

In the First Republic, 1960 to 1965, the British parliamentary system shaped the Nigerian political system. However, General Obasanjo administration's Constitution that would usher in the Second Republic advanced the American political system. The system called for a democratic government by a National Assembly consisting of a Senate and a House of Representatives, with an independent judiciary. It also called for an executive president. The Constitution touched on individual rights. Accordingly, every citizen would have complete equality before the law and all attacks on human dignity would be legally unallowable. The Constitution was, however, vague in its definition of individual rights. It was mute on the crucial issue of national citizenship versus state or ethnic citizenship.   National citizenship did not transcend the geography of federal jurisdiction. A Nigerian only has political rights-- the right to run for office-- in the state of his or her birth.

Although the Constitution followed the United States' example, it did not embrace its economic philosophy of private ownership of property and the right of the individual citizens to exploit the natural resources of the country. The Nigerian Constitution vests in the Federal Government a monopoly of control over the national economy. In the given context, crude oil and mineral exploration were nationalized. Power, energy, and communication sectors were also nationalized. Perhaps more revealing was the implicit strong influence of the Federal Government over the state governments.Furthermore, unlike the United States government, the government of Nigeria only allowed single-house state assemblies. State assemblies were not bicameral, but state governors were given executive power. However, to avail the masses the opportunity of participating in the government, the constitution emphasized the strengthening of local government. Because the state, as well as the local government, suffers from economic dependence, the Federal Government, which financed them, controlled policies for them. Consequently, the people did not have meaningful and decisive participation in governmental affairs.

Perhaps detrimental to the creation of an effective and corrective press was the constitution's failure to give special guarantees for freedom of the press. This failure would be exploited by the state in its attempts to muzzle the press.

Regarding other aspects of the Constitution, not all the sections of Nigeria were satisfied with all the provisions. For instance, constitutional provisions for the creation of a Federal Court of Appeals caused disagreement among members of the Constituent Assembly. Muslim delegates in the Assembly demanded that a Sharia Court of Appeals should also be created. The Constituent Assembly rejected the demand, but adopted a recommendation for compromise by Simeon Adebo. It was recommended that in place of a separate Sharia Court of Appeals, there would be special sittings of the Federal Court of Appeals at which only Justices of Appeal who are versed in Islamic law would sit to consider cases that are contextually Sharia. The Sharia controversy indicated a future area of crisis in Nigeria's political development. During Obasanjo's second tenure, Sharia controversy resurrected and Nigeria's unity was on the brink of disintegration.

It is also worth noting that the constitution rejected a provision that would have made military coup d'etat illegal, but approved compulsory military training for Nigerian citizens. It was suggested that this training should begin in schools.[37] It should be pointed out that the Constitution was silent on the issue of financing political campaigns in terms of source and limitations, and that it failed to address the debilitating national problem of corruption in all its ramifications.

Return to Party Politics

As the constitutional drafting committee completed its assignment, the Federal Military Government set down rules for political participation. A multi-party system was encouraged, but the parties must reflect a national outlook, in their names, manifestoes and membership. Nigerians who attained the age of 18 and over were eligible to vote in elections, but must have paid income tax in full for three years anywhere in Nigeria before elections. Moslem women in Northern Nigeria were franchised for the first time.[38] Anyone running for a senate seat must be at least 35 years of age, and anyone with dual citizenship would be ineligible to vote or be voted for. Also disqualified for participation in politics are those found guilty of corruption or other malpractice since Nigeria became independent. And to protect the political parties from foreign influence, the state would subsidize the political parties but also forbid them to hold funds in foreign accounts. Civil servants were not eligible to contest for election. They had to resign from their jobs to be eligible. When civil servants and university professors, the more educated percentile of the country's population, are denied the right and opportunity to participate in the governance of the nation, what are then left are the career politicians whose records have been unimpressive and who, to the greatest extent, were responsible for Nigeria's misfortunes as well as developmental retardation.

On September 21, 1978, General Obasanjo, in his broadcast to the nation said, "From now on let the game of politics be played . . ."[39] Once the ban on political activities was lifted, more than twenty-five political parties were formed. Of these, the Federal Electoral Commission approved only five. The approved ones were: the Nigerian Peoples Party (NPP), National Party of Nigeria (NPN), Great Nigerian Peoples Party (GNPP) Unity Party of Nigeria (UPN), and Peoples Redemption Party (PRP). Although the parties reflected national outlook in their names, they were to a great extent regionally based; in fact they were largely ethnically based. For instance, the NPP controlled the Igbo dominated states, the UPN the Yoruba states, GNPP, PRP and NPN dominated the Northern states. The chemistry of the political parties underlines a major weakness of Obasanjo's Constitution. The constitution, in this context, failed to deal with the ethnic nature of Nigerian politics. Ethnic politics has been an effective obstacle to Nigeria's efforts to build a viable nation.

The five political parties contested for 1,347 constituencies for State Assemblies, 19 State governorships, and their running mates, 95 Federal Senate seats, 449 Federal House of Representatives seats, and Federal President and his running mate.[40] The governments that resulted from the elections were inaugurated on October 1, 1979, giving birth to the Second Republic. The peaceful transition from the military regime to a democratically elected one earned General Obasanjo the respect and admiration of Nigerians, whose patience with military intervention in politics had been exhausted. Many Nigerians, nonetheless, suspected that the Second Republic would at best be an aberration in a nation whose political landscape had increasingly become militocratic.

OBASANJO: AN ASSESSMENT

As all historians know, the future reflects the past. As the next chapter indicates, the regime that supplanted Obasanjo's was an abysmal disappointment to the Nigerians. Squandermania, corruption, nepotism, godfatherism, unfavorable balance of power among the regions, moral bankruptcy and lack of national purpose defined the next administration. If, indeed, the future is a reflection of its past, could it be that Obasanjo's Nigeria experienced the ugly state that characterized its successor. Perhaps one could say that Obasanjo's government failed to sanitize the cesspool of Nigerian dirty-body politic. Perhaps his administration was overwhelmed by the enormity of the nation's socio-political pathology. Perhaps his leadership lacked the resolve to deal with the ills that tormented Nigeria. Answers to these questions would provide the foundation on which Obasanjo's administration could be put in proper perspective.

The government of General Murtala Mohammed, which Obasanjo succeeded, was seen as one that made commendable efforts to cleanse Nigeria. The measures that were introduced challenged the entrenched social decay of the nation. Civil servants who were perceived to be unproductive or corrupt were removed. Mohammed emphasized accountability in the execution of public responsibility. However, he did not introduce policies that would foster the nation's unity. Despite this particular failure, Nigerians were enthusiastic about his regime. His measures, which essentially aimed at bringing out the best in the Nigerians, resonated profoundly with the people. Unfortunately his life was untimely terminated. His assassination united the Nigerians around his memory and made them determined to support the measures which he had put in place. Indeed, as the smoke of anger surrounding his assassination evaporated, General Obasanjo was in a position to galvanize the nation's sympathy to foster Mohammed's vision of a great Nigerian nation. He failed to do so. In the area of education, however, Obasanjo performed well. In the area of foreign policy, he demonstrated Nigeria's independent posture defined by the nation's interest. In the development of the nation's economy, the performance of his regime was uneven. For instance, the indigenization measures, though well intentioned, did not promote the nation's economic growth. His government inaugurated the first post-civil war loan, necessitated by the need to implement the Third Development Plan. Obasanjo's regime should not be blamed for inaugurating this loan since the global oil glut at the time lowered the price of crude oil. Nigeria's revenue was largely derived from crude oil sales. However, the little economic growth that occurred was not evenly experienced by all Nigerians. Indeed, Obasanjo's presidency witnessed the continuation of the evolution of two economic classes in Nigeria—the generously rich and those living in economic margins of society. Nigeria became a society without a meaningful middle class, a society without the fabric of sustenance. The aristocratic class went to extremes to get richer, the poor devised whatever means possible to be like the rich. In historical context, a meaningful middle class, more often than not, maintains the infrastructure of a nation's economic growth. Its absence argues poorly for a nation's development. Nigeria under Obasanjo had no viable middle class. Also, his administration seemed to have relaxed his predecessor's efforts to inculcate in Nigerians a culture of financial accountability, social discipline and responsible work habits. It could be argued that while Murtala Mohammed's measures essentially got Nigeria moving again after the post civil war inertia, the Obasanjo administration failed to seize the initiative to continue Nigeria on the path of socio-economic sanitation. The salutary education measures which Obasanjo's regime introduced were negated by the failure of the regime to sanitize the nation's social fabric. The youth, after completing their education, and guided by the ethic of get-rich-quick-by-any-means-possible syndrome which engulfed the nation, became less concerned with how to promote a disciplined society where the rule of law should be pre-eminent.

General Obasanjo's administration did not do much to promote balanced domination in Nigerian body politic. From its independence to the regime of Obasanjo, Nigeria had witnessed five executive heads of state. Three of these were of Northern origin, while two were from the south. The two from the South, however, only governed for three and a half years. The Obasanjo regime continued a policy which strengthened Northern domination of Nigerian political landscape. Its cabinet, the Supreme Military Council, contained an overwhelming disproportionate representation from the Northern region. Heads of Parastatals were largely of Northern provenance. Nigerian ambassadors appointed to the important western countries (United States, Britain, France, and Germany) were generally of Northern origin. Many of the military generals in Nigeria were Northerners. The nation's military university was built in Kaduna. The Nigerian Institute for Strategic Studies was located in the North. All the essentials that define Nigeria's nationhood, including the nation's capital, were located in the Northern region. Even the nation's currency bears Arabic inscription, symbolic of political deference to Hausa-Fulani religious and cultural affiliation.

Furthermore, the Obasanjo administration continued the marginalization of the Biafrans. On all accounts, the regime as well as its predecessor consigned the Biafrans, the Igbo in particular, to the periphery of Nigeria's socio-economic and political promise. In the above context, the regime failed to translate the verbal pronouncement of healing the wounds of the civil war into a solid accomplishment. This marginalization of a section of the Nigerian ethnic groups frustrated the affected and fed the centrifugal elements in the country's ethnic composition.

General Obasanjo would go down in history as the military Head of State who voluntarily returned the nation to a democratically elected government. Ironically, he ill-prepared the people of Nigeria for the responsibility of democracy. The democracy that succeeded his military regime collapsed after four years of its inception. Perhaps, General

Obasanjo may have taken for granted that democracy would succeed in Nigeria following his administration. But it is doubtful that either he or the military establishment realized that democracy is an essential ingredient of nation-building. It is this failure to understand the significance of democracy's role in nation-building, from 1965 to 1979, that determined the military's inability to erect a well-ordered and viable Nigerian nation. The military's role in building a Nigerian nation was essentially an exercise in failed effort.

If Obasanjo's regime realized that democratic government following his exit from power would fail, he would have perhaps re-prepared the Nigerians for the democratic experiment. The British had nurtured the Nigerians in the ideals of western democracy before they granted independence to them. That democratic experiment endured for only five years at which time the Nigerian military killed it and consigned Nigerians to fourteen years of dictatorship and corruption. Obasanjo's regime failed to adequately provide Nigerians with the necessary training for the country's return to democracy. Patriotic Nigerians expected that the regime could have made "democracy" a major theme of discussion in high schools, colleges and universities. Rallies on how to run a democratic state should have been held on many occasions in different and many sections of Nigeria. The values of transparency in government should have been instilled in the psyche of Nigerians. After a diet of dictatorship for fourteen years, one would expect that Nigerians would not easily digest a new diet prepared with democratic ingredients. It is fair to state therefore that the military, more than any other institution, bears a greater responsibility for the corruption, political destablization and the absence of systemic leverage that now plagues Nigeria. It is one of the ironies of fate indeed, that Obasanjo would be elected in 1999 to preside over a Nigeria compelled to run on the locomotion of democracy. In 1976 Obasango had become the Nigerian Head of State by the grace of the military. It was the military that defined his governance style and shaped his perception of Nigeria. In 1999, in his second coming, he became Nigerian Head of State by the grace of the Nigerian electorate. History would judge his ability to create a balance between his military background and his new role as a civilian, democratic political leader who is expected to flush the cesspool of thirty years of misgovernance filth created by the military. How General Obasanjo performs this task will define his enduring leadership legacy.

ENDNOTES

1. *Africa Research Bulletin*, Vol. 13, No. 2, March 15, 1976, 3933.
2. Olusegun Obasanjo, *My Command* 1980, 121-130.
3. *West Africa*, February 23, 1976, 233.
4. *Africa Research Bulletin*, Vol. 13, No. 2, March 15, 1976, 3932.
5. *Tribune* (Nigeria) March 23, 1975, 4, 9.
6. *New African*, February 1979, 48.
7. *Ibid.*, 51.
8. *Ibid.,.*58.
9. *Ibid.*, 69.
10. L. Nwachuku, "Nigeria's Uncertain Future," *Current History*, November 1976, 167.
11. *Africa Research Bulletin*, March15, April 14, 1978,.4646
12. *The Renaissance* (Nigeria), August 30, 1975, 3.
13. *West Africa*, August 26, 1974.
14. *West Africa*, September 13, 1976, 1385.
15. *The New York Times*, March 6, 1975, E15.
16. *Ibid.,* July 10, 1976,1313.
17. *Ibid.,* October 25, 1976, 1601.
18. *West Africa*, September 5, 1977, 1844.
19. *Ibid.*, October 21, 1977, 2223.
20. *Ibid.,* March 13, 1978, 530.
21. *Ibid.*, March 29, 1976, 439.
22. *Ibid.*, May 3, 1976, 620.
23. *Africa Research Bulletin*, March 15-April 15, 1979, 5077.
24. *West Africa*, January 30, 1978, 122.
25. *West Africa*, May 22, 1978, 995.
26. *Ibid.*, November 1, 1976, 1646.
27. *Ibid.*, November 8, 1976, 1960.
28. *Ibid.*, December 18, 1978, 2608.
29. *Ibid.*, January 2, 1978, 38.
30. *Africa Research Bulletin*, October 1-31, 1977, 4622.
31. *Ibid.*, July 1-31, 1976, 4080.
32. *Ibid.*, December 1-31, 1977, 4246.
33. *Ibid.*, May 1-31, 1977, 4422.
34. *West Africa*, July 3, 1978, 1312.
35. Nwachuku, *Current History, op cit*, 168.
36. "Nigeria is no Longer an Automatic Friend to US," *New York Times*, January 11, 1976, Section 4, E-3.
37. *West Africa*, February 20, 1978, 326.

38. *Africa Research Bulletin*, October 1-31, 1976, 4154.
39. *West Africa*, October 2, 1978, 1937.
40. *Africa Confidential*, Vol. 20, No. 8, April 11, 1979, 4.

Alhaji Shehu Aliyu Shagari
President and Head of State
October 1979-December 1983

Chapter Six

Vision Lost: Restoration of Civilian Rule and Shehu Shagari's Missed Opportunity, 1979-1983

G. N. Uzoigwe
with
Stella A. Effah-Attoe

INTRODUCTION

The restoration of civilian rule in October 1979 is, indeed, a major milestone in Nigerian history. By that singular act Olusegun Obasanjo immortalized his name. It was by no means certain that the transition would be done without disruption despite the careful planning that preceded it. Throughout his regime Nigerians had remained apprehensive. They had every reason to be skeptical about promises made by the military. Yakubu Gowon's nine years transition program was in danger of becoming transition without end, had not the Mohammed *coup* terminated his government. And Mohammed's reckless proceedings, which had badly dislocated Nigeria's major institutions of government within a few months had the makings of another long transition precisely because it would take time to put the pieces together, so to speak. That

Obasanjo was able to midwife the birth of the Second Republic given the circumstances of his succession was a remarkable achievement. It was the dawn of a new era in Nigeria, in Africa and the Black World

In October 1979 most adult Nigerians had had only a brief experience of anything approximating democratic government (1960-1966). In reality, the government that ruled Nigeria from 1960 to 1966 was a government that exhibited at once democratic, dictatorial and anarchic tendencies. The dictatorial tendencies were a heritage of the former colonial government, while the anarchic component may have been due to Nigeria's heritage of ethnic and religious differences. Democracy, on the other hand, reflected the new world trend in political ideals. It was seen as the ideal form of governance. Nigeria's early post-colonial experience, not unexpectedly, had been an unmitigated disaster. Among other catastrophes, Nigerian colonial experience and the actions of the post-colonial government led the country into a disastrous civil war from which Nigeria has not yet fully recovered. The experience had made many Nigerians suspicious of democracy. However, for those Nigerians too young to remember the failed early attempt at democracy—those born in 1960, for example--the thought of life under a democracy was just a dream. For them, military dictatorship had become a way of life.

When, therefore, on October 1, 1979 Alhaji Shehu Usma Shagari was sworn in as the first democratically elected Executive President of all Nigeria, few knew exactly what to expect. About 54 years old and slightly-built, the shy former school teacher from Shagari Village in Sokoto State, who had spent a lifetime in politics, was given the enviable privilege of directing the affairs of the world's fourth largest democracy. Although expectations were high, the constitutional waters were quite treacherous, and the task ahead seemed menacingly daunting. The good news was that his party, the National Party of Nigeria (NPN), was united solidly behind him. The economy was buoyant. Nigeria was again united, at least superficially. The "Kaduna Mafia" and its surrogate, the military establishment, apparently preferred his party to any of the others; and his *persona* was such that he inspired confidence, not fear. This was a welcome relief from the rumbustious ebullience of Murtala Mohammed and the starchy intolerance of Olusegun Obasanjo and Shehu Musa Yar'adua.

The bad news was that the circumstances of Shagari's election were so divisive that the parties who had lost their bids for power appeared determined to make his life miserable. The apparent unity of the country was to be severely tested in the years ahead. From the beginning there was a nagging doubt among many Nigerians regarding Shagari's ability to pilot the affairs of such a complex country as Nigeria successfully. Nigeria seems to require strong rulers but somehow is uncomfortable with them and welcomes "safe"—weak--rulers who quickly find themselves in situations beyond their control. Gradually, the interest wears out, and the leader becomes a "football" for everyone, a political scapegoat and an object of ridicule. It was feared that Shagari would turn out to belong to the second category of leaders but his admirers and supporters were convinced at the beginning that he was just the right person for the job.[1]

On paper his credentials were solid if by no means spectacular. He was no bright-eyed political genius with an articulated vision for his country, but he had been in politics continuously since 1945. Like many Hausa or Fulani of his generation who had a modicum of education, he had held--by appointment or election--many enviable political and other public offices in the country. Thus, like the experienced politician that he was, finding himself under siege, surviving in office took precedence over everything.[2] It is, indeed, interesting that while proclaiming his reluctance to rule Nigeria, Shagari had "practically worked in every facet of public life--from federal to state office--from State Commissioner to local government counselor--from honorable member of the Constitutional Assembly to [now in 1979] first Executive President of Nigeria."[3] Any neutral observer would therefore be led to conclude that Shagari had carefully been groomed to rule the country. There is, of course, nothing wrong with such an ambition. But to create the impression that he was a reluctant politician and reluctant presidential candidate is unacceptable to us, given a careful study of his political life. Behind his calculated, deliberate impersonality, Shagari was a politically ambitious individual who was largely unknown both in Nigeria and abroad.

In this chapter we attempt a critique of the Shagari Presidency, which lasted from 1979 until 1983). We feel that Murtala Mohammed's quest for a great Nigerian nation—a nation in which the entrenched culture of decadence would be purified and replaced with leadership that was energetic, competent and progressive--was a model of purposeful and socially structured consciousness. In our view this vision, betrayed by Obasanjo, was indubitably derailed and lost under Shagari. Therefore, Shagari's Second Republic lost the opportunity to lay the foundation for making Nigeria both a model for democratic federalism in Africa and a great African power that is economically prosperous, militarily strong and socially regenerated. Far from accomplishing all these, within a stewardship of four years and three months, the Shagari administration shamelessly squandered the country's enormous riches, systematically assaulted Mohammed's legacy and afflicted, so it seemed, by what may be described as a state of absentmindedness or perhaps palpable euphoria bordering on hubris the administration proceeded as if it learned nothing and forgot nothing from Nigeria's recent history. The result was that civilian rule in Nigeria was now justifiably given a bad name and the way consequently was paved for another military take-over.

SHEHU SHAGARI: A PROFILE

Since it is extremely difficult to separate the man from the politician, it is necessary to assess the impact of Shagari's early life and background on his presidency.

Shehu Shagari was born in May 1925 at Shagari Village which lies some forty kilometers south of Sokoto city. His father was Mogaji Aliyu, Shagari Village Head and a descendant of Shehu Usman Dan Fodio, the famous Fulani jihadist. His mother, Mairama (a princess of Yabo) was the daughter of Sarkin Kebbi Riskuwa, District Head of Yabo, a Fulani emirate within the Sokoto Caliphate. Shehu Shagari lived most of his youthful life with his mother under modest circumstances, his father having died when he was only five years old.

At the age of four Shagari was a pupil at a Koranic school in his village. Then he attended Yabo Elementary School. He studied at Sokoto Middle School between 1936 and 1941, where he excelled. Shagari then attended Barewa College and later took a teacher's course at Zaria Middle School. In March 1945 he was appointed a Master Grade II Science Teacher at Sokoto Middle School. In 1952 he was promoted to a Visiting Head Mastership at all Sokoto Province Schools. In 1953 he attended an education administration course in Bauchi Teacher's College and, in the same year, under the sponsorship of the British Council, he attended an education course in the United Kingdom. Essentially, his formal education was completed in 1945 when he was twenty years old. And nothing in his formal education prepared him for a political career.

Yet in 1945, as a school teacher, Shagari founded a Youth Social Circle which fought to win voting rights from Sokoto's "feudal" rulers. The Circle also expressed mild anti-colonial sentiments. This marked Shagari's tentative entry into politics. In 1948 he joined Aminu Kano's Northern Teachers' Association (NTA). He later joined the Northern People's Congress (NPC), which was one of the three major political parties in Nigeria during the 1950s and early 1960s. From then onward Shagari's politicization was complete.

Shagari's life contains a fundamental contradiction. The conventional wisdom in most Nigerian circles is that Shagari is a reluctant operator, a sort of curious non-political politician always persuaded by others to play one important political role after another against his better judgment. However, he never actually acted on this supposed reluctance. In 1954, for example, the Federal House of Representatives' election for Sokoto West Constituency was said to have been literally bequeathed to him at a meeting chaired by the late Sardauna of Sokoto, Alhaji Ahmadu Bello, leader of the NPC. It is interesting to note that Shagari was not invited to this meeting; nor-- it was reported--was his consent sought. Of course he did not refuse his nomination as a candidate: he was returned unopposed. In 1958 he was sent on a Parliamentary course to Westminster, London. On his return in 1959, the Sardauna sponsored his appointment as the Parliamentary Secretary to Alhaji Abubakar Tafawa Balewa, who later became the first Prime Minister of independent Nigeria (1960-1966). Initially, Shagari was reluctant to accept this appointment, it was reported but, as usual, he was eventually persuaded to accept the position.[4]

Thus he began his climb up the greasy pole of political power that led ultimately to the presidency. In 1959 he became Acting Minister of Commerce and Industry, once again, without his consent being sought, he claimed. He was re-elected to the Federal Parliament as a NPC member for Sokoto South West in 1959 and thereafter appointed the first Federal Minister of Economic Development. On October 1, 1960, he became Minister of Establishment and Training, an appointment, he claimed, he heard over the radio. In 1962 he became Federal Minister of Internal Affairs, an appointment he held until the first military coup d'etat of January 1966.

At the end of the Nigerian Civil War in 1970, Shagari was appointed Federal Commissioner for Economic Development, Rehabilitation and Reconstruction in General Yakubu Gowon's cabinet. At the end of 1971 he replaced Chief Obafemi Awolowo as Nigeria's Federal Commissioner For Finance. He served in this capacity until Murtala Mohammed's coup d'etat in 1975.

Shehu Shagari became a member of the Constituent Assembly in 1977 and was a foundation member of a national movement that metamorphosed into the NPN. Predictably in 1978 he was invited by the Northern Caucus of the new party to carry the party's banner as its presidential candidate. It was a tough contest in which he defeated several other top candidates. And yet he is claimed to have been the most reluctant of the other contenders for the presidency. His ambition, he later claimed, was to become a senator in the Second Republic of the Nigerian federation! "I never aspired to be President", he averred. "I just wanted to serve in whatever capacity the people wanted me to."[5]

The conventional wisdom that Shagari was a poodle of the Northern Nigerian political caucus or what some would describe as the Hausa-Fulani oligarchy is still generally countenanced today. Being one of the educated Northerners - limited as that education was as we saw - in the 1950s and also connected with the House of Usman dan Fodio, Shagari was usually regarded by the Northerners as a choice candidate for important political offices in Nigeria. Apparently he embodied their ideal of a political leader, and as a good son of the soil, he was prepared to place the wishes of his people above his own.

This, then, was the man who was called upon in October 1979 to carry the burden of Nigeria. The question arises whether this so-called reluctant politician, ostensibly without ambition and without a political ideology, who for over 30 years had been a recurring decimal in Nigerian politics, deserved to rule a multi-national and multi-cultural country as Nigeria. Clearly, he was a candidate of a powerful political clique and his hidden agendum was to preserve and frankly enhance the position of his main constituency even though that constituency did not have enough votes to elect him. Assuming for the sake of argument that this assessment is faulty, that on the contrary Shagari was, in reality, a reluctant politician, a gentle, nice fellow without an enemy in the world, who could not resist the cry of his people to lead them and the country, the implication then was that what was good for the Hausa-Fulani oligarchy was good for Nigeria and vice versa!

Whatever assessment is correct, a man so perceived was a weak person, a poodle of the oligarchy, who had not worked out any ideas about solving Nigeria's complex problems. Shagari was a safe surrogate, contented to muddle along surrounded by powerful aides and supporters. A contemporary observer wrote of him during the tail-end of his first term: "He lacks the finesse of Zik, the vision of Awolowo and the revolutionary spirit of late Mallam Aminu Kano. He also is in no way similar to the political adventurer Waziri Ibrahim nor does he possess the type of budding revolutionary fervor that marks out Tunji Braithwaite."[6] Who then was he?

That Shagari's presidency turned out to be a dismal failure was not really unexpected. And yet his supporters and admirers were quick to absolve him from all blame. The problem was not the man but his aides, they asserted Representative of such a view is an open letter written to Shagari in 1986 by one S.M.O. Aka:

I have just realized that it was not really your fault. After all, you did not apply for the post of Executive President. Your ambition and cherished wish was simply to become a Senator. Unfortunately, the timbers and the caterpillars of the Second Republic who knew that they could exploit your innocence and weakness for their own selfish ends, persuaded you that you were the only suitable material around to become Nigeria's first Executive President.[7]

Only in Nigeria can one endure this arrant nonsense. No doubt, the writer meant well but all he managed to say was that Shagari was a good man but not the right person for the job. He, of course, followed the usual gratuitous Nigerian readiness to blame aides for the failures of their boss. This type of analysis should not be taken seriously. Reluctant or not, weak or not, corrupt or not, Shehu Shagari was not a child. Nobody put a gun to his head to become a politician or even a president. He could, if he wished, have flatly said "no" to any attempt to draft him, and the oligarchy would not have had much difficulty in finding another lapdog. Moreover, the more one looks critically at his career the more one begins to be skeptical about what looks increasingly as his reluctance gimmick. Shagari is always appointed one thing or the other but he never rejects! He even sought re-election to the presidency in 1983 and reneged on the agreement that would have made Maitama Sule the NPN presidential candidate; nor did he countenance the challenge of Alhaji Moshood Abiola. Having obeyed the oligarchy throughout his political career, he could have justifiably said an emphatic "no" to any further elective office if he were really reluctant to do the job. But he braved the acrimony his decision to run generated, entered and won a massively rigged election. Available evidence would support the conclusion that Shagari's profile affected adversely his performance as Nigeria's first elected executive president

POLITICS OF SURVIVAL

If the framers of the 1979 Constitution and the departing military establishment seriously believed that their fellow countrymen shared their patriotic vision of a united Nigerian nation where ethnic considerations would, at last, be subsumed by overriding national ideals, they were sadly mistaken. The results of the 1979 elections showed that each of the three major political parties drew their main support in the areas dominated by the ethnic group of their leaders. The NPN, the unofficial heir to the NPC and still essentially a Hausa-Fulani party, won more votes and seats than any of the other parties because it was able to penetrate the Middle Belt states of Benue, Kwara and Niger by appealing to traditional loyalties. In the non-lgbo states of the East (Rivers and Cross River), the NPN exploited the fear of lgbo denomination which had been a major theme of their politics since 1953. The UPN, the unofficial heir to the Action Group and still an essentially Yoruba party, won convincingly in Lagos, Oyo, Ogun, Bendel and Ondo (Loobo States). It won no seats in nine states and, except for a respectable showing in Kwara and Gongola States, performed very poorly in the other states. The NPP, the unofficial heir to the NCNC and still an essentially lgbo party, also won convincingly in the only two lgbo states and, except for a respectable showing in Rivers State, performed very poorly in the other states. It won no seats in nine states. The GNPP, which broke away from the NPP over who would carry the latter's presidential banner, won in Borno and Gongola states. It won no seats in five states and performed generally poorly in the other states. The PRP, a reincarnation of the NEPU--essentially a Kano-based party--won only in Kano State. It received no votes in fourteen states and performed very poorly in the remaining four states. In terms of raw votes in the presidential election the two candidates who had a realistic chance to become president--Shagari and Awolowo--won 5,688,857 votes and 4,916,651 votes respectively. In terms of the percentage of the votes cast for the presidential election, Shagari received 33.77percent, Awolowo 29.18 percent, Azikiwe 16.75 percent, Aminu Kano 10.28 percent and Waziri Ibrahim 10.02 percent.

(See Tables 6.1, 6.2, and 6.3)

Clearly, thirteen years of military rule during which Nigerians fought a bitter civil war for 30 months as well as produced a brand new constitution and a brand new national anthem that emphasized national unity, had not succeeded in denting the solid wall of Nigeria's ethnic politics. Clearly also, the NPN performed better than any of the other parties, all things considered. However, any NPN government would be a minority government which would require the political skills of its leader to survive in office. Moreover, because Shagari polled at least a quarter of the votes in only twelve states which technically did not constitute two-thirds of the nineteen states required by the constitution, the other parties led by the UPN which would benefit most should a run-off election become necessary refused to concede victory to Shagari and the NPN.

Fedeco's decision, on August 16, 1979, that Shagari mathematically won the election and that the NPN satisfied the spirit of the constitution, was rejected by the other parties. As a response, the UPN and the NPP formed a temporary alliance, a West-East alliance that the Northern Nigerian political leadership had fought to forestall since independence. The disputed election was also referred to the Electoral

TABLE 6.1: 1979 NATIONAL ASSEMBLY ELECTIONS

State	Total no. of Seats		NPN		UPN		NPP		GNPP		PRP	
	S	HR	S	HR	S	HR	S	HR	S	HR	S	HR
Anambra	5	29	0	3	0	0	5	26	0	0	0	0
Bauchi	5	20	5	18	0	0	0	1	0	1	0	0
Bendel	5	20	1	6	4	12	0	2	0	0	0	0
Benue	5	19	5	18	0	0	0	1	0	0	0	0
Borno	5	24	1	2	0	0	0	0	4	22	0	0
Cross River	5	28	3	22	0	2	0	0	2	4	0	0
Gongola	5	21	1	5	2	7	0	1	2	8	0	0
Imo	5	30	0	2	0	0	5	28	0	0	0	0
Kaduna	5	33	3	19	0	1	0	2	0	1	2	10
Kano	5	46	0	7	0	0	0	0	0	0	5	39
Kwara	5	14	3	8	2	5	0	0	0	1	0	0
Lagos	5	12	0	0	5	12	0	0	0	0	0	0
Niger	5	10	5	10	0	0	0	0	0	0	0	0
Ogun	5	12	0	0	5	12	0	0	0	0	0	0
Ondo	5	22	0	0	5	22	0	0	0	0	0	0
Oyo	5	42	0	4	5	38	0	0	0	0	0	0
Plateau	5	16	1	3	0	0	4	13	0	0	0	0
Rivers	5	14	3	10	0	0	2	4	0	0	0	0
Sokoto	5	37	5	31	0	0	0	0	0	6	0	0
Total	**95**	**449**	**36**	**168**	**22**	**111**	**16**	**78**	**8**	**43**	**7**	**49**

TABLE 6.2: 1979 STATE ELECTIONS

ASSEMBLY

State	Seats	GNPP	UPN	NPN	PRP	NPP	Governor/Party
Anambra	87	1	0	13	0	73	Nwobodo/NPP
Bauchi	60	9	0	45	2	4	Ali/NPP
Bendel	60	0	34	22	0	4	Alli/UPN
Benue	57	6	0	48	0	3	Aku/NPN
Borno	72	59	0	11	2	0	Goni/GNPP
Cross River	84	16	7	58	0	3	Isong/NPN
Gongola	63	25	18	15	1	4	Barde/GNPP
Imo	90	2	0	9	0	79	Mbakwe/NPP
Kaduna	99	10	3	64	16	6	Musa/PRP
Kano	138	3	1	11	123	0	Rimi/PRP
Kwara	42	2	15	25	0	0	Atta/NPN
Lagos	36	0	36	0	0	0	Jakande/UPN
Niger	30	2	0	28	0	0	Ibrahim/NPN
Ogun	36	0	36	0	0	0	Onabanjo/UPN
Ondo	66	0	65	1	0	0	Ajasin/UPN
Oyo	126	0	117	9	0	0	Ige/UPN
Plateau	47	3	0	10	0	34	Lar/NPP
Rivers	42	1	0	26	0	15	Okilo/NPN
Sokoto	111	19	0	92	0	0	Kangiwa/NPN
Total	**1347**	**157**	**333**	**487**	**144**	**226**	

TABLE 6.3: 1979 PRESIDENTIAL ELECTION

State	Total votes Cast	GNPP	% of UPN	total votes NPN	PRP	NPP
Anambra	1,209,038	1.67	0.75	13.50	1.20	82.58
Bauchi	998,683	15.44	3.00	62.48	14.34	4.72
Bendel	669,511	1.23	53.23	36.19	6.73	8.60
Benue	538,879	7.89	2.57	76.39	1.35	11.71
Borno	710,968	54.04	3.35	34.71	6.52	1.35
Cross River	661,103	15.14	11.76	64.40	1.01	7.66
Gongola	639,138	34.09	21.67	35.52	4.34	4.35
Imo	1,153,355	3.00	0.64	8.80	0.89	86.67
Kaduna	1,382,712	13.80	6.68	43.12	3.66	4.72
Kano	1,220,763	1.54	1.23	19.94	76.41	0.91
Kwara	354,605	5.71	39.48	53.62	0.67	0.52
Lagos	828,414	0.48	82.30	7.18	0.47	9.57
Niger	383,347	16.50	3.69	74.88	3.99	1.11
Ogun	744,668	0.53	92.11	6.23	0.31	0.32
Ondo	1,369,547	0.26	94.51	4.19	0.18	0.86
Oyo	1,396,547	0.57	85.78	12.75	0.32	0.55
Plateau	548,405	6.82	5.29	34.73	3.98	49.17
Rivers	687,951	2.18	0.33	72.65	0.46	14.35
Sokoto	1,348,697	26.61	2.52	66.58	3.35	0.92
Total	**16,846,633**	**10.02**	**29.18**	**33.77**	**10.28**	**16.75**

Source: Adapted from Eglaosa E. Osaghae, *Crippled Giant: Nigeria Since Independence.* Indiana University Press, 1998, pp. 125.

Tribunal. The Tribunal promptly upheld Fedeco's decision. Awolowo's appeal to the Supreme Court also failed. Predictably the UPN-NPP marriage of convenience collapsed. The NPN and the North breathed a sigh of relief. Left out on a limb, the LOOBO states controlled by the UPN refused to display Shagari's photographs in public buildings and resolved to oppose his government on most issues.

The NPP's "about face" gave Shagari his cue. It had become clear to him that he was involved in the politics of survival in the face of a robust reassertion of ethnic politics. To strengthen his position, he needed to form a national government. Consequently, he invited all the other parties to join the NPN in such a government. But only the NPP accepted the invitation. On September 27, 1979 an NPN-NPP Accord was signed. By this accord the two parties agreed to share ministerial, high level legislative posts and patronage according to their numerical strengths in the National Assembly. The NPN also agreed to resolve such outstanding issues from the civil war as the abandoned property and marginalization of the Igbo areas. On its part, the NPP agreed to give Shagari needed legislative support that would enable him to get his bills passed and presidential appointments ratified. The two parties did not have a comfortable majority in the National Assembly. They controlled only eleven out of the nineteen states. In the presidential election, they accounted only for 50.52percent of electoral votes.

From the beginning the accord was fraught with difficulties. Faced with intra-party and inter "party disputes in and between the contracting parties", writes Okadigbo, which "led to delay and vacillation with respect to the appointment of Ministers"--a delay that lasted almost two months--"Shagari had to negotiate with his fellow party leaders and then with their NPP counterpart whenever he submitted other statutory nominations and bills to the National Assembly."[8] It would then appear that the accord was in trouble from the beginning because no bill or nomination "was ever approved without dispute and negotiation, within or outside Shagari's party and its NPP partners and besides the stiff opposition of other parties--the UPN, GNPP and PRP." He concludes: "Therefore, both the executive and legislative were ab initio [from the beginning], compromised. A national *leadership* by *negotiations* [italics supplied in original quote] borne out of *confrontation,* emerged [italics supplied in original quote]."[9]

On July 9, 1981 the accord finally broke down. The NPN accused the NPP of behaving like "Shylock"; the NPP said that it could no longer tolerate NPN's "greed and arrogance of power." It has also been suggested that the accord collapsed because of the opposition of non-lgbo as well as some lgbo elements within the NPP who felt that they reaped no benefits from the Accord. Also, the machinations of the Yoruba element within the NPN who wanted to reverse the marginalization of the Yoruba were a contributing factor. The Machiavellianism of the NPN leadership which, having used the accord to strengthen its power by building a solid network of patronage as well as a "working accord" with PRP, had no qualms about jettisoning the NPP.[10] The so-called working arrangement with the PRP meant, in fact, that the two parties controlled only nine states and had only 44.05 percent of the votes cast for the presidential election. The NPN did not, therefore, have a working majority as Eghosa Osagae suggests.[11]

Forced to run a minority government, Shagari lost focus. Surviving in office became his major concern. Negotiating with the other parties degenerated to the point of shameless horse-trading. The NPP, with a straight face, joined the opposition parties to form the so-called "Progressive Governors" Forum, named in this manner because all that they really had in common was an agreement to act as an extra-parliamentary opposition to the NPN. Even the PRP that was supposed to have a working arrangement with the NPN was the hub of the forum.

It has also been stated that the reason why the NPP jettisoned the UPN was because while an NPN alliance offered "lgbo leaders" who "were desperate to be reintegrated into the *mainstream* (italics supplied) of national politics, i.e. to have access to political patronage and benefit", a UPN alliance "would have excluded them" from these benefits.[12] The reasons for the NPN-NPP accord were much more fundamental than what is suggested above. Because of previous ethnic conflicts, no serious student of Nigerian history expected a UPN-NPP marriage to last. Moreover, a UPN-NPP alliance could not have formed a constitutional government in 1979. It would have commanded only 45.93 percent of the votes cast in the presidential election and would have won only eleven states with votes of 25 percent and above. There was, of course, the possibility that the GNPP and PRP (later to become members of the Progressive Alliance with the UPN and the NPP) might have been persuaded to join the alliance and thus ensure that the North was not excluded from power. If they wished, the UPN could have justifiably argued that when in 1960 a North-East alliance deliberately excluded the West from power Nigeria did not break up. The intriguing point is that we have not found any evidence that the above combinations were seriously canvassed. However, the readiness of the lgbo elite, no doubt prodded by former president Nnamdi Azikiwe, to join forces with the

North in spite of all the tribulations the Igbo have suffered in the North since the 1950s is one of the mysteries of Igbo political strategy! Aware that the Igbo are detested by their neighbors and would not welcome a Yoruba alliance, Shagari and his NPN were convinced that they could beat Azikiwe and his NPP "like a drum" and get away with it. And they did so with aplomb.

It is, therefore, not surprising that politics in the Second Republic became a very chaotic affair. Debates in the Senate and House of Representatives were stormy and intemperate. For the most part, consensus was never reached on very serious national issues. Thus, harassed and hassled by his opponents, Shagari was up to his eyes in the politics of the new type of democratic federation characteristic of the 1979 Republican Constitution, with its executive presidency, a system that was new in Nigeria. It was a far cry from the Westminister type of parliamentary government to which Shagari had been accustomed. It was a great learning experience but he was not even given the peace of mind to learn it properly. Nor was he a fast learner. In the circumstances, he adopted the policy of offering carrots to his friends and sometimes sticks to his enemies, British style. Behaving as someone under siege, he endeavored " to sustain the system." as Okadigbo put it, "dodging and sometimes throwing punches, conciliating with other parties or pushing ahead in spite of them." It was "indeed a journey up a slippery hill managing the government of a multi-party, multi-ethnic and multi-religious African nation-state wherein the party of the ruler is in a minority position in the Legislature and where primordial loyalties and narrow partisan considerations often override national interest and mature democratic praxis."[13]

Okadigbo is right on the mark. Could anyone else had done better in the circumstances? Possibly. The important point is that it was generally believed by non-partisan analysts that Shagari and his party failed the country.[14] Some believed that Shagari "simply lacked back-bone and should never have been in charge of a country like ours, which needed firm discretion in order to realize its enormous potential."[15] Shagari's response to his critics seems to underscore their point. He blamed his ineffectiveness on the 1979 Constitution. "Is it proper", he asked, "to refer to someone as Executive President expected to bark and bite in a given situation, but could not do so because of certain limitations and encumbrances placed on him by the organic law of the land?" He then added: "If I were really to be an Executive President, I should be given a free hand to rule according to the dictates of my mind."[16] To which a bemused journalist sneered appropriately: "If after the Executive nature of the President's powers, he still reels under hysteria that the Constitution could not allow him to become or Hitler, then there is every reason to pity the President and his plight as a politician."[17]

REASSERTION OF STATE POWER AND CENTRAL GOVERNMENT RESPONSE

One of the criticisms of the 1963 Republican Constitution is that it provided for strong regions and only for a fairly strong center. This, it was claimed, facilitated the centrifugal tendencies that had made possible the Biafran secession. The thirteen years of military rule which followed the overthrow of this constitution in 1966 created a situation which deliberately concentrated power at the center while the leadership claimed to run a federal state. This is the so-called "military federalism," simply a bogus fraud, for which General Aguiyi Ironsi lost his life at the hand of the military! It should be noted that most Nigerians, the Igbo excepted, applauded Ironsi's death. It is a characteristic of Nigerian politics that consistency is of little value. With a return to constitutional democratic government, the states which had replaced the regions were determined to reassert the autonomy which the military had seized from the them and which the 1979 Constitution that they had all helped to frame deliberately curtailed. The NPN administration, on the other hand, in an effort to shore up its embattled position, was determined to enforce the constitution. Thus, a zero sum game situation developed and the battle lines were drawn.

A major battleground was the status of local governments. The 1979 Constitution, following the Dasuki Report of 1976, conferred a limited autonomy to local governments and constituted local government as a third tier of government. Essentially, however, local governments remained an arm of the state government. A Commissioner for Local Government was placed in charge of them. In this way they were tightly controlled by the state; the limited autonomy conferred on them became a joke. Some state governors took this action because they feared that Shagari and his NPN might use the alibi of local government autonomy to undermine their authority. Many, indeed, unconstitutionally dissolved democratically elected councils and replaced then with "Care-taker Committees" made up of members under their thumb. As the 1983 general elections approached, many state governors created new local governments, hoping thereby to tighten their control over them. The inability of Shagari to call them to order was a victory for the states.

The next was the constitutional rights of the states or what the states and center respectively understood these rights were. In some instances the central government, desperate to control the states, proceeded to operate unconstitutionally. For example, without consulting the states Shagari appointed Presidential Liason Officers (PLOS) ostensibly to better coordinate federal and presidential activities and programs in the states but in reality, as far as the states were concerned, these liason officers were intended to rival the state governors and eventually undermine them. That some of these officers were either individuals aspiring to be governors in their states or those defeated in the 1979 gubernatorial elections underscored the suspicion of the states. According to B.O. Nwabueze, the Liason Officer was

> intended to represent and embody the presidency in the state,
> to provide for it the physical presence needed to establish a
> personal closeness and intimacy between the president and
> the people, which would put him at par with the governor,
> and thus enable [the president] to compete more effectively
> and advantageously for support in the state.[18]

If that was Shagari's intention, then the states were justified to oppose him. And oppose him fiercely they did but without success. On their part, some states also acted unconstitutionally in opposing Shagari. For example, the LOOBO (Lagos, Oyo, Ondo, Bendel and Ogun) states ignored the central government's ban of pools betting and gambling which had been promulgated by the Obasanjo government. In Ondo, the state government embarked on oil exploration which was obviously a central government matter. In Anambara, the state government, convinced that a particular road belonged to the state, stopped the central government from interfering with it. The LOOBO states also excluded non-indigenes from such welfarist programs as free education and free health care although they paid taxes and state levies. In Oyo the state government, convinced that land was state matter, not only prevented the central government from carrying out its housing projects, but also demolished buildings already erected. The northern states were not left out in this politics of confrontation with the center. They denied southerners social goods and jobs. Again, the Shagari administration was powerless to discipline the states. The destabilizing, chaotic situation was allowed to continue and fester.

The promulgation of the Public Order Act of 1979 by the Shagari administration brought to the boil the crucial issue of control of the police in the states. Simply put, the question was: to whom was a state Police Commissioner responsible, the State Governor or the Inspector General of Police? By empowering state commissioners and not state governors to licence public meetings and processions, this Act was unequivocal about the answer to the above question. But since public order was a concurrent matter in the Constitution, the governors saw the Act as an attempt by the central government to intimidate and control them, thereby gaining electoral advantages. The challenge of this Act in the courts did not succeed and the central government was emboldened to behave even more dictatorially in these and other matters, actions that were against the spirit of the Constitution. The struggle between the Nigeria Police Force and the Road Safety Corps controlled by some states was intensified.

Within the states, too, intra-party and inter-party conflicts were rampant. In Kaduna State which was run by a PRP Governor, Balarabe Musa, and NPN denominated legislature, the conflict culminated in the impeachment and removal from office of the Governor on June 22, 1981. He was accused of not supporting his party's working arrangement with the NPN, preferring instead to pitch his tent with the Progressive Governors Forum to which, interestingly enough, his party still belonged. His action was by no means an impeachable offence since no case of gross misconduct was preferred against him. The unfortunate development in Kaduna encouraged legislators in other states to make life difficult for governors even when they belonged to the same party. The threatened impeachment of the governors of Cross River, Rivers and Bendel states failed however to materialize, but in Ondo state the Speaker of the House was impeached, and in Sokoto and Lagos states the speakers were suspended. The NPN, determined apparently to brook no opposition, used all the forces at its disposal to cause dissension in their ranks. The PRP split into two factions--the Imoudu and Aminu Kano factions. The GNPP split into three factions--the Mahmud Waziri faction which became a part of the NPN except in name; the Yoruba-lgbo faction led by Kola Balogun, Nduka Eze, Ben Uzoukwu Nzeribe (which formally joined the NPN later); and the Waziri Ibrahim faction which remained as the rump of the original GNPP drawing its support only from Borno and Gongola states. The NPP was not left untouched. Defections from its ranks to the NPN became rampant largely encouraged by real or promised patronage. Most damaging to the party in its lgbo stronghold was the NPN- managed defection to its ranks of two great lgbo sons, Odumegwu Ojukwu and Michael Okpara, a defection that encouraged some others to decamp to the NPN but, which in the long run, cost them dearly in reputation and popularity. The aged Zik, now a mere shadow of his former self, looked helplessly on, even when abused and insulated by such lgbo urban guerrillas for the NPN as Chuba Okadigbo. The UPN, too, despite its reputed discipline, was pressed by the Yoruba NPN front to also become accommodationist, leading thereby to unprecedented defections from the UPN to the more idealistic NPN. Like Zik, Awolowo also aged, could not call the Yoruba to order. However, unlike Zik, the Yoruba supporters of the NPN did not subject him to public abuse.[19]

All these developments, as we pointed out earlier, made for chaotic politics in the Second Republic. Shagari spent so much time fending off confrontations and plotting confrontations of his own that not much time was left to accomplish anything else. Factionalized, the opposing parties, tried to regroup under a new party called The Progressive Parties Alliance (PPA) but because the Yoruba and the lgbo could not agree on a common presidential candidate for the forthcoming 1983 elections the party could not get off the ground. Consequently, what was left of the PRP and GNPP fused with the NPP to form a new party - the Progressive Peoples Party (PPP)--in preparation for the forthcoming elections. To the surprise of no one, Fedeco refused to register the party. Rejected also was the NPP's application to change its name to that of the PPP. Thus frustrated, the opposition parties were determined to oppose the government relentlessly. Even within the states it controlled the NPN also faced challenges from its membership particularly over the selection of the gubernatorial candidates for the 1983 elections.

Revenue Allocation, "the bane of Nigerian politics," was another major area of confrontation between the states and the Shagari administration. The Revenue Allocation Bill of 1981, the eighth since independence, was promulgated in the face of strong opposition from the states, including some NPN controlled states. The bill distributed federally derived revenue as follows: Federal Government, 58.5percent; States, 31.5percent; Local Governments, 10percent. The states argued that the responsibilities of the central government did not warrant its share of 58.5percent. The progressive governors took the matter to the Supreme Court, which nullified the Act on the grounds that a bill agreed by a joint committee of both the Senate and the House of Representatives (HOR) must be presented to each house for approval. Shagari accepted the decision, submitted a fresh bill, and got it passed after determined lobbying. The bill became law on January 22, 1982. The central government's share of the revenue was reduced by five percent, to 53.5 percent. The sloppy handling of the revenue allocation issue, which resulted in the defeat of the government in the court, was seen as another example of the administration's muddling inefficiency.

Politics in the Second Republic was, indeed, a learning experience for Shagari, the NPN, and the opposition parties. For individuals nurtured in the British tradition of parliamentary government as operated in an undemocratic, colonial state and forced to endure thirteen years of military dictatorship as well as fight a bitter civil war, the high expectations held out for Shagari and his government, may have been perhaps unrealistic at the time. The leadership at the top, it transpired, had neither the ability, nor the training and nor the finesse to deal with the complexities of Nigerian politics. What happened was a further demonstration that in politics as in all serious contests where the stakes are very high, ethnic preferences and a "nice guy" image are hardly enough qualifications for success.

ECONOMIC CRISIS

If Shagari's political leadership left a lot to be desired, his management of the economy has been assessed as simply disastrous. On this point most studies of the Second Republic are in agreement. The military cited Shagari's "gross mismanagement" of the economy as one of the main reasons for toppling his government. Indeed, Toyin Falola and Julius Ihonvbere, who did a fairly detailed study of the economy under Shagari, conclude that he "made no serious attempt to improve or diversify the economy and reduce dependence. Instead, he intensified all the economic problems and crisis of the country." (20) They believe that the NPN's election manifesto regarding the economy and the government's subsequent "numerous and vague promises to improve the economy" amounted to nothing .[21] And reflecting on the president's management of the economy, a senator in the Second Republic wrote some months before the 1983 coup d'etat that the country's "economy is totally depressed" and he blamed the Shagari administration for it. He noted "Nigeria's [unprecedented] demand for and supply of foreign goods", the government's discarding of "the Fourth National Development Plan" and its inability to "provide a substitute plan." He accused Shagari of allowing "the economy to drift on, without a compass, without any real sense of direction."[22] While noting the poverty of "Shagari's economic performance and the profligacy of the ruling politicians of the Second Republic", Okadigbo, Shagari's Presidential Adviser, like other apologists for Shagari and the NPN, blamed the catastrophe on the dramatic collapse of oil prices which affected Nigeria by 1981.[23]

Available data would suggest that in 1979 Shagari inherited a relatively stable economy and N6 billion from the Obasanjo government.[24] By the end of his first term in office the N6 billion had practically vanished and the Nigerian economy was in the midst of unprecedented depression. It is true that the decline in the oil revenue, which started in 1981 had a lot to do with what happened. But since this was not unexpected, could the government not have taken steps to adjust its economic policy? That was the question. Granted, indeed, that Shagari was running a rentier state, that is, a state whose income is based largely on external rents collected regularly from foreign governments, companies and agencies, and whose economy is not only uncomfortably disarticulated but also thoroughly dependent, it would appear, nevertheless, that Shagari and his economic managers lacked the vision and experience to rum such a state.

It is important to understand what happened to the Nigerian economy within two years of Shagari's presidency. In 1979 Nigeria was the ninth largest producer of oil in the world. It benefitted tremendously from the phenomenal rise in oil prices following the Iranian crisis of 1979. By 1980 Shagari, in a speech commemorating his 100 days in office, painted a rosy economic future for Nigeria,[25] an optimism underscored by the Ministry of Finance some six months later.[26]

This optimism was formally reflected in the Fourth National Development Plan, Nigeria's economic blueprint for the period 1981-1985, which was published in March 1981. The plan was based largely on income from oil production estimated to average 2.19 million barrels per day (bpd) at a selling price by 1985 of 55 dollars per barrel. The Plan contains a lot of other optimistic forecasts that space does not permit us to go into.[27] Nigeria's economic opportunities appeared so exciting and limitless that many Nigerian professionals abroad began to flock back to the country. By 1983, however, everything had fallen apart. "For two whole weeks in February 1983", writes Okadigbo, "Nigeria could not sell even one drop of crude oil!"[28] Since earnings from oil accounted for over 90 percent of Nigerian's total revenue, the development was simply crippling. Although the situation was somewhat reversed, by the close of 1983 revenues from oil totaled only N7.8 billion; in 1980 the figure was N12.9 billion. In 1980 foreign reserves totaled N5.462 billion; by 1983 the figure was N998.5 million, just enough to pay for a month's import bill. In 1980 Nigeria's external debt was 9 billion dollars (which meant that Nigeria was designated as an "under borrowed" country); in 1983 the figure had doubled to 18 billion dollars. The result was capital flight and practical stoppage of foreign investment. The total capital flight from Nigeria between 1979 and 1983 was estimated to be 14 billion dollars. Consequently, the domestic economy went into depression. The impact on social programs and the quality of life was incalculable.

This being the case, is the accusation of gross misarrangement of the economy justified? The evidence seems convincing. An ambitious Fourth National Plan which calculated the selling price of crude oil at 55 dollars per barrel by 1985 when it was already clear that the oil market was being saturated is a good example of a government that was out of step with the rest of the world. Far from responding early to the crisis, the government which was well aware of its existence by 1981,[29] deliberately chose to ignore the warning that the oil boom would be short-lived and would be replaced by an "oil doom" if appropriate measures were not taken to combat the situation. On the contrary, Shagari and his government chose to engage in reckless spending on ambitious projects and offering outrageous patronages. These profligate expenditures were undertaken apparently to make good electoral promises as well as to pay back political debts. The huge expenditure on the police force and the military was also intended to ensure that the government would be better prepared to contain domestic dissent as well as to placate the military who otherwise might be tempted to return to power. The importation of all sorts of commodities--useful and useless--further depleted the dwindling foreign reserves. This policy made a few individuals extremely rich. In the meantime, agriculture which had been the main stay of the economy was neglected while Shagari and his officials were emphasizing the danger of over-dependence on oil and the absolute necessity to diversify the economy. But instead of building factories that would also give employment to many Nigerians, the government gave precedence to the construction industry and commerce. Overnight there emerged all over the country that phenomenon in Nigerian society known as "emergency contractors", mostly party loyalists. Many among them became instant millionaires whose numbers were sufficiently large "as to demoralize the working population and dislocate their value system."[30] Another consequence of Shagari's emphasis on the construction industry and commerce was the drain of the nation's money to the countries supplying the equipment, technological know-how and commodities. Clearly this was a misplaced priority. It can, of course, be argued that the so-called construction projects, for example, were either started by previous administrations or planned by them. What Shagari did, then, was to continue with such worthy projects. Included among these were the building of the Federal Capital at Abuja, the River Basin Development projects, the Third Lagos Mainland Bridge, the Delta Steel Mill complex at Aladja, the Ajaokuta plant, and so forth. Nevertheless, it is difficult to justify the vigor with which these projects were pursued in the face of the gloomy economic realities of the country. It has, indeed, been suggested that the Ajaokuta plant was outmoded even before it was constructed and that the government knew it. The furnaces at Ajaokuta would require coking coal which Nigeria did not have at the time.[31] Why could Shagari not have opted for the use of natural gas which is used at Aladja and which Nigeria has in abundance, to the point that the excess is being burned off daily? Could the huge oil resources derived in 1979 and 1980 not have been more profitably spent on the building of factories and mechanization of agriculture which would have generated employment and led ultimately to increase in local production and, hopefully, self-reliance?

The handling of the industrial sector by the Shagari administration was also done shoddily. By encouraging the massive importation of goods the administration did a lot of harm to local industries and virtually killed most local technologies. By placing a ban on the importation of industrial raw materials without developing local ones as substitutes, an acute shortage of industrial raw materials resulted. It is interesting to note that the administration stated that the ban was imposed in order to check the drain on the country's foreign currency reserves. Critics of the administration, on the other, dismiss such a claim as spurious. As far as they were concerned the policy was irrational and myopic, motivated by greed. If the government's decision was altruistic, they asked, how could one then explain and justify a policy which, while discouraging the importation of raw materials for the nation's industrial development, at the same time encouraged the massive importation of such irrelevant goods as champaign, par-boiled rice, toothpicks, sausages, etc.?[32]

The best way, one would have thought, to have ultimately and successfully reduced Nigeria's foreign debt as well as increase its foreign reserves was to produce local substitutes for goods imported into the country. This was not done. The administration has also been criticized for being very tardy in dealing with three major industries based on Nigeria's fossil fuel resources, namely, the Liquified Natural Gas (LNG), Petrochemicals Complex and Fertilizer projects. These crucial sources of growth, if properly executed would, in the short term, as the government expected, have made it possible for Nigeria to save a lot of foreign exchange and, in the long term, earned the country much needed foreign exchange. A large number of Nigerians would also have gained meaningful employment. With respect to commerce, the government's massive issuance of import licences to individuals and firms badly damaged the economy. Even though they were not registered importers, a large percentage of party loyalists were issued these licences . They, in turn, usually sold these licences to the real importers who should have been given the licences directly in the first instance. It was alleged that "between 10 and 30 percent kickback was being demanded on import licences issued to individuals and firms."[33] The large scale issuance of import licences in the country during this period induced Nigerians to indulge in the excessive and compulsive purchase of foreign consumer goods. A lot of these goods were useless, most of which should have been avoided or produced locally. They included long grain rice, milk, sugar, stockfish, champaign, toothpicks, etc. Particularly inexcusable was the fact that although Northern Nigeria produced surplus maize in 1982, Shagari's government spent some N1 billion on the importation of grains (including maize) and similar materials for breweries.[34] It was also at this time that Shagari appointed his son-in-law, Umaru Dikko, to head a Presidential Task Force on the importation of rice and other "essential commodities" such as milk, sugar, flour, detergents etc for sale to the public. A huge amount of foreign exchange was expended on this project at a time when the country's economy was in dire straits. The government was convinced, however, that the measure was intended as a positive move to bring down the rising inflationary trend in the country. The measure, of course, did not achieve the desired goal due largely to the way it was implemented. Shagari's promise during the 1979 elections to establish one food proceeding industry in every local government area in the federation was also not kept.[35] With regard to agriculture, neither the River Basin projects nor the so-called "Green Revolution" succeeded, due largely also to poor execution. The "Green Revolution," program, for example, which was the cornerstone of the NPN manifesto during the 1979 election campaigns, turned out to be more theoretical than practical. It became over-centralized in administration which made it both needless and ruinous. The pledge that the revolution would restore agriculture to its past glory and make the country self-sufficient in food production failed also to materialize. Because agricultural loans meant for farmers were brazenly diverted to NPN supporters, a reporter lamented that the loans were given to individuals "who do not even have one acre of farmland" and who used "the money to build imposing houses, buy new cars, marry new wives, and maintain chains of girlfriends and concubines." The government was aware of what was going on and did nothing to stop it especially when it became obvious that "real farmers in the rural areas do not even smell of the loan [sic]," but only "hear NPN members talking of the huge success of the Green Revolution".[36] Not surprisingly, by 1983 food prices had increased between 200 and 300 percent. For instance, one naira could buy 15 cups or more of garri in 1979; in 1983, 3 cups sold for one naira; rice which sold for about N30 per bag in 1979, sold for N120 or more per bag in 1983.[37] This drove the *Sunday Tribune* to wonder how Shagari, "Speaking on an NTA network program, 'Face the Nation,'" could tell his countrymen with a straight face "that there was no shortage of food in the country and that food prices had not risen." The statement went on: "Every housewife and family bread winner in the urban areas know that food prices have sky rocketed." It concluded: "The truth which the President was at pains to hide is that the N1 billion invested in the Green Revolution Program had ended up in the pockets of landlords, fertilizer contractors and smart NPN men." It noted bleakly that because of high prices things had become "worse than before President Shagari came into office. The housewife, the worker and the bread winner all know this. Their shopping baskets have been depleted..."[38]

The criticism of Shagari's management of the economy is not that his government was not aware of the issues involved or that it was not concerned with the country's future. The Economic Stabilization (Temporary Provisions) Act of 1982 was a realization, however belated, that something needed to be done to avoid complete economic collapse. But since this Act was essentially a deflationary austerity measure, it was very unpopular. But since, also, the measures were not austere enough to satisfy Bretton Woods institution who demanded structural adjustment which would have devalued the currency and severely limited the role of government in economic management, Nigeria's application to them for loans to enable it get over its economic difficulties did not succeed. Shagari was, indeed, in a no-win situation. If he accepted the terms of the Bretton Woods institution he would have been accused by the Nigerian public of "selling out" the country to these external creditors. He would also be accused by his party and beneficiaries of the largess offered by the state whose fortunes are derived from the strong role of the state in the control of the economy. If he did nothing, the economy would collapse. He opted to go with his party and risk the wrath of Nigerians also. He gambled that the oil crisis was a temporary affair but, once more, he miscalculated. Had he, nevertheless, succeeded in dealing with the corruption in his government as well as its fundamental lack of will and discipline to do the right thing, the economy might have been salvaged. The government seemed to have listened to itself alone. The result was that for essentially selfish reasons, the Shagari administration abandoned the path of self reliance which it had been advocating and followed the path of misplaced priorities. Self-reliance, to succeed, requires government to show the way and put in place appropriate structures and institutions. Nothing of the sort happened. The austerity measures practically crippled the economy and later gave the military an excuse to seize power.

The responses of Shagari, his administrators and supporters to their critics did not address the fundamental issues raised. On the contrary, they dismissed these critics as ill-motivated and partisan. The problem with the Nigerian economy, Shagari stressed, was the direct result of the "lack of international market for oil from which about 95 percent of the country's revenue is derived". It had nothing to do with the government's so-called inefficiency and mismanagement or "because the nation's treasury is looted by anybody as is alleged by the so-called 'progressives.'" He then blamed Nigeria's smaller units of government: "If at all the nation's treasury is looted, it is not by the federal Government, but by those states which get federal grants and do nothing with them to benefit their people." He blamed the Nigerian press for causing his "downfall." He and his party, and not his critics, he asserted remorselessly were "the Saints."[39]

THE PUBLIC SECTOR

Shagari's preoccupation with political survival and the economic mess with which he was struggling did not allow him to make bold initiatives in the public sector. Because of the constraints of space we will only emphasize such crucial sectors as the civil service, education, the future of traditional rulership and the role of the military.

The civil service needed very badly to be reorganized in the light of the adoption of an executive presidential form of government. The idea of the civil servant as the ubiquitous generalist, a sort of Jack-of-all-trades, and of a supposedly permanent secretary, ideal for parliamentary government, was clearly not appropriate for a system that functioned best under the aegis of a professional civil service. The appointment of Shehu Musa, a seasoned permanent Secretary imbued with the tradition of parliamentary government as Secretary to the Federal Government, was a signal that it would be business as usual. And yet the destruction of the relative autonomy of the Service by Murtala Mohammed should have been enough indication that the new system needed a different type of service to run it effectively. We have no evidence that Shagari gave any thought whatsoever to restructuring the Service in such a way as to make it come to terms with the new dispensation. It is not surprising, therefore, that Shagari could not make effective use of such an experienced civil servant as Shehu Musa, because the new system could not accommodate comfortably a largely independent Civil Service. Like all institutions of government during the Second Republic, the Nigerian Civil Service was near collapse by the end of 1983. Throughout the Nigerian federation, the number of public servants increased enormously because politicians used their influence to employ their relatives and those of their associates without regard to qualifications. The concept of government as an equal opportunity employer was simply ignored. Although lip service was paid to the "federal character" idea, at the end of 1983 the Federal Civil Service was still essentially ethnically lopsided. The wage bills of both the federal and state governments became bloated. This led to a situation where it became almost impossible for state governments in particular to pay the salaries of civil servants and other public servants. There developed the practice in many states--even in those controlled by the NPN–for these servants to be owed their salaries for several months, a practice that had endured up today. This became a source of instability in the country. The Civil Service, especially, was shaken to its very foundation. Morale deteriorated dangerously in the public sector. And coupled with several strikes and industrial showdowns that were naturally resorted to, productivity became unacceptably low. The consequent financial illiquidity in the society led to a decline in the purchasing power of a large percentage of the population and the inevitable rapid fall in the standard of living of most Nigerians. Again Shagari dissociated himself and his government from the mess, and pointed accusing fingers at some state governments who, according to him, because of their reckless spending, were unable to discharge their obligations to employees. Shagari absolved the Federal Government from any responsibility "whatsoever, for the failure of these state governments to pay workers as claimed by the defaulting governments."[40] He failed to address the same phenomenon in the federal public sector where he was supposedly in charge. In the final analysis it is fair to conclude that Shagari failed to handle the problems of the public sector with any sense of seriousness. To fold his hands in utter helplessness was indicative of weak leadership. For one thing, he could have used his party machinery as well as other constitutional and legal means available to him to attempt to deal with the rot. He chose to do nothing.

It has been pointed out, however, that in spite of Nigeria's economic crisis Shagari's government managed to produce salutary results especially in the education sector. The administration, for example, is said to have appreciated the importance of education as a constructive social force and hence supported its progress. It did so by nurturing into maturity the universities of technology and the colleges of education that the Mohammed and Obasonjo regimes had created in the different parts of the country. Shagari's regime also introduced the "University Salary Scale" (USS), which raised the morale of the university instructor by placing the USS above the scale of the Civil Service.[41]

For the record, it is fair to point out that the NPN administration established 41 unity secondary schools in the 19 states of the federation and Abuja, 8 federal colleges of education as well as two national technical colleges of education: and seven new federal universities of technology. This is an impressive achievement. Unfortunately the economic crisis led to these institutions being under funded. The result, inevitably, was a gradual erosion of the standard of education in the country. The process so far has not been reversed. But instead of putting in place a policy that would deal with the situation, Shagari chose to blame state governments, especially those of Imo and Anambra controlled by the NPP, for creating the serious education crisis in their states.[42] He could not, however, explain why the seven NPN controlled states also experienced a similar difficulty. "In seven NPN controlled states," wrote a contemporary observer, "education is a mockery while school fees have skyrocketed. School children have not been going to school in Benue, Sokoto, Niger and Kwara states since 1981. What a qualitative education."[43] A closer look at Shagari's handling of the education sector reveals, indeed, an approach that was discomforting to many. His first action on assuming office was to abolish the Universal Primary Education (UPE), which was introduced by the previous military regime. The UPE scheme was a program that ensured free and compulsory education at the primary school level as a means of laying a solid foundation for the educational enhancement of Nigerians. He was accused of taking this action because he was determined "purely for partisan political considerations", to frustrate "those states who advocated free education at all levels," killing by such action "a program that would have distinguished [his] tenure."[44] This may have been an exaggeration.

Although the UPE was very popular it would have been very difficult to sustain given the grim economic situation. The repercussions, however, were serious. Starved of funds, state governments, including those controlled by the NPN, had no choice but to resort to irregular and sometimes non-payment of teachers' salaries for months. It also led to the re-introduction of school fees in those states where fees had earlier been abolished.[45] As a result of irregular and non-payment of teachers' salaries, teachers' strikes became the order of the day in many states. Most often, this led to the closure of schools for many months; and in one state-- Benue--for over two years. Many teachers were forced to abandon the classroom to engage in other activities in order to survive. Left to their own devices, indiscipline among school-aged children soon became endemic. Some used to opportunity to avoid going to school; others indulged in all sorts of unsavory activities. Performance in school examinations as well as in the entrance examinations to the institutions of higher learning began the slide into mediocrity that shows no signs of improvement even today. By the end of 1983, Shagari's election promise in 1979 of qualitative and functional education could not be realized at any level. University education in Nigeria, which had been respected throughout the world, began to lose that respect by the 1980s. Critics began to wonder aloud "whether the coiners of that slogan 'qualitative education'", that is, the NPN, "knew the meaning of what they were playing with."[46]

One of the contradictions of Nigerian society is how a supposedly republican country could chose to accommodate and sustain such a bewildering number of traditional rulers. As far back as 1957 Shagari, in a speech in the House of Representatives (March 26) regarding the status of Nigeria's traditional rulers, had the foresight to warn about the future "of a very important section of the people of this country" - the traditional rulership - and feared that their powers would "wane and dwindle" in an independent parliamentary democracy. If that happened, he asked, what would happen to them since unlike European aristocrats who retained their lands and "mighty mansions" after losing political power, they had no lands or mansions because "all they have belongs to the masses?"[47] He proposed no solution. Six years later, Nigeria became a republic but failed to abolish the institution of traditional rulership even though both the 1960 Constitution and that of 1963 gave it no meaningful constitutional role. The military governments of Ironsi and Gowon, like the colonial government, however, found it useful in maintaining contact with the people. But the 1976 local government reform, as we saw, proceeded to abolish any executive functions exercised by traditional rulers in local affairs and allowed them only a ceremonial role. The 1979 Constitution accepted the report of the 1976 reform which granted some traditional rulers membership of the National Council of State and some membership of the State Council of Chiefs. And since state governors, the real bosses of these so-called rulers also sat in the National Council, the rulers could not act independently. Precluded, therefore, from involvement in partisan politics, their role was restricted to customary and chieftaincy matters in the states, in which role they were under the thumb of the chairmen of the local governments and state governors. Since the constitution made it difficult for the Federal Government to do anything "to maintain chieftaincy in the state whose government is hostile to the institution," writes Williams appropriately, "the undertaking in the NPN manifesto to maintain chieftaincy was somewhat academic."[48] Thus, Shagari could not do anything when an anti-monarchical PRP government in Kano humiliated the Emir of Kano and got away with it. One would have thought that given his concerns for the traditional rulership, and given the decision of Nigerians to opt for republicanism, Shagari and the NPN would have at least begun the process of reconciling the paradox of republicanism and monarchism in the Nigerian state. Once more, nothing was done and another opportunity was missed.

Another opportunity missed by Shagari was his failure to make any effort to try to work out a relationship with the military that would insulate the soldiers from intervening in politics in the future. It was clear that after exercising absolute power for 13 years, it would be wishful thinking to ignore the military as a political force. Although Shagari realized this fact and did not, in fact, ignore the military, we have no evidence that he even considered the possibility of a coup against him. Indeed, his personal decision to grant Yakubu Gowon full pardon, his decision (having sought the advice of the Council of State) to release immediately from prison all those serving terms for their participation in the 1975 coup, and his politically motivated decision to also grant full pardon to Emeka Ojukwu (as a quid pro quo, it has been suggested, for his joining the NPN), may have ruffled some feathers in the military. How widespread or even deep-rooted the misgivings were, if any, is not clear. However, opposition to these decisions was not among the reasons for the 1983 coup. But, the Shagari administration was accused of transforming the Nigerian Police Force (NPF) into a paramilitary outfit and was suspected to have done so as a counterpoise to the Nigerian Army. To buttress this point it has also been noted that between 1979 and 1983 the strength of the NPF was increased dramatically from 10,000 to

100,000. The force was well equipped. And the government did not hesitate to use it ruthlessly. It was, for example, used to crush the uprising of Bakalori peasants in Sokoto State who were protesting against their displacement because of a new dam; it was used to deal with the demonstration of university students; it was used regularly to break up political rallies, party meetings and campaign meetings of opposition parties. When these activities were added to the increasingly pervasive influence of the National Security Organization (NSO), it was no surprise that the Nigerian press accused Shagari of running a "police state." And it should also be noted that as soon as the Shagari government was toppled in 1983, the military immediately dispossessed the police of its military hardware.[49] The important point to note is that Shagari, far from utilizing the great rapport he had with the military at the inception of his tenure to work toward an enduring civil-military relations in the new democratic dispensation, seemed also to be oblivious of the fact that the most effective antidote to military intervention in politics is good governance. And it will be difficult to conclude, given the evidence at our disposal, that under Shagari Nigeria enjoyed good governance. It would appear that he was unable to implement "The Essentials of Good Government and the Obligation of Leadership," taught by Usman dan Fodio which Shagari himself summarizes in a 1967 book that he authored with a Mrs. Jean Boyd. An important and relevant section of this teaching is the injunction of rulers to undertake regular "assessments" of their officials to find out if any of them has acquired "unexplained wealth." Any such wealth, it was stressed, must be confiscated. The ruler is further enjoined to listen to his people's complaints and to avoid even the appearance of favoritism.[50] There seems to be little doubt that while Shagari would have very much liked to implement the above principle of governance he lacked, however, the political will and clout to do so. But had he decided, at least, "to take the bull by the horn," (so to speak) he would have been amazed at the support of the Nigerian people and the military might not have been driven to seize power.

SOCIAL FORCES

This section will focus primarily on four major social forces with which the Shagari administration had to confront, namely, religion, corruption and indiscipline, poverty and gender. Directly or indirectly they were interwoven with the political and economic issues that we have discussed above.

After ethnicity, religion was indubitably the most divisive force in the Second Republic. When, therefore, their boundaries became blurred as happened in the period under discussion, the consequences were dire. By the inception of the Second Republic the increasing use of religion to achieve political ends had become evident. And between 1979 and 1995 some twenty-two "communal riots" motivated largely by religious considerations have been identified.[51] Although only one of them occurred during our period, what happened set the tone for future developments. The catalyst was the failure of some Muslim members of the Constituent Assembly (1977-8) to get the sharia included in the 1979 Constitution. They failed to do so because Nigeria has been a secular state and has to remain so in the interests of stability. The inclusion of sharia would have altered the secular character of the state because sharia is intended to function in a theocracy. Apparently, such reasoning did not satisfy the Muslim Students' Society of Ahmadu Bello University (ABU), Zaria who (possibly prodded by fundamentalist Muslim politicians) organized demonstrations to highlight their frustration. These demonstrations soon spread to Kaduna, a city that has a sizable Christian population, but they were mild affairs compared to the destruction caused by a chain of disturbances--popularly called the Maitatsine uprisings-- which began in Kano in December, 1980. Described appropriately as "the most militant and widespread religious protest against the secular and religious establishment in the country since independence,"[52] they were, indeed, a crystallization "into religious violence of the deep mistrust that was midwifed by Muslims and Christians in the course of the acrimonious Sharia debate at the constitutional conference."[53] From Kano the disturbances spread to Yola, Kaduna, and Maiduguri by 1982. They left a lot of death and destruction in their wake - some 5000 deaths (including the military and the leader of the disturbances himself) and property worth millions of naira were lost. The Maitatsine leader, Mohammedu Marwa, curiously, was not even a Nigerian. He was a fundamentalist Muslim cleric who had migrated to Nigeria from Northern Cameroon in 1945. He had earlier, in 1962, been repatriated to his country as a "security risk" but somehow had managed to return to Nigeria and was apparently left alone. Another interesting characteristic of the movement was the substantial number of foreigners in its ranks - from Chad, Niger Republic, Mali, Burkina Faso and Cameroon. Together with Nigerian adherents they numbered some 10,000. The movement owed its success, in large part, to the existence of a large group of the urban poor who, because of their marginalization, were a prefabricated collaborating group. The immediate cause of the uprisings, however, was the physical molestation of the sect by irate Kano citizens who were reacting to the physical attack on them by members of the sect. They were also outraged by the sect's constant denunciation of Kano as a state who citizens were consumed by materialistic pursuits. Because of the bad blood between the PRP and NPN politicians in Kano, what would have been treated as a religious problem which required a resolution using standard conflict management criteria was used as a weapon to derive political advantage. NPN politicians, particularly , were accused of blatantly supporting and mobilizing the rioters for the purpose of bringing down the PRP government. Whether this allegation was unfounded or not, what is not in doubt is that the Kano State Government and the Federal Government could not even agree on how to deal with the problem. By therefore agreeing to set up two commissions of inquiry by the respective governments, the problem was further politicized. The result was that a dangerous and divisive sect which needed to be dealt with promptly and decisively was allowed to continue to operate for nearly two years before it was formally outlawed (October, 1982). Even so, the Shagari administration was unable to curb its activities. It was left to the Buhari and Babangida administrations to do so.[54]

Corruption and indiscipline are twin brothers. Like prostitution, they are as old as history and, therefore, older that Noah's Ark. They have always had incalculably disastrous consequences in the course of human history. They led, to take a few well known examples, to the building of Noah's Ark and the destruction of the world, to the annihilation of Sodom and Gomorrah, and to the fall of the Roman Empire. In spite of all these experiences, some obviously didactic and some historical, corruption and indiscipline have continued to run rampant and to constitute one of the great nemesis of our civilization. Although these social forces are global problems, their manifestations in Nigeria became so raw and bizarre during the Second Republic that it was feared that a drastic step was needed to be taken against them to avoid the disintegration of the country. The situation was so bad that a horrified Nigerian newspaper was driven to declare on its front page: "Keeping an average Nigerian from being corrupt is like keeping a goat from eating yam."[55] And yet when confronted with this problem at the time, Shehu Shagari was reported to have retorted that the level of corruption was simply exaggerated by his opponents. This response drove a stunned Chinua Achebe to write sarcastically:

My frank and honest opinion is that anybody who can say
that corruption in Nigeria has not yet become alarming is
either a fool, a crook, or else does not live in this country.
Shagari is neither a fool nor a crook, so I must assume that he
lives abroad... So Shehu Shagari should return home, read the
papers and from time to time talk to Nigerians outside the
circle of Presidential aides and party faithful.[56]

By publicly denying the severity of corruption in Nigeria,
Shagari was saying, in effect, and in the face of overwhelming evidence
to the contrary, that it was not a priority issue in his administration. Of
course, Shagari did not reside abroad; he read the papers and he agonized
about the situation. When asked, for example, by a veteran Nigerian
journalist in an exclusive conversation what was the most intractable
problem he was facing as president he said that what worried him
particularly was the "moral decadence of our country." Among these he
noted, were "bribery, corruption, lack of dedication to duty, dishonesty
and all such vices." To deal with the problem he would prefer
"preventive" rather than "punitive" measures favored by previous
administrations. He revealed that he had referred the matter to the
National Council of State which had decided to set up a permanent
commission "to monitor all the various problems." He was convinced that
the problem, although of "a great deal of concern" to him, could be dealt
with successfully.[57] Whatever the permanent commission reported or
whatever positive steps Shagari took to confront the problem we do no not
know. We do know, however, that the government called for an "ethical
revolution" which was intended to address the country's corruption and
moral decay. Nothing, of course, was achieved through the resolution.
On the contrary, throughout his administration corruption of various
categories, indiscipline, conspicuous consumption by politicians and their
cronies in the face of economic depression, profligate spending by
government, thuggery, and so forth remained undiminished.[58] Among the
reasons the military gave for the 1983 coup were "corrupt, inept and
insensitive leadership," "irresponsibility", "forgery, fraud, embezzlement,
misuse and abuse of office and illegal dealing in foreign exchange and
smuggling."[59] Nigerians generally applauded these reasons. What
happened must have been particularly heart-breaking for a man widely
reputed for his honesty, humility, simplicity, discipline, religiosity,
incorruptibility and, even to some a saintly individual untouched by any
hint sleaze. It was not, however, until January 8, 1986 that the military
government of Ibrahim Babangida formally caused him and the
Vice-President, Dr. Alex Ekwueme, to face a six-count charge of

corruption while in office.[60] The Justice Samson Uwaifo Tribunal who deliberated on these charges returned a "no-case-to answer" verdict for both men and practically elevated them to the status of sainthood. The Tribunal, however, found most of their lieutenants guilty.[61] This verdict drew a mixed reaction from Nigerians but not unnaturally some people, particularly former NPN stalwarts, relatives, friends and sympathizers of the two men praised it. On the other hand, members of the opposing parties, the press and a cross-section of Nigerian society condemned it in no uncertain terms. For Ray Ekpu, " The whole thing was a farce, inelegantly contrived much in the manner of a Kangaroo court rendered even more Kangarooic... by the abject naivety of the Presiding Judge."[62] To which T .A. Kumolu-Johnson, Secretary-General of the Nigerian Council for National Awareness concurred: "The panel's verdict is a mockery of the judicial process," he protested. "The Presidential system [of government] puts the President on the spot as the Chief of State. He has to take responsibility for whatever happens because the aides were appointed directly by his own judgement, received instructions from him and obeyed his dictates."[63] The National Association of Nigerian Students (NANS) castigated the verdict as "an insult on the intelligence of the Nigerian people."[64] Some students of the University of Lagos marched in protest and requested the government to ignore the verdict because the corruption that plagued the country could not have grown so big if not for the indolence of Shagari.[65] In a rather cynical way, Ray Ekpu reflected the disgust felt by many Nigerians:

> Although many things were going the wrong way, the Executive President of Nigeria didn't know anything, didn't see anything, didn't hear anything, didn't smell anything, for as soon as he became the President he lost his sense of intuition, his sense of sight, his sense of hearing, and his sense of smell... the President didn't know whether... the NPN had financial problems or not, he didn't know how contracts were awarded, whether kickbacks were given or taken and by whom, although he was always present at the meetings of the party's caucus... and the government.[66]

Although we have no wish to belabor this point we must reiterate that the issue of personal incorruptibility or otherwise of Shagari is not the point. The point is that he presided over the most corrupt administration in independent Nigeria up to his time and, willy-nilly, did not try hard enough to stop the rot that could have destroyed the country.

The decline of the economy, the collapse of the civil service and educational institutions and, indeed, of all sectors of Nigerian society, inevitably resulted in a drastic drop in the standard of living of a very large percentage of the population. No one had, frankly, anticipated that within four years most Nigerians would be reduced to howling poverty. What happened was precisely what the 1979 Constitution had paradoxically set out to avoid. The constitution regarded the welfare of the people as the most essential end of government. Therefore, it enjoined future Nigerian governments to pursue this end actively. It stressed particularly equal access to the means of livelihood, acceptable quality of life, and equal employment opportunities. During the 1979 campaigns, Shagari and the NPN endorsed this principle and promised to improve the standard of living of the common man and swore to bridge the gap between the rich and the poor.[67] Unfortunately, these promises remained unfulfilled. The rich became richer and the poor became poorer. If the political leadership had seriously showed concern for the plight of the masses, it would have taken drastic steps to ensure that the country's riches were not extravagantly wasted away by first disciplining itself. Shagari seems to have turned a blind eye to the excesses of his officials and political friends. It was public knowledge that in the midst of the economic crisis many NPN top-ranking politicians were able to buy private jet planes, deposit huge amounts of money in foreign banks, some who lived in rented one bedroom flats before the inception of his administration were able to build mansions which were lavishly furnished, and some who could hardly feed themselves in 1979 became chief executives of financial empires. "What of the poor?', enquired a frustrated Nigerian rhetorically. "Even those who could afford three square meals a day in 1979 now find it extremely difficult to afford one square meal", he responded and blamed the "planlessness, squandermania, corruption and mismanagement" of "the NPN Federal Government" for the peoples condition.[68] The N1.200 minimum annual wage which Shagari approved for Nigeria workers and which, for him, was his greatest achievement as president--incredible as this claim seems to us-- was accessible only to the small percentage of Nigerians who had paid employment. The vast majority of the unemployment and unemployable did not benefit from it. Nor were the salaries of the employed regularly paid. In any case, the salary increase was simply eroded by the inflation that usually followed such increases. Moreover, the executive and legislators including the President and Vice-President were at the same time granted outrageous increases in their salaries and allowances that "were completely unrelated to the country's socio-economic realities."[69]

We are reminded, however, that when Shagari realized that he was voted N5000 naura a year more than he actually needed (how his needs could be so accurately determined was not demonstrated), pricked by conscience, as it were, he distributed the excess pay to charitable organizations.[70] The gesture, however well meaning, is also beside the point. It made no dent in raising the standard of living of the poor. If the administration had adhered religiously to its own austerity measure, the poverty might have been alleviated somewhat. But that was not done. What occurred was the rise of excess financial liquidity among a few highly placed individuals and illiquidity among the rest of the population. The liquidity resulted in suffocating inflation which further eroded the standard of living of most Nigerians.

On one important issue, however, the administration's performance is commendable. This was the gender issue. During the 1979 elections, politicians, recognizing the growing importance of women as a social force, jumped onto the bandwagon of those campaigning for their empowerment. Thus, they encouraged women to participate actively in politics both as voters and candidates. For the first time in Nigerian political history, northern Nigerian women were allowed to exercise their right to vote in the elections. It will be recollected that eastern and western Nigerian women were granted the franchise in the 1950s and 1960s respectively. As a result, between 1979 and 1983 several Nigerian women won elections to the House of Representatives and Houses of Assembly in the states. In the Senate, however, only a Ms. Franca Afegbua from Bendel State won a seat. Although women were still poorly represented, what happened was an encouraging development. Shagari clearly encouraged this development when, for the first time in Nigerian history, he appointed two women to ministerial positions. The two female ministers were Chief (Mrs.) Janet Akinrinade (Minister for Internal Affairs) and Mrs. Adenike Ebun Oyagbola (Minister for National Planning). It will be noted, however, that these were not cabinet appointments. In the civil service he approved the appointment of Mrs. Francesca Yetunde Emmanuel as the Permanent Secretary for the Ministry of Health. A number of women were also appointed State Commissioners. But as a devout Muslim he kept his wives away from public glare, his progressive ideas on gender issues at the political level notwithstanding. He is also credited with encouraging the involvement of women in the economic sector. The basis for this is the fact that during Shagari's administration the country witnessed the emergence of the greatest number of female contractors.[71] It is doubtful that what happened was his own doing but it is true that in almost all the states there emerged a large number of female contractors who competed effectively with men in the construction and supplies sectors especially. Most of these women were political party stalwarts and they made a lot of money. The Shagari regime, indeed, far from frustrating female economic emancipation actually encouraged and facilitated it.

FOREIGN POLICY

Foreign policy in the Second Republic was devoid of the drama and excitement witnessed under the previous military administrations. Basically it was cautious, routine, in some respects sensible, and vision-less. Although the civilian administration of Shagari continued to pursue the essentials and aims of the country's external relations that it inherited, no serious effort was made to keep pace with the virulently patriotic, virile and robust rhetoric of Mohammed. (This rhetoric had been sustained, to some extent, by Obasanjo.) There was a high expectation that Nigeria's oil wealth would, at last, enable it to live up to its self-conferred attribute as the giant of Africa destined to lead the ancient continent out of the bondage of the ages. Within two years that great expectation, however unrealistic, had substantially diminished.

Several reasons accounted for this development. There was, first, Shagari's personality that made it difficult for him to pursue a vigorous, populist and dynamic policy. He seemed more at ease to follow a conservative and sometimes pragmatic approach in external affairs reminiscent of the policies of Tafa Balewa and Yakubu Gowon. Second, his essentially anti-Communist, pro-Western, unapologetically capitalist ideology, militated against the pursuit of an independent and truculently confrontational policy toward the West which some felt the circumstances warranted. In his own way, he articulated Nigeria's position in opposition to that of the West, but he felt more comfortable doing so under the auspices of the decisions of such international organizations as the United Nations Organizations (UN), the Commonwealth and the Organization of African Unity (OAU), now called the African Union (AU), decisions to which Nigeria had contributed. His foreign policy, therefore, was generally unpopular because many Nigerians did not believe that he had always accurately reflected and defended Nigeria's interests. Third, the democratic, republican constitution under which he operated and which denied him, more or less, the free hand enjoyed by the military. For most issues he needed legislative approval which, given his precarious political position, he would not often get. Fourth, the economic crisis that had become evident by 1981 also seriously hampered his ability to act decisively in external affairs. It has been inferred, however, that even if Nigeria was not economically distressed the Shagari regime had neither "the zeal nor the competence" to pursue a radical foreign policy and the result consequently was that the Second Republic was "a period of recess for Nigeria's foreign policy."[72] This assessment is some what exaggerated because Shagari participated, faithfully, howbeit routinely but sincerely, in most of the major foreign policy issues of his day.

He accepted, for example, the validity of that popular--but, in our opinion, flawed--policy that Africa should be the center-piece of Nigeria's foreign policy. The authors feel that this system is flawed because Nigeria itself, not Africa, should be the cornerstone of the country's foreign policy. In pursuance of the policy, and acting as a surrogate of the O.A.U., Shagari invested a lot of Nigerian time and scarce resources in a futile attempt to keep the peace in Chad with his hands figuratively tied behind his back. According to Shagari's own admission, the leaders of Chad were adept at using Nigeria when it suited their interests to do so, threw the Nigerian peace keepers out when their expectations were not fulfilled, and never seriously listened to Nigeria. But he could not act unilaterally because he was there on behalf of the O.A.U., the body that had egged Nigeria on to be involved in Chad on the understanding that it would be responsible for the expenses incurred (but which it never repaid).[73] The Shagari administration displayed a similar impotence in dealing with the conflict with Cameroon over the oil rich Bakassi Peninsula (Rio del Rey). Because he refrained from avenging the murder of five Nigerian soldiers who were a part of the Nigerian contingent in the disputed area, leaving the crisis instead to the O.A.U., Awolowo rejected Shagari as "a coward who is playing the ostrich in the face of war".[74] On his part, Awolowo said that he would have occupied the place within 48 hours, thereby presenting the O.A.U. and the U.N. with a fait accompli and then argue the case from a position of strength. Shagari, on the other hand, argued that such an occupation--which would have certainly lasted for months or even years--"would have crippled both Nigeria and Cameroon economically." He was loath, he said, to fight an avoidable war, a war that was capable of greatly undermining "all our efforts towards economic development".[75] What he failed to reveal was that he feared that France which has a defense pact with Cameroon would have intervened in the event of war to which Nigeria would not have adequate response. This was probably a wise policy at the time but the Nigerian public did not see it that way. He attached greater importance, however, to the fight against apartheid and decolonization in southern Africa. He opposed Ronald Reagan's policy of "constructive engagement" in southern Africa but he took no action against the United States and other countries that continued to trade with South Africa. He believed, however, that apartheid could be defeated in the long run only by "persistent and determined armed struggle... by the people directly concerned; that is, the Africans in South Africa who are being oppressed, with the active assistance of independent African countries."[76] To this end, he continued with the inherited policy of a yearly allocation of 5 million dollars to aid the liberation movements in southern Africa. He was forced, however, by Nigeria's economic difficulties to stop the allocation in 1980. He managed, nevertheless, to grant 10 million dollars to newly independent Zimbabwe to enable Robert Mugabe's government acquire, not land, but (curiously enough) the Zimbabwe Herald newspaper, from its white owners. Except for the unfortunate massive deportation of illegal aliens from Nigeria most of whom came from Ghana, the Shagari administration adhered religiously to Nigeria's policy of supporting the O.A.U., ECOWAS, and other African organizations as well as ensuring good relations with all African countries, casting itself in the role of "big brother". The problem that perplexed some Nigerians was that while "the African states seem to want Nigeria to play a big role" in Africa, "at the same time somehow they don't want Nigeria to play a big role - that there is a kind of love/hate."[77] Shagari's attitude was that that was "human nature. It is somewhat similar to the role of the United States in the World ... It is a difficult position for us, that is why we always try to steer a middle course."[78] His countrymen, including the military establishment, were not impressed by this attitude.

At the global level, there were also no dramatic or enduring initiatives. Nigeria's support for all international organizations and agencies did not waver, but Nigeria was no major force in global affairs in spite of its rising profile as a rich oil-producing country for the most part of Shagari's first term in office. He was well aware that "the objective" of the industrialized counties was "to break OPEC" and "deliberately try to destabilize the economies of the developing countries in order to strengthen their own",[79] but he provided no counterpoise to these objectives. Although he believed in the "non-alignment" doctrine or the "positive neutrality" of Bandung, he was pro-Western at heart. And although during his tenure Egypt gave diplomatic recognition to the State of Israel, and Nigerians clamored for a resumption of diplomatic relations with Israel, Shagari refused to follow Egypt's lead because "of Israel's continued cooperation with racist South Africa" which was increasingly being intensified, a posture that personally "horrified" him and all Africans, given Israel's own history. He believed that Palestinians were entitled to a state of their own; and he deplored Israel's "whole attitude in the international community" which was "that of defiance."[80] What, then, should Nigeria do besides refuse to recognize Israel? Shagari merely threw up his hands in the air, as it were, and passed the blame to the O.A.U..

THE 1983 ELECTIONS AND THE
FALL OF THE SECOND REPUBLIC

Those who had expected that the Second Republic would sow the seeds of true democracy in Nigeria were thoroughly disappointed. The events of the 1983 elections seemed to show that the last four years had been wasted. It was an object lesson in how democracy should not work. Whether Shehu Shagari realized it or not, he missed another opportunity to immortalize his name as someone who not only nurtured his country into true democracy but also demonstrated the superiority of civilian rule to military autocracy. On the contrary, under his regime Nigeria was gradually but inexorably heading toward a dictatorship. Whether that was his wish or not is beside the point. The fact remains that he did nothing to check the tendency. His reaction to criticisms of his government was one of uncharacteristic churlishness for someone generally reported to be decent, gentle, disciplined and meek, qualities greatly loved by his Western media admirers. He must have shocked some of these admirers when he threatened after the elections "to use a 'big stick' on those who opposed him" and warned that states hostile to him "would continue to lose benefits because of their 'confrontational' attitude."[81] This is the speech of a dictator, not of a democrat. The record of his administration was such that had he been a democrat, or a reluctant seeker of high office, he would have found a good excuse not to seek re-election. Far from doing so, however, he fought tirelessly for re-election and, according to Moshood Abiola, reneged on an earlier arrangement that Abiola would be the NPN flag-bearer in 1983, a development that forced Abiola to withdraw from Nigerian politics. Had Nigeria been a functioning democracy, the NPN would not have had a chance to be re-elected for four more years. Yet, as we saw, by manipulation, material inducements, appointments, and intimidation, the NPN had, by 1983, so destabilized the opposition parties that the political forces in the country were realigned overwhelmingly in its favor. Nigeria had become a virtual one-party state. The dice was so loaded in favor of the NPN that many of its opponents, convinced that since even the military establishment was in support of the party, felt that there was no force capable of calling it to order. They had reached the conclusion that the sensible thing to do--if they could not beat the NPN--was to join it. It did not make sense for them to starve from the sidelines and watch while those inside grew rich and robust even in the midst of economic depression. Democracy, conceived in the very narrow sense of winner-takes-all, had its worst manifestations so far in Nigerian history.

It is fascinating to note that the NPN leadership, its overwhelming advantages notwithstanding, was not absolutely sure that the party would be returned to power. They were aware that the state of Nigeria was not good, that the majority of the electorate was very dissatisfied, and that the constant refrain of the fall in oil revenue as the only cause of Nigeria's difficulties was wearing thin. They took, therefore, undemocratic and crude measures to ensure that the elections were won at all cost.

Electoral commissioners were appointed who were widely known to be either NPN members or sympathizers; ensuring that the voters' registers in both the NPN controlled states and those the party had to win to retain power contained a vast majority of its supporters; Fedeco and its pliable chairman, Justice Ovie Whisky, were forced to reverse the order of the elections by holding the presidential election first instead of last as was the case in 1979, thereby hoping to benefit from a bandwagon effect; and permitting the registration of a sixth political party, Tunji Braitwaite's Nigeria Advance Party (NAP), believing that the party would take some votes away from the UPN.

The regime also openly employed the law enforcement agencies as a partisan instrument of intimidation and coercion of opponents. The Nigerian press, television and radio, most of which were owned by the federal government and the governments of the NPN controlled states (about 50 percent of which were founded between 1979 and 1983) were used as a partisan instrument in the campaigns, thus putting in place strategies for rigging the elections. The Nigerian public was well aware of these developments but could do nothing to stop the NPN. The opposition parties and the media controlled by them, admittedly no angels themselves, protested vigorously against these undemocratic developments but they were ignored. Consequently, they mapped out their own strategies to rig the elections but they did not possess the resources to outdo the NPN.

The elections took place between August sixth and September third. By a supposed large margin of victory, the NPN was returned to power. Although an NPN victory was expected, given the prevailing circumstances, the extent of the landslide victory in all the elections was a surprise. This seemed to be a clear demonstration that the rigging strategies had paid off. The level of protests that followed the release of the results of these elections and the amount of litigations that took place were unknown in Nigerian history. From trade unions, sections of the press, and professional unions, to ASUU and the National Association of Nigerian Students (NANS), the accusations against the NPN and Shagari poured in thick and fast. "Fedeco Awards," "Selection not election," "heavily rigged," "shameful performance," and "inexcusable" were some of the expressions used to describe the elections. "No one," wrote Falola and Ihonvbere, "except perhaps members of the defunct NPN, would argue that the 1983 elections were fair and free."[82] Obafemi Awolowo was dismayed at the extent of the malpractice that took place. He admitted that "there was rigging in 1979" but that the rigging that took place in 1983 "was so massive it would have taken a month just to prepare the [legal] case, to collect the facts and figures".[83] Wole Soyinka reminded the Western press that their "meek, unassuming detribalized Shagari, the guarantee of peace and stability etc. etc. *ad nauseam* went ahead confidently ahead", as they watched, "to commit the most breathtaking, in sheer scale, electoral fraud of any nation in the whole of Africa".[84] Finally, General Theophilus Danjuma observed: "Democracy had been in jeopardy for the past four years (1979-1983). It died with the 1983 elections. The army only buried it. They did not kill it. The politicians killed democracy."[85]

(See Tables 6.4, 6.5, and 6.6)

There is no doubt that all the parties engaged in sickening electoral malpractice, but because the NPN controlled the government at the center and therefore the security forces, the electoral processes and most of the media, no other party could compete with it. Danjuma had no doubt that "the greatest offender was the NPN" which, in his view, "had the largest gathering of the worst human beings that Nigeria could produce." (86) The judicial commission of inquiry into how fedeco conducted the 1983 elections is explicit on this point (87). Except for Ondo State where the gubernatorial election, claimed to have been won

TABLE 6.4: 1983 NATIONAL ASSEMBLY ELECTIONS

State	Total no. of seats		NPN		UPN		NPP		GNPP		PRP	
	S	HR	S	HR	S	HR	S	HR	S	HR	S	HR
Anambra	5	29	1	15	0	0	4	14	0	0	0	0
Bauchi	5	20	5	20	0	0	0	0	0	0	0	0
Bendel	5	20	5	18	0	2	0	0	0	0	0	0
Benue	5	19	5	15	0	0	0	4	0	0	0	0
Borno	5	24	5	24	0	0	0	0	0	0	0	0
Cross River	5	28	5	26	0	2	0	0	0	0	0	0
Gongola	5	21	5	21	0	0	0	0	0	0	0	0
Imo	5	30	1	10	0	0	4	20	0	0	0	0
Kaduna	5	33	5	33	0	0	0	0	0	0	0	0
Kano	5	46	0	3	0	0	0	2	0	0	5	41
Kwara	5	14	1	9	2	5	0	0	1	0	0	0
Lagos	5	12	0	0	5	12	0	0	0	0	0	0
Niger	5	10	4	8	0	0	1	2	0	0	0	0
Ogun	5	12	0	0	5	12	0	0	0	0	0	0
Ondo	5	42			Elections put off							
Oyo	5	22			Elections put off							
Plateau	5	16	2	10	0	0	3	6	0	0	0	0
Rivers	5	14	5	14	0	0	0	0	0	0	0	0
Sokoto	5	37	5	37	0	0	0	0	0	0	0	0
FCT	1	1	1	1	0	0	0	0	0	0	0	0
Total	**96**	**450**	**55**	**264**	**12**	**33**	**12**	**48**	**1**	**0**	**5**	**41**

TABLE 6.5: 1983 STATE GUBERNATORIAL ELECTIONS

State	Governor/Party
Anambra	Onoh/NPN
Bauchi	Ali/NPN
Bendel	Ogbemudia/NPN
Benue	Aku/NPN
Borno	Jarma/NPN
Cross River	Etiebet/NPN
Gongola	Tukur/NPN
Imo	Mbakwe/NPN
Kaduna	Kaita/NPN
Kano	Zuwo/PRP
Kwara	Adebayo/UPN
Lagos	Jakande/UPN
Niger	Ibrahim/NPN
Ogun	Onabanjo/NPN
Ondo	Ajasin/UPN
Oyo	Olunloyo/NPN
Plateau	Lar/NPP
Rivers	Okilo/NPN
Sokoto	Nadama/NPN
FCT	

TABLE 6.6: 1983 PRESIDENTIAL ELECTION

State	Total votes				% of total votes		
	Cast	NPN	UPN	NPP	GNPP	PRP	NAP
Anambra	1,158,283	33.36	2.06	57.79	3.12	1.39	2.38
Bauchi	1,782,122	84.57	5.55	3.66	2.09	3.05	1.07
Bendel	1,099,851	41.17	51.45	4.35	1.05	0.67	0.79
Benue	652,795	58.83	12.21	23.31	3.05	0.98	1.62
Borno	718,043	48.60	16.73	3.76	24.96	3.76	2.19
Cross River	1,295,710	54.00	39.43	3.61	1.29	0.54	0.85
Gongola	735,648	38.44	21.85	20.13	3.47	11.04	5.07
Imo	1,588,975	25.07	1.43	66.99	3.29	1.16	2.06
Kaduna	2,137,398	59.28	10.57	10.58	3.08	14.02	1.75
Kano	1,193,050	32.19	4.06	22.98	2.95	36.63	1.19
Kwara	608,422	49.25	45.22	2.66	1.26	0.61	1.00
Lagos	1,640,381	7.59	83.39	7.28	0.72	0.04	0.05
Niger	430,731	63.17	3.66	25.23	3.01	2.03	1.90
Ogun	1,261,061	3.47	95.00	0.04	0.55	0.35	0.23
Ondo	1,829,343	20.03	77.25	1.11	0.63	0.39	0.58
Oyo	2,351,000	37.55	59.39	1.48	0.57	0.39	0.42
Plateau	652,302	44.86	43.05	5.86	2.85	1.77	1.61
Rivers	1,357,715	67.88	18.55	11.15	0.95	0.34	1.11
Sokoto	2,837,786	91.83	2.66	2.23	1.65	0.85	0.78
FCT	135,351	94.10	0.81	3.07	0.81	0.47	0.72
Total	**25,454,166**	**47.33**	**30.98**	**13.88**	**2.51**	**4.08**	**1.21**

Source: Adapted from Osaghae, *Crippled Giant*, pp. 148.

by the NPN, was awarded on appeal to the UPN by the Supreme Court, the election tribunals and the lower courts -generally believed to be corrupt and most of which was under the thumb of the NPN - dismissed the litigations brought by the opposition parties on some oftentimes laughable, technical legal terms. Indeed, Awolowo, believing that it was impossible to receive justice from the courts, did not even bother to contest his defeat in the courts. Waziri Ibrahim who decided to challenge Shagari's re-election in the courts met with no success. Like Awolowo, Azikiwe left everything in the hands of the almighty and history. He noted that "It is an irony of fate that [NPN] politicians have become so intoxicated with the lust for power that they are now in league with unpatriotic Lucifers in human form to destabilize Nigeria as a democracy." He prophesied that God would "frustrate their knavery and ultimately expose their machinations and consign them to the scrap heap of forgotten tyrants." He was convinced also that "History will continue to vindicate the just and God shall punish the wicked." (88)

Shagari ignored what seemed to him to be the effete fulminations of ambitious but frustrated politicians. It did not seem to have occurred to him that something had dramatically gone wrong in Nigeria. He continued to play the saint. The more unrestrained members of the NPN began to boast openly that their party would rule Nigeria forever because only two viable political parties, namely, the NPN and the military, actually existed in Nigeria. They were confident that the NPN government would easily contain the violence in various parts of the country that was threatening to reduce the country to a virtual state of anarchy. Shades of events that preceded the Nigerian Civil War began to manifest themselves increasingly and menacingly. The Yoruba vowed to frustrate what they saw as a "cabal of native imperialism," that is, a veritable Hausa-Fulani sub-imperialism in Nigeria, and called for a confederacy of southern Nigeria, no doubt, under Yoruba leadership. This is a euphemism for secession. Although the East made no such threat, understandably, the Igbo particularly must have gained a certain degree of vindication over the justification for the Biafran secession. The rest of Nigeria did not want to see the connection.

By the end of 1983 the situation was getting out of hand. Talk of military intervention was abroad in the land. Shagari and the NPN leaders appeared unperturbed. So was one of us who also lived under the Shagari regime and witnessed first hand most of the events being described. He believed that because Nigeria was in such a sorry state not even politically ambitious soldiers would want to get themselves involved in the mess by seizing power. He was wrong. On New Years Eve 1983 the Nigerian military, for the third time in seventeen years, seized political power and the Second Republic came to a deserved end as far as most Nigerians were concerned. The aftermath of this *coup d'etat* will be discussed in the next chapter.

CONCLUSION

The literature on the performance of Shehu Shagari and the NPN during the Second Republic is overwhelmingly negative. This is not surprising given the available evidence. Clearly Nigerians expected so much and received so little. And they blamed everything on what they saw as Shagari's blundering and squandering leadership. He was accused of not only failing to pursue Murtala Mohammed's vision of an independent and great Nigerian nation but also missing the opportunity to nurture the new democratic dispensation. Far from doing so, he absentmindedly , so it seemed, presided over its destruction. Had the democratic experiment succeeded under his regime the impact on the rest of Africa, at any rate, would have been phenomenal. But that was not to be. Shagari also missed the historic opportunity to demonstrate to Nigerians the superiority of democratic civilian rule to military dictatorship. The problem was that Nigeria adopted an American political system without the benefit of American political ideals and values. The founding fathers of the American Republic, as we know, were co-conspirators in the art of class self-preservation. But they were aware that the survival of their class lay in creating a strong America and inducing the masses to believe in the efficicacy of the American system. In Shagari's Nigeria, virtually nobody believed in the Nigerian system and, in the end, nobody came to its defense.

It is difficult to credit the Shagari regime with any major policy initiative. Indeed, after a stewardship of four years the Shagari administration could not point to one simple policy initiative on which it could base the 1983 election campaigns. The "Green Revolution" program of the Second Republic, for example, the essence of which was to enable Nigeria achieve autarchy in food production was merely the "Operation Freed the Nation" of Olusegun Obasanjo under another name. In any case, it was a dismal failure. It made no meaningful impact on Nigeria's inadequate food production. The country continued to depend on food imports.

The River Basin Development Authority project, too, the subject of interminable Nigerian broadcast and print media propaganda, was the initiative of a military administration. It was intended to make the "Green Revolution" possible. And the government, in fact, required corporations working in the country to invest in the program. Consequently, a lot of money was pumped into the project. The World Bank, also, pumped a lot of money into Agricultural Development Programs (ADPS). All these efforts came to nothing. During the drought of the early 80s when their impact would have been most salutary, nothing was accomplished.

Four other development projects with which the regime's name has been associated - the Abuja Capital, the steel mills, the Third Lagos Mainland Bridge, and the Universal Primary Education (UPE) - were all initiated by the military. Under the Shagari administration they became primarily avenues for massive administrative graft and illicit profit-making by the contractor class. A few strategically placed individuals used the opportunity to fatten their bank accounts. It should also be pointed out that the administration was consequently forced to abandon some of these projects. The regime inherited also the nineteen state structure, the federal character principle, and the revenue allocation system. Its execution of these initiatives were, however, frustrated by the fractious politics of the Second Republic. On the issues of higher education and gender, it is fair to point out that the administration's level of commitment went beyond that of the previous military administrations. But because of the economic crisis its achievement in the education sector was modest.

The available evidence suggest to us that the Shagari administration left no major monuments. It had no major initiatives; it bungled everything. It was even "slow in articulating new policies, and programs," wrote a contemporary observer appropriately, "that marked a significant advance on its predecessor's." (89) It is possible, but perhaps not probable, that when the archives of this administration are opened to the hard-headed scrutiny of historians the assessment may be different. More than the lack of fundamental initiatives what has perplexed students of this administration most, however, is their inability to explain satisfactorily how Shagari and Ekwueme, two individuals widely regarded as honest and incorruptible, could preside over the most corrupt and morally bankrupt administration in the history of Nigeria up to that point (90) and did nothing concrete to stop it. On the contrary, while Ekwueme remained, more or less aloof and taciturn, Shagari continued to play the saint quietly and always passed the buck elsewhere. Of course, history is replete with examples of "good" people who demonstrated weak and poor leadership. We believe that Shagari belongs to this undistinguished group. Those who suspected, right from the start, his lack of proper equipment to pilot the affairs of Nigeria have been justified. Furthermore, because he was a leader whose mission was essentially the protection of the interests of a powerful minority group (91), it was difficult for him - as indeed it would have been for all those in a similar position - to be an acceptable leader of all Nigeria. The fact, too, that he lacked a comfortable majority caused him to place the highest priority on survival in office to the detriment of all else. We discount totally his trumpeted lack of interest in the presidency as a political goal precisely because the facts negate such a claim.

ENDNOTES

1. See, for example, David Williams, *President and Power in Nigeria: The Life of Shehu Shagari.* London: Frank Cass, 1982; A.A. Nwafor Orizu, *Insight into Nigeria: The Shehu Shagari Era.* Ibadan: Evans Brothers, 1983; Okion Ojigbo, *Nigeria Returns to Civilian Rule.* Lagos: Tokion Company, 1980.

2. Chuba Okadigbo, *Power and Leadership in Nigeria.* Enugu: Fourth Dimension, 1987, 90.

3. *Ibid.,* 84.

4. See Williams, *Shehu Shagari.* Cf. Ohi Aleghe, Timothy Bonnet and Olu Akerele, "The Reluctant Operator," in *The African Concord,* vol. 5, no. 19, September 10, 1990; Okon Osung and Oqua Itu, "The Man Shagari: A Profile", *The Nigerian Call,* Sunday, May 7, 1983, 7.

5. *Nigerian Call,* May 7, 1983, 7.

6. Otutu orji, "The Man Called Alhaji Shehu Shagari," *Daily Star,* Friday, July 22, 1983, 5.

7. See *Daily Times,* July 17, 1986.

8. *Power and Leadership,* 88.

9. *Ibid.,* p.88.

10. O. Omoruyi, "Federal Character and the Party System in the Second Republic" in P.P Ekeh and E.E. Osaghae (Ceds), *Federal Character and Federalism in Nigeria.* Ibadan: Heinemann, 1989, 205.

11. Eghosa E. Osaghae, *Nigeria Since Independence: Crippled Giant,* Bloomington: Indiana University Press, 1998, 129.

12. Osaghae, *Crippled Giant,* 129.

13. Okadigbo, *Power and Leadership,* 90.

14. The reasons given by the military for seizing power and the overwhelming favorable response it received support this conclusion.

15. See David O. Oke, "The Transgressions of the Shagari Administration," in *Daily Sketch,* June 17, 1983, 7.

16. Cited in *Satellite,* April 13, 1983, 3.

17. See Fan Ndukwe, *Sunday Statesman,* March 27, 1983, 9.

18. Cited in Osaghae, *Crippled Giant,* 137.

19. For more details of the events covered in this section see Osaghae, *Crippled Giant,* 130-144 and Okadigbo, *Power and Leadership,* 86-92.

20. *The Rise and Fall of Nigeria's Second Republic, 1979-1983.* London: Zed Books, 1985, 94.

21. *Ibid.,* 100.

22. Oke, "Transgression," 7.

23. *Power and Leadership,* 92-93.

24. See Dick Oranusi, "Shagari's Failure," *Punch*, May 11, 1983, 5.

25. Falola et all, *Rise and Fall*, 99.

26. *Ibid.,* 100.

27. See *Ibid*, 100-103 for details.

28. *Power and Leadership*, 93.

29. *Ibid.*, 104.

30. Oke, "Transgressions," 7.

31. Williams, *Shehu Shagari*, 221.

32. Oke, "Transgressions," 7.

33. *Ibid.*, 7.

34. *Ibid.*

35. Rowland Anokwu, "Shagari's Promise and Achievements," *Sunday Post*, July 10, 1983, 10.

36. *Ibid*

37. *Ibid*

38. "Shagari and the Housewife," April 24, 1983, 3.

39. Shehu Shagari, "We Are The Saints," *Tempo Newspaper*, October 31, 1996, p. 15; idem, *New Nigerian*, April 20, 1983, 9.

40. *Daily Nation*, Thursday, April 7, 1983, 1; See also *Nigerian Tide*, Wednesday, May 11 1983, 1.

41. Levi Nwachuku, private communication, August, 2000.

42. *Daily Times*, July 21, 1983, 1.

43. Oranusi, " Shagari's Failures," 5.

44. *Satellite Newspaper*, February 22, 1983, 3.

45. *New Nigerian*, Friday, April 8, 1983, 1; *Sunday Post*, July 10, 1983, 10; cf. Sanya Onabmiro, "Educational Development in Shagari's Regime," in *New Nigerian*, Tuesday, July 12, 1983, 5.

46. *Satellite Newspaper*, February 22, 1983, 3.

47. Williams, *Shehu Shagari*, 192.

48. *Ibid.*, 193.

49. For more details see Osaghae, *Crippled Giant*, 132-133.

50. Williams, *Shehu Shagari*, 41-42.

51. Iheanyi M. Enwerem, "An Assessment of Government's Formal Responses to Ethnic/Religions Riots, 1980-1990s". in Ernest E. Uwazie, Isaac O Albert and Godfrey N. Uzoigwe (eds.), *Inter-ethnic and Religious Conflict Resolution in Nigeria.* New York: Lexington Books, 1999, 121.

52. *Ibid.*, p. 124.

53. *Ibid.*

54. See Chapters seven and eight below.

55. Cited in Chinua Achebe, *The Trouble With Nigeria*. Enugu: Fourth Dimension, 1983, 38.

56. *Ibid.*, 37-38.
57. See Peter Enahoro, *Shagari in Conversation.* London: Africa Now, no date, but likely 1983, 31.
58. For details, See Falola et al, *Rise and Fall*,107-114.
59. *Ibid.*, 222-231.
60. See *Newswatch Magazine*, February 3, 1986, 48.
61. *Ibid.*, 49.
62. *Ibid.*, 4.
63. *Ibid.*, 53.
64. *Ibid.*
65. *Ibid.*
66. *Ibid.*, 4.
67. *Sunday Post*, July 10, 1983, 10.
68. *Ibid.*
69. *Ibid.*, 38.
70. *Ibid.*, 40.
71. Cited in Falola et al, *Rise and Fall*, 218.
72. *Ibid.*, 216.
73. Cited *Ibid.*, 216.
74. Cited *Ibid.*, 217.
75. Cited *Ibid.*, 219.
76. Cited *Ibid.*
77. See Babalakin Report (Lagos: Government Printer, 1991); see also Osaghae, *Crippled Giant*, 150.
78. Cited Osaghae, *Crippled Giant*, 150.
79. Cited in Fred Onyeoziri, "Civilian Regimes: Policies and Progams," In Tekena N, Tamuno and J.A. Atanda (eds.), *Nigeria Since Independence: The First Twenty-Five Years,* vol. IV, Govt. and Public Policy. Ibadan: Heinemann, 1989, 40.
80. The Shagari administration, more than that of Yakubu Gowon, set the stage for what happened under Ibrahim Babangida and Sani Abacha.
81. See, for example, Okechukwu Okeke, *Hausa - Fulani Hegamony: The Dominance of the Muslim North in Contemporary Nigerian Politics.* Enugu: Acena Publishers, 1992.
82. *Ibid,* 216.
83. Cited *Ibid,* 216.
84. Cited *Ibid,* 217.
85. Cited *Ibid,* 219.
86. Cited *Ibid.*
87. See *Babalakin Report.* Lagos: Government Printer, 1991; see also Osaghae, Crippled Giant, 150.

88. Cited Osaghae, *Crippled Giant*, 150.

89. Cited in Fred Onyeoziri, "Civilian Regimes: Policies and Progams,"in Tamuno and Atanda (eds.), *Nigeria Since Independence.*

90. The Shagari administration, more than that of Yakubu Gowon, set the stage for what happened under Ibrahim Babangida and Sani Abacha.

91. See, for example, Okechukwu Okeke, *Hausa - Fulani Hegamony, op. cit.*

Major General Muhammadu Buhari
Head of State
January 1984-August 1985

Chapter 7

Crisis of Purpose: General Muhammadu Buhari's Renaissance of National Sanitation, 1984-1985

Levi A. Nwachuku

INTRODUCTION

On December 31, 1983, the Nigerian army overthrew the Second Republic. It asserted that the defunct Second Republic had mismanaged the nation's political and economic fortunes and that corruption in the society had become pervasive. Furthermore, the perceived absence of direction in the national government, in conjunction with the apprehension of an imminent economic collapse, made Nigerians wish an end to the administration of President Shehu Shagari.[1] In the above context, Nigerians accepted the leadership of General Muhammadu Buhari with optimism.[2] To many Nigerians, the intervention of the army was timely ,and to an extent, expected or invited. Before August 1983, there were at least ten unsuccessful coup plots. Aware of all of them, President Shagari communicated this information to Obafemi Awolowo and to Nnamdi Azikiwe, leaders of the Unity Party of Nigeria and the Nigerian Peoples' Party respectively.[3] Obafemi Awolowo and Nnamdi Azikiwe were the presidential candidates for their respective parties.

They contested the 1983 presidential election against President Shehu Shagari. Indeed, the army itself seemed to be anxious to overthrow the Second Republic. General Buhari who in 1982 was the brigadier commanding the third armored brigade in Jos, spoke to the press about the necessity for the military to be involved in the general elections of 1983. The army's eagerness to pull down the Second Republic was reinforced in February 1983 when demonstrators in Lagos called for the return of the military following the burning of the Nigerian Telecommunications Building.[4] Nigerians believed that the 36-storey Telecommunications Building was deliberately set on fire in order to cover up financial misdoings. During the same period, fire gulped other public buildings including the Post and Telegraph House in Lagos, the Anambra State Broadcasting Corporation in Enugu, the Republic Building at Marina, Lagos, the Federal Ministry of Education in Lagos, and the Federal Capital Development Authority account office at Abuja. These buildings contained documents that would have revealed fraudulent practices; thus, burning them covered up the frauds. The frequency of fraud scandals supported the contention that the fires were an act of arson derived from national disapproval of the government.

Although many factors have been suggested for the fall of the Second Republic, economic forces, in my view, were at the center. Nigerians had become disenchanted with the general economic condition. This view is corroborated by this comment in the magazine, *West Africa*: "The feeling that the country is on the brink of economic disaster seems to have been the principal factor which spurred the top echelons of the armed forces into their collective action."[5]

The frustrations arising from the depressed economy were aggravated by the corruption and indiscipline, which characterized the government of President Shehu Shagari. Government contracts were inflated to support kickbacks, imports were over invoiced, forgery and fraud were rampant, officials embezzled public funds and no effective measures were taken against smuggling. Many state governors were found in possession of large sums of money when the army took over the government. The most striking one was Governor Bakin Zuwo of Kano State. In office for only three months, he had $4,590,000[6] (exchange rate in 1984 was ₦1 = $1.35) in his residence.

Furthermore, as mentioned earlier, the army was eager to overthrow the government of President Shehu Shagari. The army had developed contempt for the capacity of the civilian politicians, on the strength of their performance over the past four years, to guide the country through the difficult economic period. This explains why the military did not allow President Shagari's redemptive measures--austerity measures of 1982, and the appointment of able ministers--the opportunity to prove their merit.   General Buhari's suggestion of the army's involvement in conducting the general elections of 1983 betrayed the military's lack of confidence in the ability of Shagari's government to deal with national political issues. Indeed, by June 1983, in a "secret" meeting of senior officers, including Muhammadu Buhari, top ranking military officers decided that the army would not support President Shagari politically.[7] The withdrawal of support meant a vote of no confidence in the regime. General Buhari, who suggested the army's involvement in the general elections of 1983, would at the end of that year become the Head of the Nigerian Government.

GENERAL MUHAMMADU BUHARI: A PROFILE

Nigerians may never know how and why the power brokers and king makers in the army chose General Buhari to lead the country. However, in any military regime, the civilians do not influence the choice of the leader. If Buhari had stood for popular election, he may not have won. However, he gained enough confidence of his peers to be regarded as the *primus inter pares*. Buhari's administrative experience was impressive. Age was also in his favor, for he became Nigeria's first citizen, fourteen days after he had celebrated his forty-first birthday.

Buhari joined the army in 1962 and was commissioned the following year. In 1975, the Murtala Mohammed government appointed him Governor of North Eastern State. In March 1976, General Olusegun Obasanjo who succeeded the assassinated Mohammed, appointed Buhari Commissioner for Petroleum and Natural resources. Later in 1976, the Nigerian National Petroleum Corporation (NNPC) was created. Buhari was appointed the chairman of the corporation. He held this position until 1978. When the civilian government was inaugurated in October 1979, Buhari returned to military assignment. In 1980, he was appointed the General Officer Commanding (GOC) the Fourth Division of the Nigerian army. At the time the curtain was brought down on the Second Republic, Buhari was the G.O.C. in charge of the First Mechanized Division of the army in Jos. With these experiences, one would feel that he would be equipped to solve the problems, which plagued the country.

Muhammadu Buhari ruled Nigeria for 604 days (December 31, 1983 - August 26, 1985). Indeed, in the history of a nation, 604 days do not constitute enough time to assess the achievements of a ruler. However, some leaders whose tenure in office had been untimely ended, have left positive legacies for posterity. For instance, John F. Kennedy's 1000 days left a legacy, largely in the social context, which has inspired many Americans to a greater pursuit of civil rights for all Americans.[8] Indeed, after Kennedy's death the Congress passed many civil rights bills. In Nigeria, Murtala Mohammed led his nation for 202 days. During the short period, his policies acquired a respected image for Nigeria abroad. Internally, efficiency and accountability characterized societal activities, and the spirit of nationalism was kindled. Also, General J.T.U. Aguyi-Ironsi, Nigeria's first military Head of State, ruled for 194 days. He was assassinated in the counter-coup (called by some the "Return Match") of July 1966. Although, during his tenure in office, he seemed to have misunderstood the psychology of Nigerian politics, he nonetheless, passed a measure, the "Unitary Decree" which to a large extent accounted for his untimely death. The "Unitary Decree" practically abolished federalism in favor of unitarism, while maintaining the façade of federalism. Ironically, successive military regimes after General Ironsi have, by their policies, moved Nigeria closer to centralization. In essence, Ironsi saw the need for political and administrative centralism as a therapy for national unity. The successive military regimes put his idea into practice[9]--the very ideas for which he was brutally murdered!

Before the military ostensibly disengaged from politics in 1979, it drew a constitution for the incoming Second Republic. That constitution of 1979, although avowedly federal, nevertheless reflected a tendency toward centralism. The tendency toward centralization has been intensified especially since the second advent of the military. The states are regarded as provinces in their relations with the national government. Major political and administrative appointments in the states must receive the approval of the national government.

In his inaugural address to the nation, Buhari stated the problems he thought induced the military intervention. He said that there was a serious economic predicament resulting in a crisis of confidence, betrayal of the nation's political aspirations, corruption and in discipline.[10] Against this background, Buhari and his team felt that they have been called upon to rake the debris and rebuild a shattered nation. Buhari's administration could be assessed better in the context of how successfully the problems he inherited were solved.

ECONOMIC, SOCIAL AND POLITICAL INHERITANCE

At the time of the Second Republic's death, the country's economy was suffering from severe depression. There was a budget deficit of $8.27 billion.[11] Foreign loan, which was $2.16 billion in 1979, had climbed to $13.77 billion.[12] Worse still, some politicians, exploiting the inertia of the leadership of the Second Republic, carted away more than $10 billion to Europe and the United States.[13] Nigeria's foreign reserve, which in 1979 was $6.75 billion, had gone down to only $1,080 million in 1983.[14] Also, in international trade, Nigeria was experiencing an unfavorable balance. Thus, the military regime inherited a trade deficit of $6.75 billion from the overthrown Republic.[15] Given the condition of the economy, the state governments could not pay the civil servants their salaries. The federal government placed an embargo on hiring as a cost-saving device. However, in taking this measure, the federal government aggravated the unemployment situation. The worst hit were the youth, particularly those in the fifteen years and twenty-four years bracket. This group accounted for thirty-four percent of the unemployed.[16]

Economic depression attracted political instability. The politicians failed the hopes of the masses. Concerned more with their personal aggrandizement and less with finding solutions to issues of national interest, they saw a career in politics as the easiest means of looting public wealth. This resulted in a situation whereby the national treasury emptied as fast as individual politicians became rich. As the elections of 1983 proved, politicians realizing the financial rewards of a career in politics, adopted any feasible approach to ensure their continuity in political office. Thus, callous political hooliganism, cut-throat party competition, and over-rigging were some of the characteristics of the 1983 elections. Polling agents were driven away if they were members of opposition parties. Several Electoral Commission officials were bribed to report results at their own discretion. Votes were often inflated. In some constituencies, there were more votes cast than the number of registered voters.[17]

The results of the 1983 general elections gave an erroneous impression that Nigeria was moving toward a one-party state. This impression derived from the fact that the National Party of Nigeria (NPN) controlled 15 out of the 19 States. There are now 36 states. The elections were not free and fair. The political party with greatest financial resources established the best rigging organization and mechanism and was, thus, best able to secure illegal votes. After the elections, Nigerians lost confidence in the government established through rigging and functioning under false pretenses. With the erosion of confidence in the government, political instability continued. On the whole, Nigeria's Second Republic was a cesspool in which all the weaknesses of the nation gathered. The cesspool thrived on the absence of an enduring constructive leadership. The army watched the country's tragic journey to perdition and felt it had an obligation to redeem the nation. In the light of the above, General Buhari said: "The Armed Forces came into the control of affairs of his country to arrest the drift caused by the ousted regime. . . The objective was to give the country a purposeful sense of direction and thereby advance the march of progress of our people."[18]

REDEMPTIVE ECONOMIC MEASURES

Muhammadu Buhari believed that the depressed economy was largely the result of the political, social and economic orientation of Nigerians. Thus, in order to revamp the economy, the foundations of the nation's sociopolitical and economic existence would have to be rebuilt along the realities of Nigeria's austere economic condition. The rebuilding would involve the pruning of excesses in national expenditure, expunging corruption from Nigeria's social ethics, shifting from dependence on public sector employment to an emphasis on self-employment, encouraging import substitution industrialization based largely on the use of local raw materials, and a tightening of screws on importation.[19]

These redemptive measures were not really a deviation from the economic measures, which the deposed Republic had embarked upon. Buhari's administration put life into what was Shagari's stillborn budget. On May 7, 1984, Buhari unveiled the 1984 budget, after he had reviewed his predecessor's 1983 budget. He made the review in order to make expenditures match available resources. The essentials of Buhari's budget were: I. 15% spending cut from the budget presented in 1983, II. raising of interest rates, III. halting of capital projects, IV. prohibition on borrowing by state governments, V. realignment of import duties, VI. continuation of the ban on recruitment of labor for the federal public service sector, VII. reduction of balance of payment deficit by continuing to cut imports, and VIII. giving priorities to imports of raw materials and spare parts needed for agriculture and industry.[20] Buhari believed that Nigeria's economic solution, to an appreciable extent, depended on diversifying the economy by breaking away from the cycle of an economy dependent upon oil. To this end, Buhari encouraged reviving local industries as well as exploring the nation's agricultural potentials. He was confident that his measures would improve the country's economy. He expressed this confidence when in the 1985 New Year message, he said, *inter alia*, "we have seized the initiative and [we] are on the road to recovery."[21]

Other therapeutic economic measures, which Buhari inaugurated, included counter-trade, currency change and retrenchment in the public sector. In 1984, Nigeria joined a growing number of countries, particularly in Eastern Europe and Latin America, in a counter-trade exercise. Counter-trade, a modern version of barter-trade, was an economic survival strategy for the countries that engaged in it. Indeed, in that year, counter-trade claimed more than 25% of the world trade. In cash terms, that amounted to more than $580 billion. Brazil was Nigeria's first counter-trade partner. In an agreement between the two countries, Brazil lifted 40,000 barrels of Nigeria's crude oil per day for a 12-month period. The crude oil was valued at about $500 million.[22] In return, Nigeria received automobile assembly kits and manufactures worth the same amount. Other countries; Austria, France and Italy, also negotiated counter-trade agreements with Nigeria. By the time Buhari was forced out of office in August 1985, Nigeria had involved itself in counter-trade worth $1,850 million.[23]

After careful and clandestine planning over several months, Buhari's administration announced on April 23, 1984, a change of currency. The exchange exercise was carried out between April 25 and May 6. In the exchange, the N1 note became the color of the existing N20 note, the N5 note that of the N10, the N10 note that of the N1 note, and the N20 note that of the N5 note. The 50 Kobo note remained unchanged. Land borders were closed for the duration of the exercise. Individuals were allowed to change only up to N5000 in old notes for new ones. Any amount over that had to be first deposited in a bank, with an accompanying affidavit attesting to the source and ownership of the notes. The currency change yielded the following results: (i) Large scale currency smuggled, within and beyond Africa, was rendered useless, since they were no longer of legal tender. There were no opportunities to exchange the old currency in foreign countries. (ii) The amount of currency in circulation was drastically reduced. The central bank issued only N3.5 billion of new notes as against the N5.3 billion previously in circulation. (iii) The scarcity of cash flow reduced inflation. For instance, detergent that sold for N2.50 at the time Buhari assumed office was sold for .60K, a 24 percent reduction, at the time he left office. Also, the price of milk plummeted from .80K a tin to N.50K a tin. (iv) The exercise pauperized some Nigerians. Many farmers suffered penury. The farmers who lived in areas, which had no convenient access to banks, were unable to complete the exchange exercise before the deadline. Some did not know the process involved in the exchange exercise. Just as the exercise made some Nigerians poor, it enriched others. All those who were in a position to assist in the exercise realized a financial reward. They served as agents and received 10 percent of the amount to be changed.[24] Bank workers exploited the opportunity.

The most controversial economic adjustment measure was the retrenchment of workers. For Nigerian workers, Buhari's economic recovery therapy was regarded as a crucifixion experience. By the end of 1984, more than 2,000,000 workers in the private sector had lost their jobs.[25] The federal and state civil servants also fared badly. Since the colonial days, to be a civil servant was the dream of most educated Nigerians. This was because employment in the civil service meant job security, as well as advancement in the social and economic ladder of the society. In 1975, Murtala Mohammed shattered the grand notion of the security of tenure in the public service. In that year, at least 10,000 civil servants including 840 from the universities lost their jobs.[26] Buhari, who regarded his regime as an offshoot of that of Murtala Mohammed, reintroduced retrenchment in the public service. Thus, in 1984, more than 200,000 civil servants were either retrenched, dismissed, or retired.[27] Although both Murtala Mohammed and Mohammed Buhari retrenched workers, each did it for a different reason. During Murtala Mohammed's regime, the Nigerian economy was strong enough to sustain the expenditure on the civil service. He regarded retrenchment as a cleansing mechanism to expunge the "deadwood," and assure greater bureaucratic efficiency and accountability. On the other hand, Buhari believed that retrenchment was a cost saving device.

EDUCATION

Buhari's tenure in office was for Nigerian universities a time on the cross. His policy of retrenching university academic and nonacademic staff destroyed morale, fueled the flame of instability in the university system and made academicians a poster child for national ridicule. Since there were no defined parameters for retrenchment, heads of institutions could manufacture reasons for getting rid of any lecturer they felt did not dance to their drumbeat. Veteran professors whose services were a *sine qua non* of academic integrity, felt disgusted with a system that impeded academic progress. Many of them left for overseas and took appointments in many prestigious universities of those countries. However, to the credit of some Vice Chancellors, the retrenchment exercise was not carried out. In some other institutions, the exercise was suspended in bureaucratic limbo. For the Buhari regime to even think of retrenching university dons, when there was a shortage of qualified dons, when in some universities foreign instructors were appointed to fill academic openings at a time the country could ill afford the expenses involved in attracting well-qualified foreign instructors, demonstrates not only a lack of carefully thought out policy, but also shows Buhari as a non-visionary leader.

Realizing Nigeria's need to promote science education, the Obasanjo and Shagari regimes respectively established universities of technology in different parts of the country. Cities such as Owerri, Yola, Abeokuta, Bauchi, and Minna became sites of new universities of technology. The intent for creating these institutions was to bring Nigeria up to speed in the field of technological development. Apparently, Buhari's regime did not appreciate the importance of science in the development of a nation. His administration annulled the charter that empowered the new science universities to develop independently. By that annulment, the universities of technology were merged with the traditional universities. For instance, the Federal University of Technology in Yola was merged with the University of Maiduguri under the latter's administrative lordship. The one in Abeokuta was merged with the University of Lagos. This apparent decision not to give priority to science education contributed to making Nigeria lag in technological progress.

Historians would no doubt wonder about the rationale for Buhari's posture toward education. Retrenchment in universities was carried out as foreign instructors were imported into the country. Science education was deprioritized when other developing nations made technological development a priority. Measures and policies were introduced which demoralized academic constituencies of the university, although morale boost is an essential ingredient for enhancing any institution's productivity. One could rightly argue that Buhari's policy on education was built on philosophical confusion characterized by a misplaced mission.

ETHICAL PURIFICATION

Muhammad Buhari felt that it was not just enough to restore life to the nation's ailing economy. It was equally important to purify the ethics of the Nigerians as a base on which to re-establish a socially, economically and politically healthy society. In the above spirit, he detained 475 former politicians including all the former civilian governors.[28] Those detained were alleged to have corruptly enriched themselves or increased the funds of their respective parties at the expense of the national treasury. Rightly, the culture of corruption had often negated efforts at building a viable nation. Buhari, in keeping with his stated commitment to rid the country of rampant corruption, believed that drastic punishment for the politicians found guilty of corruption would deter future politicians from indulging in corruption. To this end, Buhari's administration set up military tribunals for the trial of former politicians. The members of the tribunals were sworn in, in Lagos on April 11, 1984. There were five chairmen and twenty members. These tribunals were grouped into Enugu, Jos, Kaduna, Lagos and Ibadan zones. The tribunals derived their authority from Decree Three, "Recovery of Public Property." The members of the tribunal could impose a range of penalties on those found guilty. The court of law could not review their verdicts. The tribunals acted slowly and consequently, a majority of the detainees remained in prison throughout the tenure of Buhari's leadership.

Buhari was not the originator of ethical purification. His predecessors had initiated the quest for a disciplined society. General Olusegun Obasanjo, who handed political power to the civilians in 1979 in his Jaji address on September 12, 1977, had called for a fair, just, disciplined and humane society. Obasanjo's Jaji declaration was essentially a call for moral rearmament, which would eliminate a culture of "get-rich-quick" at any price and by any means. During the Second Republic, President Shehu Shagari had also inaugurated an "Ethical Revolution," appropriately placed in the ministry of National Guidance. However, the Ethical Revolution did not achieve its objective; if anything, corruption took charge of Shagari's regime. On the other hand, Buhari seemed determined to succeed where his predecessors had failed. In appointing his cabinet, he indicated that he was "searching for competent Nigerians of proven integrity, a high sense of discipline, public probity and transparent honesty."[29]

Buhari argued that a national war was needed to tackle the country's ethical problem. He, therefore, invited all Nigerians to a collective assault on societal ills. Accordingly, Major General Tunde

Idiagbon, Buhari's chief of staff, Supreme Head Quarters, in his address at the close of the session of the National Council of Information on March 20, 1984, exhorted the nation's leadership to instill the ideals of national consciousness, patriotism and discipline in the citizenry. Idiagbon initiated a series of blueprints for achieving the goal. The blueprints were embodied in what became "War Against Indiscipline" (WAI). Idiagbon identified thirty-five personal, moral and environmental offenses. The eradication of each of the offenses constituted a phase of the war against indiscipline. Public enlightenment centers were set up in the different states. These centers were directed by a "committee for enlightenment and consciousness." The committee in each state was responsible for organizing and launching the phases of W.A.I. By August 1985 when Buhari was overthrown, only five phases of W.A.I. were launched. A determined effort to sustain W.A.I. did not survive the ouster of General Buhari. At the time of its inauguration, Nigerians responded positively. However, the positive response was due to fear of possible punishment, for not complying with the rules of W.A.I. For Nigerians, it needed a holistic societal transformation to effect a positive change in the social, economic, and political attitude. In any case, tormented by economic adversity and haunted by the uncertainty of the future, the generality of Nigerians became more concerned with economic survival than with ethical regeneration.

FOREIGN POLICY

In principle, Buhari's foreign policy positions did not deviate from those of his predecessor. In his New Year broadcast, Buhari assured the world that his government would maintain and strengthen existing diplomatic relations with other states and would honor all treaty obligations.[30] However, the financial restrictions, which Nigeria was experiencing, was expected to force Buhari to curtail some of the country's foreign policy commitments. In general, Buhari would demonstrate his own style of diplomacy. His approach was cautiously assertive. The region of emphasis shifted slightly to Africa and particularly to Nigeria's neighbors. In line with the above, Dr. Ibrahim Gambari, Buhari's minister of External Affairs, stated the foreign policy priorities of Buhari's administration thus: (i) Africa was regarded as the centerpiece of Nigeria's diplomatic activities. Africa's central position derives from its being Nigeria's primary environment. (ii) A good relationship with Nigeria's neighbors was emphasized. This policy was necessary for Nigeria's security, since the neighbors could be used by other nations to excite upheaval in Nigeria or the neighbors themselves could threaten Nigeria's territorial integrity.   (iii)   Promoting the prosperity of the West African state. (iv) Strengthening of the security of the West African region by emphasizing the need for the states to collectivize their efforts in resisting and repelling external aggression.[31]

It was indeed necessary for Buhari to develop a policy of good relations with Nigeria's neighbors. Nigeria and Cameroons had clashed over a piece of land in Cross River; there was also a conflict over a village in Sokoto State between   Nigeria and Niger.   These developments underlined the necessity to establish a good working relationship between Nigeria and her neighbors. But some of Buhari's actions did not support the "good neighbor" policy. Indeed, four months after becoming the Head of State, in April 1984, Buhari closed the borders between Nigeria and her neighbors. The borders remained closed until February 28, 1986 when Buhari's successor re-opened them. The closure of the borders had greater economic underpinning than political. The following factors influenced Buhari's action: First, to stop or at least minimize currency smuggling across the border; Second, to achieve a successful currency exchange; Third, to assure that former politicians did not escape through the borders; and Fourth,   to control the in-flow of illegal immigrants.

In addition to closing the borders, Buhari repatriated illegal aliens, a majority of whom, were from the neighboring countries. Shehu Shagari had begun the process of expelling illegal aliens when about 2,000,000 were asked to leave Nigeria by January 31, 1983. Buhari continued the policy. The expulsion of illegal aliens dimmed the glow of Nigeria's relations with her neighbors and greatly undermined the "good neighbor policy" which many Nigerians had expected the Buhari regime to follow. The expulsion of an estimated 700,000 illegal aliens could be defended on economic, and perhaps security, grounds.[32] However, the clinical ruthlessness with which the exercise was executed traumatized the victims. Thus, critics emphasized that the approach was inhuman.

In the other regions of Africa, Buhari's policies were commendable, at least from the perspective of African nationalism. His administration took the initiative in finding solutions to the problems of the regions. Nigeria made great financial commitments to the O.A.U. Liberation fund. The process of Namibia's independence negotiations troubled Buhari's government. In particular, his government opposed linking the withdrawal of the Cuban troops with the granting of independence to Namibia. The Nigerian government urged O.A.U.

member-states to carry out economic sanctions against the countries that were obstructing the progress of Namibian independence negotiations. Furthermore, Buhari appealed for greater O.A.U. moral, political and diplomatic support for the frontline states in the latter's efforts to consolidate their security. In regard to the conflict in Western Sahara, the Buhari administration supported the Polisario's application to attend O.A.U. summit meetings and O.A.U. council of ministers meetings. In the Chad crisis, Buhari's administration continued to adhere to the principles which guided Shehu Shagari's approach and these were: First, that the Chadians, themselves, were best able to find solutions to their nation's problems. In essence, external involvement would be counter-productive in terms of peace in Chad. Second, that national reconciliation is regarded as a *sine qua non* of peace in Chad. In this context, the different parties in conflict should dissolve their differences in order to achieve a lasting peace among themselves. And, Third, that all foreign troops in Chad should evacuate the country to allow for national reconciliation.[33]

Nigeria's relation with Britain was sour. This was largely because the Buhari regime felt that Britain did not cooperate with Buhari in his effort to repatriate political fugitives in Britain who had looted the country during the Second Republic. Alhaji Umaru Dikko was one of the fugitive offenders wanted by the Buhari regime to answer charges of enriching himself during the Second Republic. It was alleged that Dikko had deposited $250 million in a bank in Central London. Buhari's administration had asked the British government to repatriate Dikko, but the former did not honor the request. On July 5, 1984, attempts were made in London to kidnap Umaru Dikko. The effort failed. There was suspicion that the Buhari government had knowledge of, and indeed master-minded, the abortive kidnap attempt. Although it could not empirically be proven that the Nigerian government was an accomplice in the episode, the kidnap drama provoked a diplomatic row that resulted in retaliatory expulsion of diplomats. The development led to a chill on the traditionally cordial relationship, which had existed between Britain and Nigeria.[34] Besides the Dikko affair, Britain's Export Credit Guarantee Department insistance on an IMF program before it could reschedule insured trade arrears, displeased the Buhari administration.[35] Buhari and Nigeria had much to lose if they failed to sustain the symbiotic relationship, which had existed between them since Nigeria's independence. Britain had been Nigeria's major-trade partner, a partnership that weighed more in favor of Britain. She would hate to lose Nigeria's import market. Furthermore, in major world issues, Nigeria, in the spirit of commonwealth comradeship, often followed Britain's lead. On the other hand, Nigeria enjoyed, perhaps, not realizing it, psychological dependence on Britain. Consequently, although the diplomatic relationship between the two countries during Buhari's tenure seemed uneasy, nonetheless, that uneasiness did not lead to an irreparable diplomatic rupture.

During Buhari's regime, Nigeria did not enjoy high priority in American foreign policy considerations. Nigeria argued that the United States had not done much to hasten Namibia's independence and the dismantling of South Africa's Apartheid structure. Furthermore, far from employing activistic approach to support the aspirations of the Namibians and the majority population in South Africa, the United States government, under President Ronald Reagan, advocated a policy of "constructive engagement" as a solution to the southern Africa problems. Buhari's regime felt that mere dialogue would not result in quick solution. It could be argued that American posture, towards African aspirations, was perceived by Buhari's government as counter productive. At best, Nigeria's relation with the United States during Burhari's administration was cautiously pragmatic.

President Ibrahim Babangida who ousted Buhari alleged that the latter anchored his diplomacy on "vengeful considerations" by conducting his foreign relations "in a policy of retaliatory reactions."[36] In fairness to Buhari and placed in proper perspective, "retaliatory reaction" is an important component of diplomacy. No nation voluntarily turns the other cheek for a second diplomatic slap. If anything, a sovereign state reacts aggressively when slapped diplomatically. On an overall assessment, it is fair to state that an air of stiffness characterized Buhari's diplomatic style. This posture argued poorly for Nigeria in its negotiations with international interests to reschedule the country's external debts. It was partly in this context, that 44% of Nigeria's budget was used in servicing debts. This measure aggravated the country's economic depression.

CONCLUSION

General Buhari hoped to instill in Nigerians a sense of purpose and direction. He moved Nigerians away from taking shelter in self-delusion and urged them to adjust their lives along the economic realities of the country. In pursuit of this purpose, Buhari subjected the generality of Nigerians to a stringent economic life. All were forced to adapt to a life of austerity. Also economic discipline went concurrently with social discipline. Nigerians had to cultivate respect for order. In what could be regarded as the crisis of survival, Nigerians took comfort in the hope that the drastic economic measures were an aberration, which would pass away with time.

Although General Buhari's intentions were genuine since he hoped that his economic measures would save the country, some of the policies ruined the lives of Nigerians. Workers were retired before their time, others were retrenched on the flimsiest excuses, and still some were either terminated or dismissed from heir jobs. Most of those who were retired experienced the agonizing protocol of the bureaucracy in receiving their entitlement. In a country without social security, those who lost their jobs, for whatever reason, resigned themselves to a life without hope. Buhari's administration did nothing to ameliorate the plight of the suffering Nigerians. In the given situation, the victims of the economic measures would not see a meaningful purpose in Buhari's regime. Thus, Buhari's purpose of redemption became a crisis for Nigerians.

As workers were being retrenched, the government instituted different types of levies. There were levies for education, despite the re-introduction of school fees in many states, levies for community self-help projects, and literally speaking, the mere existence of an individual was levied, for it appeared that to be alive meant to be levied. Indeed, the regime was so characterized by all sorts of levies that Dr. Stanley Macebuh, a respected journalist satirized Buhari's regime with the name, "call me levy."[37]

Critics have argued, and to a great extent with merit, that Buhari encouraged "Northernocracy." In this context, "Northernocracy" is the political hegemony of Northerners over the South. The pendulum of political power leaned in favor of the Northern region of Nigeria. Of the 19 members of Buhari's Supreme Military Council, 12 were Northerners, and 11 of the 18 ministries were presided over by ministers of Northern provenance. Furthermore, the North enjoyed the leadership of strategic ministries. Northern ministers were in charge of Education, Defense, Foreign Affairs, Internal Affairs, Works and Housing, Mines, Power and Steel. The term, North, in this respect, refers to the conventional geographical north as opposed to the Muslim North. Because Buhari promoted "Northernocracy" his regime experienced an intense call for confederation and a bitter criticism of his "federal character" policies. Ironically, the call for confederation came loudest from some senior military officers who had fought the civil war to assure the political unity of Nigeria. This phenomenon eroded the confidence of some Nigerians in the ability of the army to unite the country.[38]

Buhari must have regarded himself as a disciple of benevolent despotism. Believing that he understood better than anyone else the intricacies and dynamics of power, he expected unquestioned loyalty from Nigerians. He turned a deaf ear to public opinion. Buhari's insensitivity to public opinion made Professor Wole Soyinka, West Africa's first Nobel Prize Winner, say that the government was "a deaf one."[39] For the 19 months he was in power, Buhari enacted 30 decrees. Of particular note are Decrees No. 2 (State Security Detention Order), and Decree No. 13 (The Supremacy and Enforcement of Powers). These decrees denied Nigerians their fundamental human rights as well as their rights to due process and granted Buhari broad powers, which were oligarchically hegemonic in nature. All aspects of the lives of Nigerians experienced oppressive imperial over-reach. Decree 20, (Miscellaneous Offenses Decree) gave the administrators power to imprison individuals whose acts the government deemed offensive to societal decency. It placed strict limit on the funds that private newspapers can use to import newsprint and other essential materials. Beyond the import restriction, the Decree also provided prison sentence for a journalist who publishes what the government considers false information about a government official or information that brings an official into contempt. Under the Decree, Duro Onabule of the National Concord was detained for two weeks. The government did not state the charges against him. Nduka Iraboh, assistant news editor and Tunde Thompson, senior diplomatic correspondent, both of the Guardian newspaper were sent to jail for one year.[40] In the end, Buhari succeeded in making Nigerians feel that they were his enemy and that he designed his policies to punish them, rather than ameliorate life for them.

It is proper to regard General Buhari's regime as one characterized by a crisis of purpose. The implementation of his purpose produced unsavory effects on the Nigerians. The redemptive measures appeared so stringent that they ruined the lives of those they sought to elevate. The tragedy is that Nigerians would never know if at the end of it all, the nation would have been rejuvenated by Buhari's measures. It could be said with certainty that Buhari's administration did not leave an enduring legacy on Nigeria's political landscape. Devoid of success in restoring a healthy economy, and punitive in administrative style, the Buhari regime came to an abrupt end. Ironically, the Nigerian masses, who suffered much under the regime did not demand the regime's demise. It was the army which created it that also killed it. General Ibrahim

Babangida, who overthrew Buhari argued that he came to put a human face on a military regime and in the process correct the maladministation of his predecessor. But, in the final analysis, it was difficult for General Buhari to reconcile the good intentions of his measures with their devastating effect on the lives of the majority of the Nigerians. The failure to create a balance induced a crisis, which undermined Buhari's purpose and contributed to his ouster.

ENDNOTES

1. "Nigeria: The Inevitable" *Africa Confidential*, Vol.25, No.1. January 4,1984, I.

2. *West Africa*, January 9, 1984, 53.

3. *Africa Confidential*, *op cit*, 1.

4. "Nigeria: The Inevitable" *op cit*.

5. *West Africa*, *ibid*, 51.

6. *West Africa*, January 30, 1984, 242.

7. *Africa Confidential*, January 4, 1984, I.

8. Arthur Schlesinger. *John F. Kennedy: A Thousand Days*. Boston, 1965

9. Levi A. Nwachuku, "A Past in the Present: General J. T. U. Aguiui Ironsi, A Captive of History." Paper delivered at Social Science Seminar, University of Maiduguri, Maiduguri, Nigeria, June 5, 1987.

10. See "Moment of Truth," Buhari's New Year Broadcast, *West Africa*, January 8, 1984, 56-57.

11. *Daily Times* (Nigeria) April 4, 1985, 5.

12. Arthur Nzeribe, *Nigeria: Another Hope Betrayed*, London, Kilmanjoro Pres, 1985, 48.

13. *New Africa*, July 1984, 19.

14. Arthur Nzeribe *op cit*, 72.

15. *Newswatch* (Nigeria) June 17, 1985, 15.

16. *African Business,* February 1984, 14.

17. In a discussion with a former polls agent, this writer learned that some poll agents simply added several zeroes to the total votes of any party that controlled any given constituency, thus inflating the votes. See also *Africa Confidential*, September 21, 2983, 2.

18. See General Buhari's interview with *Africa Now*, October 1984, 49

19. *Africa Now*, *ibid*, 55.

20. *African Events*, February 1985, 13.

21. *Africa Report*, July-August 1984, 5.

22. *Newswatch* (Nigeria) July 15, 1985,14.

23. *Ibid.,* 11-12.

24. This was revealed to this writer by several victims who wish their identity to be protected.

25. *Africa Events op cit*, 1984, 12.

26. Levi A. Nwachuku, "Murtale Mohammed: A Revolutionary Leader" *Journal of African-Afro-American Affairs*, Spring 1979, 40.

27. *Africa Events, op cit*, 12.

28. *Africa Research Bulletin*, vol. 21, no. 4. April 1-30, 1984, 7219.

29. *Facts-on-File*, January 27, 1984, 61.
30. *West Africa*, January 9, 1984, 57.
31. See Ibrahim Gambari interview with *Africa Reports*, May/June 1984, 45.
32. *African Research Bulletin*, May 31, 1985, 7712.
33. See Ibrahim Gambari, *Africa Report. op cit*
34. *West Africa*, July 16, 1984, 1462.
35. *Africa Report*, July-August, 1985, 9.
36. *Newswatch* (Nigeria) September 9, 1985, 24.
37. *The Guardian* (Nigeria) January 26, 1985.
38. *African Concord* (Nigeria) August 7, 1986, 12.
39. *Newswatch op cit ibid.*
40. *Africa Report*, January-February, 1985, 36.

General Ibrahim Badamasi Babangida
Military President and Head of State
August 1985-August 1993

Chapter Eight

Collapse of Purpose:
Ibrahim Babangida, 1985-1993

J. I. Dibua

INTRODUCTION

General Ibrahim Babangida came to power through a military coup, overthrowing the regime of General Muhammadu Buhari in August 1985. Serious social, political and economic problems had plagued Nigeria from the Second Republic (1979-1983). The debilitating economic crisis and the tensions that arose from the obvious rigging of the December 1983 elections had almost brought the country to the brink of collapse. The Buhari regime, which came to power after the coup of December 1983, as we saw, had given itself the task of getting the country out of the quagmire into which it had been thrown. The regime stated that indiscipline was the primary cause of the various problems that plagued Nigeria. It therefore launched a campaign against indiscipline, officially called the War Against Indiscipline (WAI). Campaigns were also launched against corruption, there were massive retrenchment of workers in all sectors of the government service, and various attempts were made to promote economic and budgetary discipline. But these programs were carried out with high handedness: human rights were frequently violated under this authoritarian regime, a situation that alienated many people.

One way in which Buhari had sought to ameliorate the economic crisis was through a balance of payment support loan from the International Monetary Fund (IMF). Like the Shagari administration before it, there were serious disagreements with the administrators of the IMF over their insistence on programs like devaluation, privatization and removal of subsidies from social sectors before such a loan could be granted. Thus, there was an impasse with the IMF. This was the situation when Babangida carried out his coup on August 27, 1985.

In contrast to his predecessor, Babangida stated right from the beginning that the cornerstone of his administration's policies would be respect for human rights. This would include involvement of the people in government policies through widespread consultations and public debates, amelioration of the economic crisis and the breaking of the impasse with the IMF. In fact, his commitment to resolve the logjam with the IMF tended to create the impression that his coup was a pro-IMF coup. To convince the people about his commitment to human rights, one of the first steps Babangida took was to abrogate Decree 4 under which some journalists had been detained by the Buhari regime for publishing what was said to be false information. He also released the detained journalists. In addition, pressure groups and professional associations such as the National Association of Nigerian Students (NANS) and the Nigerian Medical Association (NMA), which had been banned by the Buhari regime, were now made legal. To demonstrate Babangida's resolve to involve the people in public policy, the IMF loan was subjected to a far-reaching public debate. The outcome was a massive popular rejection of the loan. Although the Babangida regime had stated that it would respect public opinion on the loan by not taking it, Babangida went ahead to introduce the Economic Emergency Act of October 1985 and implement all the conditions of the IMF which had been rejected by the people. This amounted to a subversion of the popular will.

Upon his assumption of power, Babangida promised to set in motion a transition program to lead to the handover of power to a democratically elected civilian regime. Initially this changeover was set for October 1990 but later it was extended to 1992, and then to 1993. He stated that in order to avoid the pitfalls of previous democratic experiments, far-reaching steps were to be taken to set in motion the processes that would promote an enduring democracy and development in the Third Republic. Sam Oyovbaire and Tunji Olagunju, two leading

Nigerian political scientists who occupied important positions in the Babangida regime, have argued that through the systematic activation of particular decisions, policies and programs by an historically informed leadership, Babangida set in motion revolutionary policies which helped to lay the foundations for a new Nigeria. According to them, this is the main factor that distinguished the Babangida administration from previous ones.[1] The aim of this chapter is to examine the extent to which Babangida was able to establish the conditions for sustainable development and an enduring and democratic Third Republic. In any case, while the human rights policies and the conduct of public debates helped at the initial stage to win some degree of legitimacy for the Babangida regime, the major step he took was the setting up of the Political Bureau in January 1986. This was aimed at assuring Nigerians that unlike the Buhari regime, which did not set out a clear program for transition to civil rule, Babangida's regime was committed to fashioning out a program for transition to a sustainable democratic system. The next section examines the report and recommendations of the Political Bureau.

THE POLITICAL BUREAU

The Political Bureau was set up with the mandate of providing a roadmap for the establishment of an enduring democracy and sustainable development in the future Third Republic.[2] Its recommendations were to constitute the blueprint for the program of transition to civil rule. The Political Bureau, which had among its sixteen members some of the most articulate and intelligent Nigerians, was to base its recommendations on the wishes and aspirations of the majority of the people. It therefore organized wide-ranging consultations and debates all over the country among various interest groups, sections and classes of Nigerians. To ensure that as many Nigerians as possible were involved, debates were conducted in indigenous languages for those people who could not speak English. Since so many attempts were made to involve all segments of the Nigerian society in the debate, the outcome was bound to be a reflection of the popular will. In March 1987, the Bureau submitted its report.

The report, which was a thorough and comprehensive analysis of all aspects of Nigerian society, was divided into three parts. The first part, which examined the background to Nigeria's political experience, stated that Nigeria is a class society. It noted that colonialism had created dependent structures in Nigeria, that have subjugated her economy and politics to the interests of international monopoly capital. The report argued that the reproduction of these structures in post-colonial Nigeria is responsible for the continued state of underdevelopment.

Part Two of the report discussed the need for a new political order for Nigeria: it dealt extensively with various aspects of society. The report regarded proper identification of a specific philosophy of government, which derived its values, mores and aspirations from the Nigerian people, as vital for the development of a new social, political and economic order for Nigeria. The Nigerian masses were emphatic in their contributions to the political debate on the need to establish adequate social, economic and political rights, which were regarded as indispensable to the existence and realization of social justice. Consequently, the Bureau noted the indispensability of a new political economy for the evolution of political and social systems that would be self-reliant, just, democratic and durable. As a result the report recommended that

> Nigeria should adopt a socialist socioeconomic system in which the state shall be committed to the nationalization and socialization of the commanding heights of the national economy.... [The] private sector should be limited to agriculture and small/medium scale industries.[3]

Furthermore it stated that

> Socioeconomic power should be democratized through political and economic participation in all structures and organizations of power. The economy should be restructured largely along the socialist pattern with emphasis on self-reliance and social justice. Leadership should derive directly from the masses of the people in consonance with the ideology and philosophy of socialism.[4]

In order to be able to develop and consolidate this proposed new democratic social, political and economic order, the Political Bureau emphasized the indispensability of a new political culture. Such a culture must emphasize things like public enlightenment and education, mass mobilization towards the achievement of set objectives, discipline, loyalty, true patriotism, commitment, dedication and accountability to the Nigerian state. It should be noted that a mass mobilization exercise would only be relevant within this context of a new political economy. We shall return to this issue later.

The third part of the Political Bureau's report was mainly concerned with the program of transition to civil rule. It noted that for a transition to civil rule program to be successful there was the need to democratize all the processes and institutions of government and that the majority of the people should be involved in the process. It called for a broadly spaced transition in which democratic government can proceed with political learning, institutional adjustment and a re-orientation of political culture at sequential levels of politics and governance, beginning with the local government and proceeding to the federal level.

What logically follows from the Political Bureau's report is that, given the comprehensive and far-reaching nature of its recommendations and the fact that there were inputs from a majority of Nigerians from all segments, classes and ethnic groups, the report represented the wishes and aspirations of most Nigerians. In fact, for the first time in Nigeria's post-colonial history, an opportunity was given to the people to make vital inputs into the process of governance. A faithful implementation of the recommendations would have been capable of laying the foundations for an enduring and self-sustaining democratic Third Republic, which was what Babangida had mandated the Bureau to do. However the Babangida administration missed the opportunity of performing this historic role when it rejected the two key recommendations of the Bureau, namely, a socialist ideology for Nigeria and the termination of the neo-colonial political economy. It claimed that to accept socialism would amount to imposing an alien ideology on the people. But as we have already noted this recommendation was based on the expressed wishes of the people. This point becomes more glaring when it is realized that only four of the sixteen members of the Bureau had socialist leanings and so they could not have imposed their wish on the majority of the members.[5] Some scholars have argued that while the recommendation of a socialist ideology was based on a thorough analysis of the problems that have inhibited the country's development and therefore the need to effectively come to terms with the problems, the recommendation can only be properly understood if situated within the context of the liberal political theory that underlined the entire report. Hence they argued that the socialism of the Bureau was "the socialism of social democracy."[6] This then makes the rejection of the socialist ideology more untenable.[7]

Secondly, the recommendation that the International Monetary Fund (IMF)-induced adjustment policies and programs should be terminated because they were helping to exacerbate the problems of neo-colonial dependency and underdevelopment in Nigeria was rejected. On the contrary, the Babangida regime argued that the Structural Adjustment Program (SAP) was vital for laying the basis of a self-reliant economy in the country.[8] Yet SAP was an alien imposition.[9] The Babangida regime's position therefore amounted to a subversion of the people's will.

Having rejected the kernel of the Bureau's report on the need for a new philosophy of governance, the regime went ahead to implement other recommendations which would have been relevant only within the context that they would have helped to establish and sustain the new governmental philosophy. A. T. Gana has observed that "taken outside this context, the entire corpus of activities and institutions articulated in the transition program provide no more than an edifice whose foundations are as fragile as the materials used." What is apparent so far is that programs of transformation that were based on this position of the regime were from the beginning fatally flawed. Another point that should be made is that while dismissing the key recommendations of the Bureau, the programs that were implemented were in the main influenced by the World Bank.[11] It is within this context that we are going to examine the various policies and programs that were put in place by the Babangida administration. The policies and programs that will be examined are mass mobilization, administrative reforms, rural development, economic policies, and the transition to civil rule program. The regime's foreign policy will also be examined.

MASS MOBILIZATION

As we have already noted, a cardinal recommendation of the Political Bureau was the need for the establishment of a new social order, which would promote social justice, viable and enduring democracy, and self-sustaining development. The Bureau regarded the inauguration of a new political culture as an indispensable condition for the success of the new social order. It recommended that public enlightenment and education, as well as mass mobilization should be pursued in order to be able to achieve the new social order. Toward this end, the Babangida regime established the Directorate for Mass Mobilization, Social and Economic Reconstruction (MAMSER) as one of the transition agencies. It is important to note that in line with the Bureau's report this mobilization is only meaningful within the context of contributing to the termination of the neo-colonial dependency and the democratization of socioeconomic power. This would be done through popular political and economic participation in all structures and of power in such a way that leadership would derive from the masses of the people.

Oyovbaire and Olagunju have argued that the establishment of MAMSER was one of the very bold and far-reaching decisions of the Babangida administration. They noted that compared to previous attempts at mobilizing Nigerians, like the campaign to "Keep Nigeria One" under Gowon, "Operation Feed the Nation" under the military regime of Obasanjo, "Ethical Revolution" under Shagari and the "War Against Indiscipline" under Buhari, MAMSER's mandate was no doubt the most fundamental and far-reaching. It was, after all, an agency that was to mobilize all Nigerians for the attainment of social justice and economic self-reliance.[12]

But as we have already pointed out, the Babangida administration rejected the key recommendation of the Bureau, that is, the attainment of a new social order through terminating neo-colonial dependency. On the contrary, it put in place policies that were helping to entrench this dependency. It thus follows that, right from the beginning, MAMSER was not in the position to achieve any meaningful result. Perhaps the best that can be said about MAMSER is that it ended up to mobilize Nigerians fitfully in support of the sustenance of the existing neo-colonial structures, as well as the increasingly corrupt and autocratic Babangida regime. This fundamental contradiction made MAMSER to lack a clear focus and militated against its success.

Rather than recognize this fact Oyovbaire and Olagunju began their search for scapegoats to blame for the failure of the program. According to them:

> True to the volatile and democratic nature of the Nigerian society, MAMSER has incurred a measure of indifference, cynicism and indeed, hostility of members of the elite class who engage in a running battle with the Directorate and the Government.
>
> Some of such people, including elements in government agencies, are puzzled that the regime could create an institution to prod it and awaken the people who now ask serious and searching questions at community meetings, gatherings, etc.[13]

It is however, clear from the foregoing discussion that this analysis is far from correct. MAMSER was at best a deformed child from birth.

ADMINISTRATIVE REFORMS

One important recommendation of the Political Bureau was that in order to successfully carry out the policies, which were to be put in place to promote the new social order, there was the need to fundamentally restructure governmental institutions. Particularly significant in this regard were the civil service and local governments. From the attainment of political independence in 1960, there had been calls for the reform of the civil service, which had retained its inherited colonial character of merely helping to maintain law and order and to routinely implement policies. The civil servants had not been given much room to use their initiative. As a result of this colonial heritage, the civil servant did not appreciate the fact that his primary responsibility was to help to promote the welfare of the generality of the people. Rather there was the tendency of adopting a paternalistic attitude towards the common people.

The schism within the civil service, especially between professional and administrators cadre did not help matters. Due to the emphasis on routine administrative functions, the administrative class had come to occupy a superior position over the professional class. It was only from among the administrative class that appointments could be made to the prestigious post of permanent secretary and it was from among the latter group that the Head of the Civil Service was appointed. In addition, there was the feud between the Permanent Secretary and the Minister or Commissioner (as they were designated under successive military regimes before that of Babangida) who was the political head of the ministry. This feud arose mainly out of the position of the Permanent Secretary as the chief accounting officer, in line with the provisions of the 1963 constitution. This situation was worsened by the powerful position Permanent Secretaries occupied under the military regime of Yakubu Gowon. Some of the functions normally performed by ministers were delegated to Permanent Secretaries with some of them, the so-called "Super Permanent Secretaries," being in the position to undermine and frustrate their commissioners (as they were then called) who were statutorily supposed to be the head of their respective ministries.

An appreciation of the above problems and the need to resolve them had led to the setting up of various review commissions in the period between 1963 and 1985. The commissions included the Morgan Commission of 1963, the Adebo Commission of 1971, the Udoji Commission of 1974 and the Dotun Phillips Study Group of 1985. Although the various commissions had made recommendations on how to make the civil service more effective, apart from the issues that had to do with salaries, no meaningful steps were taken to implement the other recommendations. For instance, the Udoji Commission had recommended that the post of Permanent Secretary should be abolished and the Phillips Study Group not only reechoed this recommendation but also made other important recommendations on how to restructure the civil service to make it relevant to the developmental requirements of Nigeria. Not until the Babangida civil service reforms of 1988 were meaningful attempts made to address the issue.

As already noted, the Political Bureau recommended the reorganization of the civil service in order to reorientate the civil servant to see his primary responsibility as helping to attain the aims and objectives of the government and to promote the welfare of the majority of the people. Under the 1988 reform, the Minister or Commissioner became both the Chief Executive and Accounting Officer of his ministry. The position of Permanent Secretary was abolished and replaced with that of the Director General. This became a political position since unless reappointed by the incoming administration the Director General was to leave office with the government that had appointed him or her. Also, the dichotomy between the administrative and professional cadres was removed since the civil service was professionalized and every officer would now make a career within a particular Department and Ministry. Toward this end each Ministry or extra-ministerial department was not to have more than eight departments. Out of these, three were mandatory-- the Departments of Personnel Management; Finance and Supplies; and Planning, Research and Statistics.[14]

It is clear that, at least in theory, that civil service reform planners made some attempts to address the various structural and organizational problems in the service and that they sought to eliminate internal feuds. In this regard, Babangida showed a greater appreciation of the problems that confronted the civil service than previous administrations. However, some criticisms that have been made against the reforms are that by making the position of the Director General a temporary political appointment, many seasoned and efficient civil servants, particularly relatively younger ones might not be willing to accept the position. Also since important decisions regarding the fate of career civil servants were to be taken by political appointees, there was the danger of politicizing the civil service. In addition, the fact that both the Minister and Director General know that their appointments are temporary could encourage them to abuse their positions through corrupt practices.[15] Perhaps more significant is the fact that in certain respects the reform was carried out half-heartedly. Some important recommendations of the Political Bureau, which were crucial for the success of the reforms, were not implemented. These included ending the very low morale of civil servants through motivational factors such as improvement in their conditions of service and the provision of adequate staff development and training facilities.

Another significant aspect of the administrative reforms pertained to local governments. This was particularly necessary in view of the very important role that the report of the Bureau assigned to local governments as the tier of government closest to the people. Before 1988, meaningful attempts had not been made to improve the position of local governments, which lacked autonomy and remained subservient to the state governments. The 1976 local government reforms had sought to rectify this situation by providing for an autonomous local government system with a statutory grant of revenue and specific allocated functions, some of which were exclusive to the local governments. The Fourth Schedule of the 1979 constitution concretized these developments by clearly spelling out the functions of local governments.[16] But these measures at best remained nothing more than a mere declaration of intents.[17] The recommendations of the Dasuki Committee in 1985 on the imperative of an autonomous local government system if it was to effectively perform its role did not elicit any better response.[18] It is against this background that Babangida sought to tackle the issue of the local government system.

The first major step the regime took in this regard was contained in Babangida's Independence Day address of October 1, 1988, in which he stated inter alia:

> From our experience, we have realized that local government is closest to the people. It is also the bedrock of our projected democratic order and is admirably well-placed to tackle and resolve most of the issues and problems that confront our people... (Local governments) are there to ensure collective participation in governance, motivate physical and economic development, create the conditions for employment opportunities, and provide social services which can improve the well being of our people.[19]

Babangida went on to announce measures which would make local governments more effective. They include the abolition of state-run [or] federally-run local government ministries in all the states of the federation and the sending of local governments' share of the federation account directly to them. State governments were asked to take their hands off those functions that were exclusive to local governments.

These measures represented the first systematic attempts at enhancing the status of local governments. But this autonomy was vitiated by some of the provisions contained in the guidelines for the application of the civil service reforms to the local government service. For instance, although the elected local government Chairman was the chief executive and accounting officer and presided over the finance and general purposes committee, this elected official was not a signatory to the accounts of the local government council. These were the responsibilities of the local government secretary and the local government treasurer who were appointees of the state government, thereby subordinating the Chairman to these state government officials.[20] It was in an attempt to resolve this anomaly that in 1991, it was provided, among others, that these elected Chairmen should be signatories to local government accounts and should appoint their local government Secretaries whose tenure were to be tied to those of the Chairmen. While the reforms to some extent helped to improve the position of local governments, an important recommendation of the Political Bureau on the democratization of local governments in order to make them more effective instruments of mobilization of the people and for rural development was not implemented.[21]

RURAL DEVELOPMENT

The Political Bureau noted that for the new social order in which there would be self-reliance, social and economic justice to be achieved, it was imperative that the majority of the people should be mobilized and involved in the various processes and institutions of governance. Toward this end there was the need to transform the rural areas where about 70 percent of the people live. In this regard local governments were to play a crucial role in the development and social transformation of the rural areas. They were also to play a significant role in the mobilization of rural dwellers for popular and democratic participation in governance. In fact, local governments were to act as a preparatory stage for future political leaders at higher levels of government.

The Bureau recommended that for an effective performance of the above roles, local governments must be democratized. This democratization would involve both structural and functional linkages between the local governments and the institutions that have been developed by the rural dwellers over time. The Bureau recommended a democratic three-tier system of local government comprising the village or neighborhood council as the lowest tier, the development area council as the intermediate tier, and the local government council as the highest tier. But this crucial recommendation was not implemented. On the contrary, various institutions like the Directorate of Food, Roads and Rural Infrastructure (DFRRI) and the Better Life Program for rural dwellers (BLP), led by urban elites, which duplicated the functions of local governments and detracted from their autonomy, were put in place.

The DFRRI was established in 1986. Its goals were to promote rural development through the improvement of the quality of life of the inhabitants; to use the resources of the rural areas to lay a solid foundation for the security, social and economic growth of the nation; and to ensure a deeply rooted development process based on mass participation at the grassroots level.22 However, DFRRI identified the development of agriculture and the provision of rural infrastructures as crucial areas of concentration for the fulfillment of its objectives. The mandate of DFRRI clearly conflicts with the functions of local governments, which as key agents of development at the grassroots, are better placed to bring about rural development.

An examination of the mode of operation and activities of DFRRI clearly demonstrates that the organization was not in the position to promote any meaningful rural development. For one thing DFRRI was a highly centralized, bureaucratized and urban-based body: This contradicted the Political Bureau's recommendation that rural dwellers should be fully involved in initiating and executing programs for rural transformation. It can be argued that by establishing DFRRI the Babangida regime further helped to entrench the paternalistic attitude of urban-based bureaucrats towards the rural population. Perhaps much more important is the fact that DFRRI functioned primarily to serve as a source of primitive accumulation of capital for Nigerian elites. This was particularly so because the emphasis on the provision of infrastructures like earth roads, pipe borne water, and culverts, resulted in the award of highly inflated contracts by DFRRI officials in return for various kinds of bribes and kickbacks. The end result of these corrupt practices as demonstrated by the reports of various monitoring teams and the results of field research, was that many projects that were supposedly executed were either non-existent or abandoned while most of those that were completed were of very poor quality.[23] Thus, DFRRI negated the ideal of mobilizing rural dwellers for grassroots development and socio-economic transformation.

The BLP was launched in September 1987 with the aim of working out "effective strategies for mobilizing rural women for development and to exchange ideas on how best to maximize the productivity and effective contribution of rural women to the development of their respective communities in general and their individual lot in particular."[24] In short, the program aimed at raising the social consciousness of rural women about their rights, and their social, political and economic responsibilities, as well as stimulating their productive energies toward achieving a better level of life and laying the foundation for a self-reliant development in Nigeria.[25]

It is generally agreed that although women occupied relatively important positions in various aspects of pre-colonial Nigerian societies, their status deteriorated under colonialism, a situation, which persisted in post-colonial Nigeria. The Political Bureau identified the factors that were responsible for the deterioration of the status of women as cultural and religious beliefs, colonialism and the introduction of capitalist relations into Nigeria.[26] Although at the theoretical level it can be said that the BLP was based on a correct premise, in practice, the program served purposes other than bettering the lot of rural women. Being a creation of a dictatorial neo-colonial state, the program rapidly became a reflection of the undemocratic and decadent structures of the Nigerian state as epitomized by authoritarian and corrupt practices. Rural women were not involved in the initiation and execution of projects that were supposedly aimed at improving their material and social conditions. On the contrary, the whole process was dominated by urban-based elite women who assumed that they knew what was best for the rural women. This patronizing and condescending attitude was rationalized by Mrs. Mariam Babangida, the prime mover of the program, when she stated:

> The blind cannot lead the blind. The people at the top are educated, more educated and more comfortable than the people in rural areas. They need educated urban women who must map out strategies to assist in solving problems of the rural poor. We have the privilege, we are very influential and so we are certain and well assured that whatever plans we have would be for the benefits of the rural people.... The rural people are voteless and powerless. How then can they lead themselves- It is the urban educated women that would have to lead them.[27]

Given the pomp and pageantry that surrounded "better-life" activities, it is difficult to escape the conclusion that the BLP was more of a publicity stunt for Mrs. Babangida and her clique. Moreover the rationale for the establishment of the BLP can further be understood if situated within the context of the SAP of the Babangida regime. In this sense, the program was to serve the dual purpose of encouraging rural women to play a more active role in the production of raw materials for Western capitalist industries and encouraging the production of more food for urban markets in order to minimize the harsh impact of SAP on the urban dwellers, thereby preventing or reducing urban riots.[28]　On the whole, both DFRRI and the BLP negated the ideals of local government autonomy and the promotion of democratization at the grassroots level.

ECONOMIC POLICY

One of the ways through which both the Shagari and Buhari administrations had sought to resolve the economic crisis that became acute in Nigeria from the early 1980s was through a balance of payment support loan from the IMF. But disagreement with the IMF over stringent conditions like devaluation, the removal of subsidies from petroleum products and social services, deregulation and privatization deadlocked the negotiations. Although the loan was rejected by the public after a national debate, as we saw, the Babangida regime went ahead to implement the IMF conditions as a first step towards introducing the SAP. The subsequent recommendation by the Political Bureau against the adoption of SAP was rejected by the regime. Some writers have argued that the stand of the Bureau was based on a hasty reaction to, and a protest against, the government for going ahead to implement SAP when the Bureau was still carrying out its task.[29] This explanation is not convincing. On the contrary, the recommendation was a clear reflection of the position of the majority of Nigerians.

The cornerstone of Babangida's economic policy was the SAP which was introduced in July 1986. The program aimed at the diversification of the productive base of the economy in order to reduce the degree of dependence on the oil sector. The program also devalued the naira. Greater reliance was placed on market forces for the allocation of resources. Subsidies were removed, especially on petroleum products and certain social services. Previously public enterprises were rationalized, commercialized and privatized. These steps were clearly in line with the orthodox adjustment programs prescribed by the IMF. In short, the center-piece of SAP was demand management policies through tightening of credit, economic liberalization and the substantial devaluation of the naira through the interplay of "free" Western-dominated market forces.[30]

Proponents of SAP have pointed to the abolition of the obnoxious import license system and the promotion of primary production as some of the benefits of the program. According to them this production boost was a product of the boost in export prices and had the effect of increasing the income of primary producers. While it is true that the abolition of import licenses and the attendant over-invoicing helped to ease access to foreign exchange, the fact remains that the corrupt practices associated with the import license system were merely shifted to the banking system which became the bastion of corruption. The sudden unrealistic high rates of profits led to the proliferation of banks, which became the main source of primitive accumulation for the Nigerian bourgeoisie. With the primary focus of the banks being on foreign exchange speculation, they neglected normal banking services, which are more beneficial to the economy. The level of speculation and corruption associated with the banking system got to the point that they could no longer be sustained by the economy: this resulted in a crash in the banking sector with adverse consequences for the economy as a whole. The initial gain of primary producers was short lived as it was merely an opportunity for some European and Asian middlemen whose resources were held up in the country to repatriate them, thus causing capital flight.[31] With regard to cocoa, Fadahunsi noted that

> Between 1987 and 1989, bogus cocoa merchants invaded the cocoa trade once government yielded to IMF/World Bank pressure to disband the cocoa and other commodity marketing boards. The newbreed cocoa merchants turned out to be mostly foreigners and their Nigerian fronts who were desperately trying to repatriate some of their genuine and ill-gotten profits that had accumulated in Nigeria during the regime of controlled exchange rates. Because these foreign entrepreneurs no longer had confidence in the viability of the Nigerian monetary system and economy, they were seeking for means to take their money out of Nigeria at all cost.[32]

It is generally agreed that the negative effects of SAP far outweighed its so-called benefits.[33] The extreme devaluation of the naira had adverse effects on the economy as the resultant spiraling inflationary situation disrupted economic activities at both the levels of the producer and the consumer. As a neo-colonial economy whose industries depended on imported machinery, spare parts and other inputs, the very high prices of these imported inputs and local raw materials, led to extremely high production costs, which led to an increase in the prices of manufactured goods. The outcome was a considerable decline in the demand for locally manufactured products.[34] There was substantial decline in the capacity utilization of the industrial sector. Between 1987 and 1993, capacity utilization did not exceed 40 percent and was in fact below 30 percent in 1991, for instance. Moreover, many industries--particularly small and medium-scale ones--declined and folded up. Thus SAP promoted deindustrialization in Nigeria.[35]

The purported aim of using SAP to diversify the economy turned out to be an unmitigated failure. The country continued to rely on oil as the primary source of foreign exchange. Throughout the period of Babangida's regime, there was no year that revenue from non-oil sources reached 10 percent of the total revenue derived from exports. Worse still, in the face of the very low purchasing power of Nigerians, salaries did not only remain stagnant but the Babangida regime went ahead to substantially raise the prices of petroleum products thereby making life extremely difficult for ordinary Nigerians. The debilitating effects of SAP virtually discouraged any form of productive activities. Educated people left for better-paying foreign jobs. There was capital flight, and disinvestments. Worst of all, Nigeria's markets were flooded with used and substantially worthless goods dumped from various Western capitalist countries, a situation which Musa Abutudu has appropriately described as the "tokunboh" culture.[36] The removal of subsidies as well as the drastic reduction in funding for social services like the educational and health sectors resulted in the virtual collapse of these sectors. These are manifested in the poor conditions of service for staff and the consequent extremely low level of morale, lack of facilities, libraries that were devoid of current books and journals, and hospitals that became glorified consulting clinics and virtual mortuaries. This was equally the case with various forms of infrastructures like roads, pipe-borne water and electricity, which declined considerably because of lack of adequate funding.

On the whole, SAP promoted a great amount of poverty, hardship and misery for the overwhelming majority of Nigerians. Commenting on the impact of SAP, Dotun Phillips noted that the program had increased the cost of development to the point that Nigeria was virtually pricing herself out of the market for development.[37] In fact, the program has constituted a dead-end for Nigeria's development.[38] Even worse is the fact that given the monumental negative impact of SAP and the fact that it has worsened rather than resolved Nigeria's economic crisis, the program did not help in laying the basis for an enduring economy. This was supposedly a crucial objective of Babangida's economic policies. Indeed, the Political Bureau's assessment of the impact of SAP in March 1987, when the program was still a few months old, has turned out to be prophetic. It states:

> While the overall effects of these current (SAP) measures are yet to be lived through, they are already redistributing social hardship and incomes sharply against labour, the peasantry and other members of the poor population, and sharply in favour of capital, both domestic and foreign.... (I)t is quite clear that through boom and bust, the Nigerian people remain victims. This is the critical problem of Nigerian politics and economy and its significance for the evolution of a just, viable, self-reliant and new social order. It is critical because peace, progress, stability and self-reliance cannot emerge alongside contemporary inequalities, mass poverty and economic dependence.[39]

In any case given the widespread hardship that was promoted by SAP there were various forms of resistance, which were ruthlessly suppressed by the Babangida regime. For instance the anti-SAP demonstrations of April 1988, May 1989, and May 1992, which were championed by students in higher institutions of learning and supported by various segments of the Nigerian society like market women, workers and the unemployed, were viciously suppressed. Also trade unions and professional groups which were critical of SAP, like the Nigerian Labour Congress (NLC) and the Academic Staff Union of Universities (ASUU), were routinely proscribed with some of their leaders imprisoned. Insisting that there was no alternative to SAP, the regime did not entertain any opposing viewpoint. An attempt by a group of Nigerians to hold a national conference on alternatives to SAP in 1991 was prevented by the federal government. Some of the organizers of the conference were detained, while a similar conference, which was externally initiated and largely pro-SAP was allowed to take place in Lagos. The intolerant attitude to critics of SAP clearly belies the supposed posture of the regime, with its public consultation and trumpeted respect for human rights posture of the regime. This act of authoritarianism would become more apparent when the program of transition to civil rule is examined.

TRANSITION TO CIVIL RULE PROGRAM

The centerpiece of Babangida's policies was the transition to civil rule program. From the inception of his administration, he had announced that the primary preoccupation of his regime would be to put in place a viable transition program. This was one of the factors that helped to confer an initial amount of legitimacy on his regime among the Nigerian public. Indeed, all the other policies of the regime like mass mobilization, administrative reforms, grassroots development and economic policies, were meant to be integral parts of the transition process and to help ensure a successful and stable democratic Third Republic. As we have already seen, the main mandate of the Political Bureau was to recommend a viable program of transition to civil rule.

However, a cardinal objective of the transition program was the consolidation of the SAP in the Third Republic. In his 1991 budget speech, Babangida stated *inter alia*:

> The reform package of this administration is constructed on two pillars. The first is on the economy which some have seen as being concretized in SAP. The second is the political programme which we have articulated in the Transition to Civil Rule Programme. These two elements are mutually reinforcing; and both must be faithfully implemented for us to be able to construct a new social order that is democratic, viable and self-reliant.

Thus in spite of the massive opposition to the adjustment policies, the transition program was to reinforce SAP at every stage of the process.[40] As a result, Babangida made it clear that opponents of SAP - whom he described as 'extremists' and 'radicals' - would not be allowed any say or participation in the transition process. He thus set in motion an authoritarian, carefully teleguided and `test-tube' transition program. One other reason for the authoritarian nature of the transition process was the desire to perpetuate Babangida's rule. Hence critics who had stated all along that Babangida did not have the intention to hand over power were conveniently dubbed as 'extremists' and 'radicals'. But the self-serving nature of the transition program soon became apparent.

The first step in the transition program was the setting up of the Constitution Review Committee (CRC) in September 1987. The task of the 46-member Committee was to review the 1979 Constitution. It submitted its report in February 1988. In May 1988, the Constituent Assembly (CA) was inaugurated to deliberate on the CRC's report and make recommendations to the Armed Forces Ruling Council (AFRC). By disqualifying progressives from participating in the elections, the National Electoral Commission (NEC) ensured that these two bodies were made up primarily of conservative and pro-SAP individuals. In fact, right from this moment, the NEC became a tool for justifying and supporting the regime's authoritarian attempts at constructing a "democratic" order.[41] Furthermore, both the CRC and the CA were precluded from discussing SAP which was regarded as a "no go" area. Moreover, the AFRC used its power of ratifying the CA's report to remove those sections with which it disagreed. Thus, the 1989 constitution was expectedly a conservative and pro-SAP document.

An important stage in the transition process was the formation and registration of political parties. The stringent guidelines for the registration of political parties which included the presentation of the passport photographs of all registered members and the establishment of well-manned and functioning offices in the federal capital, the capitals of all the states of the federation and in all local government headquarters were such that the subordinate classes were put in the position of not being able to effectively participate in the transition. Even members of the domestic bourgeoisie found it difficult to fulfil these requirements. Oyovbaire's and Olagunju's attempt at rationalizing this through the argument that the guidelines were deliberately made tough in order to eliminate frivolous, sectional and undemocratic political associations from the electoral process is not tenable.[42] On the contrary, it would seem as if the electoral process was deliberately designed to provide the regime with the opportunity of carrying out an already premeditated act of tightly controlling the affairs of the political parties in line with the authoritarian and self-serving nature of the transition process.

It is therefore not surprising that of the thirteen political associations that eventually succeeded in applying for registration as political parties, only six were deemed to have marginally met the conditions that were laid down by the NEC. The associations were said to have been hijacked by "money bags", and that they were unable to transcend ethnic, geopolitical, religious and class lines, while three of the four leading associations were said to be reincarnations of political parties of the First and Second Republics. However, none of the six associations were approved for registration as political parties by the AFRC. The body went ahead to establish two "grassroots" political parties, the National Republican Convention (NRC), which was said to be "a little to the right", and the Social Democratic Party (SDP), which was said to be "a little to the left". The manifestos of the two political parties were written by the

National Election Commission, which also chose the symbols of the parties. The national, state and local government headquarters of both parties were built by the federal government. Since political parties are supposed to be made up of individuals with similar ideals who voluntarily come together, this authoritarian way of legislating them into existence is not only fundamentally wrong but equally negates and subverts the democratic order.

It was stated that in order to successfully establish the new social order in the Third Republic, politicians who had participated actively in the politics of the previous republics, referred to as the "old breed", and all those who had been indicted for corrupt practices, would be banned from participating in the transition politics. This ban was ostensibly to ensure that the "new breed" of politicians being nurtured by the regime were not corrupted by the "old breed": in reality, the ban was self-serving. For one thing, some of the greatest critics of the authoritarian nature of the transition program and those who were likely to seriously challenge the Babangida design of perpetuating himself in office were from among the "old breed" politicians. Babangida calculated that the "new breed," many of whom depended upon his regime's goodwill for influence and new sources of accumulation, would not pose as much threat. Moreover, the ban was intended to cause a split between the older established politicians and the new ones, a situation that would work to Babangida's advantage. But members of the "new breed" political class, which could not counter the influence of the older politicians, particularly in their home bases, were in practice forced to become proxies to the "old breed". Having failed in this design, Babangida decided to lift the ban on the older politicians in December 1991, as a way of achieving the same objective, since the resultant insecurity and competition was likely to promote disunity among the political class.

Thus, rather than use the transition program to put in place structures that would promote an enduring democracy in the Third Republic, it became one for promoting Babangida's personal rule.[43] In this enterprise, the NEC became a very handy tool. Its reports became a subterfuge for shifting the hand over to civil rule date on three occasions (first from October 1990 to October 1992, later to January 3, 1993, and then to August 27, 1993) under the guise that the politicians were not yet in the position to ensure the success of democracy in the Third Republic. For instance, the cancellation of the first and second presidential primaries in 1992, which became an excuse for shifting the handover date, was based on the NEC's reports. The desire of Nigerians for more states and local governments was also exploited. In 1991, Babangida saw the creation of new states and local governments as another excuse to extend the hand over date.

Apart from these formal structures, Babangida employed the services of surrogate bodies like the shadowy "Third Eye" and the Arthur Nzeribe led "Association for Better Nigeria" (ABN) to campaign for the continuation of military rule. Although under the transition decree this could be interpreted as capable of derailing the transition process and therefore an offence, the individuals were never taken to court for any offence. Yet critics of the authoritarian nature of the transition program who accused Babangida of having a "hidden agenda" to succeed himself were routinely taken to court and incarcerated for allegedly trying to "derail the transition."[44] Even though the Campaign for Democracy (CD), the umbrella body for the human rights and pro-democracy groups in Nigeria, obtained a court order in May 1993, prohibiting the ABN from continuing with its campaign for the perpetuation of the Babangida regime, no steps were taken to enforce this order. In fact, this same association, the ABN, obtained an order from an Abuja high court prohibiting the June 12 presidential elections from being held. This was just two days before the elections. After the elections eventually took place, and were generally hailed as very free and fair by both the local and international observers, and the clear-cut winner was generally known, the ABN went to the same Abuja high court and obtained an order stopping further announcements of the election results. This ruling was met with general disapproval by Nigerians, which resulted in a tense atmosphere in the country. Yet Babangida used the so-called "confusion" arising from the two court orders, the tense atmosphere, and other flimsy excuses to annul the results of the elections on June 23, 1993. This decision was met with general disapproval as it threw the country into a very serious crisis which eventually resulted in Babangida hastily handing over power to a hand picked and inept Interim National Government (ING) under the leadership of Ernest Shonekan on August 27, 1993.

The annulment of the June 12, 1993 elections clearly demonstrated the self-serving nature and the lack of sincerity of purpose that characterized the whole transition program of the Babangida regime. Having failed to come up with an excuse to further postpone the hand over date, he had hoped that the ruling on the ABN motion by a sympathetic and inexperienced judge would create enough confusion that would justify the cancellation of the elections.[45] But this was not to be. Moreover, working in concert with the NEC, the regime deliberately refused to build polling booths even though it was substantially an open ballot election. As opposed to a secret ballot system, the open system requires voters to line up before the ballet box of the candidate of preference. The election was held at the peak of the rainy season, with the hope that rain would help to disrupt the elections in parts of the country. But it turned out to be a very dry day. The second court order and the annulment were, therefore, an act of desperation on the part of the Babangida regime.

FOREIGN POLICY

As was the case with the previous regimes in Nigeria, Babangida claimed that Africa was the centerpiece of his foreign policy. However, the regime did not have a consistent and coherent foreign policy. This was partly reflected in the frequent change of the minister in charge of foreign affairs. In fact there were five ministerial changes under his regime. In any case, most of Babangida's foreign policy merely toed the line of previous policies as in the case of the relationship to the Organization of African Unity (OAU), now called the African Union (AU), the support of the struggle against the apartheid system and white minority regimes in Southern Africa, the restating of the belief in the policy of non-alignment, the support of United Nations activities, the commitment to the Organization of Petroleum Exporting Countries (OPEC) and the support of the Economic Community of West African States (ECOWAS). However, there were a few novel initiatives that were introduced by the regime. These were mainly in the areas of the so-called economic diplomacy, the attempt to form a "concert of medium powers", the introduction of the Technical Aid Corps (TAC), the joining of the Organization of Islamic Conferences (OIC), and the establishment of diplomatic relations with Israel. Perhaps the most controversial foreign policy initiative was the formation of the ECOWAS Monitoring Group (ECOMOG).

As has already been pointed out, Babangida made it clear in his inaugural speech that he was committed to breaking the impasse with the IMF. The regime's economic diplomacy therefore largely centered on the issue of debt rescheduling, extension of new forms of credits by the international financial institutions and various Western nations, and the attraction of foreign investments. Central to this economic diplomacy was the demand that Nigeria should implement the SAP. We have already seen that in spite of popular opposition to the adjustment program, Babangida went ahead to subvert the popular will by implementing it. One outcome of this so-called economic diplomacy was the entrenchment of Western imperialist interests and control over Nigeria's economic policies. For instance after the massive rejection of the I.M.F. loan through a public debate, IMF and the World Bank executives worked covertly with the Babangida regime to fashion out a SAP policy. They sent "experts" who worked secretly with Nigerian officials in an inter-ministerial committee set up by the Babangida regime to formulate a SAP program. At the same time, they used their position to obtain the appointment of a former World Bank official and one of the strongest proponents of SAP, Kalu Idika Kalu, as the finance minister in Nigeria.[46]

Babangida attempted to portray Nigeria not just as a regional power but as some kind of intermediate global power. As a result the country played a leading role in the attempt to form the short-lived "concert of medium powers". This also accounted for the formation of the TAC in 1987 under which Nigerian experts and professionals were seconded to various African, Caribbean and Pacific countries, entirely at Nigeria's expense. This attempt at advancing Nigeria's image and power globally also accounted for the regime's unsuccessful sponsorship of Obasanjo's bid for the office of Secretary General of the United Nations.

In view of the political and religious polarization at home, the regime took two foreign policy measures that can be considered as both bold and controversial though pragmatic from the perspective of the administration. The first of such measures was the making of Nigeria a full member of the OIC. This has been a divisive issue that has generated great disagreement between Christians and Muslims in Nigeria. Given the strong opposition of Christians, no regime had been bold enough to openly make Nigeria a full member of this body. But given Babangida's increasing reliance on the conservative Northern Muslim groups for his self-succession bid, joining this Islamic organization was seen as one of the ways of appeasing them. The second measure involved the restoration of diplomatic ties with Israel. This paradoxically was in the face of the historical opposition from conservative Northern Muslim groups. However, Babangida's virtual dependence on Israel for security made such a restoration pragmatic if not inevitable.

In terms of the relationship to ECOWAS, Nigeria continued to play a major role in sustenance of the organization. It was the largest single financier of the ECOWAS, contributing about thirty-three percent of the organization's annual budget. It maintained its secretariat, and on occasions extended oil concessions and financial aid to members of the body. However the major and controversial foreign policy initiative that was taken during this period was the formation of ECOMOG which was ostensibly supposed to promote peace in war-torn Liberia. The decision to form ECOMOG in 1990 was pioneered by Nigeria, which equally bankrolled the body.

ECOMOG came under serious criticism from both within Nigeria and externally. Given the obvious friendship between Babangida and Samuel Doe (then Head of State of Liberia), some charged that Babangida had championed the formation of ECOMOG in order to prop up an embattled friend. This amounted to the personalization of Nigeria's foreign policy. People who held this opinion pointed to the visit which Doe made to Nigeria in April 1990, the fact that Nigeria was a major arm supplier to Doe and that Nigeria only decided to intervene after the forces of Charles Taylor's National Patriotic Front of Liberia (NPFL) gained control of about 90 percent of the country and threatened to overrun Monrovia. In addition Babangida had enormous investments in Liberia: he had contributed $2 million dollars to the establishment of a graduate school of international studies which was named after him, at the University of Liberia. Seven Nigerian scholars paid by the Nigerian government were seconded to this school. Incidentally, Doe was pursuing a graduate program in this school and the Nigerian scholars had to teach him at the presidential mansion. Babangida's intervention was therefore seen as a means of protecting his enormous investments in Liberia.

There was also the belief among Nigerians that the intervention constituted an enormous waste of Nigeria's human and capital resources. Furthermore, the mission was criticized for lack of an exit strategy and the lack of a clearly defined mission and mandate. It was not clear whether they were to be involved in peace keeping, peacemaking or peace enforcement. Increasingly, they found themselves embroiled in what was turning out to be an internecine war. Given the obvious closeness between Babangida and Doe, Charles Taylor was right from the beginning suspicious of ECOMOG's motive and refused to cooperate with it.

At the sub-regional level, a number of West African countries, particularly the French speaking African nations led by Cote d'Ivoire and Burkina Faso, were opposed to the intervention. They saw it as an intervention in the internal affairs of a member country and therefore against the charter of ECOWAS. According to Blaise Campaore, the President of Burkina Faso, ECOMOG was not "competent to intervene in a member state's internal conflict but only when the conflict is between one member and another" as stipulated in the ECOWAS charter.[47] This tended to cause disagreement within the ECOWAS and therefore affected the ability of the body to coherently deal with the Liberian conflict.

Although the formation of ECOMOG could be seen as a bold initiative aimed at developing a regional approach to addressing the problem of peacekeeping in West Africa, the relationship between Babangida and Doe and the personal interests that Babangida sought to protect in Liberia vitiated this otherwise laudable objective.[48] From this perspective it can be seen as a foreign policy failure. It was, unfortunately, an extension of Babangida's personalization of domestic policies into the international arena.

CONCLUSION

Babangida came to power with the promise of setting in motion a transition process that would promote sustainable development and an enduring democracy in the Third Republic. He claimed that such changes would help to prevent future military coups, thereby making his administration the last military regime in Nigeria. We have seen that the far-reaching nature of the report of the Political Bureau provided enough grounds for the achievement of this objective.

This opportunity, however, was squandered on the altar of self-interest. The various programs of socio-economic transformation which were put in place failed, not only because of wide-ranging corruption and poor implementation, but perhaps more importantly because of the lack of sincerity of purpose on the part of Babangida. His primary concern was to use the programs to perpetuate himself in office. In the end, he over-reached himself and out of desperation annulled the results of the June 12, 1993 presidential elections. The consequences of this annulment swept Babangida out of office and marked the collapse of his publicly stated purpose of installing an enduring and democratic Third Republic, as well as his hidden agenda of perpetuating himself in office.

ENDNOTES

1. S. Oyovbaire and T. Olagunju, eds., *Foundations of a New Nigeria: The IBB Era*, London: Precision Press, 1989, 1-2. It should be noted that the two authors together with Adele Jinadu constituted the intellectual backbone of the Babangida regime. They played significant roles in the initiation of the political programs of the regime; authored most of his speeches; and were right from the beginning concerned with using their writings to ensure a favorable place for Babangida's regime in Nigeria's contemporary history. Given this fact, the authors were expectedly biased in their assessment of the regime's policies. But the point should be made that given their intellectual status, the book is most likely to profoundly influence the perspectives of many Nigerians; hence the work deserves to be taken seriously. For a critical review of the book, see J. I. Dibua, "Babangida and the Foundations of a New Nigeria: A Review Article," *ITAN*, Vol. 1, 1990, 121-133.

2. Federal Government of Nigeria, *Report of the Political Bureau*, Lagos: Government Printer, 1987, 4-6.

3. *Ibid.*, 56.

4. *Ibid.*, 67-68.

5. A. T. Gana, *The Limits of Political Engineering: A Critique of the Transition Programme*, Jos: Covenant Press, 1990, 15.

6. T. Olagunju, et. al., *Transition to Democracy in Nigeria, 1985-1993*, St. Heller, UK, and Ibadan, Nigeria: Safari and Spectrum Books, 1993, pp. 128-129.

7. The fact of the demise of socialist regimes in Eastern Europe (which occurred after the work of the Political Bureau) does not provide a justification for the stand of the Babangida regime. A careful reading of the Bureau's report will show that the socialism it recommended for Nigeria was a product of extensive examination of the peculiar Nigerian situation and was aimed at promoting democratization, social and economic justice, and self-reliant development.

8. Federal Government of Nigeria. *Government's Views and Comments on the Findings and Recommendations of the Political Bureau*, Lagos: Government Printer, 1987, 9-14.

9. The point should be made that SAP is a product of the liberal/conservative ideology of the World Bank, the IMF and the Western creditor nations. Implementing it amounts to imposing an alien ideology on Nigeria and so contradicts the regime's reason for rejecting socialism. See J. I. Dibua, "Structural Adjustment Programme and the Subversion of Popular Will in Africa: The Case of the Transition to Civil Rule in Nigeria," in S. G. Tyoden, ed., The Transition to Civil Rule: The Journey So Far - The Proceedings of the 19th Annual Conference of the Nigerian Political Science Association, Lagos: The Nigerian Political Science Association, 1992, 158-169; and idem, "The Structural Adjustment Programme and the Transition to Civil Rule in Nigeria," in L. A. Thompson, ed., *Democracy, Democratization and Africa*, Ibadan, Enugu and Abuja: Afrika-Link Books, 1994, 185-203.

10. Gana, *The Limits of Political Engineering*, 16.

11. See World Bank. *Sub-Saharan Africa: From Crisis to Sustainable Growth, A Long-Term Perspective Study*, Washington, D.C.: The World Bank, 1989; and

idem, *Adjustment in Africa: Reforms, Results and the Road Ahead*, Oxford University Press, 1994.
12. Oyovbaire and Olagunju, eds., *Foundations of a New Nigeria*.
13. *Ibid.*, 59.
14. Federal Government of Nigeria. *Civil Service (Re-organization) Decree 1988*, Lagos: Government Printer, 1988; and Dotun Phillips, *Essentials of the 1988 Civil Service Reforms in Nigeria*, NISER Monograph Series, No. 2, Ibadan: NISER, 1988.
15. S. O. Jaja, "Towards the Third Republic: Strategies and Role of the Reformed Nigerian Civil Service," *ITAN*, Vol. 1, 1990, 63-77; and E. Osiruemu, "Towards an Efficient and Effective Nigerian Civil Service in the 1990s and Beyond: A Case Study of the 1988 Civil Service Reforms," in A. O. Udeagha et. al., eds., *Managing the Nigerian Public Sector in the 1990s: Issues and Analysis*, Enugu: Lako Press, 1991.
16. Federal Republic of Nigeria, *The Constitution of the Federal republic of Nigeria*, Lagos: Government Printer, 1979.
17. A. Gboyega, *Political Values and Local Government in Nigeria*, Lagos: Malthouse Press, 1987.
18. Federal Government of Nigeria. *Views and Comments of the Federal Military Government on the Findings and Recommendations of the Committee on the Review of Local Government Administration in Nigeria* (The Dasuki Committee), Lagos: Government Printer, 1985.
19. Ibrahim B. Babangida, "Text of National Day Address," *The Guardian* (Lagos, Nigeria), October 3, 4, 5, 1988.
20. Federal Government of Nigeria. *Implementation Guidelines on the Application of Civil Service Reforms in the Local Government Service*, Lagos: Government Printer, 1988.
21. J. I. Dibua, "Democratisation of Local Governments as a Way of Mobilising Nigerians for Rural Development," in J. B. Adekanye et. al., eds., Institutions and Processes of Democratization in Nigeria: Proceedings of the 16th Annual National Conference of the Nigerian Political Science Association, Ibadan: Nigerian Political Science Association, 1989, 98-113; and idem., "Babangida and the Foundations of a New Nigeria."
22. Directorate of Food, Roads and Rural Infrastructures. *Rural Development: The Mobilisation Approach*, Lagos: Government Press, 1987, 4-5.
23. A. O. Olutayo, "Poverty as a Barrier to Democracy: The case of Local Government in Nigeria," in Thompson, ed., *Democracy, Democratization and Africa*, 205-218.
24. Better Life Program. *Better Life Fair for Rural Dwellers*, Lagos: Alimbar Tribune, 1988, p. 9.
25. Oyovbaire and Olagunju, eds., *Foundations of a New Nigeria*.
26. Federal Government of Nigeria. *Report of the Political Bureau*, 157.
27. *The Guardian*, (Lagos, Nigeria), September 28, 1991.
28. J. I. Dibua, "Better Life Programme and the Empowerment of Rural Women in Nigeria: An Appraisal," Paper Presented at the 37th Annual Congress of the Historical Society of Nigeria, Held at the University of Calabar, Calabar, Nigeria,

May 18-20, 1992; H. Abdullah, "Transition Politics' and the Challenge of Gender in Nigeria," *Review of African Political Economy*, No. 56, 1993, pp. 27-41; and A. Mama, "Feminism or Femocracy- State Feminism and Democratisation in Nigeria," *Africa Development*, Vol. XX, No. 1, 1995, 37-58.

29. T. Olagunju, et. al., *Transition to Democracy in Nigeria*, 129-131.

30. Federal Government of Nigeria. *Structural Adjustment in Nigeria*, July 1986-June 1988, Lagos: Government Printer, 1986.

31. S. Dittoh and A. J. Adegeye, "Is There a Structurally Adjusted Induced Boom in the Nigerian Cocoa Industry," *The Nigerian Journal of Economic and Social Studies*, Vol. 36, No. 2, 1994, 68-378.

32. A. Fadahunsi, "Devaluation: Implications for Employment, Inflation, Growth and Development," in A. O. Olukoshi, ed., *The Politics of Structural Adjustment in Nigeria*, London: James Currey, 1993, 48-49. Also see E. A. Walker, " 'Happy Days are Here Again': Cocoa Farmers, Middlemen Traders and the Structural Adjustment Program in Southwestern Nigeria, 1986-1990s," *Africa Today*, Vol. 47, No. 2, 2000, 151-169.

33. M. E. Akor, "The Structural Adjustment Programme as Antithesis to Nigeria's Economic Recovery," The Nigerian Journal of Economic and Social Studies, vol. 36, No. 3, 1994, pp. 486-494. Also see B. Founou-Tchuigoua, "Africa Confronted with the Ravages of Neo-Liberalism," *Africa Development*, Vol. 21, Nos. 2-3, 1996, 5-24.

34. For details, see J. I. Dibua, "Devaluation and Economic Crisis: A Political Economy Analysis," in A. Oyebade, ed., *The Transformation of Nigeria: Essays in Honor of Toyin Falola*, Trenton, NJ: Africa World Press, 2002, 261-288.

35. I. U. Ukwu, "Industrialization and Economic Development in Nigeria: The Significance of Structural Adjustment Program," The Nigerian Journal of Economic and Social Studies, Vol. 36, No. 2, 1994, 434-448.

36. Tokunboh which is derived from the Yoruba language and usually given as a name to someone born overseas, was popularized in the SAP era in Nigeria by a company named Tokunboh which specialized in the importation of used motor vehicles. Generally the term is used to describe the massive importation of used consumer goods like motor vehicles, electrical and electronic equipment, clothing and shoes, etc from Europe. See M. I. M. Abutudu, "Globalization and 'Tokunboh': Tentative Notes on Structural Adjustment, Culture and Politics in Nigeria," Paper for the 22nd Annual Conference of the New York African Studies Association, Held at Binghamton University, Binghamton, April 24-25, 1998.

37. A. O. Phillips, "A General Overview of SAP," in A. O. Phillips and E. C. Ndekwu, eds., *Structural Adjustment Programme in a Developing Economy: The Case of Nigeria*, Ibadan: Nigerian Institute for Social and Economic Research, 1987, 7.

38. Dibua, "Devaluation and Economic Crisis," and idem., "Journey to Nowhere: Neo-Liberalism and Africa's Development Crisis," *Comparative Studies of South Asia, Africa and the Middle East*, Vol. XVIII, No. 2, 1998, 119-130.

39. Federal Government of Nigeri. *Report of the Political Bureau*, 37.

40. Dibua, "The Structural Adjustment Programme and the Transition to Civil Rule in Nigeria,"185-203; and A. Momoh, "The Structural Adjustment

Programme and the Transition to Civil Rule in Nigeria (1986-1993)," Africa Development, Vol. XXI, No. 1, 1996, 19-37.

41. M. I. M. Abutudu, *The State, Civil Society and the Democratisation Process in Nigeria*, Dakar: CODESRIA, 1995, 19-20.

42. Oyovbaire and Olagunju, eds., *Foundations of a New Nigeria*.

43. K. Amuwo, "Democracy by Fiat: Why it Will Not Work-," Africa Quaterly, Vol. 35, No. 3, 1995,19-31.

44. M. I. M. Abutudu, "Confronting Political Shock: Civil Society and the Annulment of the 1993 Presidential Election in Nigeria," Unpublished Research report Submitted to the SSRC, New York, 1996.

45. The Abuja high court judge was appointed to this position barely six months before the election. The manner in which she handled the ABN motions contravened clearly established procedural and institutional processes (for instance, her sitting late at night to rule over the motions). This tended to create the impression that the main reason for her appointment as a judge, was to enable Babangida acting through surrogates to use her court to achieve his ambition of personal rule.

46. See T. M. Callaghy, "Lost Between State and Market: The Politics of Economic Adjustment in Ghana, Zambia, and Nigeria," in J. M. Nelson, ed., *Economic Crisis and Policy Choice: The Politics of Adjustment in the Third World*, Princeton: Princeton University Press, 1994, 306-309; and Dibua, "Journey to Nowhere," 125-126.

47. *Newswatch* (Lagos, Nigeria), August 27, 1990, 16.

48. A. M. Vogt, ed., *The Liberian Crisis and ECOMOG: A Bold Attempt at Regional Peace-Keeping*, Lagos: Gabuno Publishing Co., 1992.

Chief Ernest A. Shonekan
Interim Head of State
August-November 1993

Chapter Nine

Legacy of National Paralysis:
Ernest Shonekan and Sani Abacha,
1993-1998

Okechukwu Okeke

RISE AND FALL OF SHONEKAN

Before January 1993, Chief Ernest Adegunle Shonekan, then 56, had been the Chairman and Managing Director of Nigeria's largest conglomerate, the United African Company (UAC). He was a leading exponent of the Structural Adjustment Program (SAP) that the Ibrahim Babangida regime had adopted in September 1986. Impressed by Shonekan's corporate stature and probably by his support for SAP, Babangida appointed him a member of the Transitional Council in late 1992. The Transitional Council had been formed for the purpose of guiding Nigeria toward civilian rule. It was the last Executive Council of Ministers of the Babangida era. In January 1993, the month the Transitional Council assumed office, Shonekan was unanimously elected to be Chairman of the Council by his colleagues. Thus he became the *de facto* Prime Minister of Nigeria. Partly because Shonekan's new post had raised his political stature, and partly because Babangida was anxious to conciliate the Yoruba (the ethnic group of chief Moshood Abiola, the undeclared winner of the presidential election of June 1993), Babangida picked Shonekan, an Egbaman like Abiola, to head the Interim National Government (ING). On August 26, 1993, the military president handed over power to this interim government.

But the appointment of Shonekan as the head of the transition government did not please all the Yoruba. Many still supported Abiola. While politicians and political activists of the Northern and South-Eastern sections of Nigeria tolerated the Interim National Government, those of the South-West, particularly the Yoruba, were strongly opposed to the regime. To the Yoruba ethnic group, the ING was illegal and Shonekan was a renegade who had been used by the Northern power elite to rob a fellow Yorubaman - Moshood Abiola - of his mandate. Thus Shonekan's kinsmen, as it were, formed the bulk of the "progressive" politicians and civil rights activists who waged a campaign to force the ING out of power.[2]

Shonekan's response to this anti-ING campaign was feeble. As one columnist put it: "Shonekan apparently believed in turning the other cheek, and not in counterpunching..., a somewhat naive policy of appeasement."[3] But Shonekan's enemies were not appeased, and continued to attack him and the ING. The result was that political tension in the country increased.

Political tension rose in Nigeria and the rate of inflation soared. A useful index of the rise in inflation is the exchange rate of the naira vis-a-vis the United State dollar in the "black" or "parallel" market. Before the June 1993 election, one dollar could be exchanged for about twenty naira in the black market. In the heat of the political crisis that followed the annulment of that election, the value of the naira fell drastically: by late August (when Babangida handed power over to Shonekan), one dollar exchanged for about fifty naira. As the advent of the ING exacerbated the country's political crisis, the value of the naira further declined: in October-November 1993, one dollar could be exchanged for about one hundred naira.[4]

Despite the high rate of inflation, the interim government was more concerned about improving its finances than reducing inflation. In early November 1993 it officially raised the domestic price of all petroleum products by approximately 61 percent. But the actual retail price was much higher. For instance, the price of gasoline, the most widely-used fuel, was increased from N 0.70 to N 5.00 per liter, a six hundred percent increase. This price hike drew the ire of Nigeria's trade union leaders, who began to mobilize workers for a strike. Thus the enemies of the Interim National Government increased, and the prospects of its survival became more gloomy.[5]

The person who stood to benefit most from the unpopularity of the ING, and from Shonekan's inability to dominate the forces that threatened his regime, was General Sani Abacha. Born in Kano, Abacha was of Kanuri extraction. His parents had been citizens of the present Republic of Chad. An officer in the Nigerian Army, Abacha had been Minister of Defense and Chairman of the Joint Chiefs of Staff since 1990. When Babangida was about to leave office in August 1993, he retired all his service chiefs except Abacha, whom he allowed to retain both posts in the ING.

To many observers, it seemed clear from the first that, with Abacha retaining his two key posts in the ING, Ernest Shonekan was merely a titular Commander-in-Chief. Indeed, Abacha was his own boss, and seemed anxious to become Shonekan's successor. He began his quest for the top post by taking measures which undermined Shonekan's authority. For instance, on September 3, 1993, he singlehandedly removed Lieutenant-General Joshua Dogonyaro (whom Babangida had appointed Chief of Defense Staff the previous month) from his post, replacing him with Lieutenant-General Oladipo Diya. About three weeks later, he retired several senior army officers who were believed to be friends of Babangida.[6] Then on November 17, 1993, eighty-three days after the ING was inaugurated, Abacha led a group of senior army officers from Lagos to Abuja and forced Shonekan and the executive members of government to resign. The next day, Abacha went to the radio station in Abuja. As Commander-in-Chief of the Armed Forces, the new Head of State announced that the two political parties of the Babangida and ING eras were now outlawed, and that all the elected branches of government in Nigeria--the National Assembly and the state assemblies and elected state governments---were dissolved. He said that his major reason for seizing power was to ensure the unity and stability of Nigeria. He assured the nation and the world that military rule would be brief, adding that, to prepare the country for a return to civil rule, his government would soon convene a Constitutional Conference with "full constituent powers."[7]

Map of Nigeria showing the 36 states and the Federal capital, Abuja.

General Sani Abacha
Head of State
November 1993-1999

POLITICAL DEVELOPMENTS UNDER
THE ABACHA REGIME

Abacha's coup led to a temporary easing of political tension in Nigeria. At first, the bulk of the political elite either welcomed the new regime or were not hostile to it. Many of the leaders of the banned political parties accepted ministerial appointments in Abacha's government. Their support helped to give legitimacy to the new regime.

However, less than six months after Abacha assumed power, some of the prominent individuals and groups who initially supported him began to attack his regime. These were mainly Abiola and the progressive politicians (who were predominantly Yoruba) and some civil rights groups (most of whom were also Yoruba-dominated). These groups wanted Abacha "to restore Abiola's mandate" (that is, hand over the presidency to Abiola) or at least adopt a transition program that would lead to a quick return to civil rule. Abacha did not seem inclined to do either, but, in January 1994, his government announced plans for convening the Constitutional Conference he had mentioned in his initial address.

By May of 1994 the progressives had formed an association, called the National Democratic Coalition (NADECO), which, among other things, rallied round Abiola and urged him to declare himself President. On June 11,1994, the eve of the first anniversary of the 1993 presidential election, he did so. Immediately, the federal government arrested him. Still, the members of NADECO continued to campaign against the Abacha regime. They succeeded in persuading the leaders of the Nigerian Labor Congress (NLC), the central organization of all trade unions in Nigeria, to pressure the federal government to release Abiola. But the government was adamant.

On July 5, 1994, two labor unions in the oil industry–the National Union of Petroleum, Energy and Gas Workers (NUPENG) and the Petroleum and Natural Gas Senior Staff Association (PENGASSEN)-- began an indefinite stride in support of Abiola's cause. On July 6, 1994, the military government began prosecution against him for treasonable felony. Three days later, pro-democracy riots broke out in Lagos, Ogun, Oyo, Ondo and Edo states. The strike and the riots paralyzed social and economic life in Nigeria for nearly two months and raised political tension in the country.[8]

The Abacha regime waited for nearly a month and half before deciding to take on the trade unions. On August 17, the Head of State dismissed the executive committees of NUPENG, PENGASSEN and the

NLC, and replaced them with Sole Administrators.[9] Subsequently, the regime used force, threats of force and threats of possible replacement to get the oil workers back to work. The Abacha regime also detained some of the leaders of NUPENG and PENGASSEN. During the period of the strike the government had closed down three Lagos - based newspaper companies–the *Concord, Punch* and *Guardian* groups– and later issued decrees banning further publications by them. The ban was not lifted until late 1995.

In January 1994, the Abacha regime announced plans for convening a Constitutional Conference later that year. In the same month, the regime appointed a body called the National Constitutional Conference Commission (NCCC) and gave it the task of receiving and analyzing memoranda on Nigeria's future constitution and then drawing up an agenda for the Constitutional Conference. In late May 1994, elections into the conference, called the National Constitutional Conference (NCC), were held all over the country. NADECO had campaigned for a boycott of the elections, and several prominent Yoruba politicians who would have been candidates withdrew just before the commencement of voting, thus enabling less prominent and/or unpopular (pro-federal government) politicians to win the elections in Yorubaland. But in other parts of Nigeria, NADECO's boycott campaign had no effect, and prominent politicians participated in the NCC elections. On August 27, 1994 Abacha inaugurated the NCC in Abuja. A year later, the NCC submitted the proposed constitution to General Abacha. On October 1, 1995 the Head of State announced a three-year (1995-1998) transition program. As Abacha's ruling council had not fully made up its mind on what should be in the Constitution, no action was taken to bring forth a new Constitution.

However, he did announce some important constitutional decisions. For instance, he proclaimed that his ruling council had decided to discard the American-type presidential system of government (which the NCC had proposed) and adopt a "modified French system" having the offices of both President and Prime Minister, as well as Vice-President and Deputy Prime Minister. Contrary to an NCC recommendation that the office of President be held alternately by qualified candidates from the Northern and Southern regions of Nigeria, Abacha also announced that the country would be divided politically into six zones, three in the north and three in the South, with each zone producing in rotation one of the following six principal officials: President, Prime Minister, Vice-President, Deputy Prime Minister, President of the Senate and Speaker of the House of Representatives. Curiously, the Head of State did not define the powers of the President and Prime Minister and avoided announcing a decision as to which of the six zones would first produce the President.[10]

The transition program announced by Abacha provided for the holding of two local government elections in 1996, one in March (to be contested by non-party candidates) and the other in December (to be contested by political party candidates). It also proposed the registration of new political parties in 1996; the creation of more states and local government areas in 1996; and the holding of state and federal elections, in 1997 and 1998. More will be said about these below.[11]

There are two events that occurred in 1995 that deserve to be mentioned in this account. One is the trial of alleged coup plotters; the other the execution of nine Ogoni activists. In March 1995, Nigeria's Defense Headquarters announced that it had uncovered a plot by some serving and some retired or dismissed military officers to overthrow the federal government. This led to a secret trial of the alleged plotters, after which most of them (including a former Head of State, Olusegun Obasanjo, and his deputy, Shehu Yar'Adua) were convicted and sentenced to death or long terms of imprisonment. Some journalists and civil rights activists who expressed doubts about the government's allegations were called "accessories after the fact of treason," and were also tried and sentenced to long terms of imprisonment. The Abacha regime's ruling council later commuted the death sentences to life imprisonment terms and reduced the imprisonment terms of those were not sentenced to death.[12]

On November 10, 1995, Kenule Saro-Wiwa, an Ogoni-born writer and environmental activist, and eight other Ogoni activists were executed in Port-Harcourt. They had been sentenced to death about three weeks before that day for allegedly being responsible for the murder of four prominent Ogoni men in May 1994. At the time of the execution, the Heads of State of the Commonwealth were meeting in New Zealand. They quickly condemned the Abacha regime for "judicial murder", and suspended Nigeria from the Commonwealth. This was a serious disaster for the Abacha regime, and a great tragedy for Nigeria.[13]In March 1996 the Abacha regime conducted local government elections "on a non-party basis." The elections were marred by several administrative flaws. For instance, the electoral commission, called the National Electoral Commission Of Nigeria (NECON), conducted the elections without a voters' register. Also, NECON arbitrarily disqualified many candidates. Most of the disqualified were politicians associated with NADECO. There were also some other prominent politicians whom the Abacha regime did not trust. The elections were neither free nor fair. Newspapers critical of Abacha referred to the results as "selections" rather than "elections." However, the new chairmen and councillors for Nigeria's local government councils assumed office within a month.[14]

In the second quarter of 1996, the National Electoral Commission started the process that would lead to the registration of political parties later in the year. On September 30, it reported to Abacha's ruling council that only five of the many political parties which had sought registration met the requirements which it had laid down. And the council (whose official name is Provisional Ruling Council, PRC) permitted NECON to register the five associations as political parties. They are: the National Center Party of Nigeria (NCPN), the Democratic Party of Nigeria (DPN), the Grassroots Democratic Party (GDM), the United Nigeria Congress Party (UNCP), and the Congress for National Consensus (CNC). NECON's registration of only five parties was controversial. Some of the political associations which were not registered, notably the Social Progressive Peoples Party (PPP), were made up of the most prominent politicians in Nigeria. It seems unlikely that these associations were less capable of meeting NECON's requirements than the associations which were registered. It is reasonable to assume that they were not registered because the Abacha regime did not want Nigeria's most prominent politicians to participate in the politics of the transition period.[15]

It was suspected that the associations of prominent politicians were not registered because the Head of State had made up his mind to run for President and feared that this class of politicians would make it difficult for him to succeed. Signs of Abacha's ambition began to emerge shortly after NECON announced the registration of political parties. First, some prominent supporters of Abacha, including a former Chief Justice of the Federation, took turns to tell the press that he had has as much right as any other Nigerian to run for President. Then several leaders of the newly-registered political parties started urging him to run on the ticket of one or all of the parties. Soon, crowds of people began to appear in Abuja, urging the Head of State to succeed himself. But there were indications that these people were hired. Abacha's wife then spoke on the issue: she saw nothing bad in it; after all, she added, army generals had been messiahs of some other Third World countries. At last Abacha himself decided to speak on the issue. He did not deny that he had plans to succeed himself and added that his "constituency," which he did not define, would decide whether he would run or not. Those campaigning on Abacha's behalf said that he alone could ensure peace and stability in Nigeria. According to them, only "someone with a military background", could hold the country together and stop the frequent occurrence of coups. President Suharto of Indonesia was held up as a model for Abacha.[16]

After the registration of political parties, the next important items on Abacha's transition program for the year 1996 were the creation of more states and local government areas and the holding of local government elections "on a party basis." Contrary to advice from both Nigerian and foreign economic experts and organizations, Abacha's ruling council created six new states on October 1, 1996 and later created 183 new local government areas. The regime's objective in creating more political units despite the force of argument of the economic opinion against it was probably to win political support. And the Abacha regime probably won more admirers for doing so.

In mid-December 1996, NECON announced that the local government elections scheduled to be held later that month had been postponed to March 1997. The commission pleaded lack of preparedness, which was obvious. But NECON and the Abacha regime had been given enough time (almost nine months, March-December 1996) to prepare adequately for the elections. Thus lack of preparedness seemed to be a ploy to start a process that, like in the Babangida era, would lead to the postponement of subsequent elections and thus prolong the life of the Abacha - led junta. Thus the postponement of the December 1996 local government elections tended to give credence to claims by Abacha's opponents--NADECO members and a large proportion of Lagos-based journalists and civil rights activists--that the Head of State did not really intend to implement the transition program to institute civilian rule.

It would be well to add here that, in addition to NADECO members and other Nigerian critics of the Abacha regime, the governments of many western European and North-American countries were not persuaded that the regime genuinely wished to restore democracy in Nigeria. For instance, the European Union (EU) was doubtful about the credibility of the Nigerian government in this respect. In November 1996 the EU reviewed Abacha's transition program and came to the conclusion that it was not "credible". Hence the European Union extended its sanctions against Nigeria for another six months.[17]

ECONOMIC AND SOCIAL DEVELOPMENTS

It is difficult to write a chronological account of economic and social changes in Nigeria under Abacha. This is because there are so many issues and events to mention, and almost all of them overlap in time, so that it is difficult to achieve coherence if a chronological approach is adopted. Hence we use a thematic treatment, with each issue or event treated under a sub-heading.

Politics and Inflation

We have seen how the political crisis of June-November 1993 reduced the value of the Nigerian currency, the naira. The relaxation of political tension brought about by the advent of Abacha led to a rapid appreciation of the naira. Between November 17 and December 31, 1993, the value of the naira doubled from its initial exchange rate of about 100 naira to the dollar.[18] Thus Abacha's rise to power initially had a beneficial effect on the rate of inflation in Nigeria.

Fuel Prices and Industrial Unrest

The Shonekan regime, we have seen, raised fuel prices sixfold. After Abacha ousted Shonekan, Abacha's government negotiated with labor unions over fuel prices, and, as a result, the new regime reduced the prices announced by its predecessor by one-third. For example, the price of a liter of petrol was reduced from N5.00 to N3.25. Perhaps this was partly responsible for the appreciation of the naira which occurred in November and December of 1993.

Fuel prices were to rise again during the oil workers' strike in July and August of 1994. The immediate effect of the strike was scarcity of petroleum products. Scarcity led to hoarding, and hoarding created the black market. Black market prices of some fuels, notably petrol, diesel, kerosene and cooking gas, were often more than ten times higher than official prices. As fuel prices rose (and as political tension increased), the naira's value depreciated heavily once again: from an equivalency of about fifty naira to the dollar before the strike, it fell to about ninety naira to the dollar during the strike. As fuel prices rose, transport costs increased, causing a general inflationary effect. Factories which depended on diesel-powered machinery found it difficult to operate. In most urban homes the scarcity of kerosene and cooking gas meant cooking with firewood and sawdust. In order to use these "primitive fuels," however, those of them who lived in the upper floors of storied buildings had to relocate their kitchens to their courtyards. Generally, the strike made life more miserable for Nigerians.

In late September 1994, after the strike had ended, the Nigerian National Petroleum Corporation (NNPC) dramatically increased the prices of petroleum products. To illustrate, the price of a liter of petrol rose from N3.25 to N15.00. But soon after, in early October, Abacha reduced the new prices by about 26 percent. Thus the price of petrol was reduced from N15.00 to N11.00 per liter. The supply of fuel in Nigeria has been fairly stable since then.

Fiscal Policy, Foreign Exchange Management and Foreign Investment

In his first budget (January 1994), Abacha reintroduced many government controls which, in keeping with the principles of SAP, had been abolished in the Babangida era. The controls included: a ceiling on interest rates (21 percent); a fixed exchange rate of 22 naira to the dollar; and import licensing. These measures were contrary to prevailing economic practices in the countries of the Third World which were experiencing rapid economic growth, and were thus criticized by Nigeria's corporate leaders, the World Bank and the International Monetary Fund (IMF), and even by the Central Bank of Nigeria (CBN).[19] By mid-1994 it had become clear that the above measures were not helping the economy: they encouraged corruption, were a disincentive to exporters, and (precisely because the federal government sold its foreign exchange at rates that were far below their market value) helped to balloon the federal government's budget deficit. Yet the Abacha regime did not revise the budget.[20]

Also in January 1994, the federal government introduced a five percent Value Added Tax (VAT) on most locally manufactured and imported goods in Nigeria. The tax caused an immediate inflationary effect. One report in February 1994 showed that it had led to a 50 percent increase in the prices of manufactured goods. However, as the economy became accustomed to the tax and since its rate has remained the same, its inflationary effect has not been continuous. The VAT has since been an important source of revenue for Nigeria's federal, state and local governments. It yielded N8.1 billion in 1994 (two billion naira higher than the projected revenue from the tax), N21 billion in 1995 and N29 billion in 1996.[21]

In his 1995 budget, Abacha abolished import licensing, but maintained the fixed exchange rate regime (still at 22 naira to the dollar) and the ceiling on interest rates (still at 21 percent). In March 1995, however, the federal government adopted a dual exchange rate, whereby foreign exchange would be sold at the fixed rate for official business and religious pilgrimages, and at its real market value to individuals, associations and companies. Since then the federal government, through the CBN, has from time to time auctioned foreign currencies to banks at rates that are competitive with black market rates. The CBN calls its action "intervention." Since then, and largely due to CBN's interventions, exchange rates have hovered between \$1=N80 and \$1=N85. Thus the government has succeeded in stabilizing exchange rates. This achievement has had certain advantages. For instance, it has helped to stabilize prices, to facilitate medium-term planning by governments, companies and individuals, and has been enabling the federal government to earn money in naira from the sale of its foreign currencies.[22] But it has had one important disadvantage: the rate (or the range of rates) at which stability was achieved has ensured that the value of the naira was, in 1998, almost as low as it was during the fuel crisis and strike of 1994. This was not favorable to wage earners, all of whom are paid in naira.

Also in the 1995 federal budget, the Abacha regime announced the abrogation of two laws which were considered to be impediments to foreign investment. These are the Exchange Control Act of 1962, which empowered the federal government to regulate the amount/proportion of foreign exchange any individual or business organization could take out of Nigeria, and the Enterprises Promotion Decree of 1972, which reserved certain categories of enterprises either partially or exclusively for Nigerian citizens. The decree repealing the above laws was promulgated in July 1995. However, foreign investors continued to shun Nigeria. Political crises, the bad reputation of Nigerians abroad, and the IMF's and World Bank's unwillingness to endorse the federal government's economic policies: these have been identified as the remaining impediments to foreign investment.[23]

The most powerful critics of the Abacha regime's economic policies were the International Monetary Fund and the World Bank. In 1994 the regime felt it could ignore them, and reintroduced the controls of the pre-SAP era. But after early 1995 (when that year's budget was announced), the regime took these two institutions more seriously. Basically, the IMF and World Bank wanted the Nigerian government to achieve "fiscal discipline" (essentially to stop deficit spending), stop running business enterprises, and devote a greater proportion of its revenue to debt servicing. To achieve these, they compelled the government to, among other things, reduce its work force, privatize all government-owned companies, reduce expenditure on social services, and scrap unviable projects like the Ajaokuta Steel project. They also required the government to minimize the cost of its transition program, increase the prices of petroleum products, devalue the naira, abolish controls on interest rates, and abolish protectionism of all sorts. The Abacha regime had tried to do almost all of this. Some of the measures it had taken have been mentioned above; others will be mentioned under some of the sub-headings below. As a result of the government's effort to achieve fiscal discipline, it was possible for the CBN and the Federal Ministry of Finance to announce that the federal government had a budget surplus of eight billion naira in the first half of 1996.

Some foreign observers, like the British High Commissioner and the United States Ambassador to Nigeria, had praised the 1995-96 economic policies of the Abacha regime.[24] But the IMF and the World Bank were not impressed. They were even doubtful about the government's claim that it achieved a budget surplus in the first six months of 1996. According to a World Bank official,

> Both institutions [the CBN and the Federal Ministry of Finance] were wrong in that they did not include the revenues and expenditures of the Petroleum Special Trust Fund and did not deal transparently with the differences in revenues caused by the higher than projected price of petroleum..., interest paid versus interest accrued in external and internal debts.[25]

Thus, the IMF and the World Bank wanted the federal government to adopt more stringent measures to reduce its expenditure before they could endorse its economic program.

For their part, Nigeria's corporate leaders had commended the Abacha regime for achieving "macroeconomic stability." In late 1996, as the announcement of the next budget approached, they urged the federal government to stick to the fiscal measures of 1995 and 1996. To make the measures already taken by the government even more effective, they advised the government to abolish the official exchange at prevailing market rates.[26] The IMF and the World Bank also pressed the government to do this. However, Nigeria's corporate leaders (who call themselves the Organized Private Sector) acknowledged that macroeconomic stability has not alleviated poverty and has probably worsened the unemployment situation in Nigeria. According to a report by Nigeria's National Association of Chambers of Commerce, Industry, Mines and Agriculture (NACCIMA, one of the arms of the Organized Private Sector), "the misery index is still critically appalling as no meaningful result has been achieved in poverty and unemployment, NACCIMA and other corporate organizations wanted the government to, among other things, increase the purchasing power of Nigerians, through higher wages and investments in public works.[28]

In its 1997 budget, the Abacha regime stuck to its macroeconomic policies of 1995 and 1996. Contrary to the wishes of corporate leaders, the government did not scrap the dual exchange rate system, and Abacha said nothing about increasing public sector wages. Instead he announced a new policy that probably had the opposite effect: in the name of encouraging the practice of "true federalism," he abolished the uniform salary structure under which the federal, state and local governments had been operating since the 1970s and advised each state and local government to pay as it could afford.

Education

In 1994 the federal government had taken over from the local governments the responsibility for funding primary education in Nigeria. This led to regular payment of teachers' salaries and to significant efforts to improve the infrastructure of primary schools in the country. But these gains were not significant enough to improve the reputation of public primary (as well as public secondary) schools. Hence the Abacha era witnessed the opening of large numbers of private primary and secondary schools in almost all parts of Nigeria. Public schools were being left for the poor.

Because of Abacha regime's fiscal discipline and the low purchasing power of the naira, the federal and state governments spent increasingly less in real terms on the provision of facilities in secondary and post-secondary institutions in the country. Hence the facilities they had were miserably inadequate. Also because of the above factors–fiscal discipline and inflation–and the fact that there had been no review of the salaries of teachers in public schools and the universities since Abacha assumed power, teachers at all levels of the educational system had become so poor that they could not reasonably be expected to offer their best. Poor salaries and inadequate facilities contributed to several strikes by secondary school and university teachers in the Abacha era. For instance, since November 1993, there had been several strikes by secondary school and university teachers in Nigeria. Two long strikes took place from July 1994 to January 1995 and from April to September of 1996. These conditions had also led to a rather massive "brain drain" from Nigerian universities. Large numbers of educators had also resigned their appointments and taken up more lucrative jobs in multinational corporations and in some branches of the civil service, like the departments of Customs and Immigration (whose staff were also very poorly paid but who had ample opportunities, in the course of their duties, to get rich through taking bribes).

To meet increased demands for higher salaries and funds in the educational sector, many state governments (for example, those of Edo, Imo and Abia) had increased or introduced fees in their secondary schools and universities. After the 1996 strike by university teachers, which lasted from April to September, the federal government indicated that it would soon start "sharing the burden of education," particularly post-secondary education, with parents. "Economic fees" in universities, and hence the inability of children of low income earners to receive post-secondary education, and the promotion of the idea that higher education is not a right but a privilege: These ideas will probably be the educational legacies of the Abacha regime's fiscal discipline.[29]

Health

Poor funding, poor salaries to medical staff, irregular payment of those salaries, and the resulting industrial unrest were recurring problems in the health sector after Abacha became Head of State. Another problem has been the flight of qualified medical staff out of Nigeria to North America, Europe and the Middle East, and from public to private hospitals. Thus the Abacha era witnessed a deterioration in the quality of health care delivery in Nigeria. To illustrate, the comprehensive infant immunization program faithfully implemented by the Babangida regime, was neglected by the Abacha regime. Often, vaccines were not available. If they were available, they were administered to infants for a fee. Generally, public hospitals had declined so badly that, as one columnist wrote in late 1996, they were "centers for those waiting to die."[30] Patients literally waited to die in public hospitals when health workers were on strike or when they were unable to pay the "economic fees" required for their treatment.

Roads

The deterioration of federal and state roads, both highways and urban roads, which had begun in the last two years of the Babangida era, reached an alarming extent in the Abacha era. As one columnist wrote of Lagos roads, Nigerian roads "present vivid pictures of valleys, craters and gullies crisis-crossed by brooks and rivulets...[because of] failed and abandoned drainages."[31] The federal and state governments did very little to rehabilitate roads in 1994 and 1995. But in the second half of 1996, a government trust–the Petroleum Trust Fund (PTF)– started an extensive road rehabilitation program in all parts of the country.

The PTF was an "intervention fund" established in March 1995 to use the additional earnings from the 1994 increases in the prices of petroleum products to help rehabilitate infrastructure: roads, hospitals, schools, water works. By late November of 1996, the PTF, which seemed almost like a parallel federal government, had, among other things, awarded contracts worth N33 billion for the rehabilitation of 12,500 kilometers of federal and state highways and urban roads.[32]

The Civil Service

Since the 1975 purge of federal and state civil servants by the Murtala Mohammed regime, employees of the civil services of the federal, state and local governments of Nigeria had been traumatized by a strong feeling of insecurity. The 1975 purge, which was done with little sense of discrimination, was a precedent which subsequent regimes (including Abacha's) followed. For example, there was a large-scale retrenchment in the federal civil service and federal parastatals in 1995. Job insecurity often causes loss of morale and a certain desperation (desperation to survive by rough-and-ready means) among workers. This was probably why there was a marked decline in the morale and efficiency of public servants in Nigeria.

In addition to insecurity, Nigerian civil servants had been badly hit by inflation. During this time, no civil servant could rely on salary alone to meet his basic needs, and the bulk of them were alarmingly poor. Yet civil servants, including the very poor, survived. But they survived mainly by private business and corrupt practices. Those of them who were comfortable were often the ones who used their positions to make much money through corrupt practices. The few civil service jobs which were still attractive were those, like the Customs Service, which enabled the officers who hold them to enrich themselves by corrupt means.

In 1995, the Abacha regime effected an important change in the leadership of the civil service. On the recommendation of the NCC, the regime restored the civil service rules of the pre-Second Republic era. Under the rules which had been in operation since 1979 (the year the Second Republic began), the position of Secretary to Government, formerly held by the most senior Permanent Secretary, became a political appointment, and non-civil servants were often appointed to that post. The 1979 rules were strengthened by Decree No.43 of 1988, which gave a freer hand to political heads of the federal and state governments in appointments to important civil service posts. It permitted the governor of a state or president of the nation to appoint any person they liked--any person who was literate and had no criminal record--to the post of Director-General (the new name for Permanent Secretary). The 1988 decree also took away the function of Chief Accounting Officer of ministries from the Director-General, and gave it to the Minister/Commissioner. Indeed this decree gave so much power to the Minister/Commissioner that the functions of the Director were hardly more than those assigned to him by the Minister. Clearly, the 1988 reforms tended to ignore knowledge and experience and encouraged the arbitrary exercise of power. The restoration of the old order is therefore commendable.

The Gender Issue

As in other countries of the world, the gender issue has been the question of how to improve the socio-economic and political status of women in relation to men. The cause of women is usually championed by feminist groups which, among other things, pressure governments to discriminate affirmatively in favor of women and to help end cultural, religious and statutory discrimination against women.

When Babangida was at the helm, the First Lady, Maryam Babangida, was Nigeria's leading campaigner for the upliftment of women's status and for improvements in the living conditions of women. Abacha's wife, whose name is also Maryam, as the country's First Lady, also assumed responsibility for improving the lot of Nigerian women. In early 1995 she launched a program, called the Family Support Program (FSP), which was designed to alleviate the economic and health problems of the country's women. Using her husband's influence rather than her own reputation, she raised hundreds of millions of naira for the program on the day it was launched. Much of the money came from government ministries and parastatals. The highest donation of N100 million was made by the NNPC.[33] The wives of military governors of states (who, unlike their civilian counterparts, are not permitted to bear the title of First Lady) took a cue from Mrs. Abacha, and later raised millions of naira for the program in their various states. These fund-raising ladies used the monies they realized to build hospitals and health centers for women and children. They also campaigned against early marriages by girls and the withdrawal of girls from school, and for more top political and other appointments for women.

In 1995 Abacha created a Ministry of Women's Affairs, to coordinate government efforts to improve the conditions of women.[34] He also appointed three women into the reconstituted federal cabinet of 1995. With the support of the federal government, a large Nigerian contingent, led by the First Lady, participated with fanfare in the 1995 Beijing Conference on Women. When they returned to Nigeria, the Abacha regime promised to implement the recommendations of the conference.

It would be well to observe here that for decades before the first ladyship of Maryam Abacha, even before that of Maryam Babangida, Nigeria had several activist feminist organizations whose objectives were even broader than those of the FSP. Under Abacha, however, the wives of military leaders were the leading champions of the women movement. Perhaps because of sheer lust for power, the new champions of feminism were concerned to control the country's feminist associations. It is widely believed that only nominees of the First Lady had any chance of being elected to executive positions in large women's organizations like the National Council of Women's Societies (NCWS). Thus, independent-minded feminists (for example, Laila Dogonyaro, former President of the NCWS, who lost her position to a nominee of Mrs. Abacha) were compelled to become inactive or, if they insisted on remaining visible, to fawn for patronage in the offices of soldiers' wives (most of whom had no feminist past). Clearly, the feminist movement was, in common parlance, hijacked by the government, and, even though it might have profited by this in terms of money, jobs and publicity, its participants lost their freedom of thought and action.

Crime

As in the times of Abacha's post-civil war predecessors, armed robbery remained a menace to the safety and happiness of Nigerians. Until late 1996, when several state governments began to use soldiers to track down armed robbers, the Abacha regime proved unable to minimize the incidence of armed robbery. One of the reasons for the regime's failure in this respect was probably its neglect of the police. The conditions of service of policemen were as wretched as those of other public sector workers, and, particularly after Abacha became Head of State, policemen's salaries were not paid regularly.[35]

The Abacha era also witnessed several assassinations of prominent Nigerians.For example, Kudirat Abiola, wife of the detained ex-presidential candidate Moshood Abiola, was killed in June 1996. There were at least five bomb blasts, in Kaduna, Ilorin and Lagos. The Nigeria Police, some prominent members of Abacha's government, and indeed most Nigerians, believed that these crimes were politically motivated. But during Abacha's regime, nobody was charged to court, let alone convicted, for any of the assassinations and bomb blasts.[36]

Like previous military regimes, the Abacha regime early assumed the responsibility for leading the fight against corruption in Nigeria. Abacha had reportedly amassed much wealth by corrupt means before he became Head of State. So he could not adopt the principle of "first remove the log in your own eye, and then you will see clearly to remove the speck in your brother's eye." Yet Abacha did take some bold anti-corruption measures.

Perhaps the most important, certainly the most remarkable, of Abacha's anti-corruption measures was the enactment of the Failed Banks and Other Financial Institutions Decree of 1994. This decree provided for the setting up of tribunals to try some bank officials and their customers who were believed to be responsible for the failure of many commercial and merchant banks in the country. The tribunals started sitting in 1995 and had recovered hundreds of millions of naira from the culprits and jailed many bank officials and others (customers), who, by taking loans without adequate collaterals and not bothering to repay them, caused the crash of the failed banks.[37] In his budget speech of January 1997, the Head of State promised that two decrees similar to the Failed Banks Decree–a Failed Parastatals Decree and a Failed Contracts Decree–would soon be enacted.

The Abacha regime also made serious efforts to control drug trafficking and Advance Fee Frauds (popularly called "419") which had been prevalent in the Babangida era. The National Drug Law Enforcement Agency (NDLEA) was quite effective, if somewhat overenthusiastic.[38] To help minimize "419," offices for local and international telephone and fax services, which had been used by fraudsters to contact their overseas dupes, were closed down by the federal government in 1996. Rich fraudsters and drug barons became less visible on the streets of Nigeria. The above anti-crime measures won much popular support for the Abacha regime. This resulted in a widespread belief in Nigeria that Abacha had changed: that he had become "born-again" and, thus, he was a blessing to Nigeria and the best Head of the State the country has had since independence.[39]

FOREIGN AFFAIRS

As we have seen above, Canada, the United States, Japan and the countries of the European Union all applied some sanctions against Nigeria after the annulment of the June 1993 presidential election. The sanctions remained in force after Abacha came to power. These countries insisted that the Abacha regime adopt a credible program for the restoration of democracy and keep a good human rights record before they would lift the sanctions on the country. As we have also seen, the Abacha regime was unwilling or unable to take these steps. Thus its domestic policy was a drag on its foreign policy.

Abacha's first foreign minister, Alhaji Baba Kingibe (Abiola's running mate in the 1993 presidential election), adopted a diplomatic attitude toward the West. Under him, the Ministry of External Affairs tried to convince the West that the seizure of power by the military was in response to popular demand and in the interest of national unity and stability. The ministry wanted the West to give the Nigerian government more time to restore democratic rule, stating that the Constitutional Conference would establish the constitutional framework and determine the timetable for elections for the restoration of civil rule. The ministry also criticized the imposition of sanctions on Nigeria, arguing that sanctions hurt the poor more than those leading the government.

These statements were attacked by the Nigerian opposition, led by NADECO and prominent individuals like 1986 Nobel laureate Wole Soyinka. The opposition campaigned abroad for the application of more sanctions against Nigeria, including a boycott of Nigeria's crude petroleum. We are not able to determine the exact extent to which the efforts of the opposition influenced official policy in the West. But the policy adopted by the West was closer to what the opposition wanted than to what the Abacha regime desired. The highlights of this policy were a continuation of the sanctions imposed in 1993, and criticisms of Nigeria's human rights practices at international forums. In several subtle ways, Nigeria was treated as a pariah state.[40]

In the second quarter of 1995, Abacha reconstituted his cabinet, appointing Tom Ikime, a former Chairman of one of the two political parties of the Babangida era, as his new Minister of External Affairs. Unlike Kingibe, Ikimi was combative in his diplomacy. In a manner reminiscent of leftist academics in Nigeria in the 1970s and early 1980s, Ikimi condemned the countries of the West, accusing them of trying to undermine Nigeria's sovereignty, of neo-imperialism, and of being hypercritical of the Abacha regime.[41]

Within Ikimi's first year in office, in November 1995, the Commonwealth expelled Nigeria for the alleged judicial murder of Ken Saro-Wiwa and eight other Ogoni activists. In addition to the Commonwealth countries, the European Union and the United States condemned the execution of the Ogoni men, recalled their ambassadors from Nigeria, asked Nigeria's ambassadors in their various countries to go home, and perhaps most importantly, increased the range of the sanctions they had applied against Nigeria.[42]

To make up for its losses in the West, and probably also as a way of putting pressure on the West to change its policy toward Nigeria, the Abacha regime began to strengthen the country's ties with non-Western countries like Indonesia, China, India, Iran, Iraq and Turkey. Lucrative contracts in oil mining, railway rehabilitation and supplies of motor vehicles were given to some companies based in these countries. For instance, a Chinese company was given the contract for the rebuilding of Nigeria's railway system, and an Indian company was given a contract to supply light trucks to NECON. Thus the Abacha regime put pressure on Western companies in Nigeria to continue lobbying their home governments to soften their stance on Nigeria. To add to this pressure, in 1996 the government broke diplomatic relations with Canada, which had become highly critical of the regime's human rights practices. In this manner, the Nigerian junta warned other Western powers that it could afford to dispense with its diplomatic relations with the West.

There were several Western companies in Nigeria which would have wanted their home governments to be more tolerant of the Abacha regime, so as to protect their commercial interests in the country. But it does not seem that their governments were persuaded by the Abacha regime's measures. In November 1996, the European Union extended its sanctions against Nigeria for another six months.

Although Nigeria in 1996 was a pariah in western Europe and North America, its leadership role in African international affairs (especially in the West African sub-region) was not significantly threatened. In West Africa, Nigeria's armed intervention in the Liberian civil war remained her most important diplomatic effort. This effort, as we have seen in a previous chapter, began in 1990, when Babangida was at the helm, under the auspices of the Economic Community of West African States (ECOWAS). In his first broadcast as Head of the Interim National Government (ING), Shonekan had said that his government would soon end Nigeria's involvement in the Liberian crisis. But the ING did not, and probably could not, do this before it was overthrown. Unlike the head of the Interim National Government, General Abacha seemed committed to keeping Nigerian troops in Liberia for as long as it took to achieve the objective for which they were sent there.[43]

Interestingly, Western countries were supportive of Nigeria's mission in Liberia. Despite the disagreements with Nigeria's internal policy, in October 1996, the United States' government gave 10 million dollars in assistance to the ECOWAS Monitoring Group (ECOMOG), the Nigerian - led force which was stationed in Liberia.[44] But the mission was not popular in Nigeria, mainly because of its high costs in money and lives. As of April 1996 there were several estimates showing that the country had spent over 4 billion dollars in Liberia.[45]

CONCLUSION

There had been much hope for a peaceful transition to civil rule in Nigeria in June 1993. The annulment of the June 12,1993 presidential election by the Babangida regime dimmed that hope and raised political tension in the country. Ignoring the repercussions of Babangida's action on his own transition program, Abacha's political ambition drove him to ruin his own transition program as well. Had he suceeded, he would had frustrated the desire of enlightened Nigerians for the institutionalization of Western-type (not Indonesian-type) democracy in Nigerian and dashed the hope of southern Nigerians (and perhaps northern progressives also) for the rotation of presidential power between the northern and southern sections of the country.

The Abacha regime managed to achieve "macro-economic stability" in Nigeria. Several measures appropriate to its goals of attracting more foreign investment to the country were also adopted. However, the regime was not able to improve the living conditions of most Nigerians. The Abacha-led federal government did not bother to stabilize the rate of inflation until it had risen by over 100 percent above the rate that had been in effect before June of 1993. With the federal government's efforts to reduce the budget deficit, the high rate of inflation was not counterbalanced by a commensurate rise in wages and employment. Most Nigerians were less capable of meeting their basic needs in 1998 than in the period before Abacha became Head of State. Macro-economic stability has meant the stability of impecuniousness among Nigeria's low and middle income earners.

THE ABACHA REGIME, 1997-1998: A POSTSCRIPT

Perhaps it is best to start by mentioning the major successes of the Abacha regime since March 1997. The most remarkable one was undoubtedly the July 1997 restoration, albeit temporary, of peace and democratic rule in Liberia. Even though this was done under the auspices of ECOWAS, the world knew that Nigeria had rallied other West African countries to found ECOMOG and had been urging them to remain committed to their mission in Liberia despite its high costs. The world also knew that Nigeria had provided the bulk of the money, troops and weapons used by ECOMOG to bring peace and install an elected government in Liberia. So the United Nations, the Organization of African Unity and several individual countries in the world, including the Western powers, praised Nigeria for its role in Liberia.[46]

About two months before the election in Liberia, on May 25,1997, a group of Sierra Leonean soldiers led by Major John Koromah overthrew the elected government of their country, which had been headed by Alhaji Tejan Kabbah. ECOWAS leaders met shortly after the coup, condemned it, and sent ECOMOG to Sierra Leone to block the country's air and sea links to the outside world. By these actions, they put pressure on the junta to quit. In March 1998, Nigerian troops in Sierra Leone military government, and paved the way to the restoration of the civilian government to office.[47] Even though Nigeria did this without the consent of other ECOWAS states, and even though Nigeria itself was under a military government, international organizations and several of the world's leading nations hailed Nigeria for its effort.

Another effort of the Abacha regime that was largely successful was its road rehabilitation program, which led to the rehabilitation of hundreds of federal and state highways and urban roads by the Petroleum Trust Fund (PTF). The regime's major failure in this respect was that a large majority of the roads that were rehabilitated were in the northern states of the country: the PTF did not work on most of the roads it had undertaken to rehabilitate in the southern states.[48]

Apart from the above, it is difficult to identify any major success of the Abacha regime during his last year or two in power. The regime's performance during this period was very poor. It appears that the government suddenly became bereft of energy and patriotic feelings, with the result that, apart from implementing its transition program, it could hardly do anything to arrest social and economic drift, let alone promote economic development, in the country.[49]

In the year or so immediately preceding his death, Sani Abacha and his ministers virtually stopped the anti- corruption crusade they had launched in 1994. They did not promulgate the Failed Contracts Decree and the Failed Parastatals Decree which they had promised to enact in early 1997. And they unduly delayed the setting up of new Failed Banks Tribunals until May of 1998. These new tribunals were to try the cases of suspects who had been in detention since 1994 or 1995 but had not appeared before any of the existing tribunals. The large number of tribunals--ten in all--that were set up in 1998 indicates that the number of cases that been left unattended was quite high.

By mid-1997 all four of the petroleum refineries in Nigeria, with a combined capacity of refining 445 barrels of crude oil per day, had broken down. The federal government was unable to repair them, and began to import fuel into the country. But it could not import enough to meet the country's needs. From late 1997 until the present day there have been periodic acute fuel shortages in Nigeria. The economic and social costs of acute fuel scarcity are staggering. [50]

Apart from the problems with refineries, the Abacha regime also presided over the closing of Nigeria's National Fertilizer Company (NAFCON) and almost all the steel rolling mills and cement companies in the country. In April-May 1998 cement production virtually stopped in the country, which was compelled to depend almost exclusively on imported cement for some time. It was evident that the quantity imported could not meet the country's needs at the time. The price of a bag of cement rose from about N500 to between N800 and N1000.[51] The breakdown of NAFCON also affected fertilizer supply in the country, and fertilizer became a scarce commodity. To meet pressing agricultural demands, some state governments, like those of Niger and Oyo, rushed to establish their own fertilizer plants.

Throughout this time of acute scarcities of fuel, fertilizer and cement, the Abacha regime evinced little concern for the plight of the Nigerian people. There was no obvious sense of urgency on the part of senior government officials to end the scarcities, not even to offer explanations for them or to raise hopes that normal supplies would soon resume. As on newspaper report said of Abacha: "despite all the agony that the perennial fuel crisis in the country... inflicted on the people, ... [Abacha] never spoke to the people, not even to make excuses for what was happening."[52]

One might raise the question:"Why did Nigeria decline so badly in the last year of the Abacha regime? This is a rather difficult question, but we will attempt to give as detailed an answer as space permits. A number of reasons can be readily identified.

One reason for Nigeria's decline was the cumulative effect of the sanctions applied by the West in 1993, and again in 1995. This made it difficult for Nigerian companies to get spare parts. Even spare parts for very important facilities like those for oil refining, and cement and fertilizer production were hard to come by. The sanctions also made it difficult for the country to reschedule its debts and to obtain new investments. Nigeria's new Asian "friends" did not help in any meaningful way to mitigate the effects of the sanctions imposed by the West.[53]

Another reason was that Abacha may have been ill. If so, he concealed it effectively. Certainly he did not devote much time each day to affairs of state. During this time, it was common knowledge that Abacha came to work late and left early. Thus, among other failings of the regime, meetings of the Provisional Ruling Council, cabinet meetings and those of the National Council of States were rarely held. And it was extremely difficult for ministers and other senior government officials to meet with Abacha when they wanted or needed to do so.[54]

Yet another reason for the decline was corruption, especially at the highest levels of government. Reliable media sources reported that Abacha and some of his ministers, security chiefs and business friends were looting billions of naira from the national treasury. One such report, of October 1996, revealed that the Minister of Petroleum Resources, Chief Dan Etete, had been duped of $200 million (about N17 billion). The report was not denied by the minister, who remained in Abacha's cabinet until the end.[55] Abacha himself reportedly acquired about N500 billion (over $6 billion) during his administration,[56] with properties and investments of about CF500 million (about N60 billion) in Britain alone.[57] These are indices of the degree of corruption in the country. Not surprisingly, one German-based non-governmental organization reported sometime in the last few years that Nigeria was the most corrupt country in the world. Unlike corruption in Asia, which was said to be "productive" in that the bulk of the loot was invested at home in enterprises that promote further economic growth and development, official corruption in Nigeria was not "productive." The bulk of what was acquired by corrupt means was taken abroad (mainly to Europe) and much of what was left at home was squandered on expensive consumer goods imported from Europe and Asia. It is precisely because corruption led to capital flight of enormous proportions from Nigeria that hardly any economic development plan could have worked in Nigeria during the Abacha era.

But the most important reason was the series of domestic political decisions taken by the Abacha regime. Determined as he was to succeed himself, Abacha pressed ahead with the transition program he had announced in October 1995. Thus, in March 1997, the regime conducted local government elections "on a party basis," and, in the same month, swore the elected councillors and chairmen into office. In December 1997 the regime conducted state legislative elections. The elected assemblymen were to wait until October 1998 to assume office.[58]

In late December 1997 political tension rose suddenly in the country following an announcement that the government had uncovered a plot by some senior army officers and some civilians, who were allegedly led by Abacha's deputy Lieutenant-General Oladipo Diya to overthrow the Abacha regime. Diya and those who allegedly planned the coup with him were arrested in December 1997. During March and April of 1998, they were tried in camera (in closed judicial sessions) by a military tribunal. Six of the accused-- Lieutenant. General Diya and five other persons (all of whom were Yoruba)-- were sentenced to death by the tribunal. The others were either acquitted or sentenced to various terms of imprisonment. The Provisional Ruling Council had yet to review the sentences before Abacha died, and Diya's sentence was never carried out.

Meanwhile Abacha continued implementing his self-succession program. In April of 1998 the regime conducted National Assembly elections. These elections were heavily marred by fraud. Terrible voter apathy led to low voter turnout, estimated to be less than one per cent. Also in April 1998 each of the five political parties registered by NECON, obviously following a script written for them, adopted General Abacha as their presidential candidate. It appeared that Sani Abacha was going to emerge as civilian President of Nigeria without undergoing the process of election.

As Abacha and his aides were working toward his transformation to a civilian President, the Nigerian opposition were making their own plans to stop them from realizing this objective. Among other things, they intensified their campaigns abroad for economic sanctions against, and for diplomatic isolation of, Nigeria. One of the oppositions groups, the one led by Wole Soyinka, set up a radio station to wage a propaganda war against the Abacha regime. Some of the other groups, especially those which had activists who were resident in Nigeria, chose to oppose the regime through rallies and demonstrations in the streets. Three of such public protests are notable. One was a rally staged in Lagos from the third to the fifth of March 1998. It was organized by a coalition of civil rights groups to counter a pro-Abacha rally being staged in Abuja during the

same period. The other two protest rallies were staged in Ibadan in April
and May 1998. The April rally, which was also meant to counter a
pro-Abacha rally in the city, ended violently. The second Ibadan rally,
held on May Day, also ended violently and with the detention of several
opposition leaders. However, despite the shooting of protesters and the
detention of their leaders, the opposition remained defiant, vowing to hold
more anti-government demonstrations.[59] The stage was thus set for more
confrontations in the streets between the government (in the form of the
police and the army) and the opposition in the months ahead.

With Abacha at the helm, and with the armed forces apparently
loyal to him, it seemed there was no stopping him. It seemed certain that
more opposition elements would be gunned down in the streets, that those
in power would intimidate other Nigerians opposed to the ruling regime,
and, that Sani Abacha would be taking the oath of office as President of
the Federal Republic of Nigeria and Commander-in-Chief of the Armed
Forces on October 1, 1998. It also seemed certain that, with General
Abacha imposing himself on Nigerians as their civilian President, political
tension in the country would escalate, the sanctions on Nigeria would not
be lifted, foreign investors would continue to shun the country, and the
"leaders" of Nigeria would continue to loot the treasury without restraint.
But Sani Abacha died on June 8,1998. Suddenly, Nigeria had fresh
opportunities to resolve its political crises, review its foreign policy, and
revive its economy.

ENDNOTES

1. For biographical sketches of Ernest Shonekan, see the *Guardian*, 27/8/93; and *Newswatch*, 6/9/93.
2. See cover stories of *Newswatch*, 13/9/93 and 1/11/93.
3. *Newswatch,* 6/12/93.
4. Information from the author's notebook/diary.
5. *Ibid.* See also newspaper reports of Abacha's first week in office, 18-25 November 1993.
6. See reports in *Newswatch*, 27/9/93 and 4/10/93.
7. See all Nigerian dailies, 20/11/93.
8. See Nigerian newspapers and magazines of the period. For instance, see the *Guardian*, 12-13/6/94 and 6-8/7/94.
9. See the *Daily Times* and the *Vanguard*, 19/8/94.
10. Reports on and analyses of the Head of State's speech can be found in Nigerian newspapers and magazines of the first week of October 1995.
11. *Ibid.*
12. Information from the author's notebook/diary.
13. See the Sunday *Vanguard*, 12/11/95 and *Tell*,20/11/95.
14. For a report on and a denunciatory review of the elections see *Tempo*,4/4/96.
15. See the *Guardian*, 3/10/96, *Tell* and *Newswatch*, 14/10/96.
16. See: comments by S.G. Ikoku, a veteran politician and member of the Abacha regime's Transition Implementation Committee, in the Punch, 22/10/96; an interview with Abacha's wife, in the *Guardian* on Sunday, 12/1/97; and excerpts of an interview granted by Abacha to an American newspaper, in the *Guardian*, 6/2/97.
17. See reports on the front pages of the *Guardian* and the *Vanguard*, 27/11/96.
18. Information from the author's notebook/diary.
19. For instance, see the cover story of *The Nigerian Economist*, 14/2/94.
20. See report on the economy in *Ibid.*, 16/5/94. See also an interview with economist Rasheed Gbadamosi in the same issue of *The Nigerian Economist.*
21. See report on the economy, with emphasis on VAT, in *The Nigerian Economist*, 14/2/94. For an assessment of VAT after its first three years, see the *Vanguard*, 21/2/97.
22. See reports on the economy in the *Nigerian Tribune*, 1/11/96 and *Tell,* 14/10/96.

23. See comments by the United States Ambassador to Nigeria in the *Nigerian Tribune*, 1/11/96 and the report on EU sanctions in the *Guardian*, 27/11/96.

24. *Ibid.*

25. Dr. H.L. Hutcheson of the World Bank Resident Mission in Abuja, in a speech at a seminar in Abuja. Speech is reproduced in the *Post Express*, 4/12/96.

26. A detailed report on the economy is in *Newswatch*, 9/12/96.

27. Quoted in *Ibid.*

28. *Ibid.*

29. On the state of education, especially tertiary education, see Advertiser's Announcement by the National Chairman of the proscribed Academic Staff Union of Universities in the *Daily Champion*, 10/10/96.

30. By Onome Osido-Whiskey, in *Tell*, 2/9/96.

31. *Ibid.*

32. See the editorial of the *Guardian*, 29/11/96 and reports in *The News*, 3/6/96 and the *Daily Times*, 3/12/96.

33. Information from the author's notebook/diary.

34. See the 1995 budget speech of the Head of State.

35. Information from policemen at Uturu, Abia State.

36. See the front-page report of the *Vanguard*, 14/2/97, on the most recent bomb blasts in Lagos.

37. Information from the author's notebook/diary.

38. See story entitled, "The Many Victims of Bamaiyi" in *The News*, 4/4/96. Major-General Musa Bamaiyi is the head of the NDLEA.

39. For instance, see S.G. Ikoku's comments in the *Punch*, 22/10/96.

40. For instance, see the *Daily Champion*, 5/6/95 (p.3).

41. See Nigerian Television Authority (NTA) network program, "Tonight at Nine", of Saturday 18 November 1995.

42. See Nigerian newspapers of 12-15 November 1995.

43. See the cover story of *The News*, 29/4/96.

44. See page 23 of *Tell*, 14/10/96.

45. See *The News*, 29/4/96.

46. See Aka Akpuru Aja, "Nigeria's Peace Roles in Liberia and Sierra Leone: Strategic Analysis," in Okechukwu Okeke et al (eds), *Issues in Contemporary Nigerian History* (Port-Harcourt: EBI, 1998), 270-298.

47. *Ibid.*

48. Personal observation. To further illustrate, sometime in the last week of July 1998, the Secretary to the Osun State Government, a highly-placed civil servant who would not be expected to talk carelessly, called for a probe of the PTF. According to him, the PTF, which had reportedly done

much in some other states, had not made its presence felt in his state. The Secretary of the PTF's reaction to the allegation was carried by the NTA in its network news of 3/8/98.

49. See the editorial of the *Guardian*, 29/7/98.

50. See page 9 of the *Vanguard*, 18/4/98 and *The News*, 27/10/97, (p.9).

51. See *The News*, 27/10/97 (pp. 32-33) and the *Vanguard*, 18/4/98 (p.21).

52. See report in the *Guardian*, 15/6/98 (p.15).

53. See the *Vanguard*, 18/4/98 (p.21).

54. See the cover story of *Tempo*, 18/6/98 and the *Guardian*, 15/6/98 (pp.15-16).

55. See *The News*, 20/10/96 and 27/10/96, and *Tempo*, 28/5/98.

56. See *The News*, 27/7/98.

57. See the *Guardian*, 3/8/98 (p.55).

58. See Nigerian dailies, 6-9/12/97.

59. See the *Vanguard*, 18/4/98 and 2-4/5/98.

Major General Abdulsalaam Abubakar
Head of State 1998-1999

Chapter 10

Abdulsalaam Abubakar's Interregnum, 1998-1999

Gloria IfeomaChuku

INTRODUCTION

After the sudden death of General Sani Abacha on June 7, 1998, Abdulsalaam Abubakar became Nigeria's ninth military ruler since independence. A Major General who had served as Nigeria's Chief of Defense Staff under Abacha's regime, Abubakar was promoted to the full rank of General on June 9, 1998 during the ceremony when he was appointed as Nigeria's new Head of State by the Provisional Ruling Council, the country's highest governing body.

Abdulsalaam Abubakar was born on June 13, 1942 in the town of Minna near Abuja into the devout Muslim family of Alhaji Abubakar Jibril and Hajiya Fati Kande Mohammed. He has been described as a career serviceman who was thoroughly professional. He was a very well-respected military officer who did not appear tainted by a political past.

It is generally believed that it was because of these qualities that his colleagues appointed him to succeed Abacha. Abubakar was seen as the person who had the capacity to bring together the factions in the army, including hardliners such as Abacha loyalists and hangers-on as were all ambitious young officers. Abubakar's ascension to Nigeria's top political post was seen as a step to hold the military together, improve its image, and bring stability to the fluid political situation in the country.

After his swearing-in as the Head of State, during the celebration of the thirty-eighth anniversary of Nigeria's independence, Abubakar announced programs and reforms his government would accomplish. Among such proposals were his commitment to hand over power to a democratically elected government on May 29 1999; restoration of the rule of law and protection of individual rights and freedom; ensuring a free political environment and protecting the human rights of all citizens. He also promised to produce a constitution that reflected the feelings and aspirations of all segments of the Nigerian society by setting up a committee to review the 1995 Draft Constitution. The discussion that follows examines to what extent these program and policies were accomplished. We will group our discussion under the following themes: the transition to civil rule, social policy, the economy, and foreign policy.

One month after ascending to power, Abubakar dissolved the 34-member Cabinet he inherited from his predecessor General Sani Abacha. He however, left in place the Provisional Ruling Council, the core of the military junta that had ruled Nigeria since 1993.

TRANSITION TO CIVIL RULE

The greatest achievement of Abdulsalaam Abubakar, of course, was the successful completion of the transition to civil rule in May 1999. On assumption of office, Abubakar inaugurated a new electoral commission. He passed a series of decrees formally scrapping the transition program that had been adopted by his predecessor. All five of the registered political parties under Abacha's regime had endorsed and made him the sole candidate for the presidency in the transition process even though his rule had been marked by a series of human rights and political abuses. Total lack of political freedom and fear of being locked up in detention, or even killed, warranted this decision.

When Abubakar came to power, he created a political atmosphere that encouraged people to participate freely in politics. He scrapped Abacha's transition program including the elections held before Abacha's death and the Nation Election Commission that organized them.

Abubakar instituted a fresh transition program under conditions of greater openness. The Independent National Electoral Commission (INEC), headed by Justice Ephraim Akpata, released the guidelines for voter registration and the elections. INEC's guidelines stipulated that political associations must pay 100,000 naira (about 1,250 US dollars) to get provisional approval to function as a political party. Unlike in the past, they did not need a particular number of card-carrying members to get approval. But they must have received at least ten percent of the votes in 24 states during the local government elections. This arrangement was a marked departure from Abacha's regime, when all political associations were required to show proof of voters' registration and to maintain offices in all the states of the federation and local governments, (as well as headquarters in Abuja) before being registered as a political party. With these new arrangements, the politicians and civilians had a free hand to form parties and manage the elections independently under the scrutiny of the Commonwealth and the United Nations.

Some innovations were adopted in the voting process. For example, knowing that politicians had bought up millions of voter cards, Abubakar's government ordered that voters must queue up to register, and once registered, must stay in polling stations[1] until registration was completed and voting started. This rule, and the transparent ballot boxes used during the elections, at least limited multiple voting and fraud. On December 5, 1998, Nigerians went to the polls for the local government elections. Elections for state governors were carried out in January 1999, and those for the National Assembly and the Presidency of Nigeria took place on February 20 and 27, respectively. On May 29, 1999, the newly elected president, retired General Olusegun Obasanjo was sworn-in as the Executive President of Nigeria. While the United States of America and Britain praised Abubakar's government for its swift moves to bring about political reforms, Canada offered financial and technical assistance for the country's transition program.[2]

Abubakar's transition to civil rule was a success, though not without some problems. The first problem was the opposition from the Southern Minorities Front of Nigeria (SOMIFON), and the National Democratic Coalition (NADECO). According to these groups, Abubakar was placing the cart before the horse by insisting on elections before the resolution of the real causes of Nigeria's unending political instability. NADECO supported the presidential claim of Moshood Abiola and demanded a national unity government to be headed by Abiola (who was still being held in prison) to oversee the transition to democracy, a demand that Abubakar rejected. Elections in the Niger Delta states were particularly problematic because of the inhabitants' long fight for justice, better treatment, equal opportunity and reward for oil produced in the region. Generally, the elections were marred by bribery, of which all parties were guilty. But the result was widely agreed to have reflected the will of the Nigerian people. The presidential election was a competition between the Peoples Democratic Party (PDP), which won majority votes that brought Obasanjo to power, and the All People's Party (APP), whose candidate was the former finance minister, Olu Falae. The successful handing over of power to a democratically elected government erased the fears of most Nigerians and their friends, and proved Abubakar's critics wrong.

SOCIAL POLICY

The administration of Abdulsalaam Abubakar pursued a number of reforms in the country. Abubakar released more than 140 prisoners[3]-- including senior military officers, politicians, and journalists, who had been unjustly incarcerated by Abacha. He freed all detained opponents of the Abacha regime, a long-standing demand of Western Governments and pro-democracy activists at home and abroad. Discussions were taking place regarding the conditions to release Chief Moshood Abiola, who had been incarcerated since 1994 by Abacha, when he died suddenly on July 7, 1998. The resulting riots caused the death of more than 60 people. Abubakar also announced that government had withdrawn all charges against Nigerian exiles to pave the way for their return to the country. A good number of them did return.

Abubakar scrapped major decrees banning trade union activity. He released some labor union leaders imprisoned by Abacha. Although tough military decrees remained in place, including a decree that allowed for indefinite detention without trial, and hordes of detainees were still in detention, there was a general feeling and belief that Abubakar had begun to lift the sense of terror that had weighed on the country during Abacha's iron-fisted regime. In general, the level of individual freedom, freedom of expression and freedom of association among others greatly improved. Cases of people detained without trial, and some cases of persons already convicted were examined and appropriate decision taken. Because of these reforms, Nigeria was removed from the United Nation's list of human rights oppressors.[4]

In his July 20, 1998 address, Abdulsalaam Abubakar announced the suspension of the exercise on rationalization of staff in the public service to avoid an action capable of spreading large-scale discontent in the service. The announcement showed Abubakar's sensitivity to the plight of the public servants, who had been subjected to irregular salary, lack of promotion, poor wages, and non-payment of retirement benefits. Suspending the rationalization exercise was not enough in view of the poor working conditions of the public servants. In September 1998, he announced a raise in the minimum wage of the public sector. Unfortunately, the government could not meet this promise. Instead, it climbed down on the increase in civil servants' wages. Abubakar's interim government's inability to stick to its earlier decision on the raise in the minimum wage resulted in protest demonstrations and several weeks of strikes. With poor wages, the people were restive over high inflation, fuel shortages, and collapsing infrastructure.

One of the most serious problems that confronted the interim government of Abubakar was how to deal with the people of the oil-producing areas. On July 20, 1998, Abubakar announced that the concerns of the people of this region remained a priority of his government. Apparently, his announcement was not followed-up with constructive actions to resolve the problem in the oil-producing areas. Thus, a few weeks after the announcement, an organization of militant youths of the ljaw ethnic group (who called themselves the Federated Niger-Delta Izon Communities) seized twenty flow-stations demanding more say in local government and representation on how revenues from oil produced in their land were shared. They also closed taps, shutting off about a third of Nigeria's two million barrels a day exports.[5] On December 11, 1998 the ljaw issued the Kainama Declaration. By this declaration, they claimed ownership of all natural resources found in ljaw territory. Protesters occupied oil industry flow-stations and stopped production. They took some oil workers hostage. The protesters gave the oil companies in their land until December 30 to withdraw from the ljaw area pending the time the issue of ownership and control of resources would be settled. The oil companies responded by asking the interim government for improved security.

Within a few weeks of this wave of unrest in the oil-producing areas, Abubakar was forced to use some measure of force to restore at least temporary peace in the region. The situation in this region became a test of Abubakar's authority and ability to maintain peace and order in the country. Military personnel were deployed to the region to crack down on the protesters. Many felt that excessive force was used to quell the unrest. According to a 200-page publication[6] of the Human Rights Watch in February 1999 on the human rights violations connected to the suppression of protest at oil company activities, there was evidence of the use of excessive force against the protesters in the region between December 1998 and January 1999. The publication reported the death of several dozens of people, torture and inhuman treatment, and arbitrary detention of many. The demonstrations of the Ijaw youths in Yenagoa, the capital of Bayelsa State and in Kaiama community had been met by sporadic shooting, resulting in the killing of these unarmed youths. Soldiers, as the report shows, remained deployed in Bayelsa and Delta states. Although the report acknowledged the genuine security concerns relating to kidnapping of oil workers and inter-community conflicts in Delta State, it strongly opposed the deployment of soldiers in the region.

Amid widespread criticism, the government appointed a committee to consider the needs of the Niger Delta. The committee recommended immediate disbursement of 15.3 billion naira (170 million US dollars) on development projects, and the establishment of the Niger Delta Consultative Council (NDCC) to be made up of government figures and representatives of the oil companies to oversee the development projects. Although government held discussions with selected Ijaw leaders in relation to this plan, there may be a problem with the committee's recommendation regarding those who should constitute the membership of the NDCC. It is very absurd to constitute a committee to oversee the development of the Niger Delta region without representatives drawn from the indigenes. The non-inclusion of the indigenes in this committee is not unprecedented in Nigeria's development policies. Historical evidence has shown that laudable urban and rural development projects of government in Nigeria failed partly because of the imposition of such projects on the people. Those involved should be given the opportunity to participate actively and be part of any development projects that directly affect them, be it by the government or corporate organizations.

Abdulsalaam Abubakar also announced anti-corruption measures such as open competitive tendering for government contracts, elimination of the dual exchange rate, a more transparent system for the importation of petroleum products and a requirement that all senior military officials in government declare their assets. Most of these measures were mere rhetoric, for as we shall see below, corruption as well as lack of resources was a factor in the state of disrepair.

THE ECONOMY

When Abdulsalaam Abubakar took power in June 1998, he announced a number of economic reforms his government would pursue. He tried to put in place a transparent regulatory framework for competition and nondiscrimination in all sectors. He repealed all major laws inhibiting competition in every facet of the economy. Apart from announcing government plans toward privatization, commercialization, and liberalization, Abubakar's government issued a decree to privatize and commercialize some government-owned parastatals such as Nigerian Telecommunications Limited (NITEL), which had had negative impacts on the country's economic growth. But these were only on paper, for no actual privatization took place during the interim regime of Abubakar. Some forms of liberalization took place, but not enough to attract enough immediate responses from foreign investors. Part of the problem was the high level of corruption in Nigeria, which made foreign investors reluctant to do business in Nigeria. Of course, this situation was on-going before Abubakar came to power.

Abubakar reached agreement with the International Monetary Funds (IMF) and creditor governments in an attempt to reschedule Nigeria's debts totaling $37 billion dollars[7] for an extended structural adjustment facility (ESAF). The Nigerian government agreed to an IMF-monitored program. The first step of this agreement was to abolish the controversial dual-exchange rate. The dual-exchange rate, which allowed official institutions linked to the government access to cheaper foreign currency, and which also fueled corruption, was scrapped by government. Under the dual exchange rate system, favored individuals had had the right to change Nigerian naira at the rate of N22 to the dollar, when the official rate was N86. As part of the IMF deal, the Nigerian government devalued the naira by 4.2 percent. Already in 1998, the naira currency had lost more than 14 percent of its value against the US dollar as a result of Nigeria's political instability and worries over its future.[8] There was also a renewed commitment to the privatization process in the 1999 budget. Abubakar's government also deregulated the fuel market causing petrol prices to double. In all this, the lower manpower and the masses bore the greatest burden of survival.

An acute fuel shortage was one of the problems that confronted Abubakar's administration. Petrol was rationed. At times, some cities witnessed closure of petrol or gas stations due to non-availability of fuel. In a country that produced more than 2 million barrels of oil a day, these were bitter circumstances. Some Nigerians resorted to smuggling and stealing of fuel. For example, there was the Atiworo fire outburst on October 17,1998 when people illegally opened fuel pipes or valves and started fetching the urgently needed fluid with buckets and other containers. In this incident, more than 700 people were burnt to death and about a thousand more suffered horrific injuries.[9] Part of the shortage was that only one of the country's four oil refineries was working. The importation of fuel, which had been going on before Abubakar took office, was increased, as chronic fuel shortages began to cripple the economy and even the government. In order to increase productivity, Abubakar reorganized the Ministry of Petroleum Resources and the state-run Nigerian National Petroleum Corporation (NNPC). For some weeks, the Petrol Resources Ministry had no minister, but was run by a civilian technocrat. Abubakar took this action because he believed that part of the problem of the ministry had to do with its ministers. Abubakar also issued clear guidelines on who could take part in oil marketing.

A detailed plan released by the finance minister, Ismaila Usman, outlined measures to be taken to diversify the economy, accelerate the privatization program, and give the Central Bank of Nigeria some autonomy in monetary policy. Some of the country's debts were paid. For example, the amount of 630 million dollars owed to multinational oil companies was paid. These reforms were well received by the international community especially in the business circle. It was reported that foreign interest in Nigeria was beginning to pick up. Inquiries about trading possibilities had multiplied by five at the Deputy British High Commission in Lagos since Abubakar took over office.[10]

When Abubakar came to power, he promised to track down the hundreds of millions of dollars stolen by Abacha and his cronies. In August 1998, it was reported that the government uncovered about 500 million US dollars stashed away illegally in bank accounts and safe houses by Abacha's former national security adviser, Ismail Gwarzo. This recovery was an encouraging development. However, that was one of the several cases of looting of the Nigerian government treasury by the Abacha administration. If the government had recovered more than the above amount, the citizens were not informed. Many Nigerians believed that they knew who the thieves were and how much they stole from the treasury, how much was recovered and for what purposes the recovered money had been used. Such thieves, they insisted, should be punished according to the law of the land.

It was not surprising that Abubakar's administration could not handle the issue of government officials stealing money from the Nigerian treasury. After all, this was the same circle of people who had been in power since 1993. Thus, from the military's action, it was clear that Abubakar's government was only a little better than its predecessor when it came to plundering Nigeria's wealth. There were reports of a last-minute spending spree by Abacha's ministers, of oil prospecting licenses going to friends of the regime, and of palatial retirement homes being built for leading members of the interim government by "grateful" foreign contractors. The awarding of lucrative oil exploration concessions to firms run by senior military officers at prices lower than what foreign companies were willing to pay attracted widespread criticisms especially from the international bankers and the incoming government of Obasanjo. Abubakar was personally responsible for approving oil and defense contracts. Almost a billion dollars disappeared behind the mysterious screen of "defense spending," and no one outside the inner circle of the military knew how the money had been allocated. Most of the contracts awarded--for oil exploration, for events such as the hosting of the Youth World Cup in Nigeria, and for the license to print money--went to military officers. The Nigerian press said that while Abubakar had a stake in four of the oil contracts, Admiral Mike Akhigbe, Chief of the General Staff, got dozens of the lucrative government contracts in hard currency. The interim government never denied these allegations.

On March 8, 1999, the government awarded without tender eleven oil exploration blocks and eight oil lifting contracts on Nigerian waters to a group of companies (some of which were not even registered) owned by well-connected military officers and local businessmen. The national government also awarded a twenty-two million dollar contract for the construction of a new national assembly, a similar amount to build a new defense headquarters, and 100 million for a new police center. About 600 million dollars worth of last-minute deals for the renovation of old structures and revival of schemes abandoned twenty years ago were signed just in April 1999, barely one month before Abubakar handed over power to the civilian administration.[11] This action was seen more as a sort of golden pensions for some of the country's top military men than as a way of getting the best deal for Nigeria. There was a lack of accountability in these awards. All these contracts were dressed up as "indigenization" of the oil industry and the Nigerian economy.

Abdulsalaam Abubakar's interim government faces public scrutiny over billions of dollars worth of unbudgeted and unaccountable government expenditures. For example, one billion dollars worth of miscellaneous contracts were awarded in the last five months of his military regime. Up to this day, no explanation has been given on how the above amount as well as the sum of another 2.5 billion US dollars was spent under Abubakar's authority, amounts about which there are few or no records at the Central Bank of Nigeria.[12] According to Abubakar, part of the money, about one third of the country's reserves, was spent on propping up the naira, which had plummeted by more than 10 percent. He blamed the rapid fall in reserves on a sharp drop in oil revenue, the main base of the country's external trade, from 17 US dollars per barrel in the 1998 budget to nine US dollars per barrel in 1999; the cost of holding three sets of nationwide elections; and the return to civilian rule. He also blamed the cost of hosting the Youth World Football (Soccer) Championships in Nigeria in 1999; and the financing of Nigeria's military leadership of the Economic Community of West African States Monitoring Group's (ECOMOG) peacekeeping operations in Sierra Leone after the rebel invasion of Freetown in January 1999. Although these projects and operations cost a lot of money, they do not in any way account for the suspicious and unexplained depletion of Nigeria's foreign reserves, and the outrageous last-minute contracts that Abubakar's interim government awarded.

Amid public outcry, Abubakar called for a halt to new public spending after it was revealed that foreign reserves were drawn down by 2.7 billion US dollars to four billion US dollars between the end of December 1998 and the end of March 1999. On March 9, 1999, at the donors' meeting in Paris, finance minister Ismaila Usman pledged to restore some order to government spending. But all these promises seem to have been mere rhetoric. Within the same period, the interim military government approved projects of dubious merit and of no particular urgency for some of the lesser government ministries to a value of an astonishing 280.3 naira (3.1 billion US dollars).[13]

The pilfering continued right until the end of General Abubakar's transitional government. The recklessness in government spending and expenditures shrank the Nigeria's foreign exchange reserves from seven billion dollars at the end of June 1998 to $3.1 billion dollars at the end of April 1999.[14] This amount was further depleted by the time Abubakar handed over power to the civilian government because, as we saw above, he continued to award contracts even until his last days in office.

General Abubakar also did something in his last days in office that suggested how insensitive he really was to the economic plight of Nigeria.   Amid the impoverishment of majority of the Nigerian population, Abubakar signed into law a retirement package for Nigeria's heads of state and their deputies. According to a government gazette, Number Seventy of May 11, 1999,[15] which was signed by General

Abdulsalaam Abubakar, the Nigerian government would pay 350,000 naira as monthly upkeep allowance for each former president or head of state for life. Also, all former vice presidents and chiefs of general staff (CGS) would be paid 250,000 naira annually. In addition, each would be given a diplomatic passport, three cars renewable every five years, a grade level-twelve officer bodyguard, free medical treatment within and outside Nigeria, a five-bedroom bungalow, a paid annual vacation for a month abroad, and three security men drawn from the police, army and state security service. Many Nigerians expressed surprise and anger at this extravagant retirement package. They saw it as Abubakar's final effort to impoverish the country. This was signed into law at a time when there was a nation-wide teachers' strike caused by the inability of government to approve and pay teachers a minimum wage of 3,500 naira a month. The strike lasted for four months. It had devastating effects on the education of Nigerian children and increased the economic woes of Nigerian families.

FOREIGN POLICY

In his July 20 address, General Abdulsalaam Abubakar promised that his interim military government would devote a substantial part of its time to improving the country's external image as well as to actively participating in the promotion of global peace, stability and progress. Nigeria would be a responsible and respected member of the international community. He stepped out to have further cooperation with African countries, and to restore relations with Nigeria's friends abroad. In August 1998, Abubakar went to South Africa on his first official visit abroad where he assured the South African government of his commitment to democratic reforms. In the gathering of non-aligned countries in South Africa in September 1999, and at the opening of the United Nations' General Assembly in New York, Abubakar succeeded in charming fellow heads of state especially with his program of transition to civil rule. He sent his foreign minister, Ignatius Olisemeka, a respected ex-diplomat, to London to request Nigeria's full readmission to the Commonwealth. The mild sanctions on Nigeria were lifted except for the ban on arms sales.

Abubakar showed serious commitments to the operations of the Nigerian-led West African ECOMOG peacekeeping force in Sierra Leone when the president of that country, Ahmad Tejan Kabbah, who had no army of his own, was faced with rebel attack. He did not act unilaterally, however. Abubakar sought and got some assistance from such foreign countries as Canada, Britain, the United States of America, Italy and the Netherlands.

CONCLUSION

Abubakar's interim government has been criticized for its inability to reform the army to ensure that in future the military keeps out of politics. The greatest criticism, however, concerned his administration's plundering of the country's financial reserves. He ran down Nigeria's foreign reserves and left his successor, Obasanjo, a poisoned chalice. The general decline of the Nigerian economy, utter disrepair of infrastructure and high level of corruption compounded to make Nigeria among the poorest twenty countries in Africa.[16]

However, Abubakar won worldwide applause for bringing his transition program to a successful conclusion. As a Nigerian politician put it, "Abubakar may have the shortest reign of all political rulers in Nigeria but he may become the hero of a new Nigeria, and best remembered" because of this singular act.[17]

ENDNOTES

1. One hundred and ten thousand (110,000) polling stations were built for the elections.

2. It should be recalled that Canada cut her aid to Nigeria in 1995, and removed its embassy in 1997 following repeted civil and human rights abuses of the Abacha regime. But it has continued to support pro-democracy groups in the country. See *Electronic Mail and Guardian*, August 27, 1998.

3. On June 15, 1998, Abubakar announced the release of Frank Ovie Kokori, Milton Dabili, Retired General Olusegun Obasanjo, Dr. Beko Ransome-Kuti, Chris Anyanwu, Alhaji Ibrahim Dasuki, Chief Olabiyi Durojaiye, Uwen Udo, and Chief Bola Ige, referred to as prisoners of conscience.

4. *Electronic Mail and Guardian*, September 8, 1998; and BBC *News Online Network*, Tuesday, August 11, 1998.

5. *The Economists*, October 24-30, 1998.

6. *The Price of Oil: Corporate Responsibility and Human Rights Violations in Nigeria's Oil Producing Communities*. New York: Human Rights Watch, 1999.

7. *BBC News Online Network*, December 31, 1998, put Nigeria's external debts at $37 billion including arrears.

8. *The Associated Press*, June 9, 1998, and *The Economist*, January 9-15, 1999.

9. *The Economist,* October 24-30, 1998.

10. *The Economist,* August 29-September 4, 1998.

11. *The Economist,* March 27-April 2, 1999; and *Daily Mail and Guardian*, May 25, 1999.

12. *African Confidential*, vol. 40, no. 17-27, August 1999.

13. *African Confidential*, vol. 40, no. 10-14, May, 1999; and *Daily Mail and Guardian*, May 25, 1999.

14. *The Economist,* May 22-28, 1999.

15. *Post Express*, July 8, 1999, "The Rewards of Coup-plotting and Nation-leading."

16. A World Bank Report, *BBC News Online Network*, December 31, 1998.

17. Chukwuemeka Ezeife quoted in *Electronic Mail and Guardian*, August 27, 1998.

Chapter 11

The Future of Nigeria: Problems and Prospects in the Twenty-first Century

G. N. Uzoigwe

THE PARADOX OF NIGERIA

Having examined comprehensively in the previous chapters the post-civil war history of Nigeria from the administration of Yakubu Gowon to that of Abdulsalaam Abubakar, we conclude this book by taking stock and looking forward to the future. Here both the historian and the reader must tread carefully. No one is equipped, of course, to forecast the future, and there is no intention to do so in this chapter. Nevertheless, the historian is permitted to attempt a look at the future by drawing from the past and the present, bearing in mind all the time that, in the final analysis, the past is really all that we know.

The post-civil war history of Nigeria contains several paradoxes. There is the contrast of unitarianism versus federalism, republicanism versus monarchism, national identity versus ethnic identity, secularity versus theocracy, enormous resources versus great poverty, high expectations versus poor performance. These paradoxes puzzle and infuriate Nigerian scholars, including contributors to this book. Particularly inexplicable to them is how a country so profusely endowed with enviable human resources and an embarrassment of natural resources could find itself mired not only in the foggy bottom of confusion but also even more seriously in a state of almost total stasis.[1] For many scholars, the predictions are dire, the future very bleak.

Will these problems continue in the twenty-first century without resolution? If the answer is yes, then there seems to be no way the nation-state of Nigeria can endure. But this is a conclusion no historian can risk. This is why contributors to this book exercise cautious optimism. It appears probable that the future of Nigeria will be characterized by a slow and painful yet purposive regeneration and, eventually, renaissance--because almost everything that could have possibly gone wrong for Nigeria has already done so: genocide, political assassinations, civil war, colonial domination and more. Nigeria has demonstrated an uncanny ability to bend without breaking. Given the country's evolution and heritage, it would be naive to expect events to move smoothly in the post-independence period after the British colonial administration left so many fundamental issues unresolved. Nigeria's problems will likely work themselves out gradually under patient, sound and progressive leadership operating within the framework of a constitution that creates an acceptable potestas.[2] The desire of Nigerians to establish a workable democracy and correct the evils of the past is a clear indication that a nationwide rebirth is in progress. No doubt, this rebirth will be severely challenged and tested by unprogressive and anarchic forces. Having dealt with the nightmares of imperialism and colonialism, Nigerians are better prepared to face the complexities of the twenty-first century.

Informed opinions may differ legitimately about what will constitute the core issues for Nigeria in this century and even in what order to rank them. They may also differ about what solutions to propose. But Nigerians must deal with these issues if their country is to realize its great potential.

IMPORTANCE OF NIGERIA

It is not often realized that Nigeria is today one of the world's largest democracies. Nigeria can be regarded as a microcosm, or metaphor, for all of Africa.[3] Its many problems and experiences are shared by other African countries to a lesser or greater degree. And given the country's importance in the continent --one in five Africans is a Nigerian---Nigeria's future is certainly more than of tangential interest to African countries.

By any measure, Nigeria is clearly the major player in the West African sub-region, and a front-line country in Africa, (with the potential to be the leading actor in the continent), and not an insignificant power at the world stage, (with also the potential to be one of the great powers) by the close of this century. It is the most populous African country in the world with an estimated population of between 120 and150 million. It should, therefore, constitute a future formidable power with Africa and the global African diaspora behind its leadership. Nigeria is the biggest oil producer in Africa with about a quarter of the continent's crude oil reserves; and among African nations it is second only to Algeria in natural gas reserves. These reserves, estimated to be more than 182 trillion cubic feet (TCF) and expected to last for 450 years, double the quantity of the country's substantial mineral fuel reserves. This places Nigeria in the ninth position among gas producers in the world.[4] Within the Organization of Petroleum Exporting Countries (OPEC), it is the sixth largest producer. Globally, Nigeria is the sixth largest crude oil exporter and the twelfth largest producer of oil. Its current reserves of 25 billion barrels are expected to be boosted to 50 billion barrels by 2010; and the current productive capacity of 2.13 million barrels per day is expected to rise to 5 million barrels.[5] Indeed, according to David Frost, Mission Manager of the Birmingham Chamber of Commerce, in ten years Nigeria would be at par "with the Middle East Oil producing countries, regarding to what use revenue generated is being put, rather than using most of it to pay off debts as is currently the case."[6] It is important to note also that Nigeria and South Africa account for 58% of Africa's Gross Domestic Product (G.P.D.).[7] Nigeria's first fuel export under colonialism, coal, is found in thirteen states. Reserves are estimated to rise to more than two billion metric tons.[8] Nigeria's oil resources are of strategic value to the North American and European economies. The future of Nigeria, therefore, is of significant global interest today, especially as Mid-Eastern sources of petroleum become enmeshed in political instability.

And yet, to many observers Nigeria has become a subject of ridicule, myopic assessments, several irreverent commentations, and predictions that are totally lacking in historical foundation. To a large extent the Nigerian leadership since independence is responsible for this development. It fought one of the largest post-Colonial civil wars in Africa in the twentieth century. And because of the unpleasantness with which the country has been associated under indigenous leadership,

Nigeria has become an example of wasted opportunities for significant, economic and socio-political development in Africa and the world. It has become an example of how "so little can be achieved from so much," and an example of how pervasive and deleterious the effects of poor governance can be. Thus one outraged writer has castigated Nigeria as Africa's "open sore".[9] Another has accused the Nigerian leadership of "losing the twentieth century."[10] Yet another has dismissed Nigeria as a "Crippled Giant."[11] What these assessments have failed to point out--and should have noted--is that on the bright side, there is a growing feeling that a political and economic upturn in Nigeria is possible and even probable; that Nigeria has a realizable potential to be the new economic frontier which is expected, under proper management, to lead the next generation of emerging economies in this century. After all, the Nigerian state, like any other state, is a living organism. And it is a grave mistake to consign such an organism to oblivion. Certainly, no historian worth his or her salt would dare to do so.

PRIMACY OF POLITICS: "SEEK YE FIRST THE POLITICAL KINGDOM"

Nigeria's problems are political and congenital, that is, historically the leadership--British and indigenous--has been unable to fashion workable constitutional mechanisms that would hold the large and complex country together. This is unfortunate because Nigeria, far from being a mere geographical expression and a historical abstraction, is a natural geographical and historical unity.[12] The failure of the makers of modern Nigeria to realize this fact right from the start led to the conventional wisdom that Nigeria is an artificial creation of British companies and the British government.[13] Policy decisions arising from this idea inevitably resulted in the political incoherence and instability that eventually led to the Nigerian Civil War of 1967-1970. Most of the defining issues that will be discussed in this chapter derive essentially also from this failure. Until they are properly resolved Nigeria's problems will intensify. Those who believe that after forty years of indigenous rulership Nigerians should stop blaming British colonial government for their woes should be reminded that historical legacies die hard and that Britain, in large measure, created Nigeria's dilemmas.

Federalism Versus Centralism

Let us take, for example, the constitutional problem of federalism versus centralism, which has been described as a "British Dilemma,"[14] but which was to become a Nigerian nightmare.[15] This dilemma has its genesis in the Lord Selborne Report of 1898, modern Nigeria's first constitutional document whose fundamental principles have remained more or less intact.[16] Simply put, the problem facing White Hall at the inception of colonial rule in Nigeria was this: how to govern hundreds of vibrant national groups with Imperial resources that were very limited. The British colonial administration, always suspicious of federal constitutions, and afraid of the consequences of a unitary constitution in a colonial environment, chose deliberately to employ the time-tested colonial device of divide and rule. Subsequent constitutions from Clifford to MacPherson introduced some changes but left the fundamental principles largely undisturbed. And although the Independence Constitution of 1959 ensured the triumph of federalism over centralism it was a curious type of federalism that was adopted. This constitution has been described appropriately as "an object lesson in unbalanced federalism."[17] It maintained the three regions structure in which one region (the North) was bigger both in population and territorial extent than the other two regions (the East and the West) combined. The replacement of this constitution with a unitary one by the government of General Aguiyi Ironsi in 1966 was intended to bring into line the military concept of centralized command. However, this step was misunderstood by the North. This led, in part, to the Nigerian Civil War. Ironsi's assassination led to the restoration of what was thought to be a federal constitution. But was it really? We know that confronted with the anomalous character of this constitution there developed quietly a myth whereby the country was recognized officially as a federation but in reality was ruled unitarily. In short, Gowon's "federation" was essentially Ironsi's centralism without the name. This fabrication continued up to the interregnum of Abdulsalaam Abubakar.

Nigeria's essential disunity is inherent, in large part, in this constitutional incongruity. Until this anomaly, which has deep roots in British colonialism, is resolved, not even a saint or a genius can effectively solve Nigeria's problems. This is why Nigerians must follow the advice of Kwame Nkrumah and "first seek the political kingdom," hoping that other things dear to their hearts will follow after the achievement of basic national unity. This is not mere wishful thinking. A leader is the product of a country's historical forces, and he or she is as good or as bad as the country he leads. The Nigerian leadership since the end of the civil war has not been unaware of the primacy of politics in the solution of the country's problems. That is why continuous efforts have been made to create more states and local governments since 1970. But it is also true that although by 1996 thirty-six states and 775 local governments have been created the fundamental constitutional dilemma has remained unresolved. The Hausa-Fulani continue to see the Middle Belt as an indivisible part of the North in which they would brook no interference whatever some nationalists in the region may want. The Yoruba and the Igbo do not have a similar problem. Not even the current division of the country into six ethno-regional zones has made any significant difference. This division for the purpose of rotating the presidency as well as for sharing executive posts has not yet been enacted as part of fundamental law. The legacy of the military mind, which is very noticeable in the proceedings of Obasanjo and the desire of Nigerians to always require strong central intervention in state affairs, demonstrate that neither the military nor most Nigerians understand the limits of federal government and presidential authority in a federation.

To buttress this point, a look at the current Constitution of the Federal Republic of Nigeria (Promulgation) Decree 1999, Decree No. 34[18] demonstrates that the Nigerian leadership is still wedded to the ideas of the earlier constitutions that have not worked. The fairly radical 1989 Constitution proposed by Ibrahim Babangida, itself a revision of the Olusegun Obasanjo 1979 Constitution, was more or less rejected by the Constitutional Assembly of 1994. For all practical purposes, it was ignored by both Sani Abacha and Abdulsalaam Abubakar. The most perplexing, however, of these constitutions is the current 1999 constitution which, thankfully, is being revised. Some constitutional lawyers have appropriately dismissed it as "a false document," "Pure Tokunbo" ("foreign make"), a "federal arrangement unitarised," "a unitary federal constitution,"[19] and so forth. Essentially, the problem with this constitution is that it is an unimaginative means of perpetuating the myth of running a unitary state-with its central concentration of power--under the guise of federalism. And yet even the critics of this document seem to be irrevocably committed to the idea that true federalism must only be a two-tier arrangement in which power is shared between the central government and the federating states. This standard textbook concept of federalism may be ideal for states in which there is really only one culture, broadly defined. But it has always worked badly in multi-cultural states such as Nigeria. This being the case, Nigeria's constitutional dilemma can only be resolved if the country can devise a document which provides for a proper three-tier federation in which responsibilities are relatively shared between the local governments, the states, and the central government.[20] Each of the tiers will have clearly defined responsibilities within which it is completely autonomous. The 1999 document does not do this. It empowers the central government to legislate on all important issues. It does not permit the states and local governments to have exclusive, residual legislative power. By thus providing the center with an overwhelming amount of legislative autocracy--as well as giving it an unprecedented right to interfere in the affairs of the states and local governments--this so-called "federal" constitution grossly violates the principles of federalism. Equally importantly, the present revenue arrangement (for example) whereby the central government retains some 55 percent of budgetary allocations makes the center simply too powerful. As Bola Tinubu, Governor of Lagos State laments: "The Federal Government does not want to give away what it perceives as an empire. They are operating an empire system of government in a republic... We want a republic, not an empire... the cumulative total of what the Federal Government takes is about 70 percent. We are only left with about 30 percent to share between the 36 states and the 775 local governments."[21] That is why electing the Nigerian president is a "do or die" struggle. It is being suggested, therefore, that for Nigeria to have the internal peace and stability that it requires to be an African or even world power in this century, the country needs to be restructured constitutionally. Nigerians must now go back to the drawing board, and debate the future with no holds barred. No subject will be too sacred to touch; cosmetic improvements will be rejected. This debate may take place under the auspices of a sovereign national conference or under any other arrangement that the Nigerian legislature approves. Decisions arrived at must be subjected to a national referendum. Whatever is the case, the ideal is to make the center less seductive but sufficiently attractive to talented Nigerians who are drawn to politics at the level not solely for monetary gains (as seems to be the case presently) but largely for an opportunity to serve and govern in the best interests of the vast majority of Nigerians.

This is admittedly a rather tall order, but it is an ideal nonetheless worth pursuing for the next millennium. Since most Nigerians seem to believe that Nigeria must continue to exist, and since the present two-tier arrangement has woefully failed, giving a proper three-tier arrangement a trial cannot hurt. On the contrary, it offers a real possibility for resolving Nigeria's constitutional dilemma.

Republicanism Versus Monarchism: Future of Traditional Rulership

Related to the constitutional dilemma discussed above is the intriguing paradox of republicanism versus monarchism. Historically, a republic originates from a death - that of monarchism. The situation, however, becomes anomalous and contradictory when a nation-state is at once a republic and a curious motley of monarchies rolled into one. President Yoweri Museveni of Uganda, I know, has restored some of the monarchies but I know enough of the history of Uganda to know that he will find the experiment difficult if not eventually regrettable.

Throughout the colonial period Nigeria was ruled as a monarchical state, the King or Queen of the United Kingdom being the Head of State. The appointed Governor-General who was seen as his or her representative acted as the executive Head of Government. In 1963 Nigeria became a parliamentary republic with a President as ceremonial Head of State and a Prime Minister as executive Head of Government. In a real sense, then, the Nigerian monarchical state was replaced by Nigeria's first republic. Somehow, however, the republican government forgot or did not have the political will to pension off the monarchs. Nigeria's turbulent history between 1964 and 1966 did not make matters any easier for the government. The overthrow of the first republic by the military in January 1966 and the subsequent civil war allowed the anomalous situation to continue almost unnoticed by the general public. The military knew, of course, that since they themselves had never been approved by the electorate, the traditional rulers offered them at least some sort of link with the people. They were thus quite satisfied to believe that these monarchs were the true representatives of their communities. Thus recognized by government, but not by any constitution, the traditional rulers took themselves very seriously. Understandably, many non-monarchical communities in the pre-British period, began to either resurrect or invent royal pedigrees to take advantage of the importance attached to monarchical communities. They sought government recognition of their kings which was invariably granted. Almost unobtrusively the traditional title of chief came to be reserved for distinguished or wealthy individuals as a sort of honorific title. The framers of the 1979 Constitution, quite aware of what was taking place, stoutly refused to assign the kings any constitutional role. Even though he had a close relationship with the traditional rulers, Shehu Shagari, who ruled under this constitution, could not do anything to make them constitutionally relevant. The return of the military in 1984 meant, however, a return to treating these rulers as representatives of their people, a role that continued until the restoration of civilian rule in May, 1999.

Clearly, this anomalous situation will continue in the future and most likely, as the Nigerian democracy solidifies, lead to conflict and instability. What, then, is to be done? The following alternatives may be worth considering. Nigerians could pension off the traditional rulers and thus remove the dichotomy between republicanism and monarchism. But since this was not done in 1963 when Nigeria's first republic was declared, a decision to do so now may result in more instability. This would be especially true in the non-Muslim states because the traditional rulers in these areas would be left without any meaningful role to play. In the Muslim areas, the emirs (the traditional rulers) will continue, of course, to perform their religious functions. This option is therefore not advocated.

Second, one could strengthen the monarchies by assigning to them some constitutional role. But this cannot be a viable option in a democratic republic. Moreover, it will be difficult to justify tax money expenditure on what amounts clearly to a sinecure institution.

Third, the new constitution should allow communities which have strong monarchical traditions or which have monarchical predilections to preserve their traditional leadership on the strict understanding that such communities will be solely responsible for their upkeep. Thus, the institution will be purely a community affair and the monarchs will have no need to seek the recognition of government. This seems to be the most viable of the three alternatives. If the proper position of monarchism in a democratic republican dispensation is not clarified, there eventually will be a clash between democratically elected deputies and traditional rulers who, although expected to be non-partisan, have been known to favor openly or discretely certain political parties. This is not healthy for a democracy. A monarchy thrives best in a centralized system of government; a republic thrives best in a federal or confederal structure. In a monarchy, rulership resides in one royal family: in a federal republic, power is decentralized with appropriate checks and balances.

Nationalism versus Ethnicity: Dangers of Ethnic Arithmetic

Inseparable also from Nigeria's constitutional dilemma is its ethnic configuration. Over the years governance has been treated as a sort of ethnic arithmetic. That the country is an ethnic or national mosaic is true; but was the ethnicization of Nigerian politics which began in the colonial period as a competition for dominance first between the Yoruba and the Igbo, later between the North and the South, and lastly between the three biggest ethnic groups (Yoruba, Igbo, Hausa-Fulani) and the others (called the minority groups although put together they actually constitute the majority),[22] and which is one of the core issues inhibiting the rise of a great Nigerian nation unavoidable? The survival of colonialism often depended on the ability of the colonizing power to divide and rule. And Britain was a master at this game. In Nigeria, Britain, in fact, may be said to have invented the concept of "tribes" (ethnic groups) to further imperial aims. Having arbitrarily divided the country into three regions - North, West and East - it was amazing, if not amusing, to watch British political officers placed in charge of the respective regions compete with one another as if they were serving different European countries. Led by F. D. Lugard, many Northern political officers, in particular, became so fascinated with the Muslim North that the interests of the rest of the colony did not appear to have been of any concern to them. All that seemed to have mattered to them was that the North must be subsidized by the south financially as well as shielded from what they regarded as pernicious southern influences. British academics, too, joined the act and created their own pet "tribes" even within each region. The current images Nigerian traditional groups have of one another were created by the British.

Those who ignore historical legacies do so at their peril because just as a good doctor cannot initiate the treatment of any ailment without first discovering what the problem is and perhaps its cause, any discussion of ethnicity in modern Nigerian politics must take into serious consideration its colonial antecedents. This is not to absolve Nigerians and their leaders from any accountability in regard to the country's ethnic problem, which is a major defining issue for the future. Because of the hunger of Nigeria's political and religious leadership for power and material accumulation, they have found the appeal to ethnic particularisms too tempting to resist. The numerous ethnic nationalities have become for them useful prefabricated collaborating groups. By promising their respective groups their fair share of the "national cake" if they captured the center, it became of paramount importance to them to support a constitutional arrangement that would make it possible for them to achieve this goal. Such a constitution, first and foremost, must make the center sufficiently enticing in terms of both power and material accumulation to make its capture worth the bother. The inevitable consequence of this centralization was the Nigerian Civil War. The bitter lessons, which were supposed to have been learned from the war have not, in fact, really been learned. Since the end of the war Nigeria's journey to nationhood, political and socio-economic development has been very much troubled. Ethnic or sub-national competition has greatly intensified. Political and religious leaders, instead of putting a stop to this destabilizing development have, in fact, openly encouraged it.

The various national governments of Nigeria, on the other hand, have tended since independence to favor some ethnic groups and deliberately marginalize others while at the same time pleading for ethnic reconciliation and national unity. This obvious insincerity has become more noticeable since the end of the war. The slogan of "no victor no vanquished" initially made somewhat meaningful by Yakubu Gowon has, since his fall from power in 1975, become a joke. Unconvinced, therefore, that these governments meant well some disaffected groups have been unwilling to bestow credulity to their protestations. Consequently, some of those who feel particularly marginalized have been gradually disengaging form the state, so to speak, and have formed parallel institutions which solve problems relevant to themselves. Initially, this development was particularly noticeable in Igbo states and took the form of self-help projects without which Igbo societies would be much worse off than they are today. In recent times other groups have also begun to complain loudly about their own marginalization, implying, so it seems, that the Igbo situation is not unique but is the general in the unique. Particularly interesting and, indeed, surprising, is the recent claim by the Hausa-Fulani that the Obasanjo administration is victimizing them.[23] For the students of contemporary Nigeria the facts must be left to speak for themselves. What is more disturbing, however, is that some Nigerian ethnic groups, instead of adopting the Igbo self-help approach, have formed aggressive, ethnically - based groups not only for the purpose of highlighting their dissatisfaction with the Nigerian state but also to protect the interests of their respective groups against encroachment from other similar organizations. In a sense, this is a declaration of no confidence in the efficacy of the Nigerian state. This raises an important question, namely, if the central government is unable or unwillingly to protect their interests or help them actualize themselves within the Nigerian federation, what, then, is the use of that government?[24] Their answer to this question has been, as we saw, to disengage from the state by forming parallel institutions (armed vigilante groups) to those of the center. "Already," laments Odumegwu Emeka Ojukwu, "One half of the country has opted out of the police force of the nation. OPC* here, Bakassi there, APC there and so on. All these are symptoms of a very big malaise in our society. I will like to see more action to achieve a true reconciliation of Nigeria."[25] A day earlier, writing in the same newspaper, Gbolabo Ogunsanwo, had underscored Ojukwu's point more pessimistically: "As of today, there are many Ijaws, many Yorubas, many Igbos, many Hausa-Fulanis and few Nigerians. The nationality question is still unresolved. Except you have the gift of extra-terrestrial knowledge, nobody can quite say confidently based on the facts on the ground that Nigeria will survive unto the end of the millennium."[26]

Legally speaking, this development may not be secessionist in intent; it is nevertheless dangerous and disturbing. True to form, some Igbo youth--reflecting a total lack of subtlety but, nevertheless, representing the view of other aggrieved Nigerian groups more reluctant to come out in the open--have founded a Movement For the Actualization of the Sovereign State of Biafra (MASSOB). This has driven the Obasanjo government, its patience apparently exhausted, to swoop down on the movement's leadership. But incarcerating the leaders of MASSOB or even executing them for treason will not solve the problem that led to their desperate action in the first instance.

The major issue in Nigerian politics has been the problem of devising the best equitable means of sharing power in a federation. Over the years successive Nigerian governments have addressed this problem. The fact, however, that the problem still persists demonstrates that it has not been candidly and properly addressed. For a federation to endure, the federating units should not be forced to cohabit. Like a marriage the partners must have reasons that make the union compelling and attractive to them; for the union to endure these reasons must continue to be relevant. Now, after forty years of nationhood, and faced with the obvious lack of confidence in the Nigerian state by most Nigerians, the Nigerian leadership should go back to the drawing board, as it were, and demonstrate to Nigerians the reasons why it is in their best interest to remain together. To do so meaningfully, the interests of the four major components of the Nigerian federation, namely, the Igbo, the Yoruba, the Hausa-Fulani, and the minorities, must be candidly ascertained and, as much as possible, satisfied, bearing in mind that in any union sacrifices are inevitable. Let us, therefore, look at these groups, drawing from available information, to determine what they conceive their interests to be. Let it be made clear, right from the start, that I lay no claim to total knowledge of their respective interests; nor am I totally free of bias. If, nevertheless, I am adjudged to have been relatively fair to all, I will be quite satisfied.

"The Igbo," I wrote recently, "are at the center of the ethnic relations in Nigeria, and their issues cannot be swept under the carpet."[27] I was saying, in effect, that in Nigerian politics the Igbo are like a big elephant in the middle of a room and not a quiet one at that. They started by being arguably the most Nigerian of all the other groups; they ended by being the first group to be sufficiently disaffected with Nigeria to risk everything by seceding from it and creating the short-lived state of Biafra. After the collapse of Biafra, they found themselves at the crossroads. Their situation has been characterized by self-doubt, self-examination, frustration, and sometimes, anger.[28] This feeling is most discernible among those Igbo born after 1960 who have no experience of the centrality of the Igbo position in Nigerian politics during the colonial period. Their elders, resourceful as ever, have tried unsuccessfully to provide an appropriate response to the Igbo dilemma. There has developed an obvious disconnect between the young and the old in Igboland. This is a dangerous development not only for the Igbo but for Nigeria as well. What, then, do the Igbo really want? As far as I can determine, they seek understanding of the question of what being a Nigerian means since the end of the civil war and why they should want to continue to be proud Nigerians. They complain that they have systematically lost ground to the other groups particularly in terms of the provision of infrastructure; representation and promotion in the security forces, the federal civil service and federal corporations; in producing a president for all Nigeria; and in the education sector largely due to the formula for admission to federal secondary schools and tertiary institutions that was devised, in their view, to penalize them in the one area that they were "level-pegging" with the Yoruba before the war. They question how, for example, the child of a Kano millionaire can be said to be educationally disadvantaged in competition with that of a poor farmer from Abakaliki! They stress that while the Yoruba monopolize the federal civil service and control the commanding heights of the economy and the Hausa-Fulani monopolized political power from independence until the accession of Olusegun Obasanjo, a Yoruba, the Igbo do not monopolize anything in Nigeria. They believe that in spite of the slogan of "no victor nor vanquished", successive Nigerian governments have continued to treat them as the vanquished. They have determined to put a stop to this deception.

      The Yoruba, too, have not been satisfied with their position in Nigeria since independence. They note that the Hausa-Fulani and the Igbo conspired in 1960 to exclude them from power. They conspired also to carve out the Mid-West from the West shortly after independence while leaving the North and East intact. They believe that Shehu Shagari did not win the 1979 presidential election and that the Igbo and the minorities failed to support actively Obafemi Awolowo's challenge to Fedeco's "award" of the presidency to Shagari. They believe that Moshood Abiola won the June 12, 1993 presidential election which Ibrahim Babangida annulled. They resent the fact that the rest of the country failed to give them adequate support. The Yoruba believe that the situation badly inhibits the country's development. They see the solution in the formation of a confederal government in which each participant has the freedom to develop according to its own abilities and pace.

The Hausa-Fulani and their surrogates have dominated Nigerian politics since independence. This was the case even during Aguiyi Ironsi's six-month interregnum which they terminated when it suited them to do so. During Obasanjo's interregnum between 1976 and 1979, Shehu Musa Ya'radua was generally believed to be the real power behind the throne, and Ernest Shonekan's short-lived interregnum was terminated by Sani Abacha when it suited him to do so). Because of this, they have found it difficult to make a coherent case regarding why they should be unhappy with Nigeria. Naturally, they want the status quo to continue. They believe that since the North comprises some two-thirds of the Nigerian landmass and slightly more than half of the population, any sharing arrangement that does not take these realities into consideration would be rejected and resisted as unfair. Democracy, they argue, is a game of numbers and that that sacred principle must be respected if Nigeria is to endure. While they accept the principle of admitting students to federal institutions without regard to merit, they do not seem to see why the same principle should have general application in the other sectors of the federal institutions that have favored them. They want the North to remain intact because a Middle Belt region that separates itself from the North dominated by the Hausa-Fulani renders their case based on the existence of a monolithic North bogus. They seem to believe that since the south controls economic and intellectual power in Nigeria, the North must balance the equation by controlling political and military power. At the same time they insist that the North must be allowed to practice its way of life by instituting an effective Sharia theocracy in both civil and criminal matters. This desire is complicated by the fact that the North is not made up entirely of Muslims.

The minorities may also arguably claim to be the most Nigerian of all groups precisely because they used to believe that they needed a strong federal government as a counterweight to their domination by the Igbo, Yoruba and Hausa-Fulani respectively. Thus, their love for Nigeria, like that of the other groups, is based largely on self-interest. Their demand for the creation of their own states, which began in the 1950s, has now been met, more or less. However, the southern minorities, which produce most of Nigeria's wealth (based mainly on mineral resources), believe that they are inadequately compensated. Oil and gas, they argue, are perishable resources; the exploitation of them pollutes their environment and renders their agricultural lands unproductive; and they fear that when these resources are exhausted, their people will slide back into poverty unless some income from these resources are ploughed back to develop their states. Others argue that in a proper federation, states control their natural resources and only pay tax to the federal government. They want the constitution to be changed to reflect this principle. But what they fail to point out is that in a country like the United States of America where a similar principle applies, such resources belong to the individual who owns the land where they are discovered. The owner exploits them and pays local, state, and federal taxes on the income derived from them. The Nigerian constitution stipulates that all mineral resources belong to the Nigerian Federal government. The minority states in the Middle Belt feel frustrated because, appealing to old loyalties, the Hausa-Fulani have continued to exercise a stronghold over them. They complain that the south treats them as if they are an integral part of the Hausa-Fulani and fail to realize that there are great differences between them and the former.

It may, of course, be pointed out that successive Nigerian governments have addressed some of these problems through the creation of states, local governments, the federal character principle, the zoning of certain offices, the revenue derivation principle, and so on. But it is also true that these devices have not worked. On the contrary, every ethnic group and every region complains about their increasing marginalization. The present attitude of studied indifference by the central government regarding protestations about marginalization in various forms will become counter-productive if not seriously addressed. One also gets the impression that the central government is not concerned that it is itself being rendered irrelevant.

If the Nigerian state is to survive the twenty-first century and achieve the great things expected of it, the political leadership should listen to the complaints of the dissenters as outlined above, at any rate, and do its best to restore their equanimity. Democracy is a most difficult form of government, but its weaknesses notwithstanding, it is the fairest of all forms of government. It requires patience and maturity especially on the part of the leadership particularly in a country that has become used to being ruled by decree. A serious effort, should be made, even in the face of flagrant provocation by anarchist or other elements, to pursue a policy of inclusion and not of deliberate and churlish exclusion of any group. Diversity for Nigeria is beautiful because if properly managed it will become a source of great strength rather than of weakness and instability. The federal character arithmetic, which to some is a policy of inclusion, has not worked properly because it is not sufficiently comprehensive to satisfy every group. If this were not the case, the issue of marginalization should not have arisen.

This problem can be remedied in one or two ways: Make the federal character arithmetic more comprehensive; or scrap it since it has been in existence more or less since 1954 and cannot - and should not - operate in perpetuity. Any imbalance in the Nigerian nation-state can also be remedied by constitutionally creating a democratic federation which grants states and local governments more specific authority and responsibilities which are inalienable. Many Nigerians and interest groups, ignorant of the limits of federal government, have developed the expectation that the center will intercede in their affairs. But a major characteristic of federal government - and perhaps its beauty - is the minimalism of its authority.

SECULARITY VERSUS THEOCRACY: RELIGION AS THE OPIATE OF THE PEOPLE

Bertrand Russell once advised in his own inimitable way that the best way to settle an ethical argument is with a big bash on the head or words to that effect. He was saying, in short, that ethical issues cannot be resolved by appealing to reason and logical argument. He was drawing, no doubt, from his study of European history, specifically from that struggle for supremacy within the *Respublica Christiana* (Christian Commonwealth), popularly known as the Investiture Contest, which may be said to have started with the coronation of Charlemagne as Emperor of the Holy Roman Empire on Christmas day 800 A.D. Simply put, the question was this: who was boss in this Commonwealth - the emperor or the pope? The question was answered when Philip IV the Fair of France (1285-1314) invaded the Vatican, defeated the army of the powerful Pope, Boniface VIII, captured him, tied him to his horse with his head facing the tail, and rode him in triumph to the Castle of St, Angelo which is situated about 1 mile from the Vatican. There he was imprisoned. This event led to the banishment of the papacy to Avignon in France for about a hundred years - the so-called Papal Captivity. But it was not really until the Council of Trent in 1545 which ended The Reformation and

Counter-Reformation controversy that the separation of Church and State in Europe was finally accomplished. This separation meant that in things temporal (secular) the state is supreme and in things spiritual (religious) the church is supreme.

This short summary of a huge subject has been supplied simply to provide the background to the current conventional wisdom in modern democracies that regards the separation of religion and state as the ideal solution to religious and political problems. If it is an ideal, it is one that was realized after centuries of sweat, blood and tears. I believe that Nigeria would not want to revisit that European experience. That is why all Nigerian constitutions since colonial times have emphasized the secularity of the Nigerian state as well as the right of every Nigerian "to freedom of thought, conscience and religion, including freedom to change his religion or belief, and freedom (either alone or in community with others, and in public or private) to manifest and propagate his religion or belief in worship, teaching, practice and observance." The current constitution, which embodies this ideal, states categorically further:

> No person attending any place of education shall be required to receive religious instruction or to take part in or attend any religious ceremony or observance if such instruction, ceremony or observance relates to a religion other than his own, or a religion not approved by his parent or guardian.
>
> No religious community or denomination shall be prevented from providing religious instruction for pupils of that community or denomination in any place of education maintained wholly by that community or denomination.[29]

And with regard to either the federal government and the state governments it states very clearly: "The Government of the Federation or of a State shall not adopt any religion as State Religion."[30] It does not require a constitutional lawyer to know that this provision unambiguously prohibits the adoption of any state religion. It is therefore difficult to understand how Alhaji Ahmed Sani Yerima, Governor of Zamfara state, in establishing his state as the first Sharia state in the country declared:

> There will never be a conflict between the law that we've established and the constitution because we have been able to study the constitution very well and take into consideration every loophole that is likely to come up because one of the fundamental provision [sic] in the

constitution is the freedom of religion, and we are trying as
best as possible to ensure that we practice our religion one
hundred percent without any hindrance. The constitution has
guaranteed the right to freedom of religion.[31]

The rights to freedom of thought, conscience and religion which the
constitution specifically enjoins as already noted does not permit any state
to make a law constituting itself into a theocracy. For the avoidance of
doubt the constitution also declares. "If any other law is inconsistent with
provisions of this Constitution, this Constitution shall prevail, and that
other shall to the extent of the inconsistency be void."[32]

The Sharia controversy has many serious implications. For
example, if a Muslim and a non-Muslim are involved together in a
criminal or civil case, which court will try them? If the non-Muslim
chooses not to be tried in a Sharia court but is forced to do so, what will
the federal government do? The solution is to make the choice as to what
court to be tried in voluntary for all concerned. But this is the prevailing
situation. If so, what is the need for the action of Zamfara state? Since the
police force is under federal control, who will enforce Sharia laws? Can
the Aid-Groups--a voluntary organization--drafted to enforce these laws
legally act as a state police without violating the constitution? Can a
Sharia state allow freedom of religion in schools and ensure that
non-Muslims are not discriminated against in any shape or form and still
be regarded as a Sharia state? If the answer is no, what will the federal
government do? These are just a few of the grave issues raised by the
Sharia controversy. And supposing the states in which Christians
command a majority in retaliation declare themselves legally as Christian
states and enforce the Canon Law, what will the federal government do?

The conventional wisdom seems to be that the Sharia issue is
motivated more by political than religious reasons, that religion is being
used as an opiate of the people. If that is so, the solution should be
political and constitutional, not religious. After all, it has been constantly
pointed out that the civil aspects of the Sharia law have been in operation
in the Muslim states of the North since colonial times. Successive
Nigerian constitutions (including the 1999 Constitution) have recognized
that fact. Why Zamfara state chose the time it did to mount what is clearly
a challenge to the Nigerian constitution has become a matter of disturbing
interpretations. That Zamfara's example has been followed by those
Northern states where the Muslims are in the majority has made the
challenge more ominous. It is interesting that Alhaji Azeez Arisekola, the
Aare Musulumi of Yorubaland, has joined the bandwagon

and called for the adoption of Sharia in Oyo state.[33] The problem is thus being further compounded.

The paradox of secularity and theocracy in the Northern states of Nigeria whether motivated by political or religious considerations, if not quickly and decisively resolved, poses the greatest danger not only for Nigerian democracy but more seriously for the country's corporate existence. A fundamentalist Islamic state or any theocratic state for that matter cannot be a democratic state. If "Sharia is sabotage" as Chukwuemeka Odumegwu Ojukwu (the leader of the defeated secessionist state of Biafra) asserts [34] and if "Sharia is similar to Ojukwu's declaration of Biafra,"[35] a point made earlier by the Igboezue Cultural Association (ICA)[36] the implications are clear. And if these implications lead to their logical conclusion, the consequences will be dire: the great Nigerian enterprise will perish, an outcome that will stun the whole world.

It is clear, then, that if Nigeria is to have any prospects whatsoever for the twenty-first century the Sharia problematic should not be allowed to become unmanageable. What, then, is to be done? Since the Sharia is, at bottom, a constitutional matter, the Nigerian federation should be restructured as already outlined in this chapter and thus end, as Ben Nwabueze has put it, "the existing inequity, injustice, undue concentration of power at the center and its monopolization by one section of the country, and the installation of a new system that would assure to all the ethnic nationalities a feeling of belonging, a sense of participation engendered by an agreed power share [sic] of the national wealth."[37] The next step will involve a serious consideration of the tripartite legal system now being advocated by Kaduna State, namely, customary, Islamic and common laws. This system will function in such a way as not to "violate the constitution of Nigeria" but to "accommodate all shades of interests."[38] If Nigerian leaders fail to give serious consideration to this reasonable modification of the constitution, then, there is little hope that the country will survive this century. There are several Muslim countries that take their religions very seriously but which do not apply Sharia laws fully. Among these are Egypt and Turkey (each over ninety percent Muslim), Senegal, Indonesia, Morocco, and Jordan. The argument that a complete application of Sharia is vital for the survival of Islam in Nigeria is invalid.

THE MILITARY FACTOR: THE SOLDIER AS CITIZEN

It is not always realized that the military factor in the rise, development and fall of states is as old as history itself. Nor is it also emphasized that the military interpretation of history is at least as valid as any other interpretation for that matter.[39] Consequently, the role of the military in Nigeria's post-colonial history has often been regarded as an aberration. The reality, indeed, is that both the Nigerian colonial state and the Nigerian post-colonial state may be characterized in their different ways as law and order military states. In this capacity the military exercised a dominating influence over Nigerian affairs for over one hundred years. The colonial government (which in the case of the Lagos Colony may be dated to 1861 and for the rest of the country to different dates after that), was essentially a military government, a law and order state. The successor civilian administration, which came to power in 1960 and lasted for a little more that five years, turned out to be as most Nigerians had not expected, an interregnum. Although the Nigerian colonial situation was not unique as a law and order state, the country's experience with military rule since independence has been of maximum severity, to say the least, even in the context of African states.

In all but nine and one half years of Nigeria's 40 years of independence, the country had been under eight different military dictatorships, and had experienced several failed coup d'etats. During our period only two civilians ruled the country - Shehu Shagari (1979-1983) and Ernest Shonekan, who reigned (he did not rule) for a few months in 1993 under the shadow of the military. Thus, it can be reasonably concluded that most Nigerians under fifty years of age have no real experience of democratic civilian rule. This is also true of most of the members of the Nigerian military establishment. For our period, then, military rule was a way of life. But because military regimes, thought to be corrective regimes, and supported on that score, had failed Nigeria even more woefully than the civilian regimes that they overthrew, distrust of the Nigerian military and what they stand for is now abroad in the land.

But old habits die hard; the allure of the perquisites of political power in the context of Nigeria's present constitutional and political structure will, sooner or later, and in spite of the encouraging policy statements made by the Obasanjo administration, lead the civilian rulers to continue to misbehave (as we have already noticed) as their military predecessors had done. It is being stated here that there is no evidence to suggest that the present civilian leaders have learned much from the past or forgotten anything from it. On the contrary, we are being haunted by shades of the Shagari administration as discussed in chapter six above. It is amazing how things tend to change but continue to remain the same.

If Nigeria is not restructured, another military take-over of the country may not be ruled out. The Nigerian military, already smitten with the political bug essentially because of the material benefits they derive from the dictatorial exercise of political power, will look for one excuse or the other to re-enter the political arena while avoiding the ballot box. The Nigerian public, fickle, unreliable, always predictable and driven by ethnic or religious considerations--or both--will legitimize the take-over. And the Nigerian elite, including some of the overthrown politicians and academics, driven by the same considerations as the military, will accept appointments in the new dispensation. The result will be another military --civilian government in which the civilian partners will undoubtedly continue as underdogs. Nigeria will then be afflicted with another transition to civilian rule with the concomitant political instability, elite factionalization, economic crisis largely the consequence of mismanagement, corruption, capital flight, lack of foreign investment, institutional decay and widespread poverty. The international community, powerless to restore the status quo ante, will make the usual pleas to the swashbuckling coup leader and his volatile aides to restore democracy "as soon as possible." And if the military leader is politically astute he will come out with another transitional timetable for a return to democracy, which, of course, will easily be extended to suit the military government. The international community will respond by imposing a variety of limited sanctions that in reality will hurt Nigeria and Nigerians more than the military dictators.

Students of Nigerian history and politics and, indeed, politically conscious Nigerians, are familiar with the picture painted above with regard, at any rate, to the past. But they may well have their own ideas about the future. Whatever these ideas may be and whatever they may be worth, the fact remains that one of the core issues that will define the character of Nigerian society, history and politics in the twenty-first century will be the role of the military. The military cannot be wished away because they have a crucial role to play in the protection of the country and in projecting a quantum of power and reach that confers on Nigeria international respect. How to focus their attention on their essentially military role and prevent them from seizing power is a major worry. To get the military to disengage totally from politics, given the picture I have painted, will not be an easy task. The diarchy option proposed by the late Nnamdi Azikiwe and now being canvassed by some will be, in my opinion, fatal to democracy. If, for example, the military are guaranteed a constitutional role in the governance of Nigeria just because they possess the means of physical coercion bought and paid for by the Nigerians specifically for their protection, what of those segments of civil society which also possess the means of production, or the means of distribution, or who control labor, education and health services - segments that, if effectively organized and mobilized, can equally hold the Nigerian state to ransom and cripple it? Will they also be given a similar role? What of women-who, to me, are more crucial than soldiers? Diarchy, therefore, is not a rational or an acceptable option in a democracy.

A better alternative will be to encourage politically-minded military personnel[40] to take premature retirement with appropriate inducements, join a political party of their choice, and run for office just like any other Nigerian. The state of Israel has a similar arrangement and it has been working well. In the twenty-first century the indications are that a diarchy arrangement will be resented, and probably resisted, and therefore will lead to further instability; and a violent overthrow of a democratically elected government will have a similar effect. The other solution of introducing a constitutional provision to specifically ban coup d'etats is both illogical and foolish because the military can violently overthrow the constitution and consign the provision to the dustbin.

The most effective antidote to military rule, let it be stressed, is good governance. And since that is impossible given Nigeria's present structure, the next best solution is a hard-nosed, constitutional re-engineering in Nigeria which provides for a meaningful three-tier federation as already outlined above. In this way each group is assured that its basic needs are in its own hands, that it is not marginalized, and that it has the freedom to live its own way of life within the limits of the fundamental law of the land. By thus creating various centers of power, a military take-over of the government will be a most hazardous and unwise undertaking. The chances of success are not certain; the dangers of losing the coup leaders' lives real because the undertaking will no longer be the usual, effortless military promenade. In the belief that a group of ambitious soldiers, nonetheless, will be foolhardy enough to attempt to seize power the type of constitution notwithstanding, the Nigerian political culture of the century must fortify the three-tier federal constitution by educating civil society--the press, students, labor unions, the professions, churches, mosques, women's organizations, ethnic associations and so forth - to mobilize their constituencies to say "never again" to military rule. If the center has been rendered less attractive and the military have become aware that they have lost the confidence and respect of Nigerians, and cannot convince anyone that their governance will be a success in the future, they will reconcile themselves to their traditional duties. It has been demonstrated in the last few years in Russia and recently in Serbia and Ivory Coast that an aggrieved and determined citizenry cannot only foil a coup but can chase military dictators from power.

If it becomes clear that the Nigerian military are not fully occupied, and that they are really "the largest welfare organization in the world" as an American observer once described them, their number must be gradually reduced. The demobilized soldiers would then be retrained in such a way as to make them productive members of society. What will be left in active service will be a leaner, better equipped, better trained, more disciplined and a more efficient fighting force that will be a credit to Nigeria when deployed internationally, and at home, they will cooperate with civil society to make Nigerian the great country that it has the resources to aspire to be. Thus will be formed a compact with civil society that will create stability, enhance democracy and help to define Nigeria's role in the world of the twenty-first century.

FOREIGN POLICY: CHARITY BEGINS AT HOME

Nigeria's foreign policy since the end of the civil war and, indeed, since independence, as has been demonstrated in this book, has been remarkably consistent in spite of who ruled the country. The style and tempo varied, of course, with the personalities who conducted the country's external relations. Except for a few successes in the last thirty years, Nigeria has not generally played the influential role expected of it in foreign affairs. This was due largely to the weaknesses and instability of its domestic situation; economic woes in the midst of plenty, military dictatorships in a world that has been moving inexorably toward democracy, massive corruption, indiscipline, religious crises, institutional decay, etc. This is not surprising because a strong and effective foreign policy is a reflection of a country's domestic strength.

This being the case, that sacred canon of Nigerian foreign policy, namely, that Africa is its centerpiece, should be revisited and changed as urged in chapter six. Charity must begin at home. Nigeria itself should henceforth be the centerpiece of foreign policy. The emphasis should be on the ability of the Nigerian leadership to project and defend Nigerian interests by cultivating a wide range of international alliances. Only when Nigeria is economically buoyant, militarily strong, domestically stable, politically democratic, able to enforce the rule of law and human rights, and seriously able to embark on a well-structured policy of moral rearmament can it begin the long journey toward realizing its manifest destiny in Africa and the world.

ECONOMIC AND SOCIAL IMPERATIVES: LEADERSHIP AND REFORM

Enormous Resources Versus Great Poverty

Once an acceptable politico-constitutional structure has been erected as outlined above, and stability and harmony achieved, the appropriate conditions would then have been created for economic reform and social regeneration. To achieve this goal, intelligent and progressive leadership--and not eloquent and gratuitous speeches--must be an absolute necessity. This means that the managers of the country's economy and its political and cultural leaders must be well-trained professionals rather than political cronies. And, most importantly, the government must resist the temptation to be a farmer, merchant, trader, professional educator, or newsperson, and confine itself to providing appropriate regulations and general direction for socio-economic development. President William Clinton of the United States of America was reflecting a similar sentiment when he advised the Nigerian leadership during his state visit to that country to "do the intelligent thing" by expanding the nature of the country's economy, putting in place "the right government policy", initiating economic reforms, rebuilding collapsed infrastructures and providing greater access to information technology. [41] The economic and social history of independent Nigeria is enough testimony that centralized planning has been a dismal failure. The Clinton administration in America demonstrated that economic growth and prosperity can be achieved without adopting the "trickle down" economic policy of President Ronald Reagan.

In an official memorandum the government of Obasanjo stated that Nigeria's "role in the world economy has diminished since the late 1970s and its economic performance has fallen far short of its potential."[42] At best, this is an understatement. Perhaps the most perplexing of Nigeria's problems is economic stagnation and great poverty in a country that is embarrassingly endowed with wealth and talent. Mismanagement of the economy has been, in fact, a central feature of Nigerian economic history since 1960. There has been a consistently traumatized economy even in periods of high prosperity. The collapse of institutions, virtual disappearance of the middle class, extreme poverty, tensions in all segments of the country's life and culture, and what is called derisively the "Nigerian way" of doing business and other things. This Nigerian way or system, although dispassionately considered is, in reality, a global phenomenon. However, in Nigeria it has been exhibited very crudely and openly. Essentially, it is a system in which public resources are widely and improperly diverted to private ends. In this divisive system, patronage is shamelessly made to work along regional, ethnic and religious lines. It has thus led to unequal distribution of politics which, in turn, encourage group competition and mistrust. For Nigeria to be a major power in this century a serious economic reform is inevitable.

But if the most perplexing of Nigeria's problems is economic stagnation in the midst of plenty, the most embarrassing is the decay of public institutions. This is, of course, the direct consequence of political instability, economic recession, and prodigious corruption. Basic utilities such as electricity, water supply, telecommunication and so forth, cannot be depended upon. The postal services are among the most inefficient in the world. These are deficiencies which are easily correctable by good leadership. So far Nigerians have managed to survive through the self-help efforts of religious, community and civic organizations; by using extended family and individual initiatives; and through money sent home by Nigerians abroad to their relatives and friends in Nigeria. Indeed, some communities, especially among the Igbo, forced by continuous neglect, have continued to operate as if the government does not exist by looking after themselves the best way they can. In this century, and given current trends since the return to democracy, this development will have to change dramatically.

Failed Expectations

Why have Nigeria's great economic and social expectations failed? I tackled this question briefly in a presidential address I presented to the Historical Society of Nigeria in 1989. In the section sub-titled

"The Material Basis of the Nation."[43] I began by noting the most popular reasons given why the great expectations of the economy have not materialized, namely, massive corruption, debt burden, archaic banking and tax policies, centralized planning, failure to achieve scientific, technological, and management competence in the educational system, failure to revive the universities and other tertiary institutions, and so forth. I accepted the importance of these reasons but added what, in my view, was the core problem. I wrote:

> . . . [A] study of the post-independence economic history of Nigeria reveals certain characteristics. The first is the inexplicable neglect of agriculture which had been the mainstay of the economy during the pre-European and colonial periods. The second is the failure to develop the manufacturing sector starting initially with agro-based and cottage industries and graduating to light-heavy and heavy industries in a coordinated fashion. I understand that our various development plans which advocated some of these policies were not implemented by successive governments strictly as the economic planners had advised. On the contrary, political and ethnic considerations were allowed to dictate economic policies. The British colonial government did no such thing. Hard economic factors determined where industries were sited, where railways and airports were built, where agricultural settlements were established... Economics shares a common characteristic with history. If you toy with its basic principles, it makes you pay heavily.

The statement continues:

> There is also our incredible managerial inability especially in the public sector. There is no parastatal that operates in the black in spite of heavy financial support by governments; there is none that operates efficiently even if it shows no profit. The universities are run as inefficiently as any other parastatal for a basically similar reason: the chief executives are chosen not necessarily on the basis of competence but primarily for political considerations. This is the case in most countries. But in these countries if a political balancing act is a major criterion, governments spend considerable time in choosing the right candidate from the favored group. And in some of these countries, once the candidate gets the job he operates in the national

> interest and not in the sectional interest. [But] this is not the case in Nigeria.[44]

I have no reason to believe that the situation has changed appreciably since 1989. On the contrary, it has worsened. It was revealed recently by Vice-President Atiku Abubakar that, incredibly as it seems, the country's official financial accounts have not been audited in twenty years, and that successive governments since 1960 had failed to supply the public with enough information regarding the nation's economy.[45] It has also been revealed recently that in spite of the "162.3 percent extra earnings from oil," Nigeria recorded a budget deficit of N59,945.2 million between January and June 2000.[46] Surely Nigerians cannot realize their great expectations if their governments continue to operate so unprofessionally and irresponsibly.

Socially, the expectations of Nigerians have not also materialized. The latest World Bank's World Development Report for 2000/2001[47] exposes the alarming poverty depth into which Nigeria has sunk in spite of it being ranked among the eight richest countries in natural resources in the world.[48] According to this Report out of 206 countries surveyed Nigeria is the twenty-eighth poorest in real terms; and in terms of purchasing power, it ranks 193 out of 206 countries. "In no other country in Africa," Reinold H. Van Til, the International Monetary Fund(IMF) Senior Resident Representative in Nigeria points out, "has the deterioration in living standards been so severe as in Nigeria." The reason, according to him is, in part, because the Nigerian leadership failed to reap the benefits of their country's abundant natural resources in the last twenty years, thus operating below its potential. He noted further the disastrous effect of managing an economy whereby "90 Kobo of every naira spent is raised from oil export revenue which has the same economic impact as monetary financing of expenditure."[49] Massive corruption is also another reason. In another recent publication released in Berlin in September 2000 by a non-governmental organization called the Transparency International (TI), Nigeria is rated the most corrupt of the 90 countries surveyed.[50]

In the section of the above Presidential Address titled "The Intellectual Basis of the Nation,"[51] I mentioned how, beneath the Christian and Islamic heritages which dominate the thinking and behavior of the Nigerian elite, is the persistent tintinnabulation of something that cannot be wished away--namely, African cosmology, a world view whose traditions predate more organized systems of belief. Failure to reconcile comfortably these three sources of tradition is the core problem that Nigeria's cultural maximizers have faced since well before independence. As I pointed out previously, Japan found itself faced with a similar problem several centuries ago. Japanese historians of the time were reacting against the infatuation of their people with Chinese civilization, just as Nigerians today are infatuated with European and Arab civilization.[52] Yamato damashi connotes "Japanese sense" while Kara-jie connotes "Chinese knowledge."[53] Assiduously cultivating and marrying together these two concepts aroused Japanese national consciousness. It is generally believed that it was in this period that the foundations were laid for Japan to eventually become a great power. This consciousness developed later to become what the Japanese called *kokutai* ("national entity") which became linked also with the famous *kokugatu* ("National Learning or Movement"), a sort of national history. This development climaxed in the Shinto revivalism during the Tokugawa period of Japanese history (1600-1868).[54] In short, the consequence of the acquisition of technological knowledge and the concomitants of *kokutai* was dynamite. It must be stressed, however, that at no time during this development did the Japanese allow the humanities and social sciences to be sacrificed at the altar of science, technology and the professions. They regarded the triad as holism, all nourishing one another in the pursuit of fundamental national goals. Needless to say, the Japanese faced numerous and severe bumps in the long journey but the political leadership and the men of learning, working together, preached perseverance and resilience, rather than regional, ethnic and religious exclusiveness. Their message to the youth of Japan came from the heart. "Young people," they admonished, "do not be discouraged." To bring this message home, the first toy that was traditionally given to a Japanese child was a sort of roly-poly doll called Okiagari Koboshi (literally, "little self-righting monk"). To this doll was linked the teaching: Nana Korobi ya oki, meaning "seven falls, eight rises."[55] Concluding this section, I wrote:

> . . . our nation has a lot to learn from the Japanese experience. We have invested an astronomical amount of money in education. Even the worst detractors of our successive governments must concede this point. We have tried the "Ethical Revolution" and fought the "War Against Indiscipline" to no avail; we are now preaching the much maligned MAMSER whose success is doubtful. Success has not attended our efforts, not for want of trying, but because their applications lack intellectual [and honest] rigor precisely because we have been unable to consummate a

marriage between kokutai and kokugatu. In short, our nation still lacks an intellectual basis for its existence. We have also failed to apply Nigerian Yamato damashi to European kara-jie. Nor have we been able to convince our young that when they fall on their faces, they will always get up. MAMSER is not the answer.[56]

The debate that I had hoped these ideas might generate did not materialize. I am not even sure that the Nigerian political leadership or the Nigerian people of learning care to read what simple historians write. The notion that once an individual is elected to a political office or shoots his way to one, he automatically and mysteriously becomes the philosopher king of Nigeria, must be reconsidered. The Nigerian mind must be opened to learning; the political leadership and the people of learning must stop looking at one another as enemies. They must complement one another in the national interest.

VISION 2010 REPORT: A RETROSPECTIVE LOOK

It may be useful at this point to have a retrospective look at the Main Report of the Vision 2010 Committee, the white paper on which, as far as I am aware, has not been published. The Report is available, however, for private circulation. It is the outcome of the work of a committee inaugurated on September 27, 1996 by the "interim" government of Sani Abacha. Called the Vision 2010 Committee, it was chaired by Ernest Shonekan, the very person Abacha had only recently ousted from power for alleged incompetence. Shonekan, incredible as it may seem, accepted the chairmanship with enthusiasm and Nigerians, somehow, failed to see the irony.

Among other things, the Committee was charged with the responsibility of determining the economic and social direction of the country by the year 2010. In addition to Shonekan(Chairman), Gidado Idris (Secretary to the Government of the Federation) and Ibrahim M. Ida (Director--General (Economic Affairs), the Presidency), the committee comprised 247 members representing a cross-section of the Nigerian population, 24 resource persons, 7 consultants, and a variety of facilitators. It was the largest and most inclusive, in terms of membership, committee of its kind in Nigerian history.

On September 30, 1997, a little over a year after it was inaugurated, the committee issued its main report which it sub-titled "A

Call to Action."[57] The Vision 2010 Report makes far-reaching suggestions for economic reform. It starts by the members asking themselves the following questions:

> "Where we are (and why)?
> Where do we want to be?
> How do we get there?"

As the report deals with the first two questions, it traverses well-known and well-trodden ground. Its major value in this regard lies, therefore, in the specific strategies it lays down meticulously for making Nigeria "A United, Industrious, Caring, and God-fearing Democratic Society committed to making the basic needs of life affordable for everyone and creating Africa's leading economy."[58] The report proposes to achieve this goal through the adoption of "Immediate, Short-Term, Medium-Term and Long-Term measures" which would "stimulate economic growth and transform Nigerians into patriotic citizens."[59]

That the Central Bank of Nigeria (CBN) called for the adoption and implementation of the Report[60] seems to suggest that the Report still needs to be acted upon. And since the year 2010 is around the corner, it is likely to be as stillborn as most other reports in Nigeria in recent years. It would appear also that Obasanjo's most recent 10-year economic plan[61] is not based on it. This may be why the CBN requested this action. It is hoped that the Obasanjo administration will take a dispassionate look at this report, as well as considering a "blueprint and action plans for translating this shared vision into reality."[62] Economic reform based on the Vision 2010 blueprint is an imperative.

An important omission in the Report, however, is the failure to deal with the important issue of how many Nigerians there really are. The census controversies in Nigeria from colonial times to the present are mentioned in the second chapter of this book. The Report failed to make it clear that a country's population figure derived from a census enumeration goes far beyond its political implications. For one thing, it is crucial in economic planning. Many of the failures of Nigeria's various economic plans since independence are largely attributable to census failures, the refusal of Nigerians to count themselves accurately because of their practice of using population figures to maximize their political and economic advantages. In the twenty-first century the Nigerian political leadership should do the right thing by emphasizing the crucial importance of an accurate population count to national development.

The Vision 2010 Committee may also be faulted for failing to show vision by not documenting for posterity the wealth of Nigerians, that is, by producing--or, at any rate, advising government to produce--a modern version of the *Domesday Book* for Nigeria. By thus documenting a record of assets owned by individual Nigerians, especially lands and houses, the committee would have called the attention of government to assets which, if properly harnessed and utilized, might be invaluable for economic development and growth. It is well known that these assets located largely in the non-urban areas are not taxed. Nor are they acceptable by commercial and government banks as viable collateral for loans because they are not capital assets. In other words, as economic assets for development, they are essentially worthless. Admittedly, the documentation would take more than one year to complete. However, this would have been accomplished within a reasonable amount of time if it were coordinated through the local governments and the states. It is being suggested, therefore, that in reviewing the Report government should take the above suggestion into account. If it does so, it will be amazed to discover that the assets of individual Nigerians run into trillions of American dollars.

Admittedly, to accomplish what the government is being urged to do is fraught with grave problems. In the first place, the government would be faced with a major obstacle - cultural traditions and a worldview, which make it extremely difficult to turn these assets into capital assets that can be used by banks as collateral for loans. Secondly, because traditional lands cannot be sold to outsiders, it would be an irrational act for companies and individuals to invest in these lands and houses for development purposes. Herein lies perhaps the greatest obstacle to development in countries such as Nigeria. To ignore the problem and hope for the best is no solution. The point being made is that the Vision 2010 Committee should, at least, have identified the problem and recommended appropriate strategies for dealing with it.

ECONOMIC REFORM

It is, of course, common knowledge that every Nigerian administration since the end of the civil war has embarked on some sort of economic reform. That the Nigerian economy has remained distressed is evidence of the relative failure of reforms. Perhaps the most disastrous of these reforms is the Fourth Development Plan (discussed in chapter six of this book) that was, for all intents and purposes, out of date before it was published. I believe that if seriously implemented the economic strategies advocated in the Vision 2010 Report will go a long way to realizing Nigeria's great economic expectation. The Report aims to "stimulate economic growth" and to "really place the country en route to becoming a developed country by the year 2010."[63] This may be a rather tall order. It may not be realized in the time envisaged but it is certainly realizable within a generation. However, as Shonekan warned, everything will depend "ultimately . . . on how effectively its recommendation are implemented" by the governments in power.[64]

The government is urged, therefore, to do the following. First, create an environment that stimulates savings and investments in the private sector; provide infrastructural support; build human capital especially in education, healthcare, and technology; govern in the public interest, diversify the economy and emphasize the conventional Walpolian mercantilism by exporting more and importing less.

Secondly, the private sector thus must not only be "the engine of growth of the economy" but must also "support government in a truly progressive partnership." And, thirdly, at the macro-economic level, the government must support "free markets and global competition," foster "high domestic saving and investment," pursue "consistent economic policies," achieve low inflation, and emphasize "strong fiscal/monetary discipline!."[65] The important thing about this report, as I have previously stated, is that it provides a systematic, detailed "Implementation Action Plan." Its weakness, as I have stated, is that it does not deal with the importance of an accurate population figure for economic development.

It is also regretted, however, that in the important sub-section dealing with Nigeria's "Core Economic Objectives,"[66] the report is surprising silent on the debt burden. At the time the report was being prepared, the country's foreign debt was generally believed to be about thirty billion dollars. And yet in the 1980s the debt was estimated to be only five billion dollars.[67] Since there was no significant borrowing afterward, it is obvious that most of the later debt of thirty billion dollars constitute of interests and penalties on late payments. As Dauda Garben Bundof, Chairman of the House of Representatives Committee on Banking and Currency, lamented: " It was discovered that for borrowing five billion dollars, Nigeria has paid an interest of 18 billion dollars and we are still owing 31 billion dollars." He obtained his figures from Treasury officials in Britain's House of Commons .[68] Despite the fact that the country spends a mind-boggling forty percent of its annual budgets in servicing foreign debts, the debt is still estimated by another source to have stood at twenty-eight billion dollars as of December, 1999.[69] A year later, according to Bundof, the figure was thirty-one billion dollars. A major problem with Nigeria's foreign debt is that a proper assessment of its accuracy has not been made.

Surely, such a huge debt burden poses a great threat to the country's economic development. Since rescheduling the debt has resulted in "debt inducing rather that debt reducing,"[70] such an exercise should be reconsidered. What, then, is to be done? Of course, Nigeria could simply refuse to pay the debts and dare the various creditors to do their worst. This would only succeed if all the debtor countries were to work together to do the same. But since this seems improbable, reneging on the debts is not a viable option. Possibly, the country could borrow more money to pay off arrears and then ensure that future debts are paid on schedule to avoid penalties. This is also not a viable option because the debts have still to be paid and the burden on the economy is not meaningfully reduced.

Perhaps more realistically, debt forgiveness or relief should be sought. This is apparently what the Obasanjo administration is committed to doing. Although some of the creditor countries like Italy and Canada are said to have agreed to write off some debts as a friendly gesture, there is no official confirmation in Canada's case of such a decision. Even if the report is true, the big creditors are unlikely to follow suit because, in their view, Nigeria is not a poor country and must keep its obligations. That the Paris Club, Nigeria's biggest creditor, has agreed to reschedule--not cancel--the 23.4 billion dollars Nigeria owes to it underscores my point.[71] No doubt, the Club's decision seems to be a great relief to Nigeria and a credit to the Obasanjo administration, but this remains to be substantiated. The debt owed to the Club represents 73.14 percent of total debt. About twenty-one billion dollars of the rescheduled amount consists of arrears due to be repaid by August, 2000; the rest consist of the principal and interest which are due to be repaid by July, 2001. The debt moratorium is for only three years and will expire by 2003, after which Nigeria will have between eighteen and twenty years to have the total debt repaid. It is hoped that the Nigerian government will use this opportunity to apply the savings toward economic and social reform.

Fourth, the creditor nations should be persuaded to pay off Nigeria's foreign debts by using the country's money looted by Nigerians and deposited in the respective creditor countries. The argument here is that "If it is wrong to steal, it surely must be wrong to accept and harbor stolen money."[72] This may be a compelling argument but it is not likely to be heeded. Capitalism has no conscience. The best recipe for economic progress is for the country to do what any sensible family does when overburdened with debt; namely, resolve to borrow no more and religiously continue to pay a little more than the required minimum payment until the debt is fully repaid. This will instill financial discipline and responsibility, enhance the country's image and, perhaps, persuade some creditors to write off the interests on the loans. Without finding a solution to the debt burden, Nigeria's prospects for economic growth and development in the twenty-first century will continue to be uncertain.

SOCIAL REFORM

It bears repeating that without political stability and economic growth, social reform will continue to be limited and ineffectual. But it is also true that if political stability and economic growth are not used by the Nigerian leadership in the service of social reform, Nigeria's dream of greatness will remain a chimera.

In Section 11 of Chapter 3 of the Vision 2010 Report ("Political Socio-Cultural And Economic Direction: The Underpinnings of Fundamental and Sustainable Development.")[73] emphasizes several issues, including "corruption, which pervades all facets of society including the political realm"; poor revenue allocation which resulted in the "weakness and inefficiency of the Public services"; the Prison Service, whose prisons "have now become a breeding ground for criminals"; the value system which showed "signs of the state of decay"; a lack of openness in governance; inadequate governmental and private sector support for Nigeria's cultural heritage; education which "is currently experiencing a deep crisis"; the development of science, engineering and technology (SET) which "is characterized by policy and institutional constraints as well as poor infrastructure;" an environment which presently "makes it difficult for the youth [who] over the years, made significant contributions to national development... to continue to exploit their full potential"; failure to utilize Nigeria's women, who after all, make up half the population, "to the fullest for sustainable national development"; a dangerously decayed health care system; and a need for population management. The report then injects this upbeat note:

Notwithstanding the pervasive negative characteristics of
Nigeria's political and socio-cultural conditions highlighted

above, Nigerians, as individuals, have continued to excel in
various fields of human endeavor within and outside the
country, such as in science and technology, medicine,
literature, jurisprudence, sports and administration. All these
give tremendous hope for the future.[74]

It proceeds to provide the goals of social reform and "How to get there."[75]
It will be tedious to summarize these goals and strategies here. The
interested reader is urged to read the report. I believe that a rational
application of its recommendations as well as a determination to apply
Nigerian sense to Western knowledge will constitute a *sine qua non* for
achieving the social reform that will anchor Nigeria's drive toward unity
and greatness in this century.

CONCLUSION

Although, for reasons generally agreed upon, the state of Nigeria
since the Civil War has not been good, for, it will be a dishonesty to the
discipline of history to write off the country as a failed project. Like any
other state, the Nigerian state is an organism. Thus, the possibility--and,
indeed, the probability--exists that Nigerians are better prepared to deal
with the complexities of the twenty-first century than they were in dealing
with the nightmares of the twentieth century. There is nothing that has
happened in Nigeria that is historically unique. Examples abound, and
lessons can be learned, from the historical experiences of other countries,
who have experienced similar problems. It frequently happens that the act
of finding solutions to difficult problems has helped propel a nation to
greatness. There is hope that Nigerians, too, will somehow manage to
solve their problems under progressive and focused leadership.

Yet from the same evidence on which some observers base their
forecasts of uncertainty-even doom--for Nigeria, it can be shown that a
Nigeria which is politically restructured, transformed along the lines
sketched out in this chapter, will be characterized by a slow but purposive
renewal. Thus will future Nigerians be assured that they will realize that
manifest destiny which their inherent abilities and abundant resources
entitle them to expect.

ENDNOTES

1. See, for example, Chinua Achebe, *The Trouble with Nigeria* (Enugu: Fourth Dimension Press, 1983); R. A. Joseph, *Democracy and Prebendal Politics in Nigeria: The Rise and Fall of the Second Republic* (Cambridge: The University Press, 1987); idem, "Nigeria: Inside the Dismal Tunnel," *Current History*, 95, 601 (1996); P.M Lewis, "Endgame in Nigeria? The Politics of a Failed Transition Programme," *African Affairs*, 95 (1994); idem, "From Prebendalism to Predation: The Political Economy of Decline in Nigeria," *Journal of Modern African Studies*, 34 (1996); Wole Soyinka, *The Open Sore of A Continent: A Personal Narrative of the Nigerian Crisis* (New York: Oxford Univ. Press, 1998); Levi A Nwachuku, "Nigeria's Uncertain Future," *Current History*, Nov. 1970.

2. For a development of this idea see G. N. Uzoigwe, "Toward Constitutional Re-engineering: A Three-Tier Democratic Federation as the Future of Nigeria," Special Feature in *West African Research Association (WARA) Newsletter*, Madison: University of Wisconsin, Fall, 2001, 34-41.

3. See Ali A. Mazrui, Keynote Address, First Nnamdi:Azikwe Symposium On Africa and World Affairs on the theme Nigeria and The Future of Africa: Defining Issues for the twenty-first Century, Center For Public Policy and Diplomacy, Lincoln Univ. Pennsylvania, April 29- May 1, 1998.

4. See speech by Imeh Okopido, Minister of State For Environment. *The Comet*, Nov. 15, 2000; cf. *The Guardian*, Sept. 11, 2000.

5. Olusegun Obasanjo, "Message to the 10th Yearly Conference of the Nigerian Association of Petroleum Explorationists," *The Guardian,* November 14, 2000.

6. Cited in *The Guardian*, September 20, 2000.

7. Gerry Gana in *The Guardian*, Sept. 14, 2000.

8. See *The Comet*, November 15, 2000.

9. Soyinka, *Open Sore*, op. at.

10. Achebe, *Trouble With Nigeria*, op. cit.

11. Osaghae, *Crippled Giant*, op. cit.

12. Obaro Ikime, *In Search of Nigerians: Changing Patterns of Inter-group Relations in an Evolving Nation State* (Ibadan: Impact Publishers, 1985); cf G. N. Uzoigwe, "Assessing the History of Ethnic/Religions Relations" in Ernest E. Uwazie, Isaac O. Albert and Godfrey N. Uzoigwe (eds.), *Inter-Ethnic and Religious Conflict Resolution in Nigeria.* (Oxford and New York: Lexington Books, 1999).

13. John E. Flint, *Sir George and the Making of Nigeria* (London: 1960); C.R. Niven, *A Short History of Nigeria* (London: Longmans, 1937); Alan Burns, *History of Nigeria*, 6th ed. 9th impression (London: Allen and Unwin, 1964); Kalu Ezera, *Constitutional Developments in Nigeria* (Cambridge; The Univ. Press, 1960); Obafemi Awolowo, *Path to Nigerian Freedom* (London; Faber & Faber, 1947), 47-48; Tafawa Balewa, Legislative Council Debates, Lagos, March, 1948, 227.

14. I. A. Nwabughuogu, "Unitarism Versus Federalism: A British Dilemma," in G. N. Uzoigwe (ed.), *Foundations of Nigerian Federalism, 1900 - 1960* (Abuja: NCIR, 1996), 39 - 59.

15. G. N. Uzoigwe, "Federalism Versus Centralism in Nigeria; Continuity and Change," in Adebayo O. Oyebade (ed.), *The Foundation of Nigeria* (New York: Africa World Press, 2003).

16. For details see G. N. Uzoigwe, "The Niger Committee of 1898: Lord Selborne's Report," *Journal of the Historical Society of Nigeria* (JHSN), IV, 3 (1968), 467 - 472.

17. S. E. Majuk, "Independence and the Triumph of Federalism, 1954 -1960" in Uzoigwe, *Foundation of Nigerian Federalism*, 295.

18. Lagos: Federal Republic of Nigeria Official Gazzette, no. 27, vol. 86, May 1999.

19. See Kayode Adaramoye, "An Anatomy of Federalism and the 1999 Constitution", *The Guardian*, October 6, 1999.

20. For details see G. N. Uzoigwe," Nigeria's Third Republic States Verses Local Governments," *Comet: An Analytical News Feature* (Owerri), 1, 2(1988), 42- 44; idem, "For a Three-tier Democracy," *Sunday Guardian*, Lagos, 21 August, 1988; idem, "Local Government and Home Rule," *Focus Magazine* (Makurdi), October, 1998; idem, "Toward Constitutional Re-engineering," *Supra.*

21. *The Guardian*, January 9, 2001.

22. For further development of this analysis see Uzoigwe, "History of Ethnic/Religious Relations," op.cit.

23. See "Kano rallies North Against Obasanjo: Alleges ill-treatment of Hausa-Fulani," in *The Comet*, September 7, 2000.

24. This was why the East officially disengaged from the Nigerian State in 1967.

25. Quoted in *The Comet*, September 11, 2000.

26. Quoted in *Ibid*, September 10, 2000.

27. Uzoigwe, "Ethnic/Religious Relations," 11.

28. See the *Ahiajoku Lecture Series* (Owerri: Ministry of Information and Culture).

29. See Part 11, Chapter IV, section 38, sub-sections 1-3; cf 1979 Constitution, pp. 16-17 from where these provisions were copied..

30. *Ibid*, Part II, Fourth Schedule, section 10.

31. Cited in *The Vanguard*, October 27, 1999.

32. Chapter 1 Part 1, Section 1, sub-section 3.

33. See *The Comet*, October 10, 2000.

34. *Newswatch* interview, vol. 31, no. 11, March 30, 2000.

35. Ambassador Jolly Tanko Yusuf in *The Guardian*, July 16, 2000.

36. See *The Vanguard*, June 29, 2000.

37. Cited in *The Vanguard*, August 28, 2000.

38. Cited in *The Comet*, Sept. 3, 2000.

39. This argument is developed in G. N. Uzoigwe, "The Warrior and the state in Pre-colonial Africa: Comparative Perspectives," *Journal of Asian and African Studies*, XII, 1 - 2 (1977), 20- 47. Reprinted in Ali A. Mazrui ed.), *The Warrior Tradition in Modern Africa* (Leiden: E. J. Brill, 1977).

40. According to the *Africa Confidential* of October 13, 2000, vol. 41, no. 20, Olusegun Obasanjo stated that some 90 percent of trainee officers joined the military for a career in politics. It is also pointed out in the same publication that 93 percent of officers who retired in 1999 were Northern Muslims who had held political office and that the 80,000 strong army is still very politicized.

41. Quoted in *The Guardian*, August 28, 2000.

42. Cited in *The Comet*, Sept. 7, 2000.

43. G. N. Uzoigwe, *History and Democracy in Nigeria* (Owerri: Esther Thompson Publishing Company, 1989), 15 - 18.

44. *Ibid.*, 16 - 17.

45. Speech at the Institute of Chartered Accountants in Nigeria, Agence France-Press, October 5, 2000.

46. Sunday Okoh in *The Comet*, October 23, 2000; cf, Vanguard, October 27, 2000.

47. See *The Comet*, October 23, 2000.

48. See *The Guardian*, July 14, 2000.

49. See *The Comet*, October 23, 2000.

50. See *Agence France-Press*, Sept. 13, 2000. Finland was judged the least corrupt; the United States of America ranked 14th.

51. Uzoigwe, *History and Democracy*, 20 - 22. I am indebted to H. Neil McFarland's "The Spirit of Japan: A Thematic Review of Japanese History," Paper presented at the Tenth International Conference on the Unity of Sciences, Seoul, South Korea, Nov. 9 - 13, 1981, for the Japanese experience.

52. McFarland, "Spirit of Japan," loc.cit.

53. China colonized Japan for several centuries.

54. *Idem.*

55. McFarland, "Spirit of Japan," loc. cit.

56. Uzoigwe, *History And Democracy*, 21 - 22.

57. *Report of the Vision 2010 Committee,* henceforth *The Report*, Foreward, "The Vision Process," Section 13 (1 - 3).

58. *The Report*, Chapter 7, "Implementation Action Plan: Making Vision 2010 A Reality," 145 - 198 esp., 182 -188; 194 - 198.

59. *The Report*, Shonekan to Abacha, 30 Sept., 1997.

60. See "CBN Seeks Adoption of Vision 2010 Report," *The Guardian*, Nov. 19, 2000.

61. See *The Guardian*, Nov. 14, for summary of the Plan.

62. *The Report*, Foreward, 3 (c).

63. *Ibid.*, Shonekan to Abacha, 30 Sept. 1997.

64. *Idem.*

65. *Ibid.*, "The Economic Imperative," section 26, sub-sections a - c.

66. *Ibid.*, 79 - 90.

67. See *The Vanguard*, July 16, 2000.

68. *Ibid.*

69. See *Reuter's English News Service*, March 30, 2000.

70. *Ibid.*

71. See "Nigeria Gets Relief from Paris Club," *The Guardian*, December 14, 2000.

72. See *Reuter's English News Service* quoting Senator Victor Oyofo, April 28, 2000.

73. *The Report*, 30 - 58.

74. *Ibid.*, 42.

75. *Ibid.*, 42 - 58.

APPENDIX

Nigeria: Basic Facts

People

- Country's Name: Federal Republic of Nigeria

- Federal Capital: Abuja

- Independence: October 1, 1960 (from the UK)

- Population: 121.2 million (World Bank)

- Ethnic Groups: Multi-ethnic with over 250 different ethnic groups. Major groups are Hausa/Fulani, Yoruba, and Igbo.

- Language: English (Official) & "Pidgin" English.

- Religion: Secular state. The two main
religions are Christianity and Islam.

Government

- Units in the Federation -
  - 36 States and the Federal Capital
  Territory (FCT, Abuja)

- Democracy with three branches-
  - Executive branch (headed by elected
  President)
  - Legislative branch (with Senate and
  House of Representatives)
  - Judicial branch (with a Supreme Court
  and Federal Court of Appeal)

- Political Parties - (1999)
  - All People's Party (APP); People's
  Democratic Party (PDP); Alliance for
  Democracy (AD).

Geography

- Area: 923,770 square km (slightly more
than twice the size of California)

- Location: West Africa, approximately
between 4 N and 14 N of the
Equator.

- Vegetation: Equatorial in south, tropical in
center, and arid in the north.

- Climate: Tropical; temperatures vary between a low of about 56 F (in Dec. and Jan. in the North) to a mean maximum of 94 F (in the North). Rainfall is heavy in the south (May, June, and July) but decreases fairly sharply inland.

Economy

- **Natural resources:** petroleum, natural gas, tin, comumbite, iron ore, coal, limestone, lead, zinc.

- **Labor/ manpower:** Well-educated labor force.

- **Industries:** crude oil, coal, tin, columbite, palm oil, wood, rubber, peanuts, cotton, hides, and skins, textiles, cement and other construction materials, food products, footwear, chemicals, fertilizer, printing, ceramics steel.

- **Exports-commodities:** petroleum and petroleum products (95%); cocoa, rubber, timber, manufactured goods.

- **Exports-partners:** US 35%, Spain 11%, Italy 6%, France 6% (1997 est.)

- **Market:** Untapped market with 125 million people.

- **Some US Businesses in Nigeria:** Amoco, Ashland, British Gas British Petroleum, Chevron, Conoco, Derminex, Elf Aquitaine, Exxon, Mobil, Royal Dutch/Shell, Texaco, Total, Coca-Cola, Citibank Corps, MCI, Microsoft, General Motors, Sheraton hotels, and Hilton

- **Imports-commodities:** machinery, chemicals, transportation equipment, manufactured goods, food and animals

- **Imports-partners:** US 14%, UK 11%, Germany 10%, France 8%, Netherlands 5% (1997 est.)

- **Agriculture-products:** cocoa, peanuts, palm oil, corn, rice, sorghum, millet, cassava (tapioca), yams, rubber; cattle, sheep, goats, pigs; timber; fish.

- **GDP:** purchasing power parity - $106.2 billion (1998 est.)

- **GDP-per capita:** purchasing power parity- $960 (1998 est.)

- **Electricity-production:** 13.8 billion kWh (1996)

- **Currency:** 1 naira (N) = 100 kobo

SELECT BIBLIOGRAPHY

Achebe, Chinua, *The Trouble With Nigeria*. Emgu: Fourth Dimension, 1983.

Adamolekun, L. (ed.), *Nigerian Public Administration 1960-1980: Perspectives and Prospects*. Ibadan: Heinemann, 1985.

Ademoyega, Adewale, *Why We Struck: The Story of the First Military Coup*. Ibadan: Evans Brothers, 1981.

Aluko, O., *Essays on Nigerian Foreign Policy*. London: Allen and Unwin, 1981.

Arikpo, Okoi, *The Development of Modern Nigeria*. Baltimore: Penguin Books, 1967.

Duke-Abiola, Aksoba Z., *From Abubakar to Abubakar: Forty Years of Nigerian Foreign Policy*. Lagos: 1999.

Egboh, Edmund O., *Community Development Efforts in Igboland*. Onitsha: Etukokwu Publishers, 1987.

Ekeh, Peter and Osaghae, Eghosa (eds.), *Federal Character and Federalism in Nigeria*. Ibadan: Heinemann, 1989.

Elaigwu, J.I., *Gowon: The Biography of a Soldier-Statesman*. Ibadan: West Books, 1986.

Ezera, Kalu, *Constitutional Development in Nigeria* 2nd Edition. Cambridge: Cambridge UP, 1964.

Falola, Toyin and Ihonvbere, Julius, *The Rise and Fall of Nigeria's Second Republic*. London: Zed Books, 1985.

Gana, A.T., *The Limits of Political Engineering: A Critique of the Transition Programme*. JOS: Covenant Press, 1990.

Gboyega, A. *Political Values and Local Government in Nigeria*. Lagos: Malthouse Press, 1987.

Hatch, John C., *Nigeria: The Seeds of Disaster*. Chicago: H. Regnery Co., 1970.

Jorre, de St. John *The Nigerian Civil War*. London: Hodder and Stoughton, 1972.

Joseph, R.A., *Democracy and Probendal Politics in Nigeria: The Rise and Fall of the Second Republic*. Cambridge: The University Press, 1987.

Kayode, M.O. and Usman, Y.B., *Nigeria Since Independence: The First Twenty-Five Years*. Vol. 2., *The Economy*. Ibadan: Heinemann, 1989.

Kirk-Green, Anthony M.H., *Crisis and Conflict in Nigeria: A Documentary Source Book, 1966-1970*. London: Oxford UP, 1971.

Kirk-Green, Anthony M. H., and Rimmer, Douglas, *Nigeria Since 1970: A Political and Economic Outline*. New York: Africana Publishing Company, 1981.

Maduebo, Alexander, *The Nigerian Revolution and the Biafran War*. Enugu: Fourth Dimension, 1980.

Mahadi, Abdallahi et al. (eds.), *Nigeria: The State of the Nation and the Way Forward*. Kaduna: Arewa House, 1994.

Nnoli, Okwudiba, *Ethnic Politics in Nigeria*. Enugu: Fourth Dimension, 1978.

Nwankwo, Arthur A., *Nigeria: The Challenge of Biafra*. Enugu: Fourth Dimension, 1980.

Obasanjo, Olusegun, *Africa Embittered: Essays on Contemporary African Development.* Ibadan: Wemilore Press [Nigeria Ltd.] 1988.

Obasanjo, Olusegun, *My Command*. Ibadan: Heinemann, 1981.

Obasanjo, Olusegun, *Not My Will*. Ibadan: University Press, 1990.

Ogbudinkpa, R.N. *The Economics of the Nigerian Civil War and Its Prospects for National Development*. Enugu: Fourth Dimension, 1985.

Ojiako, J.O. *Thirteen Years of Military Rule*. Lagos: *Daily Times of Nigeria*, Ltd, no date.

Ojiako, James O., *Nigeria: Yesterday, Today and ....* Onitsha: African Educational Books, no date.

Ojibo, Okion, *Nigeria Returns to Civil Rule*. Lagos: Tokion Company, 1980.

Ojukwu, C. Odumegwu, *Biafra: Random Thoughts*. New York: Harper and Row, 1969.

Okadigbo, Chuba, *Power and Leadership in Nigeria*. Enugu: Fourth Dimension, 1987.

Okeke, Okechukwu *Hausa-Fulani Hegemony: The Dominance of the Muslim North in Contemporary Nigerian Politics*. Enugu: Acona Publishers, 1992.

Olagunju, T. et al, *Transition to Democracy in Nigeria, 1985-1993*. Ibadan: Spectrum Books, 1993.

Olukoshi, A.O. (ed.), *The Politics of Structural Adjustment in Nigeria*. London: James Curry, 1993.

Onyemelukwe, C.C., *Economic Development: An Inside View*. London: Longman, 1974.

Orizu, A.A. Nwafor, *Insight Into Nigeria: The Shebu Shagari Era*. Ibadan: Evans Brothers, 1983.

Osaghae, Eghosa E., *Crippled Giant: Nigeria Since Independence*. Bloomington: Indiana UP, 1998.

Osuntokun, Akinjide. *Equatorial Guinea- Nigerian Relations: The Diplomacy of Labour*. Ibadan: OUP, 1978.

Oyediran, O. (ed.), *Nigerian Government and Politics Under Military Rule, 1966-79*. London: Macmillan, 1979.

Oyinbo, John *Nigeria: Crisis and Beyond*. London: Charles, Knight and Co., 1971.Oyako, James O., *First Four Years of Nigeria Executive Presidency*. Lagos: *Daily Times of Nigeria*, 1983.

Oyovbaire, S. and Olagunju, T. (eds.), *Foundations of a New Nigeria: The IBB Era*. London: Precision Press, 1989.

Panter-Brick, S.K. (eds.), *Nigerian Politics and Military Rule: Prelude to the Civil War*. London: The Athlone Press, 1970.

Panter-Brick, K. (ed.), *Soldiers and Oil: The Political Transformation of Nigeria*. London: Frank Cass, 1978.

Philips, A.O. and Ndekwu, E.C.(eds.), *Structural Adjustment Program in a Developing Economy: The Case of Nigeria*. Ibadan: Niser, 1987.

Schwarz, Walter, *Nigeria*. New York: Frederick A. Praeger, 1968.

Sklar, Richard, *Nigerian Political Parties*. New Jersey: Princeton UP, 1970.

Soyinka, Wole, *The Open Sore of a Continent: A Personal Narrative of the Nigerian Crisis*. New York: Oxford UP, 1998.

Stremlau, John J., *The International Politics of the Nigerian Civil War, 1967-1970.* New Jersey: Princeton UP, 1977.

Tamuno, Tekena N., and Ukpabi, S.C. (eds.), *Nigeria Since Independence Vol. vi.*, Ibadan: Heinemann, 1989.

Tamuno, Tekena N. and J.A. Atanda (eds.), *Nigeria Since Independence: The First Twenty-Five Years.* Vol. IV. *Government and Public Policy.* Ibadan: Heinemann, 1989.

Ukwu, I..U. (ed.), *Federal Character and National Integration in Nigeria.* Kuru: NIPPS, 1987.

Usman, Y.B. , *For the Liberation of Nigeria: Essays and Lectures, 1969-1978.* London: New Beacon Books, 1979.

Usman, Y.B., *The Manipulation of Religion in Nigeria, 1977-1989.* Kaduna: Vanguard Publishers, 1987.

Uwazie, Ernest E., Isaac O. Albert, and Uzoigwe, G. N. (eds.), *Inter-ethnic and Religious Conflict Resolution in Nigeria.* New York: Lexington Books, 1999.

Uya, Okon Edet (ed.) *Contemporary Nigeria: Essays in Society, Politics and Economy.* Buenos Aires: Edipublisa, 1992.

Uzoigwe, G.N., *History and Democracy in Nigeria.* Owerri: Esther Thompson Publishing Company, 1989.

Uzoigwe, G.N. and Elaigwu, J. Isawa (eds.), *Foundations of Nigerian Federalism, 1900-1960*, vol. 2. Abjua: NCIR, 1996.

Uzoigwe, G.N., *Britain and the Conquest of Africa: The Age of Salisbury.* Ann Arbor: University of Michigan Press, 1974.

Vogt, A.M. (ed.), *The Liberian Crisis and Ecomog: A Bold Attempt at Regional Peace-Keeping.* Lagos: Gabuno Publishers, 1992.

Williams, David *President and Power in Nigeria: The Life of Shehu Shagari.* London: Frank Cass, 1982.

INDEX

NOTES ON CONTRIBUTORS

Gloria Chuku (Ph.D.) is Assistant Professor of history at South Carolina State University, Orangeburg, SC, U.S.A. where she teaches African history and World Civilizations. Dr. Chuku specializes in African and African Women's history, and gender studies. She has published many articles in journals and books.

Jerry I. Dibua (Ph.D.) is Associate Professor of History at Morgan State University, Baltimore, Maryland. He has taught in various universities in Nigeria and the United States. His research focuses on modern African history, politics and economy, on which he has published numerous articles and contributed chapters to books.

Stella A. Effa-Attoe (Ph.D.) is Senior Lecturer in history at the University of Calabar in Nigeria. Among her publications is a *History of the Biase People* of the Cross River State, Nigeria and several articles in learned journals.

Onwuka N. Njoku (Ph. D.) is a professor of African Economic History and the current Head of Department of History, University of Nigeria. Nsukka where he has taught undergraduate and graduate students for over two decades. Among his publications are *Economic History of Nigeria: 19th and 20th Centuries* (Enugu, 2001); *Ohafia: A Heroic Igbo Society*(Ebem, 2000); *MBUNDU of Angola* (New York, 1997); and over fifty articles in learned journals and books.

Levi A. Nwachuku received his Ph.D. from Michigan State University and he is currently Professor and Chair of the History Department as well as coordinator of the African-American Experience at Lincoln University, Pennsylvania. Previously he taught at the University of Michigan, Flint and the University of Maiduguri in Nigeria where he headed the department of history. His Articles have appeared in *Black World*, *Current Hisotry*, and *Journal of Black Studies*. He co-edited, with Niara Sudarkasa, Exploring the African-American Experience, (1996).

Okechukwu Okeke (Ph.D.) is a senior lecturer of African History at Abia State University, Uturu, Nigeria. His major publication is *Hausa-Fulani Hegemony: The Dominance of the Muslim North in Contemporary Nigerian Politics* (Enugu, 1992). Dr. Okeke has also a number of articles in learned journals and books.

G.N. Uzoigwe received D. Phil. From Christ Church, Oxford University, England. He is currently Professor and Head of the Department of History at Mississippi State University. Previously he taught at Makerere University in Uganda, the University of Michigan, Ann Arbor,and in a number of Nigerian Universities where he served variously as head of history departments and deans of Arts and Social Sciences as well as graduate school dean. He has also held distinguished visiting appointments at Cornell University, Lincoln University and Tulane University. He is a widely published scholar with ten books and over a hundred articles and book chapters.